Mental Disorders of the New Millennium

MENTAL DISORDERS OF THE NEW MILLENNIUM

Volume 3
Biology and Function

Edited by Thomas G. Plante

Praeger Perspectives

Abnormal Psychology

PRAEGER

Westport, Connecticut
London

Library of Congress Cataloging-in-Publication Data

Mental disorders of the new millennium / edited by Thomas G. Plante.
    p. ; cm.—(Praeger perspectives. Abnormal psychology, ISSN 1554–2238)
    Includes bibliographical references and index.
    ISBN 0–275–98781–7 (set)—ISBN 0–275–98782–5 (v. 1)—
    ISBN 0–275–98783–3 (v. 2)—ISBN 0–275–98784–1 (v. 3)
    1. Psychiatry. 2. Mental illness. I. Plante, Thomas G. II. Series.
    [DNLM: 1. Mental Disorders. WM 140 M548326 2006]
    RC454.M462   2006
    616.89—dc22   2006015096

British Library Cataloguing in Publication Data is available.

Library of Congress Catalog Card Number: 2006015096
ISBN: 0–275–98781–7 (set)
      0–275–98782–5 (vol. 1)
      0–275–98783–3 (vol. 2)
      0–275–98784–1 (vol. 3)
ISSN: 1554–2238

First published in 2006

Praeger Publishers, 88 Post Road West, Westport, CT 06881
An imprint of Greenwood Publishing Group, Inc.
www.praeger.com

Printed in the United States of America

The paper used in this book complies with the
Permanent Paper Standard issued by the National
Information Standards Organization (Z39.48–1984).

10 9 8 7 6 5 4 3 2 1

Dedicated to my sisters—Mary (Plante)
Beauchemin and Leeann (Plante) Sperduti—who have taught me much
about the human condition and have both worked tirelessly to improve it.

Contents

Preface

Tragically, the daily news is filled with stories about significant and remarkable problems in human behavior. Each morning we are greeted with news reports about murder, suicide, terrorist acts, drunken driving accidents, child molestation and abduction, drug abuse, gambling troubles, gang violence, various criminal behavior, and so forth. Other frequent stories reported in the press involve the betrayal of trust among highly respected and regarded members of society. These stories include the legal, sexual, financial, and general ethical lapses of politicians, leading sports celebrities, and movies stars. Some reports include the sexual abuse perpetrated on children and teens by school teachers, coaches, and members of the clergy. Other stories focus on the stress-related troubles soldiers experience following their duty in war. Still others focus on more and more reports of what appear to be mental problems such as autism, dementia, attention deficit disorders, panic, eating disorders, and depression, among both children and adults.

These troubles are reflected in recent cover stories in magazine news weeklies such as *Time, Newsweek,* and *US News and World Report.* Problems such as attention deficit hyperactivity disorder, autism, Alzheimer's disease, depression, panic disorder, murder-suicide, eating disorders, and child sexual abuse, among others, have been featured many times over as cover stories in these and other popular media outlets. The fact that these topics appear frequently on the covers of these news weeklies means they must impact significant numbers of people.

Perhaps just about everyone in the United States is affected by mental illness and abnormal behavior to some extent. Many people either suffer from one or more of the various mental disorders or live with those who do. It is likely that almost everyone in our contemporary society knows someone in his or her immediate family or circle of close friends and relatives who suffers from a significant abnormal behavior, psychiatric condition, or behavioral pattern that causes the person and his or her loved ones a great deal of stress.

Consider just a few of these statistics from our chapter contributors:

1. About 1 million people will die by suicide every year. The worldwide mortality rate of suicide is 16 per 100,000, or one suicide every 40 seconds. Fifty-five percent of suicides occur before age 44. Suicide is the third leading cause of death for both sexes.

2. About 1 million older Americans (1 in 35) is a victim of elder abuse each year, and between 3 and 5 percent of older adults over the age of 65 are or will be victims of abuse and/or neglect.

3. Epidemiological studies suggest the prevalence rate of child and adolescent depressive disorders ranges from 2 to 9 percent.

4. Over 18 million Americans suffer from some type of depression each year, and about 20 percent of the U.S. population will experience a significant depressive episode in their lifetime.

5. The number of probable adult pathological gamblers varies from just under 1 percent in the United Kingdom to between 1 and 2 percent in the United States and about 2.5 percent in Australia.

6. About 20 percent of all American women and 15 percent of all American men report being sexually abused by an adult while they were still a child.

7. About 4 percent of Catholic priests and 5 percent of school teachers have had a sexual encounter with a minor child in their care.

Clearly, mental illness and abnormal behavior touch the lives of just about all of us!

What's going on? How can it be that so many highly problematic psychiatric disorders, abnormal behaviors, and problems in living impact so many people? It wouldn't be an exaggeration to state that the vast troubles of the world stem from abnormal behavior. From ignoring global warming to terrorism, from murder to suicide, from divorce to gambling, from autism to dementia, it seems that abnormal behavior is at the root of so many challenges of our day.

Sadly, most of the books available in the field of abnormal psychology are not especially useful for the average educated lay reader. Much of the literature currently available tends to fall into two categories. The first includes academic books written by academics for an academic or scholarly audience. These books are often written in a very dry, jargon-filled, data-driven manner that is challenging for the general reader to get through. In fact, these books are often challenging for professionals in psychology and related fields to understand as well. The second category includes trade books that tend to be very simplistic and often tell the story of someone suffering from a particular problem. These books are often located in the self-help or inspirational section in a bookstore. Books of this type are written by those who experience the particular disorder, mental health professionals who treat the problem, or journalists who tell a remarkable story about a particular case that made news. Very few books are written for the educated lay reader that balance academic, scholarly, and clinical information with a readable, engaging, and user-friendly style.

The purpose of this series on mental disorders is to help bridge this gap between academic and self-help /inspirational books written on abnormal psychology topics that impact society—those topics that potential readers see on the covers of weekly news magazines or in daily newspapers. The series focuses on contemporary abnormal behavior topics and is compiled from contributions by experts for an educated lay audience. Leading experts who study, treat, evaluate, and reflect upon these troubles and issues have been asked to write chapters for you to help you better understand these contemporary problems. The chapters are based on the most up-to-date research and practice evidence and go well beyond the information provided in popular media outlets. Hopefully, you will find that the books are highly informative, contemporary, and readable.

If we better understand the factors that contribute to these contemporary abnormal behaviors and patterns, then perhaps we can find better ways to prevent some of these problems from emerging and better evaluate and treat those who suffer from these experiences. In an effort to create a better world for ourselves and our children we must do all that we can to prevent abnormal behavior and help those who are troubled by abnormal behavior in themselves, their loved ones, and their communities. In doing so, we will be better able to create an improved world.

Acknowledgments

Many people other than the author or editor assist in the completion of a book project. Some contribute in a direct way while others help in a more supportive manner. I would like to acknowledge the assistance of the people who worked to make this book idea a reality and who have helped me in both direct and indirect ways.

First and foremost, I would like to thank the contributors to this volume. Leading experts who represent the very best that the professional community has to offer graciously agreed to contribute quality chapters to this book project. Second, I would like to thank my associate editors, Drs. DeLeon, Kaslow, and Plante, for agreeing to serve as associate editors for this book and all the books in the abnormal psychology book series. Third, it is important to recognize the wonderful people at Greenwood who published this book. Most especially, many thanks go to Debbie Carvalko, our editor at Greenwood. Fourth, I would like to thank Santa Clara University, which has supported me and allowed me many opportunities to pursue my scholarly academic activities and interests.

Fifth, I would like to acknowledge the anonymous persons who are referred to in this book, who have allowed their life experiences and traumas to become instruments of learning for others. Sixth, I would like to thank my family patriarchs (Bernard Plante, the late Henry McCormick, and Eli Goldfarb) and matriarchs (Marcia Plante, the late Anna McCormick, the late Margaret Condon, and Marilyn Goldfarb) and my sisters (Mary Beauchemin and Leeann Sperduti), all of whom have taught me much about the human condition. Finally, I would like to thank my wife, Lori, and son, Zachary, for their love and support while I worked on yet another compelling book project.

Chapter 1

Postpartum Depression: More than the "Baby Blues"?

Rudy Nydegger

Depression is a major health problem in the United States and around the world. At any time, depression affects 15 to 25 percent of the population,[1,2] and it is estimated that the economic burden of depression in the U.S. is about four billion dollars per year.[3] One of the major problems with depression is that it is frequently undetected, and less than 25 percent of patients suffering from psychological conditions (including depression) are under the care of a mental health professional.[1,3] Of particular interest to us in this chapter is the fact that women are twice as likely as men to suffer depression, and this is most pronounced during the child bearing years of 25 to 45. There is also a particularly high incidence of depression in women during premenstrual, perimenopausal, and immediately postpartum periods.[3]

Of the four million births in this country, as many as 40 percent are complicated by some sort of postpartum mood disorder.[4] However, many patients and providers overlook these symptoms and dismiss them as normal. This fact has led many providers to feel that all mothers should be screened routinely for mood disorders, but this is not typically done. While many of these postpartum mood disorders will remit, it is true that many mothers report being depressed one year after the birth of their child.[5] Other studies have found that 10 to 28 percent of women experience a major depressive episode postpartum, and most of the studies are closer to the 10 percent figure. However, this still suggests that a substantial number of women who give birth will experience not just a mood disorder, but a *major* mood disorder following birth.[6] It is also true that women who experience a postpartum mood disorder are at high risk for a relapse or continuing psychological illness. In fact, during one follow-up study, about 80 percent of patients who were diagnosed with a postpartum mood disorder later sought help for psychological complaints.[7,8]

Some of the major reasons why there is concern for mothers suffering from postpartum affective disorders are the effects that these disorders have on mothers, infants, and others in the family. When untreated or under-treated, these problems can have significant and far-reaching effects. One study found that 32 percent of women who suffered an episode of postpartum depression dramatically changed their future childbearing plans, many resorting to adoption, abortion, or in some instances, even sterilization.[9] In many cases, depressed mothers show a more negative attitude toward their children, and a mother who is experiencing these types of difficulties may put significant emotional and even perhaps financial burdens on their families.[10] It has been demonstrated that in a 4-year follow-up study, depressive episodes in mothers were linked to poorer cognitive test scores in their children.[11] While it is not clear how pervasive or continuing these effects are, it is clear that in some children, even as late as four years after birth, there are cognitive changes that are apparently linked to previous depression in their mothers.

Other studies have found that postpartum depression can affect the bonding between mother and infant, and that this can affect infant well-being and development later. Mothers with postpartum depression are more likely to have negative attitudes toward their infant and will often see the child as more difficult and demanding. Often, mothers with postpartum depression have difficulty engaging the infant, are more withdrawn or intrusive, and have more negative facial expressions when with the infant. Children of mothers with postpartum depression are more likely than those born to non-depressed mothers to have behavioral problems such as difficulties with sleeping, eating, tantrums, cognitive development, emotional and social dysregulation, and early onset depressive illness.[5]

Postpartum depression is hardly a new discovery. We have been aware of this problem for a very long time. Even Hippocrates, in 460 B.C. described "puerperal fever," theorizing that, "suppressed lochial discharge was transported to the brain where it produced agitation, delirium, and attacks of mania."[12] Eleventh century writings of gynecologist Trotula of Salerno speculated, "if the womb is too moist, the brain is filled with water, and the moisture running over to the eyes, compels them to shed tears." Attempts to describe postpartum depression became more systematic in the mid-19th century when Esquirol wrote about the "mental alienation of those recently confined and of nursing women." Various accounts of puerperal psychosis and depression are specifically delineated by Marce in his 18th-century *Treatise on Insanity in Pregnant and Lactating Women*.[13]

While postpartum affective disorders have been described throughout history, it is interesting that they have received less attention in the professional literature than less common problems such as gestational diabetes, preeclampsia, and preterm delivery. Although we are certainly seeing more attention paid to psychological problems today, they are still frequently overlooked. In addition, there is still serious and frequent debate over the causes, definitions, diagnostic criteria, and even the existence of postpartum mood disorders.[10]

While it is true that these disorders are often overlooked at the primary care level, this is not terribly surprising since providers are often principally concerned with the welfare and health of the infant, and the mother may be too embarrassed to report being depressed when she feels that she should be happy. However, the risks of missing this diagnosis are significant. For the mother, there are the risks of a continuing and perhaps chronic depressive illness, and even the risk of suicide. For the infant, as mentioned above, there are risks of impacting maternal bonding and later child development. There is also the risk in the infant for the development of psychological problems later in the child's life.[14]

In sum, it is clear that childbirth is one of the major life stressors for women, is a risk factor for mental illness, and it has been frequently demonstrated that there is a temporal relationship between childbirth and psychiatric admissions.[12,15,16] Of course, the preponderance of psychological disorders in the postpartum period do not require hospitalization, but the increase in serious problems is quite striking. Data from 35,000 deliveries at 90-day intervals over a two-year period before and after delivery showed a seven-fold increase in the rate of psychiatric admission in the first three months after childbirth.[15] Further, the risk of psychosis was 22 times greater during the postpartum period than it was pre-pregnancy. For women admitted for psychiatric reasons postpartum, 87 percent of them were for affective disorders with the majority being for major depression.[15,16]

SYMPTOMS AND FORMS OF POSTPARTUM MOOD DISORDERS

There are several types of postpartum mood disorders, and it is important to distinguish between them, especially since the appropriate treatment depends upon accurate diagnosis. Recognizing the disorder and prescribing the appropriate type of treatment in a timely manner is very important in the treatment of any type of disorder, but certainly for postpartum mood disorders. The different types of postpartum mood disorders vary from very mild to extremely serious and dangerous.

The "baby blues" has mood swings, irritability, feelings of loneliness and anxiety, and typically lasts from a few hours to a couple of weeks. Postpartum depression may begin a few days or a few months after birth and may occur after the first or any or all subsequent births. This disorder has similar symptoms to the baby blues, but is more intense and lasts longer—up to one year or more. Unlike the baby blues, postpartum depression also significantly interferes with the mother's life. Finally, postpartum psychosis or puerperal psychosis is the most severe type of postpartum disorder. It usually has an acute onset, often within a short time after birth. The patient often hallucinates, is delusional and/or agitated, has insomnia, and shows a loss of touch with reality. This disorder usually requires hospitalization and medical intervention because the patient may be self-destructive and may also harm her children.[17]

Interestingly, some have even described a type of postpartum disorder that may be found in fathers. Some new fathers and especially stepfathers may experience some depression after the birth of a child. They are particularly vulnerable if:

+ Their partner is depressed
+ They are ending their relationship with the child's mother
+ They are unemployed
+ They are poorly educated
+ They are socially isolated
+ They are under severe stress
+ They are in a physically aggressive relationship with the child's mother[18]

Diagnosing a postpartum mood disorder is not always easy, especially in the milder variants. Weight and appetite changes as well as sleep problems are so common in new mothers that many physicians don't suspect depression. Questions need to be carefully asked to insure that it is not being overlooked.[10] Some have even begun using a 10-question scale (the Edinburgh Postnatal Depression Scale) that is used as a screening device to try and catch some of these cases that might otherwise not be diagnosed.[19,20]

Having briefly described the various postpartum mood disorders, let us now examine them in more depth. As mentioned above, the least problematic form of postpartum mood disorder is commonly called the baby blues. Typically, this is not even considered to be a disorder, and it affects anywhere between 40 to 85 percent of all mothers, depending upon which study one examines. The onset is usually in the first week postpartum and the symptoms usually peak in three to five days. This disorder usually only lasts a few weeks at most, and may spontaneously resolve in a matter of days. The symptoms of baby blues involve things like: unstable mood, weepiness, sadness, anxiety, lack of concentration, feelings of dependency, and irritability. These symptoms may be uncomfortable, but don't interfere with the mother's ability to function.[5,21,22,23,24] The etiology of baby blues is assumed to be multifactoral, and involves some or all of the following factors: rapid hormonal changes after birth, physical and emotional stress from birthing, physical discomfort, the emotional letdown after birth, awareness of and anxiety regarding increased responsibility, fatigue and sleep deprivation, and disappointments that may come from a variety of sources.[21] Since this condition usually spontaneously remits, there is not usually any formal treatment prescribed. However, rather than ignoring this, supportive care and reassurance seem to help and should be made available when the mother is experiencing this type of difficulty.[22]

Postpartum depression is a more severe type of problem than baby blues, and is considered to be a clinical disorder deserving of treatment. It is also true that this disorder itself exists on a continuum from mild to severe, and the severity of the symptoms usually determine the types and length of treatment that is used.[4] It should also be noted that in diagnosing this problem it is very important to first rule out physical causes like anemia and thyroid problems.[5] Postpartum depression can develop at any time during the first year postpartum, and usually peaks within the first four months after birth.[24]

This disorder is a unique and serious complication of childbirth, and its insidious course complicates 10 to 15 percent of all deliveries.[4,5,7,11] The majority of patients suffer postpartum depression for more than six months, and if untreated, 25 percent of the patients are still depressed one year later.[25] In adolescent deliveries, the incidence rate is usually between 26 to 32 percent of all births, and is clearly a major health risk for adolescent mothers.[26] Postpartum depression develops insidiously over the first three months after delivery although it can be acute as well, and it may be very persistent and debilitating for many mothers. Symptoms are very much like major depressive disorder (MDD) and often include suicidal thinking and thoughts of death. Occasionally, anxiety is prominent and many mothers worry obsessively about harming their baby. In addition, the disorder often causes the mothers to have negative feelings about the infant, and will interfere with the mother's ability to care for herself and her baby.[5]

The usual symptoms of postpartum depression include:

+ Dysphoric mood
+ Anhedonia (absences of pleasure in activities that are usually enjoyable)
+ Difficulty concentrating and/or making decisions
+ Psychomotor agitation or retardation
+ Fatigue

- Changes in appetite and/or sleep
- Recurrent thoughts of death or suicide
- Feelings of worthlessness and guilt—especially failure at motherhood
- Excessive anxiety over the child's health[10,13,21]

When anxiety and delusions are present, the postpartum depression may be termed *atypical*.[24]

This is a serious problem and usually requires some type of treatment when it is diagnosed. Very importantly, the risk of relapse in subsequent deliveries is 1:3–1:4.[22] This is not like the baby blues, since the symptoms must last for more than two weeks and must have dysphoria and/or anhedonia most of the day, almost every day for at least two weeks.[13] As mentioned above, postpartum depression is much like MDD, but there are some differences. For example, postpartum depression also includes:

- Difficulty sleeping when the baby is sleeping
- Lack of enjoyment in the maternal role
- Feelings of guilt relative to parenting ability
- And the mother may also have

  - Anxiety, including panic attacks
  - Obsessive fears of harming the baby[4]

Some of the signs that the mother or those around her may notice include:

- Feeling restless and irritable
- Feeling sad, depressed, or crying a lot
- Having no energy
- Physical symptoms (e.g., headache, chest pains, palpitations, numbness, hyperventilation)
- Insomnia and fatigue
- Decreased appetite and weight loss
- Overeating and weight gain
- Trouble focusing, remembering, or making decisions
- Being overly worried regarding the baby
- Not having any interest in the baby
- Feeling worthless and guilty
- Being afraid of hurting herself or the baby
- Unable to enjoy things that she usually enjoys—including sex[17]

Of course many of these symptoms can exist in a number of different conditions, and in fact are perfectly normal at times. If they are troublesome enough to interfere with normal functioning and happiness, and/or if they don't go away or even get worse, then it is time to mention them to the physician or someone else who can help.

Of all of the postpartum mood disorders, postpartum or puerperal psychosis is by far the most serious. Fortunately, it is very rare and only occurs in .1 to .2 percent of all deliveries.[5,27,28] However, this rate is 12 to 14.5 times the prenatal incidence of psychosis.[27] Typically, this has a very rapid onset, and is usually manifest in the first three weeks postpartum, and within three months at the most.[29] There is also a second and smaller peak of incidence that occurs 18 to 24 days postpartum.[4]

Patients with this condition may present with symptoms that resemble acute mania or psychotic depression, and may have hallucinations or delusions that are very frightening. This may present as a rapidly evolving manic episode with markedly bizarre behavior.[5] Many patients have additional symptoms that resemble delirium and involve distractibility, labile mood, and transient confusion.[13] Since these patients frequently suffer from both delusions and suicidal tendencies, the impact of this disorder on both mother and child are quite significant.[10] At times the delusions may take the form of the infant dying or divine or demonic intervention. Further, the hallucinations may take the form of commands that instruct the mother to harm herself or the baby. Mothers with this disorder are at higher risk for suicide and infanticide.[4,5]

People who develop this disorder usually have some history of a serious psychiatric disorder. Most commonly it is found that women who have bipolar disorder or who have previous episodes of postpartum psychosis are most at risk for developing this very serious condition.[5] It is also reported that patients with a previous diagnosis of schizophrenia are also at higher risk for this disorder.[4]

For patients diagnosed with postpartum psychosis, hospitalization is often necessary because of the risk to the mother and the child. Acute treatment also usually involves psychotropic medication, with mood stabilizers being the medication most frequently chosen. Often these are prescribed in combination with antipsychotic medications. For patients who do not respond well to medication, electroconvulsive therapy (ECT) has also been used, and has been found to be safe and effective.[5]

RISK FACTORS AND ETIOLOGY

Postpartum depression is a cross-cultural phenomenon and has not been associated with any particular ethnicity, socioeconomic class, or educational level.[4,17] In fact, any woman who is pregnant, has had a baby in the past few months, miscarried, or weaned a child from breast-feeding can develop postpartum depression.[17] There are, however, numerous risk factors that have been associated with the development of postpartum depression, ranging from biological to personal to family and social factors. The basic assumption is that the risk factors increase the experienced stress that the mother experiences, and the continuing stress then leads to depression.[10] One study done on Mexican mothers found that higher levels of emotional dysregulation made the mother more likely to develop postpartum depression.[30] Frequently, it has been found that patients with a negative world view may find a decrease in self-esteem and more distant relationships, which may lead to feelings of helplessness and depression.[4] While many studies have found such negative attitudes or emotional factors, there is no clear evidence of a consistent causal picture of postpartum depression in general. Obviously, not all patients who have negative attitudes, affect, or emotional dyscontrol end up diagnosed with depression.[10]

In most of the work that has been done, a prior history of depression and a family history of depression are the most predictive factors for the subsequent diagnosis of postpartum depression.[3,7,17,31,32,33] One study showed that a mother with a prior diagnosis of depression had a 30 percent risk of developing postpartum depression, and if there was a prior episode of postpartum depression the risk was increased to 70 percent.[3] Another study demonstrated that severe baby blues and a past history of depression were independent predictors that each raised the risk of postpartum depression threefold.[32]

While most of the studies on predictive factors focus on specific elements of the mother's condition, situation, and history, it is also true that there are things that have been found to be contributory that are related to the mother's experiences. For example, the following are things that mothers experience that are common and certainly understandable, but have also been associated with subsequent depression:

+ Feeling tired after delivery, having fragmented sleep, not getting enough rest, and this is even more true when the mother has had a C-section
+ Feeling overwhelmed with a new or additional baby, and doubting maternal ability
+ Feeling stress from the changes in work and home routines; needs for perfectionism and being the "Super Mom"
+ Feelings of loss of such things as identity, control, slim figure, attractiveness, and others
+ Having less free time, feeling a loss of control over one's time, having less time with husband and friends, and having to stay home most of the time[17]

Summarizing the most predictive factors for postpartum depression, the following are frequently found to be related to its subsequent development:

+ Previous episode of postpartum depression
+ Lack of support

- Family history of depression
- Labor difficulties or complications
- Premature or late delivery
- Being separated from the baby
- Difficulties with the baby
- Severe premenstrual syndrome
- Marital problems
- Pre-existing psychological problems[18]

In addition to these factors, some of the other things that have been related to postpartum depression in the literature are:

- Adverse life events during the postpartum period
- Young maternal age
- Infants with health problems or "difficult temperaments"[36]
- Comorbidities of substance abuse
- Anxiety or somatization[37,38]

Further, there are some other more controversial factors like:

- Primiparous women
- Breast-feeding
- Length and difficulty of labor
- Multiple gestation
- Advanced maternal age.[37,38]

Other factors include such things as abrupt weaning, mood changes when taking birth control or fertility medication, and thyroid dysfunction.[21]

One very interesting study evaluated mothers at four months and twelve months postpartum. At the twelve month period it was found that 30 percent of all mothers were depressed, and if they had been depressed at the four month period the rate increased to 60 percent. In fact, the best predictor of depression at the twelve month time period was the severity of depression at four months. It was also found that women from non-English speaking backgrounds were more likely to remain depressed after four months. Other factors that were predictive of depression at twelve months were low maternal care in childhood, maternal dissatisfaction at four months, an attachment style characterized by anxiety over relationships, and an immature defense style.[39]

One important line of research has looked at the relationship between anxiety and subsequent diagnosis of postpartum depression. Very simply, women with anxiety disorders during pregnancy were more likely to develop postpartum depression later.[35] This is true even when controlling for antenatal depression.[34]

When looking at the impressive lists of factors that have been associated with postpartum depression it is clear that prior history of depression or anxiety disorders is a major predictive factor. However, it is equally clear that things like feeling a loss of control over one's life, difficult family or personal circumstances, and lack of support are also contributory. It is also true that having a difficult baby might be a factor as well, but it is not easy to determine if the baby's problems are a cause or perhaps an effect of the mother's difficulties—or more likely, perhaps a little of both.

When looking at risk factors for postpartum psychosis, a slightly different picture emerges, but that is not surprising since it seems to be a distinct and different type of disorder. Similarly to postpartum depression, the principal predictor of postpartum psychosis is a history of psychosis in previous pregnancies. Other predictive factors include a history of bipolar disorder and a family history of psychosis.[41,45,46] Risk is also associated with initial severity. In a subset of women with onset of psychotic symptoms within two years, the recurrence risk approached 100 percent.[40]

An entirely different but entirely understandable approach to trying to understand risk and causality for postpartum depression deals with the physical and biological factors associated with pregnancy and birth. This is, of course, understandable since it is obvious that there are many changes that do occur. However, although postpartum depression may be triggered by hormone changes, it is not clear the extent to which these factors may truly be causal.[17] It does appear that thyroid changes and especially thyroiditis make a mother high risk for postpartum depression.[4,42] It is also true that hypothyroidism may be associated with mild depression, but for patients with postpartum depression there are mixed results relating depression with thyroid levels.[4] It has also been found that women with early postpartum anemia are also at high risk for postpartum depression.[43]

Much of the research in this area has focused on the "female" hormones estrogen and progesterone. This makes good sense because estrogen levels, like progesterone, fall 90 to 95 percent in the first 48 hours after delivery.[4,44] The rapid withdrawal of progesterone occurs with the delivery of the placenta, and has been proposed as a potential complicating factor in postpartum depression.[4] Hormone changes of this magnitude would certainly be expected to have some impact on psychological functioning. We know that estrogen has a role in memory and cognition as well as mood, and is linked to many elements of brain function. For example, estrogen effects dopamine, serotonin, and gamma-amino-butyric acid systems as well.[44] However, as compelling as this line of research is, there are no convincing studies linking postpartum depression to estrogen levels, and in fact, some studies link postpartum depression to high estrogen levels and other studies link it to low levels.[4] While women with postpartum depression don't appear to have different levels of hormones after birth as compared to mothers without postpartum depression, it is hypothesized that they may be more sensitive to the hormonal milieu.[5]

Some studies have focused on prolactin levels which also rise during pregnancy and fall more slowly after delivery. While prolactin has also been implicated in postpartum depression, once again there are conflicting results and no clear conclusions.[4] Similarly, a strong correlation between cortisol levels and the incidence of postpartum depression is not clear because there are studies that demonstrate both high and low levels of cortisol described in women with the disorder.[4,26,45]

One theory looking at physiological factors has looked at the dysregulation of neurotransmitters serotonin and the other biogenic amines such as norepinephrine, epinephrine, and dopamine. While there have been some studies that showed a correlation between these neurotransmitter levels and postpartum depression, there are other studies that have found no relationship at all.[4] This may be surprising to some, since these substances have been related to depression in general, but their role in postpartum depression is not clear. Further, the catecholamines have not been studied as thoroughly, but low norephinephrine levels and the severity of postpartum depression have been correlated.[4] Finally, the hypothalamic-pituitary axis has been frequently studied and implicated in depression, but its role in postpartum depression is not clear either.[45]

In summary, there appear to be no simple answers regarding the causality of postpartum depression. Clearly there are many factors that are related, but how these things combine to influence the development of this disorder is not obvious. Perhaps the best summary came from Leopold and Zoschnick: "The data suggest that the etiology of postpartum depression is multifactoral. Causative components include both organic and conditional changes arising from both parturition as well as the mother's surrounding situation, which likely combine to influence the patient's psychological function."[10] Since this is a complex and complicated disorder it should not be surprising that the causal picture is also complex and complicated.

Treatments

Although postpartum mood disorders can be a sometimes persistent and troublesome problem, there is almost always some treatment that can be applied that can be very helpful. Although the etiology of these problems may be unique in many ways, there is no reason to believe that postpartum depression responds differently to treatment than any other type of depression. As with any depression, early identification and treatment are the keys to successful interventions.[46] The range of treatments that are used generally depend upon the severity of the symptoms. Interventions typically range from things like support and support groups, group or individual psychotherapy, to medication or even to hospitalization or ECT.[4,5,26] Typically, acute treatment may be used from about six–twelve weeks, and is largely oriented toward symptom relief; continuation therapy may go for four–nine months and addresses issues like stabilizing the person and helping them to recover from the episode. Finally, maintenance therapy goes for nine months or more, and is generally used to prevent high-risk patients from having another acute episode.[46] If the postpartum depression is the first episode of depression, then it would be expected that treatment should last about six–twelve months. However, if the postpartum depression is a recurrence, then maintenance treatment might be needed. Often patients and sometimes even the providers will not carry treatment on long enough and this poses a risk to the mother and to the child. Two important things to remember are first, earlier treatment leads to a better prognosis, and second, more complete treatment will lead to better outcomes, fewer complications, and less chance of recurrence. Generally speaking, more intensive treatments like hospitalization and ECT are needed only if there are serious symptoms, psychotic symptoms, or if there is a suicidal or infanticidal risk.[5]

Treatment for the baby blues is often not formal since this "problem" tends to resolve itself in a relatively brief period. This is not to suggest, however, that it should be ignored. Patients who experience this problem can be significantly helped with very minimal interventions that will likely shorten the episode and reduce its impact. Simple reassurance and support are helpful, and emphasizing the importance of sleep and rest is usually adequate treatment; sometimes using minor tranquilizers may help with insomnia. Careful monitoring of this condition is important to ensure that it doesn't progress.[5,47]

Postpartum depression will usually benefit significantly from treatment, and unlike the baby blues, this condition does not spontaneously remit in a brief period and might last for months or even more. Consequently, it is more likely that this disorder will be the focus of formal treatment. Some of the work that has been done with postpartum depression has focused on non-pharmocological methods. Cognitive-behavioral and interpersonal psychotherapy as well as group psycho-educational therapy and supports groups have been very helpful, especially for mild to moderate postpartum depression. This is particularly true of mothers who are breast-feeding and who would rather not use medications.[5,49] It is important for all mothers to be aware of the fact that there is a broad range of treatment options available for the treatment of postpartum depression, and that this is a disorder that can be substantially helped with treatment. This has been shown in a variety of patient groups including some who are often not provided with a wide variety of treatment options. For example, one study found that using a four-session interpersonally oriented group intervention reduced the occurrence of postpartum depression in a group of financially disadvantaged women.[48]

Much of the research on the treatment of postpartum depression has focused on the medications that have been used to treat it, and this is particularly true in the recent past as more effective and safer medications have become available. Particularly for moderate to severe depression, medications are more likely to be used, and often this is in conjunction with other forms of treatment like psychotherapy. When using medications it is important to understand the role of medication in the whole treatment plan of the patient, and this should include psychological as well as medical treatment. Often, the mental health provider and the prescribing physician will coordinate their efforts to insure that the patient is getting the best effect from the treatments that she is receiving.

The most frequently prescribed medications for postpartum depression are the selective serotonin reuptake inhibitors (SSRIs) like Prozac, Zoloft, Paxil, Celexa, Lexapro, and Luvox. These are usually the first choice of medication for post-partum depression and are used in the normal dosage range. Some of the newer selective serotonin/norepinephrine reuptake inhibitors like Effexor or Cymbalta might also be helpful. Other classes of newer drugs like Remeron (noradrenaline/specific serotonergic antidepressants), Wellbutrin (norepinephrine dopamine reuptake inhibitor), and Deseryl or Serzone (serotonin-2 antagonists/reuptake inhibitors) might be used if the SSRIs aren't effective or if they produce side effects. Note that Serzone is not often used any more because of some liver problems that have been found to be associated with its use. However, it should be made clear that the SSRIs are typically the first-line drug to be tried for postpartum depression.

An older class of drugs, the tricyclics (e.g., Elavil, Anafranil, Norpramin, Sinequan, Adapin, Tofranil, Aventyl or Pamelor, Vivactil, and Surmontil) or tetracyclics (Ludiomil) can be helpful, especially if there is insomnia, but frequently these drugs are not used because they have more troublesome side effects in general. When using any of the tricyclic or tetracyclic medications, the usual strategy is to start off the patient on a lower dose, gradually move them up to the lowest therapeutic dose, and leave them there for two–four weeks. If they haven't shown any improvement by that time then the dosage should be increased. If dosage increases don't lead to symptomatic improvement, or if the side effects are too troubling, then the drug should be stopped and another tried.[5]

Occasionally, anxiolytic medications like Valium, Xanax, Klonopin, Librium, and Ativan can be used if anxiety and/or insomnia are the principle symptoms.[5] However, these drugs can also be problematic because of side effects, increased tolerance with continuing use, and the possibility of dependence. As such, they should never be used with a person who has a substance abuse history unless there are no other options, and even then they should be used with care.

At times, estrogen alone or with antidepressant medication has been used for postpartum depression, and this has been found to be helpful in some cases.[5] However, the antidepressants, and especially the SSRIs, still remain the first-line of treatment with respect to medications.

It is very important for providers to determine before delivery whether or not the mother is high risk for postpartum depression or postpartum psychosis. If there is a prior history of recurrent depression or previous postpartum depression it might be wise to start the mother on a prophylactic course of antidepressant medication before delivery. If there is a prior history of postpartum psychosis or bipolar disorder, then the physician may choose to use lithium prior to or within 24 hours of delivery. This has been found to minimize the risk of recurrent postpartum psychosis. Unfortunately, there is not much literature on prophylaxis for non-pharmacological forms of treatment.[5]

One thing of concern to many mothers is the impact of medication on their baby if the mother is breast-feeding. Of course, under such circumstances, the mother and her physician must look at the risks and make the appropriate decision.[5] In terms of the antidepressants, most of the tricyclics have a very low degree of transfer into the breast milk and are considered safe. SSRIs vary in terms of how much is transferred into the breast milk, with Prozac transferring the most, Celexa a more moderate amount, and Paxil the least.[5,18,50,51,52] In general, it would appear that with SSRIs the shorter the half-life of the drug, the less transfer of medication into the breast milk and therefore the safer it is for the child. With respect to antidepressants, reports of toxicity in breast-feeding infants are rare, but the long-term effects are unknown.[5]

Mothers who are being treated with valproic acid or carbamazapine should avoid breast-feeding because these drugs have been linked to hepatotoxicity in infants. Similarly, mothers who are taking lithium should not breast-feed since this compound is secreted at high levels in breast milk and may cause toxicity in the infant. Finally, it is recommended that mothers should avoid breast-feeding if they are taking any psychotropic medications when the infant is premature or has hepatic insufficiency. These infants may have difficulties metabolizing the medications in breast milk.[5] What really needs to be remembered here is the importance of common sense. A mother who really wants to breast-feed her baby should be able to do so unless it would be risky for the child. If the mother needs to take medication for her psychological condition, then she and her physician need to discuss the risks and strategies for keeping the mother healthy and the child safe. Further, mothers who are high risk and who are not on medications and want to breast-feed should probably be put in some type of non-pharmacologic type of treatment to make sure that the mother's and child's needs are being met, and that the mother's psychological condition is being adequately treated.

PREVENTION

Probably an area that is more important than treatment is prevention. To the extent that we can successfully prevent a problem, treatment may not even be necessary. This is not, of course, to suggest that treatment isn't important, because it most certainly is. However, it is also true that the best treatment is always prevention, and this is true of postpartum depression as well. Prevention should begin well before birth, but it must continue postpartum if it is to be effective. When discussing prevention, we can describe three different types or levels of prevention. Primary prevention refers to activities that are intended to reduce the incidence of a given disorder in the population as a whole. Thus, this would refer to activities that all expectant mothers or women who are planning to get pregnant should be involved in. In fact, these would be things that all of us should probably do anyway. For example, good nutrition, exercise, relaxation and rest, adequate sleep, recreation, appropriate socialization, having alone time, and so forth, are things that all of us should do whether male or female, pregnant or not, or even planning to be pregnant or not.

Secondary prevention has to do with working with people who are high risk for a given disorder and may even be displaying some mild symptoms, but who have not yet manifested the disorder in question. Thus, for these people, the key is to intervene in such a way as to keep the problem from getting worse and finally becoming a disorder. Tertiary prevention has to do with taking patients who have been diagnosed with a problem and intervening in such a way as to keep the diagnosed problem from getting worse or perhaps decompensating into something more serious. The goal here is to minimize the expected negative outcomes from a specific disorder.

Thus, when we look at prevention, it is important to think in terms of working at this *before* a given situation actually becomes a problem—that is, primary prevention. As with treatment, prevention too works best when it is done early. From the provider's standpoint, the key is to make sure that all women who are pregnant, planning to be pregnant, who are of childbearing age, or who have recently delivered a child are being carefully monitored for symptoms of depression or any other psychological problems for that matter. Of course, at the primary care site, patients should be monitored for these issues under any circumstances, but it is often the case that mental health issues are not monitored as carefully as medical issues. This is not always due to the provider's lack of awareness, but may also be due in part to the patient's unwillingness to discuss these issues with their physician. The provider should try to provide the kind of atmosphere that makes discussing these types of issues simply a part of what is normally done. By attending to these types of issues as part of normal health care, many of the postpartum psychological problems can be eliminated or at least minimized.

Mothers or expectant mothers can certainly do many things to help insure that they will be as healthy postpartum as they can be. As mentioned above, we these include good nutrition, exercise, relaxation and rest, adequate sleep, recreation, appropriate socialization, alone time, and so forth. Since pregnancy and birth are expected to be happy and rewarding times, we often forget how stressful and difficult they can be. When mothers don't take care of themselves physically and psychologically, there is usually a price to pay. When mothers are feeling overwhelmed or angry, it is easy to see how they might take it out on the baby or on their family. To avoid this we usually recommend:

+ Relaxation (yes, there is time—find it)
+ Cognitive restructuring (looking at things differently)
+ Problem solving (seeing what is bothering them and finding different ways to deal with the situation)
+ Communication (not suffering in silence—talking to people about how they feel and what is bothering them)
+ Humor (there is usually something humorous in any difficult situation, and this will help them keep it in perspective)[18]

It is also true that often when mothers are feeling overwhelmed or angry and they find themselves getting angry or resentful toward the baby, they then feel terribly guilty and feel that they are being a bad mother. It is terribly important for mothers to maintain and nurture the mother-baby bond, and this is even more important when the mother is having a difficult time. It is also important that mothers don't overcompensate for perceived weaknesses by doing even more than they would normally want to do. Mothers should maintain a consistent and intentional pattern of caring for the mother-child bond. This is important to the mother and to the baby. Some of the things that can be done include:

+ Nurse or feed the baby frequently
+ Provide a quiet place for the baby to rest, and rest when he/she does
+ Hold and talk softly to the infant often
+ Keep the baby warm, dry, and fed
+ Involve others in caring for the baby

- Take time with the other children (if there are any)
- Go outside with the baby when the weather permits
- Take some time for themselves[18]

Mothers should also be particularly nurturing of themselves—even more than usual. Some advice for all mothers includes such things as:

- Talk to someone about their feelings (a professional if necessary)
- Take time to talk with their spouse or partner—about how they feel and about normal kinds of things as well
- Let people help them—don't try to do everything themselves
- Do something for themselves every day—even if it is only for 15 minutes
- Rest (e.g., nap when the baby does)
- Exercise
- Pay attention to their nutrition—avoid alcohol, nicotine, and caffeine
- Keep a journal
- Set goals—they can be simple, but do so every day
- Give themselves permission to feel overwhelmed
- Don't spend a lot of time alone—they don't have to; they can get dressed, go for a walk, go to the store, visit a friend, and so forth
- Spend time alone with husband or partner
- Talk to their medical provider if they feel the need to see a mental health professional, and get a referral
- Talk to other mothers
- Join a support group[17,18]

In addition, there are some things that a husband or partner can do that will also help. For example:

- Listen and validate the mother's feelings
- Avoid criticizing or judging
- Be patient
- Give the mother some breaks from child care and home care
- Support the mother's decision to get help (medically, psychologically, around the house, or with the child)
- Talk to their physician or a mental health professional themselves[18]

One additional step that prospective or new mothers might take to help themselves falls into the realm of nutrition. All prospective or new mothers should be aware of the importance of good nutrition, and should comply with the nutritional guidelines and supplements that are recommended by their physicians. Since one of the major complaints that is heard from new mothers is the difficulty they have with weight or with gaining weight after delivery, this is often a significant and worrisome issue. Dieting while pregnant or nursing is not usually recommended, but maintaining good, well-balanced meals is very important. One line of research also suggests that prospective or new mothers use omega-3 fatty acids as a dietary supplement. There has been a lot of interest recently in omega-3s as a way to reduce the risks of cardiovascular disease. This is where most people have heard about them. However, omega-3 fatty acids are also used to help treat people with chronic inflammatory illnesses, and even more recently to help augment the treatment of certain psychiatric conditions. A recent study very convincingly demonstrated that, around the world in many different cultures and climates, there is a strong correlation between postpartum depression and how much fish is eaten. Specifically, the more fish that is consumed the lower the rate of postpartum depression, and this relationship is so strong as to be very compelling.[53] While we know that correlation does not imply causation, this high of a correlation certainly is suggestive of a functional relationship of some type.

There are a number of sources of omega-3s that are easily accessible. Fish, fish oil capsules, and flax seed oil are the most common sources. One concern about fish and fish oil capsules is the potential for toxins to be present. Unfortunately, there are probably no safe water sources in North America today, and there is no way to be certain of fish from the ocean. Many experts recommend that we not have fish or sea food more than once per week. The concern over fish oil capsules seems not to be as well-founded, however. Particularly, if the fish oil is "concentrated," this indicates that it has been processed in such a way as to eliminate the toxic substances. Also, if the fish oil has been processed under nitrogen instead of normal air, then the fish oil won't oxidize and smell fishy. To determine the safety of the product, you should read the label, ask your pharmacist, or go to the Web site www.consumerlab.com which will tell you more about the product you are looking at and what it contains.[53]

Some people will try to avoid the fish problem altogether by getting their omega-3s from non-marine sources like flax seed oil. This is certainly a good thing, and flax seed has its own advantages. However, the omega-3 fatty acids in flax seed are the shorter molecules, and don't have all of the benefits of those found in the fish oils. Consequently, it would seem that using fish oil capsules and flax seed would be a good combination, and also help reduce the likelihood of a mother getting postpartum depression.[53] Of course, it is strongly recommended that anyone who is interested in trying to use dietary supplements to augment or complement their medical care should inform their physician as to what they are doing or would like to do. The best way to proceed with these types of treatments is to make sure that everyone who is involved is aware and on board with what is being done. Do not begin supplementing your diet with a variety of substances without first discussing it with your physician.

CONCLUSION

As should be clear from the above discussion, postpartum mood disorders are complex and complicated phenomena about which we are only very recently finding out more. The most important thing to remember, of course, is that when detected and accurately diagnosed, these problems can be treated effectively and significant help can be provided. The other side of this coin is that when untreated, these disorders can create serious problems for mothers, children, and others in the family as well. Being aware of this type of problem, being willing to talk about it, and being open to appropriate preventative and treatment options are vitally important for mothers and for medical providers as well.

There is an impressive range of effective treatments that are available today, but the most obvious ones are also the simplest and easiest—awareness, concern, and support. Particularly for baby blues, these are usually adequate "treatments." When the problems are more severe, there are many very good psychological types of interventions that can be very helpful. If a patient doesn't know how to contact an appropriate mental health provider, they should discuss this with their primary care physician who should be able to make an appropriate recommendation. It is important that the mental health provider has experience dealing with mood disorders, and specifically with postpartum depression.

In addition to psychological interventions, there are also currently many good medication options to treat this condition. If a mother feels that she might be a candidate for medication, she should discuss this with her physician and the options should be considered. It should also be remembered that if the depression is serious or recurrent, medication alone will not likely be adequate treatment. Even with milder forms of depression, psychotherapy will usually reduce the probability of recurrence, and should be part of the treatment package.

Similarly, if the mother would like to consider nutritional or complementary forms of treatment like omega-3 fatty acids, they should also discuss this with their physician. While there is compelling evidence that this might be very helpful in minimizing the impact of postpartum mood disorders, this should not be undertaken without a thorough discussion with the mother's physician. Although very safe, these compounds do impact us in different ways, and care must be taken to use such complementary and/or supplemental treatments responsibly and with full awareness and coordination with the appropriate providers.

Finally, when the postpartum problems are very serious, hospitalization in addition to medication might be necessary. This is not usually long-term, and the typical treatment plan tries to get the mother back with her baby and family as soon as it is safe. When necessary, hospitalization can certainly minimize some of the serious and potentially tragic results that need not occur. Similarly, as frightening as ECT might sound, it is safer today than ever before. While never a first-line treatment, it has proven to be helpful in situations where other treatments have not worked, especially if the mother's or baby's life is at risk. It is important that all appropriate treatment options be kept open and that when a mother is suffering from a postpartum mood disorder that the most appropriate treatment be made available in a timely fashion.

The goal of this whole area of care is simple. We want to insure the safest, healthiest, most positive and supportive environment for new mothers and their babies as is possible. To the extent that this is done, we know that there will be fewer problems in the future for both the mothers and the children, and that this is good for families and for society. Treatment and prevention of these disorders is available and inexpensive—especially when we look at the costs, both human and financial, of inadequate or unavailable treatment.

REFERENCES

1. Steiner, M. (1990). Postpartum psychiatric disorders. *Canadian Journal of Psychiatry, 35,* 89–95.
2. Yonkers, K. A., Gallion, C., & Williams, A. (1996). Paroxetine as a treatment for premenstrual dysphoric disorder. *Journal of Clinical Psychopharmacology, 16,* 3–8.
3. Yonkers, K. A., & Chantilis, S. J. (1995). Recognition of depression in obstetric/gynecology practices. *American Journal of Obstetrics and Gynecology, 173,* 632–638.
4. O'Hara, M. W. (1995). Postpartum depression: Causes and consequences. In L. B. Alloy (Ed.), *Series in Psychopharmacology* (pp. 1–27). New York: Springer-Verlag.
5. Nonacs, R. M. (2005). *Postpartum depression.* RetrievedApril 24, 2006, from http://www.emedicine.com/med/topic3408.htm
6. O'Hara, M. W., & Swain, A. M. (1996). Rates and risk of postpartum depression—a meta-analysis. *International Review of Psychiatry, 8,* 37–54.
7. Kumar, R., & Robson, M. K. (1984). A prospective study of emotional disorders in child-bearing women. *British Journal of Psychiatry, 144,* 35–47.
8. Philipps, L. H., & O'Hara, M. W. (1991). Prospective study of postpartum depression: 4½ year follow-up of women and children. *Journal of Abnormal Psychology, 100,* 151–155.
9. Peindl, K. S., Zolnik, E. J., Wisner, K. L., & Hanusa, B. H. (1995). Effects of postpartum psychiatric illnesses on family planning. *International Journal of Psychiatric Medicine, 25,* 291–300.
10. Leopold, K. A., & Zoschnick, L. B. (2005). *Postpartum depression.* Retrieved April 24, 2006, from http://www.obgyn.net/femalepatient/default.asp?page=leopold
11. O'Hara, M. W., Neunaber, D. J., & Zekoski, E. M. (1984). A prospective study of postpartum depression, prevalence, course, and predictive factors. *Journal of Abnormal Psychology, 91,* 158–171.

12. Thurtle, V. (1995). Post-natal depression: The relevance of sociological approaches. *Journal of Advances in Nursing, 22,* 416–424.
13. Steiner, M. (1990). Postpartum psychiatric disorders. *Canadian Journal of Psychiatry, 35,* 89–95.
14. Ryan, D., & Kostaras, X. (2005). Psychiatric disorders in the postpartum period. *British Columbia Medical Journal, 47,* 100–103.
15. Kendell, R. E., Wainwright, S., Hailey, A., & Shannon, B. (1976). The influence of childbirth on psychiatric morbidity. *Psychological Medicine, 6,* 297–302.
16. Kendell, R. E., Rennie, D., Clarke, J. A., & Dean, C. (1981). The social and obstetric correlates of psychiatric admission in the puerperium. *Psychological Medicine, 11,* 341–350.
17. *Postpartum depression.* (2005). Retrieved April 24, 2006, from http://www.4woman.gov/faq/postpartum.htm
18. *Postpartum depression and caring for your baby.* (2005, April 7). Retrieved April 24, 2006, from http://www.kidshealth.org/search01.jsp
19. Cox, J. L., Holden, J. M., & Sagorsky, R. (1987). Detection of postnatal depression: Development of the 10-item Edinburgh Postnatal Depression Scale. *British Journal of Psychiatry, 150,* 782–786.
20. Kennerley, H., & Gath, D. (1989). Maternity Blues I. detection and measurement by questionnaire. *British Journal of Psychiatry, 155,* 356–362.
21. Bennett, S. S., & Indman, P. (2003). *Beyond the blues: A guide to understanding and treating prenatal and postpartum depression.* San Jose, CA: Moodswings Press.
22. Hamilton, J. A. (1989). Postpartum psychiatric syndromes. *Psychiatric Clinics of North America, 12,* 89–103.
23. O'Hara, M. W., Schlecte, J. A., & Lewis, D. A. (1991). Prospective study of postpartum blues: Biologic and psychosocial factors. *Archives of General Psychiatry, 48,* 804–806.
24. O'Hara, M. W., Zekoski, E. M., & Philipps, L. H. (1990). A controlled prospective study of postpartum mood disorders: Comparison of childbearing and nonchildbearing women. *Journal of Abnormal Psychology, 99,* 3–15.
25. Gregoire, A. J., Kumar, R., & Everitt, B. (1996). Transdermal oestrogen for treatment of severe postnatal depression. *Lancet, 347,* 930–933.
26. Stowe, Z. N., & Nemeroff, C. B. (1995). Women at risk for postpartum onset of major depression. *American Journal of Obstetrics and Gynecology, 173,* 639–645.
27. Nott, R. N. (1982). Psychiatric illness following childbirth in Southhampton: A case register study. *Psychological Medicine, 12,* 557–561.
28. Kumar, R. (1994). Postnatal mental illness: A transcultural perspective. *Social Psychiatry, 29,* 250–264.
29. Altshuler, L. L., Cohen, L., Szuba, M. P., Burt, V. K., Gitlin, M., & Mintz, J. (1996). Pharmacologic management of psychiatric illness during pregnancy: Dilemmas and guidelines. *American Journal of Psychiatry, 153,* 592–606.
30. Le, H.-N., Munoz, R. F., Soto, J. A., & Delucci, K. L. (2004). Identifying risk for onset of major depressive episodes in low-income Latinas during pregnancy and postpartum. *Hispanic Journal of Behavioral Science, 26,* 463–482.

31. Llewellyn, A. M., Stowe, Z. N., & Nemeroff, C. B. (1997). Depression during pregnancy and the puerperium. *Journal of Clinical Psychiatry, 58*(Suppl. 15), 26–32.
32. Henshaw, C., Foreman, D., & Cox, J. (2004). Postnatal blues: A risk factory of postnatal depression. *Journal of Psychosomatic Obstetrics & Gynecology, 25,* 267–272.
33. O'Hara, M. W. (1986). Social support, life events, and depression during pregnancy and the puerperium. *Archives of General Psychiatry, 43,* 569–573.
34. Cloitre, M., Yonkers., K. A., Pearlstein, T., Altemus, M., Davidson, K. W., Pigott, T. A., et al. (2004). Women and anxiety disorders: Implications for diagnosis and treatment. *CNS Spectrums, 9,* 1–16.
35. Sutter-Dallay, E., Glatigny, E., & Verderex, H. (2004). Women with anxiety disorders during pregnancy are at increased risk of intense postnatal depressive symptoms: A prospective survey of the MATQUID cohort. *European Psychiatry, 19,* 459–463.
36. Ryan, D., & Kostaras, X. (2005). Psychiatric disorders in the postpartum period. *British Columbia Medical Journal, 47,* 100–103.
37. Warner, R., Appleby, L., Whitten, A., & Faragher, B. (1996). Demographic and obstetric risk factors for postnatal psychiatric morbidity. *British Journal of Psychiatry, 168,* 607–611.
38. Cox, J. L., Connor, Y., & Kendell, R. E. (1981). Prospective study of the psychiatric disorders of childbirth. *British Journal of Psychiatry, 140,* 111–117.
39. McMahon, C., Barnett, B., Kowalenko, N., & Tennant, C. (2005). Psychological factors associated with persistent postnatal depression: Past and current relationships, defense styles, and the mediating role of insecure attachment style. *Journal of Affective Disorders, 84,* 15–24.
40. Sichel, D. A., Cohen, L. S., Robertson, L. M, Ruttenberg, A., & Rosenbaum, J. F. (1995). Prophylactic estrogen in recurrent postpartum affective disorders. *Biological Psychiatry, 38,* 814–818.
41. McNeil, T. F. (1987). A prospective study of postpartum psychosis in a high risk group. 2. Relationships to demographic and psychiatric history characteristics, *Acta Psychiatrica Scandinavica, 75,* 35–43.
42. Lucas, A., Pizarro, E., Granada, M. L., Salinas, I., & Sanmarti, A. (2001). Postpartum Thyroid dysfunction and postpartum depression: Are the two linked disorders? *Clinical Endocrinology, 55,* 809–814.
43. Corwin, E. J., Murray-Koln, L. E., & Beard, J. L. (2003). Low hemoglobin level is a risk factor for postpartum depression. *Journal of Nutrition, 133,* 4139–4142.
44. McEwen, B. S. (1993). Ovarian steroids have diverse effects on brain structure and function. In G. Berg & M. Hammar (Eds.), *The Modern Management of Menopause: A perspective for the 21st century* (pp 269–273). New York: Patterson Publishing.
45. Kendell, R. E., Chalmers, J. C., & Platz, C. (1987). Epidemiology of puerperal psychosis. *British Journal of Psychiatry, 150,* 662–673.
46. Nonacs, R., & Cohen, L. S. (1998). Postpartum mood disorders: Diagnosis and treatment guidelines. *Journal of Clinical Psychiatry, 59*(Suppl. 2), 34–40.

47. Cox, J. L., Murray, D., & Chapman, G. A. (1993). A controlled study of the onset, duration and prevalence of postnatal depression. *British Journal of Psychiatry, 163*, 27–31.

48. Zlotnick, C., Johnson, S. L, Miller, I. W., Pearlstein, T., & Howard, M. (2001). Postpartum depression in women receiving public assistance: Pilot study of an interpersonal-therapy-oriented group intervention. *American Journal of Psychiatry, 158*, 638–640.

49. O'Hara, M. W., Scott, S., Gorman, L. L., & Wenzel, A. (2000). Efficacy of interpersonal psychotherapy for postpartum depression. *Archives of General Psychiatry, 57*, 1039–1045.

50. Bennett, P. N. (Ed.). (1997). *Drugs and human lactation* (2nd ed.) Amsterdam: Elsevier.

51. Ilett, K. F., Kristensen, J. H., & Begg, E. J. (1997). Drugs distribution in human milk. *Australian Prescriber, 20*, 35–40.

52. Speight, T. M., & Holforg, N. H. G. (Eds.). *Avery's Drug Treatment* (4th ed.). Auckland, NZ: Adis International Ltd.

53. Stoll, A. L. (2005, June). *Fatty acids in mood disorders.* Paper presented at Natural Remedies for Psychiatric Disorders: Considering the Alternatives, Harvard Medical School and Massachusetts General Hospital, Boston, MA.

Chapter 2

Persons with Mental Retardation: Scientific, Clinical, and Policy Advances

Robert M. Hodapp, Melissa A. Maxwell, Marisa H. Sellinger, and Elisabeth M. Dykens

---

Michael is trying to wait patiently with his mom at the clinic, but he is starting to get frustrated. He is hungry and just plain tired of seeing doctors all the time. As he begins to pace around the room, his mom pulls out a book to try to entertain him, but the attempt comes too late. Michael's impatience has already escalated, and a full-blown tantrum has begun. As his mother tries desperately to calm Michael, she notices the eyes of the other patients begin to rise from their reading materials and all fix on her and her son. She takes a deep breath and braces herself for just one more event to add to the list of incidents she has dealt with in Michael's 14 years of life. "If *only* he would use his words," she thinks to herself, as she tries to calm him.

When we think of groups within our society that face special problems or challenges, we generally consider minority groups, or those encountering poverty, illness, or psychiatric disorders such as depression. Rarely do we consider children or adults with mental retardation or their families. Some would even argue that persons with mental retardation are one of our society's most unacknowledged, under-appreciated "special groups." And yet, persons with mental retardation live in every city, state, and region of our country.

Even within the world of social services, persons with mental retardation are generally accorded less respect or interest. Consider the American Psychiatric Association's *Diagnostic and Statistical Manual*, now in its 4th text revised edition (*DSM–IV–TR*).[1] In *DSM–IV–TR*, under the class of "Disorders Usually First Diagnosed in Infancy, Childhood, or Adolescence," mental retardation is the first disorder examined (pp. 41–49). But at the same time, only a small number of researchers in clinical psychology, adult psychiatry, or child psychiatry study persons who have both mental retardation and psychiatric disorders, those with so-called dual diagnoses. Moreover, various professionals have predicted that mental retardation would soon become the triumphant Cinderella of the mental health field, but such predictions were made in 1927,[2] 1966,[3] and 1997.[4] Similarly, subspecialties concerning mental retardation exist, but are not prominent, in education, nursing, social work, child development, clinical genetics, and pediatrics.

Why are persons with mental retardation so often ignored? To us, the answer involves misunderstandings of several types. First, many professionals and lay people consider mental retardation as a rarely occurring condition, something that happens so infrequently as to not require attention. Although we counter such thinking below, prevalence rates have rarely precluded scientific or clinical interest in children with many conditions that occur much more rarely than mental retardation. Second, persons with mental retardation are, by definition, less intelligent, and some (though by no means all) of these individuals are less able to advocate for themselves. Although movements are afoot to raise their levels of self-advocacy skills, the lessened ability to argue for their own needs may lead to a lessened public and professional awareness of persons with mental retardation and their families.

The third, and to us most important, factor is more subtle. Simply stated, many professionals feel that persons with mental retardation are somehow less interesting, less worthy of their professional time and attention. They judge persons with mental retardation as being of less interest scientifically, and, compared to groups with other psychiatric or medical problems, less capable of being the subject of a cure or of major advances that will increase these individuals' functioning. Partly as a result, mental retardation has assumed a less prominent role in many scientific and social service fields.

We disagree with each of these views. We start with the belief that persons with mental retardation are intrinsically interesting in their own right, with strengths, challenges, and concerns that relate to all of us. We are also intrigued by the way in which the difficulties faced by persons with mental retardation intersect with so many societal, public policy, and legal concerns. Finally, persons with mental retardation inform us about many interesting scientific issues in clinical psychology and psychiatry, developmental psychology, genetics, and other fields.

At the risk of yet again proclaiming a Cinderella-like period for mental retardation, in this chapter we emphasize the re-emergence of mental retardation as a societal, policy, and research concern. To explain this rise, we first provide the basics of mental retardation, its definition, prevalence, levels of impairment, and causes. We then describe the many diagnostic and treatment issues involving the dually-diagnosed population with mental retardation, before expanding our scope to functioning in families of a child with mental retardation, individuals with mental retardation as parents, and issues of abuse and criminality. We conclude by describing how many of the field's advances lead to further questions for researchers, clinicians, and society as a whole.

MENTAL RETARDATION: THE BASICS

When Michael was born, his mother did not notice anything peculiar about him nor during her pregnancy, as compared with his two older siblings. Yet, as weeks turned to months, she noticed he was not reaching his milestones at the same rate as his siblings did; and when he was still not sitting up or babbling at 9 months, she began to be concerned. The excessive visits to doctors and medical clinics began before Michael's first birthday, but no one could really tell her what was wrong with her son. In fact, he did not receive his first diagnosis until he was two years old—"developmentally delayed." Michael's mother began early intervention services with Michael as soon as they were offered to him, shuttling him to occupational, physical, and speech therapy once a week. When he was school-aged and placed in a special education classroom, Michael received another diagnosis, this one more upsetting to his mother—Michael had an intelligence quotient (IQ) of 54; he had mental retardation.

Definition and Diagnostic Criteria

Although most of us have an everyday, common-sense definition of the term, mental retardation is actually not so simple to define and, historically, its definition has been the source of considerable controversy. For the most part, however, most professionals subscribe to the following three-factor definition of mental retardation. To quote *DSM–IV–TR*,[1] mental retardation involves:

A. "Significantly subaverage intellectual functioning . . . ;
B. "Concurrent deficits or impairments in present adaptive functioning . . . ; and,
C. "The onset is before age 18 years" (p. 49).

The first factor involves deficits in intellectual functioning. Using appropriate, standardized psychometric tests (e.g., the latest Stanford-Binet, Wechsler, Kaufman, or other IQ tests), individuals are considered to fall within the mental retardation range when their IQs are at 70 or below. Due to errors of measurement, diagnostic manuals—including *DSM–IV–TR*[1] and the manual of the American Association on Mental Retardation (the main professional group in the field; AAMR)[5]—all allow for some leeway in this "IQ-70 criterion," usually up to IQ 75. Still, significant intellectual impairment constitutes one criterion for a diagnosis of mental retardation.

But such intellectual deficits should also involve a so-called real-world component. The second criterion therefore involves deficits in adaptive behavior. Deficits in adaptive behavior involve a lessened ability to perform "daily activities required for personal and social sufficiency" (p. 1).[6] In the newly revised Vineland Adaptive Behavior Scales, the three domains of adaptive behavior include *communication,* or communicating one's needs to others; *daily living skills,* or performing such tasks as eating, dressing, grooming, and toileting; and *socialization,* or following rules and working and playing with others. In *DSM–IV–TR,*[1] 10 domains of adaptive behavior are proposed, with deficits in two or more domains constituting evidence of impairments in adaptive behavior. Although the presence of 10 separate domains and the "2 of 10" criteria for adaptive deficits have been harshly criticized,[7] most would agree that lower intelligence should not constitute the sole criterion of whether a person has mental retardation.

The third criterion involves onset during the childhood years. Unlike both the intellectual and adaptive criteria, childhood onset has received little criticism. To most professionals, mental retardation should be differentiated from problems associated with Alzheimer's or other degenerative diseases, traumatic brain damage that occurs during the adult years, or other adult-onset diseases or conditions.

Prevalence

How many persons have mental retardation? Given the three-factor definition, this issue is not so clear-cut even in a theoretical sense. Assuming that IQ has a mean of 100, a standard deviation of 15, and follows a Gaussian or bell-shaped distribution, one would expect 2.28 percent of the population to have IQs of 70 or below (i.e., two or more standard deviations below the mean). But other considerations lead to prevalence estimates that are much less than 2.28 percent.[5]

Consider two criteria of the mental retardation diagnosis, below-70 IQ and adaptive deficits. If, in addition to IQ levels of 70 and below, adaptive deficits are also involved in the definition of mental retardation, then the prevalence rate depends on the correlation between levels of intellectual and adaptive behaviors. If all persons with IQs below 70 showed adaptive impairments, then the 2.28 percent prevalence rate would hold. But if many persons with below-70 IQs do not show adaptive impairments, then a smaller figure would result.

What is the correlation between adaptive and intellectual functioning? Different studies lead to varying conclusions. One problem concerns different correlations for groups at different levels of functioning. For persons with more severe levels of mental retardation—that is, those with IQ 50 and below—the correlation between the two is reasonably high. Most persons with IQs of 50 or below require some degree of help in everyday living. With IQs in the 50 to 70 range, however, the correlations between IQ and adaptive behavior are much lower. Considering two persons with an IQ of 60, one individual might require intensive, lifelong supports, whereas another might need no help whatsoever. The degree to which IQ and adaptive behavior are not perfectly correlated lowers the overall prevalence rate.

Other issues also enter in. Prevalence estimates of 2.28 percent assume both a constant rate of diagnosis at different ages and a life expectancy that mirrors that of the general population. Both appear unlikely. Prevalence rates of mental retardation go up from about age 6–17—roughly, the period of formal schooling—and are lower before and after these ages.[8] Similarly, the life expectancies of individuals who are at the lowest IQ levels (IQ < 20) and who are nonambulatory fall well below the 70- to 80-year average life spans currently found in the United States and other Western countries.[9] Similarly, several genetic mental retardation syndromes frequently lead to comorbid health conditions that lower a person's life expectancy (see below). Age-related fluctuations of rates of diagnosis and shorter life expectancies likely lower the prevalence rate of mental retardation in our society.

What, then, is the prevalence of mental retardation? Recent estimates are below 2 percent of the population, generally from 1.0 to 1.5 percent.[8] Given a current U.S. population of almost 300 million people, 3.0 million or more Americans have mental retardation.

Levels of Impairment

Like any group of people, those with mental retardation differ one from another. Historically, professionals have divided persons with mental retardation into four categories based on IQ: mild, moderate, severe, and profound mental retardation.

As Table 2.1 illustrates, these four levels of impairment are based on IQ levels, not on adaptive functioning. Thus, different persons—particularly in the mild mental retardation range—may vary in their ability to perform most tasks of everyday living. A second feature of the level-of-impairment classification is that

Table 2.1
Levels of Impairment for Individuals with Mental Retardation

Mild mental retardation (IQ 55-70) constitutes 85 percent of all persons with mental retardation.[1] As adults, many individuals hold jobs, marry, raise families and are indistinguishable
from those without mental retardation.

Moderate mental retardation (IQ 40-54) is the second most common level of impairment.
In contrast to those with mild mental retardation, these individuals are often diagnosed at the
preschool age. Many with moderate mental retardation have an organic cause for their mental
retardation. Although some require minimal support, most persons with moderate mental
retardation need help throughout life. Increasingly, however, these individuals hold jobs in the
outside workforce as unskilled laborers.

Severe mental retardation (IQ 25-39) refers to more affected persons, the majority of
whom suffer from clear organic causes. Many such persons show concurrent physical or
ambulatory problems, as well as respiratory, heart, or other conditions. Most persons require
special assistance throughout their lives. As adults, many live with their parents or in supervised group homes; most work in either workshop or "preworkshop" settings.

Profound mental retardation (IQ below 25) involves persons with the most severe levels
of intellectual and adaptive impairments. These persons generally learn only the rudiments
of communicative skills, and intensive training is required to teach basic eating, grooming,
toileting, and dressing behaviors. Persons with profound mental retardation require lifelong care and assistance. Almost all show organic causes for their mental retardation, and
many have severe co-occurring conditions that sometimes lead to death during childhood
or early adulthood. Some persons with profound mental retardation can perform workshop or preworkshop tasks, and most live with their parents, in supervised group homes, or
in small, specialized facilities.

no attention is given to the cause or etiology of the person's mental retardation.
Thus, individuals with different causes for their mental retardation (or no clear
cause at all) are considered together as long as they are at roughly comparable
levels of IQ.

Although this classification of mild, moderate, severe, and profound mental
retardation is well-known, the most recent AAMR classification manuals[5] have
proposed changing these IQ-level categories to those based on a person's needs
for intermittent, limited, extensive, and pervasive support. Although praise-
worthy in its focus on the interaction between the person and that person's
environmental needs (as opposed to focusing solely on the person's problems),
the AAMR approach is cumbersome. As a result, most professionals continue to use the level-of-impairment categories in describing subject groups.[10]
Similarly, in surveying mental retardation guidelines used by the 50 states plus
the District of Columbia, Denning, Chamberlain, and Polloway[11] found that
44 states continued using the level-of-impairment classification system, 4 used
the 1992 AAMR manual as the basis of their regulations, and 3 states used

neither model. To most professionals, the level-of-impairment system remains the most used system.

Etiology

Although mental retardation is caused by many conditions, the field has historically focused on the person's level of functioning, paying scant attention to the individual's cause of mental retardation. Recently, however, this situation has changed, with recent years showing a major shift toward etiology-related studies, particularly as they relate to genetic mental retardation conditions. Consider the numbers of behavioral research articles on Williams syndrome, Prader-Willi syndrome, and fragile X syndrome. From the 1980s to the 1990s, the numbers of behavioral research articles on Williams syndrome increased from 10 to 81; on Prader-Willi syndrome, from 24 to 86; on fragile X syndrome, from 60 to 149. Even in Down syndrome (DS), the sole etiology featuring a longstanding tradition of behavioral research, the amount of behavioral research almost doubled—from 607 to 1,140 articles—from the 1980s to the 1990s.[12]

Definition and Principles

Such increased numbers of research articles reflect the growing sense that groups with different genetic disorders do differ behaviorally from one to another. This sense has led to a growing field of behavioral phenotypes, which refers to "the heightened probability or likelihood that people with a given syndrome will exhibit certain behavioral and developmental sequelae relative to those without the syndrome" (p. 523).[12]

Before describing the behavioral phenotypes of different genetic syndromes, it is necessary to describe the main characteristics of behavioral phenotypes. Three aspects are especially noteworthy:

1. *Probabilistic nature.* In describing heightened probabilities and likelihoods, the Dykens[12] definition highlights the probabilistic nature of behavioral phenotypes. Many, but rarely all, individuals with a given syndrome will show that syndrome's so-called characteristic behaviors.
2. *Total and partial specificity.* The second characteristic refers to whether etiology-related behaviors are unique to only one genetic disorder (total specificity) or instead common to two or more disorders (partial specificity). Examining the many different studies so far, it appears that both total and partial specificity occur, with some etiology-related behaviors unique to a single syndrome, whereas others are common to two or more syndromes.[13] But given the vast number of genetic (and other) causes of mental retardation and the relatively few ways to show behavioral

outcomes, this second, partially specific pattern probably occurs more often.

3. *Multiple domains.* Although in this chapter we focus mainly on maladaptive behavior-psychopathology of different genetic disorders, behavioral pheno-types can be found in many domains. Different genetic disorders predispose individuals to specific cognitive, linguistic, or adaptive strengths or weak-nesses, or ages of rapid versus slowed rates of development. At times, indi-viduals with a specific syndrome may even show a propensity to display a single behavior, such as the self-hugging behavior of many individuals with Smith-Magenis syndrome.[12]

Behavioral Phenotypes of Three Genetic Syndromes

Although many genetic disorders are associated with mental retardation, we here briefly describe only three syndromes. To flesh out these descriptions, we also provide brief case vignettes of these syndromes in Table 2.2.

Down syndrome, or trisomy 21, is the best-known form of mental retardation. DS is also the most prevalent form known to be associated with a chromosomal abnormality, occurring once in every 800 live births. First described in 1866 by John Langdon Down,[14] DS has been the focus of intensive genetic and behav-ioral research. Children with DS usually have characteristic physical features including epicanthic folds around the eyes, a protruding tongue, short stature, and hypotonia (weak muscle tone). DS often occurs together with such medical conditions as heart defects and respiratory problems, particularly during the first year of life. Although in the past individuals with DS had short life spans, medi-cal treatments have improved life expectancies for persons with DS to approxi-mately 50 years.[15]

Three behavioral characteristics appear in many individuals with DS. The first involves cognitive-linguistic strengths and weaknesses. In various studies, persons with DS appear particularly impaired in language. Such impairments, which are more pronounced than overall levels of mental age (MA), occur in linguistic grammar[16] and in expressive (as opposed to receptive) language.[17] In addition, most individuals with DS show problems in articulation.[18] Conversely, persons with DS often show relatively higher performance on tasks of visual (as opposed to auditory) short-term memory.[19]

A second behavioral issue involves the rate of development, with children with DS developing at slower rates as they get older. Such slowing of develop-ment may relate to age-related changes or to difficulties these children have in achieving certain cognitive tasks (e.g., language).[20] A third, possibly related change concerns Alzheimer's disease. Neuropathological signs of Alzheimer's disease appear to be universal by age 35 or 40 in individuals with DS, although the dementia associated with Alzheimer's does not appear (if at all) in most persons with DS until decades later.[21]

Table 2.2
Individuals with Down Syndrome, Prader-Willi Syndrome,
and Williams Syndrome

Down syndrome. Erica is a 19-year-old who recently graduated from high school. Her mother is concerned because, while Erica was always very social and well–liked in school, she has now become less upbeat and more passive. She has also put on weight. To make matters worse, the vocational training program that she was slated to attend after graduation has a long waiting list, so most of Erica's days are spent watching TV alone at home, and helping to take care of a neighbor's cat. She and her mother have now decided to ask a social worker to identify alternative training programs to keep her busy. They also agreed to take walks after dinner. Erica, once an avid swimmer, is going to re-enroll in the Special Olympics swimming program.

Erica's story demonstrates several concerns for young adults with Down syndrome:

+ the propensity for adults with Down syndrome to become more sedentary and withdrawn,
+ the need for programs that foster lifelong learning in adults with mental retardation; and
+ the importance of continued social interactions as these individuals age.

Prader-Willi syndrome. Greg is a 14-year-old who loves to complete puzzles. First diagnosed with Prader-Willi syndrome shortly after birth, Greg has since demonstrated the classic features of the syndrome: hypotonia in infancy, delayed milestones, and a marked interest in eating and food that began at age five. Greg is having trouble at school because of difficulties with transitions. Greg's weight is also creeping up, as are instances of food seeking. His family has started locking the refrigerator and cabinets, as they have learned that if he knows that he can not get into food, he will get involved with other things, like his puzzles. Indeed, Greg, who has just completed a 50-piece puzzle with remarkable speed, looks up with a grin. "This one was easy," he boasts, "I thought you said you had hard puzzles!"

Greg's case demonstrates issues for many youngsters with Prader-Willi syndrome:

+ a host of behavioral concerns, especially hyperphagia and compulsions,
+ the need for the management of his diet and behavior to be carefully monitored,
+ strengths in expressive vocabulary and visual-spatial skills (e.g., puzzles), and
+ targeting strengths as incentives (i.e., "puzzle time") to ease compulsions and transitions.

Williams syndrome. Rachel is a highly energetic 12 year-old. She is very social and feels that everyone is her friend. Her parents are concerned because, while they love her friendly nature, they are worried about her poor social judgment and vulnerability as she enters adolescence. After being diagnosed with Williams syndrome at eight months and coming through a corrective heart surgery, a fussy infancy, and a period of language delay, Rachel quickly caught up. On formal testing as a first grader, her vocabulary exceeded her overall cognitive abilities. Recently, Rachel has been worrying about things more and more often. Her anxiety can at times get out of hand, but never to the point that it stops her from going outside. Along with her growing anxiety, Rachel has a growing interest in music. Her father observes that music calms her and playing the piano helps her to settle down for the night. Recently, Rachel has asked to try another instrument so that she can play in the school band, or to join the glee club, so that she can sing with others.

Rachel demonstrates many of the key behavioral features of Williams syndrome:

+ a strong social orientation coupled with poor social judgment and disinhibition;
+ well-developed expressive language skills,
+ a worried, fretful stance; and
+ an interest in music that may or may not reflect remarkable talent but that is emotionally compelling and gratifying.

Prader-Willi syndrome is caused by missing genetic material from chromosome 15—either a deletion on chromosome 15 coming from the father or two chromosome 15s from the mother (maternal uniparental disomy). Most individuals with Prader-Willi syndrome are short in stature (about five feet tall in adulthood) and show extreme hyperphagia (i.e., overeating). Indeed, hyperphagia and resultant obesity have long been considered the hallmarks of Prader-Willi syndrome, and most cases of early death in the syndrome relate to complications of obesity (e.g., type II diabetes, respiratory and circulatory problems).[22] Many individuals show obsessions and compulsions that are similar in level to those with clinically diagnosed obsessive-compulsive disorder.[23]

Intellectually, most children with Prader-Willi syndrome show relative weaknesses in sequential processing, or tasks involving consecutive, step-by-step order in problem solving.[24] In contrast, these children perform well on tasks requiring integration and synthesis of stimuli as a unified whole, or simultaneous processing. Many individuals with Prader-Willi syndrome also demonstrate particularly high-level abilities in jigsaw puzzles. Such skills, which on average exceed those of typical children of comparable chronological ages, are especially shown by those having the deletion form of this disorder—as opposed to the maternal uniparental disomy.[25]

Williams syndrome is caused by a micro-deletion on chromosome 7. Children with this syndrome generally show a characteristic facial appearance, along with heart and other health problems.[26] As many as 95 percent of children with Williams syndrome show a hypersensitivity to loud sound. Along with an overly social, outgoing personality, children with Williams syndrome also show a wide variety of anxieties and fears.[27]

Apart from these medical and psychiatric issues, recent attention has strongly focused on the interesting cognitive-linguistic profile shown by most of these children. Children with Williams syndrome show relative strengths in language; for many years it was thought that these children might even perform at chronological age-levels on a variety of linguistic tasks. Although age-appropriate performance in language has now been found in only small percentages of children with Williams syndrome,[28] these children nevertheless show relative strengths in language, as well as in auditory processing and music. Conversely, many children with Williams syndrome perform especially poorly on a variety of visuospatial tasks.

Taken together, studies on genetic syndromes highlight the many ways in which one's cause of mental retardation affects specific behavioral outcomes. Such studies also shift the ground from a research field focused on a single, heterogeneous "mental retardation" group to a field interested in various types of mental retardation, many with their own etiology-related behaviors and genebrain-behavior relations. In discussions of remaining issues, then, we consider the evidence both in terms of mental retardation in general as well as in different genetic conditions.

MALADAPTIVE BEHAVIOR-PSYCHOPATHOLOGY

Despite his cognitive limitations, his minimal expressive language capabilities, and his placement in a special education classroom, Michael always struck his mother as a happy boy. His smile always had a way of brightening even her hardest day. Michael loved to laugh and always wanted to be around people. He had a good group of friends from his neighborhood, whom he enjoyed seeing in the halls of his school.

Since he hit the teen years, however, Michael's disposition had changed. He did not seem as happy. He preferred to be alone, and he rarely went outside to play. Michael's mother noticed that fewer things made him happy, and more things threw him into a temper tantrum. His withdrawal and moodiness were what brought him and his mother to the clinic's waiting room on this day.

Historically, mental retardation has been separated from mental illness. Indeed, when clinicians encountered psychiatric symptoms in persons with mental retardation, these issues were interpreted as being a part of, or caused by, intellectual deficit. In the early 1980s, Reiss and Szyszko[29] even identified the phenomenon of "diagnostic overshadowing," the idea that, to most professionals, the mental retardation diagnosis overshadowed all other psychiatric concerns.

But in recent years, professionals have begun to appreciate that mental retardation and mental illness often go together. Persons with mental retardation are at heightened risks for mental illness, with the prevalence of comorbid psychiatric conditions in persons with mental retardation estimated to be 3–4 times that of the general population.[1] In addition, all types of mental illness are seen in those with mental retardation.

These statements, however, mask the many difficulties inherent in the study of mental illness in persons with mental retardation. For this reason, we first discuss diagnosis of psychopathology in persons with mental retardation and the many advances and challenges that have arisen in this area. We then tackle the issues of prevalence, risk factors, etiology, and treatment.

Challenges in Diagnosis

In contrast to diagnosing individuals of average intelligence, psychiatric diagnoses of persons with mental retardation are beset by several difficulties. The first concerns self-report. In order to diagnose many types of psychopathology, clinicians rely on the person's own self-report of symptoms. Thus, self-reported feelings of hopelessness and depression constitute major symptoms of mood disorders, and disorganized speech and reported hallucinations or delusions help the clinician make a diagnosis of schizophrenia. Obviously, if persons are less able to communicate their feelings and thoughts, it becomes more difficult to make these diagnoses.

Another complication concerns the distinction between one's mental age and chronological age. Particularly before mental age plateaus in late adolescence (16–18 years on most IQ tests), individuals with average IQ have mental ages that are roughly the same as their chronological ages. In children with mental retardation, however, chronological ages exceed mental ages. When a 14-year-old adolescent or a 30-year-old adult has a mental age of six years, it becomes difficult to determine which behaviors are normal for someone with his or her level of development.

Fortunately, some headway has been made on both these issues. In the case of individuals who are non-verbal or limited linguistically, diagnosis relies heavily on third-party reports.[30] However, the validity of such reports can be questionable. Moss argues that both respondent and informant should be interviewed, and have found that omission of either interview results in one-third of psychopathology going undiagnosed.[30]

Similarly, over the past decade, a movement has arisen to develop parent or caregiver-report measures of maladaptive behavior-psychopathology for children and adults with mental retardation. Because of the need to consider mental age as well as chronological age, several widely used assessment tools have been normed specifically on large, community-based samples of persons with mental retardation. These instruments include the Aberrant Behavior Checklist, the Reiss Screen, and the Developmental Behaviour Checklist. Each is specific to the concerns of persons with mental retardation and has a factor structure of maladaptive behaviors derived solely from persons with mental retardation. (For a review, see Dykens.[31])

As these measures have been developed and more widely used, several problems have arisen. First, the exact factor structures of different instruments have not always been identical. Second, problems in different domains do not always map onto *DSM* or other psychiatric categories. Although this mapping problem also occurs in children and adults without mental retardation, it becomes more of an issue in a group for which *DSM* categories may already be more problematic.[31]

Prevalence, Nature, and Correlates of Psychopathology

Despite the difficulties in providing accurate psychiatric diagnoses to persons with mental retardation, many such persons show significant psychiatric impairments. A rate of approximately 40 percent seems likely, although different studies range widely. Koller, Richardson, Katz, and McClaren[32] found that 36 percent of their sample suffered from psychiatric impairments, whereas Gilberg, Persson, Grufman, and Themmer[33] reported a rate of psychiatric diagnosis that was 64 percent. More recently, Einfeld and Tonge[34] found the prevalence of psychopathology in individuals with mental retardation to be 40.7 percent. These percentages are in stark contrast to rates of psychopathology in samples without mental retardation, which are considered to be about 6 percent.[35] In addition, although showing all types of psychopathology, persons with mental retardation appear more prone to psychosis, autism, and behavior disorders, and less prone to substance abuse or affective disorders.[36]

In considering correlates of psychopathology, one sees major differences from samples without mental retardation. Unlike those without mental retardation, age and sex generally do not seem to affect the prevalence of psychopathology in persons with mental retardation.[34] Instead, the main influence on the amount and type of psychopathology is one's level of impairment. Einfeld and Tonge[34] found that persons with profound mental retardation (IQ < 25) have lower levels of psychopathology compared to persons with mild, moderate, or severe mental retardation. In contrast, individuals with milder levels of mental retardation (IQ of 50–69) had the highest rates of disruptive and antisocial behaviors. Other studies have found that individuals with milder levels of impairment also have higher rates of schizophrenia spectrum disorders, personality disorder, and depression.

Although the numbers suggest a higher prevalence of psychopathology in individuals with milder mental retardation, there may be high levels of unrecognized psychopathology in individuals with more severe levels due to difficulties in diagnosis. In comparison to persons with milder forms of mental retardation, individuals with severe or profound mental retardation are more likely to be diagnosed with such behavioral disorders as self-injury, stereotypies, and autistic behaviors.[37] Rojahn, Matson, Naglieri, and Mayville[38] found a significant, positive, and clinically meaningful relationship between these behavior problems and psychiatric conditions, but emphasize that the relationship is complex. It is therefore difficult to assess whether individuals at the lower end of the IQ spectrum truly have less psychopathology than those with milder levels of mental retardation.

Risk Factors and Vulnerabilities

Beyond increased rates of psychopathology per se, persons with mental retardation may have specific risk factors and vulnerabilities. In reviewing why persons with mental retardation are at heightened risk, Dykens[37] suggests a variety of possible risk factors along the biopsychosocial spectrum. Psychological vulnerabilities may range from aberrant personality-motivational styles (including learned helplessness); to familial vulnerabilities stemming from family stress; to social factors such as poor communication skills and peer rejection; to biological factors such as the presence of seizure disorders or self-injurious behaviors.

In one of the few detailed studies of this issue, Dekker and Koot[39] investigated family and child factors that predicted psychopathology in children and adolescents with mental retardation one year later. Among the family factors predicting later child psychopathology, they found that parental psychopathology and single-parent families predicted later child psychopathology. Aspects of the child were also identified as risk factors, including inadequate daily living skills, chronic physical conditions, social incompetence, and negative life events.

Etiology

Etiology is another risk factor for psychopathology. We here describe separately psychopathology in DS, Prader-Willi syndrome, and Williams syndrome.

Down Syndrome

Children with DS generally show both lesser amounts and less severe types of psychopathology. Such studies include those comparing children with DS to children with (heterogeneous) mental retardation, as well as those comparing to children with Prader-Willi or other genetic syndromes. Such studies include those comparing children with DS to children with heterogeneous mental retardation, as well as those comparing to children with Prader-Will or other genetic syndromes (see Dykens[37] for a review).

Recently, however, the picture concerning psychopathology in DS has changed in several ways. First, several recent studies have examined changes in maladaptive behavior-psychopathology as children and adults get older. Dykens, Shah, Beck, Sagun, and King[40] noted that adolescents with DS may become more inward during the adolescent years, in addition to showing lesser amounts of stubbornness and other externalizing problems.[41] Although the reasons for such changes are unclear, one factor predisposing adolescents with DS to depression and other psychopathology seems to be less stimulation and programming.[42] Less activity and engagement with the world are probably risk factors for all adolescents with mental retardation, but a lack of activity may be especially harmful for adolescents and young adults with DS.

A second issue concerns a possible connection between DS and autism. Long thought to be protected from autism due to a generally social, upbeat personality (the so-called "Down syndrome personality"), recent studies have identified a small subset of children with DS who have autism or autism spectrum disorders. The percentage of such children is unknown, but a 5–10 percent figure seems likely.[43] Granted, the connection between autism and DS has received insufficient attention, and some connection between the two may occur due to lower IQ alone. Still, such ties of DS and autism are intriguing and may lead to increased understandings of both disorders.

Prader-Willi Syndrome

Although persons with Prader-Willi syndrome show high rates of tantrums, emotional lability, and peer problems,[44] the hallmark of the syndrome is its hyperphagia and impaired satiety response. Obsessive thoughts of food are common, as are unusual food behaviors such as foraging through the trash for food, stealing food, and eating unpalatable items.[44]

Although food-related problems are almost universal for individuals with Prader-Willi syndrome, these individuals also frequently exhibit other obsessions and compulsions. Common compulsions include hoarding, ordering, arranging, and needing to tell or ask, along with need for sameness in routine.[23] Such obsessions and compulsions usually begin in the two–five year period,[45] around the same age as the onset of hyperphagia and food seeking.

Recently, different types of psychopathology have also been linked to different forms of Prader-Willi syndrome. Besides having higher IQs,[46] those with the maternal disomy (versus deletion) form of Prader-Willi syndrome seem especially prone to severe psychopathology.[47] Current thinking is that the majority of individuals with maternal uniparental disomy develop severe, atypical psychosis during their early adult years. The nature, causes, and course of such psychotic disorders are all being actively investigated.[48]

Williams Syndrome

Although individuals with Williams syndrome tend to be outgoing and socially disinhibited, these individuals also show high rates of fears, anxiety, and phobia. In a sample of persons with mental retardation (but not Williams syndrome), Dykens[27] found that over 50 percent of respondents reported only two commonly occurring fears—of their parents getting sick and of getting a shot or injection. In contrast, over half of the group with Williams syndrome endorsed 41 different fears. Such fears ran the gamut from interpersonal issues like being teased (92%), getting punished (85%), or getting into arguments with others (85%); to such physical issues as injections (90%), being in a fire or getting burned (82%), or getting stung by a bee (79%); to loud noises-sirens (87%), falling from high places (79%), and thunderstorms (78%). Such fears also relate to formal psychiatric diagnoses. In this same sample, 84 percent of individuals with Williams syndrome met most diagnostic criteria for phobia, and 35 percent of these individuals had symptom-related adaptive impairment.

Treatment

The history of treatment is mixed for clients with mental retardation. In the 1930s, persons with mental retardation were often included in psychotherapy.[4] This practice waned in subsequent years, as persons with mental retardation were thought to have problems with transference and insight, poor impulse control, and a reduced capacity for change.[49] More recently, psychologists have once again begun to recognize the utility of psychotherapeutic interventions, including cognitive therapy, relaxation therapy, and psychoanalytic or developmentally-based therapies. In all approaches, beneficial modifications include being aware of the client's language ability and of his or her developmental level.[4]

In addition to talk therapies, pharmacotherapy is widely used for both specific disorders and more general behavioral problems. In a population-based study, Spreat, Conroy, and Jones[50] found that 22 percent of adults with mental retardation were prescribed antipsychotic and 5.9 percent antidepressant medications. Examining prevalence rates of drug treatments in adults and children with mental retardation in institutions from 1966–1985, Singh, Ellis, and Wechsler[51] found 30–40 percent were prescribed psychotropic drugs, 25–45 percent anticonvulsants, and 50–70 percent psychotropic drugs, anticonvulsants, or some combination of the two.

Despite the potential utility of psychotherapy and of pharmacological treatments, no single professional group has a monopoly on knowledge of how to treat this population. In fact, a collaborative team approach to treatment best ensures that services are not fragmented. This multidisciplinary approach may include psychiatrists, mental health practitioners, behavior specialists, and case managers.[52] Such a multidisciplinary team can then provide services involving case management, social skills training, supported employment, family intervention, and behavioral strategies.

Although progress has been made in treating persons with dual diagnosis, many such individuals continue to go untreated. McCarthy and Boyd[53] found that over half (64%) of their sample of individuals with mental retardation and a psychiatric diagnosis or persistent behavioral problems had not received specialist mental health care. Potential reasons for lack of care include diagnostic overshadowing by primary care physicians and a lack of specialized training in mental retardation throughout the mental health field. As McCarthy and Boyd note, the mental health of any individual is important, but it is critical for persons with mental retardation, who are particularly vulnerable to psychopathology.

MENTAL RETARDATION IN SOCIETY

The treatment of dually-diagnosed persons constitutes the tip of the iceberg relative to the societal issues concerning persons with mental retardation. We address three of these issues below.

As Michael's turn with the psychologist finally roles around, his mother begins telling her story from the beginning. She talks about how hard it was to drive him from appointment to appointment, and how all of the early intervention staff came to her home on an almost daily basis. She talks about the adjustments her family had to make, and how her two older children did not always understand why these "big people" always came to play with Michael and not with them. She ended her story, however, with all that Michael had taught her and her children. Despite some bumps in her marriage shortly after Michael was born, she realized that he was a blessing and not the stressor she originally viewed him as. She noticed that her two older children were more patient with other children with disabilities, and she loved to overhear when they defended Michael's behaviors to their friends. She told the psychologist she wouldn't have changed a thing about the past, but now, as he's growing older, she's worried about his future; will he be able to live on his own, who will care for him when she no longer can, and will he have a job?

Families of Individuals with Mental Retardation

Historically, families have been considered to suffer from raising their child with mental retardation. Following Solnit and Stark's[54] idea that mothers mourn—as in a death—the birth of the child with disabilities, various authors proposed stage models of mourning and spoke of parental depression and sibling and family problems. In the early 1980s, however, Crnic, Freidrich, and Greenberg[55] proposed a stress-and-coping model of parental adaptation. According to this model, the child with mental retardation could be considered a stressor in the family system, but, like any stressor, could result in family functioning that was worse, the same, or even improved.

This more positive, albeit realistic model of family coping changed the field in several ways.[56] Instead of considering all parents as necessarily negatively affected by their child with mental retardation, parents were now considered to vary widely. Researchers performed more within-group studies to identify which parent, child, or family factors might lead to better or worse coping. Such studies found that the parent's active (as opposed to passive or emotional) problem-solving styles were very beneficial,[57] and that children with fewer behavior problems helped in parental and familial functioning. Similarly, children whose mental retardation was caused by genetic disorders leading to fewer maladaptive behaviors (e.g., DS) and to more upbeat, positive personalities (DS, Williams syndrome) often predispose better coping by parents and families as a whole.[58]

Similarly, studies of siblings also moved from a pathological to a stress-and-coping orientation. In the past, a brother or sister with a disability was thought to negatively affect the typically developing sibling. In a review of the sibling literature, however, Stoneman[59] found that, compared to siblings of same-aged typically developing children, most siblings of children with disabilities showed no differences in self-concept, perceived competence, self-efficacy, or internalizing or externalizing problems. Taunt and Hastings[60] also reported that having a sibling with a disability does not lead to pathology or maladaptive behaviors in typically developing children, although some children are harmed by the experience of growing up with a sibling with a disability.

The sibling experience also changes as the two offspring get older. As sibling relationships progress, typically developing siblings often assume roles related to helping, teaching, and managing their brother or sister with disabilities. They also help parents with caretaking responsibilities. Although for some siblings these role responsibilities limit their time with friends and decrease their social activities, siblings of children with disabilities on average do not have fewer social contacts than other children.[59]

When siblings enter adulthood, siblings become more concerned about the future of their sibling with mental retardation and about the caretaking roles they may be expected to assume. Krauss, Seltzer, Gordon, and Friedman[61] found that, as they age, many siblings report high levels of phone contact or weekly visits, and many report living within a thirty minute drive of their sibling with a disability. Activities often involve going to a restaurant, shopping together, and going to the movies.

These adult sibling relationships may also hold the key to solving one of our society's important, but little discussed, public policy issues. As in society as a whole, the population of persons with mental retardation is aging. At present, 526,000 individuals with disabilities 60 years and older live in the United States; by the year 2030, that number is expected to triple—to 1.5 million.[62] Given that over 60 percent of these individuals live in their parents' home, who—apart from siblings—will be caring for these aging individuals when their parents can no longer do so? Such issues have clear, difficult implications for our entire society.

Parents with Mental Retardation

A second societal issue concerns parents who themselves have mental retardation. In the early 1900s, women with mental retardation were often prohibited from marriage, were institutionalized, and were involuntarily sterilized. The prevailing view was that people with mental retardation and their children were degenerate, criminally inclined, and insane.[63] In the mid-1900s, the focus shifted from fears of people with mental retardation having children, to a concern for the children of parents with mental retardation.

From the 1970s to the present, studies have dispelled many of the myths surrounding parents with mental retardation. The four most prevalent myths were that parents with mental retardation would: have children with mental retardation, have large numbers of children, be inadequate parents, and be unable to learn how to raise a child.

Children of Parents with Mental Retardation

In their review of the literature on parents with mental retardation, Holburn, Perkins, and Vietze[63] reported that approximately one-fourth of the children of parents with mental retardation will also have mental retardation. Furthermore, when both parents have mental retardation, the risk of their child having mental retardation is doubled, and the risk of having a child with mental retardation is higher when the mother as opposed to the father has mental retardation. When the parents with mental retardation are of lower socioeconomic status (SES), the children are at a higher risk for developmental delay (especially delayed expressive language) than those children born to middle-class families.[64]

Family Size

While many feared that people with mental retardation would have a large number of children, Espe-Sherwindt and Crable[64] reported that parents with mental retardation have either fewer or the same amount of children as other parents of the same SES. In addition, these parents were reported to have a realistic view of how many children they could handle raising. In addition, many parents with mental retardation reported that they did not want to have children at all.

Parents as Caregivers

Like mothers without mental retardation, most mothers with mental retardation provide adequate care for their children. Feldman, Towns, Betel, Case, Rincover, and Rubino[65] compared mother-infant interactions of mothers with mental retardation to mothers without mental retardation. Mothers with mental retardation provided less prompting, praise, looking, imitating, playing, and talking to their infant. The children of these mothers also vocalized less than the infants of mothers without mental retardation. Although Tymchuk[66] found that the incidence of neglect was greater than the incidence of abuse by parents with mental retardation, it was unclear how rates of either neglect or abuse compared to rates for other parents of the same SES. Most reported neglect and abuse, however, was the result of ill-preparation for parenting, rather than purposeful abusive behavior.

Parent Interventions

Parents with mental retardation can learn good parenting skills. Unfortunately, few programs exist that teach parents with mental retardation how to raise a child and few parents with mental retardation have received any preparation for raising a child.[64] Another confounding factor is that parents with mental retardation have never been taught to seek out services when they need help. Consequently, they are less likely to approach professionals.

Factors related to better parenting skills include an IQ greater than 50, being married, and having fewer children, adequate financial support, and a willingness to accept help and support.[64] Unfortunately, many mothers with mental retardation are single, poor women who are under extreme stress and who suffer from depression. These mothers often lack self-confidence, a stable residence, and the skills needed to be an adequate parent.[63] Fortunately, early intervention and services have been shown to help parents with mental retardation to be good, nurturing parents.

As for the offspring, many feel stigmatized by certain characteristics and behaviors their parents exhibit.[67] Some also fear they may be like their parents. The most important outcome for the parent-child relationship, however, is the child's perception of the mother's caregiving style, which can have a very positive influence on attachment.

Child Abuse

Studies consistently find much higher than expected levels of child abuse and neglect for children with mental retardation (and all disabilities). While estimates vary greatly, children with disabilities may be from four–ten times more likely than children without disabilities to suffer from child abuse or maltreatment.[68]

In the most comprehensive study of this issue, Sullivan and Knutson[69] examined maltreatment among children with disabilities in Omaha, Nebraska. By merging public school records with Central Registry, Foster Care Review

Board, and police databases, these authors were able to account for over 50,000 children, from birth to age 21, and to determine maltreatment among the populations. They found a 31 percent rate of maltreatment of children with disabilities, as compared to a prevalence rate of 9 percent for children without disabilities. Children with disabilities were also more likely to be abused multiple times and in multiple forms. Behavior disorders, mental retardation, and learning disabilities were the most prevalent disabled types of children experiencing maltreatment. Children with mental retardation were four times more likely to be abused compared to children without disabilities. While more girls than boys are abused in the typical population, more boys than girls are abused among children with disabilities.[69]

Many possible causes have been suggested for why children with disabilities are more often abused than children without disabilities. As in abusive families of children without disabilities, family and parent stress have been identified as risk factors leading to child abuse. Factors increasing such stress include parents of low SES, parent under- or unemployment, and being a single parent. Social isolation, parental substance abuse, parents with mental illness or mental retardation, and a parent's own experience of abuse have also been shown to increase the risk of child abuse.[70]

Specific child characteristics can also increase stress experienced by parents and thus lead to child abuse. These characteristics include prematurity or low birth weight, discipline problems, sexual acting out, poor school performance, permanent or chronic conditions such as developmental disabilities or medical fragility, and difficult temperament.[71] The age of the child may also interact with disability status to increase the risk for sexual and physical abuse. Children with disabilities are maltreated at younger ages, leading to the importance of early intervention and support services for families with young children with disabilities. Furthermore, children with communication impairments may be at increased risk because these impairments may prevent them from communicating, either verbally or behaviorally, what has happened to them.[72]

Criminality

A final issue concerns criminality. Although many believe that people with mental retardation are over-represented as offenders in the criminal justice system, the facts are much more complicated. Reviewing the existing literature, Holland, Clare, and Mukhopadhyay[73] found little support that people with mental retardation were over-represented. Instead, being a male and being young were more predictive than mental retardation for involvement in the criminal justice system. Mental retardation did seem to increase the risk of illegal or antisocial behavior, but this risk was also greater if the individual was socially disadvantaged in childhood and adulthood, was a substance abuser, and had a background of familial offending.

Barron, Hassiotis, and Banes[74] also investigated the characteristics of individuals with mental retardation who came into contact with the criminal justice system. They found that those with mental retardation began offending at a young age and frequently had a history of multiple offenses. In fact, 54 percent of their sample (61 individuals) first came into contact with the criminal justice system before they were 16 years old, and 21.3 percent had contact before 12 years of age. The mean number of offenses was 4.1; the most common offense was violence, followed by sex offenses and property offenses. Over a quarter of the group has spent time in prison as a result of their most recent offense. At the follow-up interview (10 months later), about half of the sample had reoffended. The group also had a high rate of psychopathology, especially psychotic illness (51.7%), and more than half had been prescribed antipsychotic medication (63.9%).

In addition to criminal behavior per se, other issues relate to persons with mental retardation within the criminal justice system. Specifically, Perske[75] reported people with mental retardation often confess to crimes they did not commit. In fact, almost half of the cases he examined had exonerated the individual with mental retardation through DNA testing. In addition, in all of the 38 cases examined by Perske, a lawyer was not present during the interrogation of the individual with mental retardation.

Such lack of attention to basic criminal rights—as well as the diminished capacity to advocate for oneself and to understand criminal proceedings—has led to an ongoing controversy about the status of persons with mental retardation within the criminal justice system. The most salient issue surrounds the death penalty. Should persons with mental retardation face death for their actions? In *Atkins v. Virginia,* 122 S.Ct.2242 (June 20, 2002), the Supreme Court held that the execution of any individual with mental retardation violated the Eighth Amendment's prohibition on cruel and unusual punishment. But this issue, like many others concerning persons with mental retardation, continues to reverberate throughout our society.

THE ROAD AHEAD

Advances in Research

Although persons with mental retardation have long been considered as so-called natural experiments, the ways in which such individuals tell us about typical or nonretarded functioning have increased exponentially in recent years. Consider three examples.

The first involves the use of different genetic disorders to examine gene-brain-behavior connections involving psychopathology. As noted earlier, children with Prader-Willi syndrome develop obsessions and compulsions beginning in the two- to five-year period,[45] and many persons with Williams syndrome show extreme levels of fears and phobias.[27] Simply put, what is the relation of specific genetic disorders, brain anomalies, and psychopathological outcomes? Although such questions are in their infancy, different genetic disorders indeed promise to tell us much about gene-brain-behavior connections and the development of psychopathology.

But the lessons of genetic disorders go beyond psychopathology and maladaptive behaviors per se. Various linguists and psycholinguistics, for example, have been intrigued by the way in which children with Williams syndrome show high levels of language in the relative absence of high-level cognition. Which aspects of language are less impaired or unimpaired, what is the connection between cognition and language, and what are the various modules of language itself? All are issues increasingly informed by individuals with Williams syndrome.

A third issue concerns the effects on others of individuals with specific types of mental retardation. If, for example, most families of children with DS are coping better than families of other children with mental retardation, which aspects of the children themselves, of parent groups, and/or of societal knowledge accounts for such better functioning? Conversely, why are children with mental retardation so much more likely to be abused, and are some groups more or less likely to be abused? In short, what is the elicitor of either positive or negative reactions from others?

Advances in Treatment

A similar set of advances involves treating persons who are dually diagnosed. Again, many findings point to treatment implications for specific genetic syndromes. Consider Williams syndrome and the way in which most such individuals show extreme fearfulness and phobias. These individuals also often show high levels of interest, participation, and (sometimes) skill in music.[76] Moreover, Dykens[77] has recently discovered that, in Williams syndrome, anxiety and music may be linked, such that participation and skill in music is associated with lessened levels of anxieties and fears. Granted, the direction of this association remains unclear. Can less anxious children better participate in music or does participation in music make children less anxious? Still, the connection is intriguing. Ultimately, music therapies may be especially promising in persons with Williams syndrome.

Advances in Society

So far, we have focused on the many societal problems associated with persons with mental retardation. We have considered issues of caring for aging persons with mental retardation and how our society seems ill-equipped to address the three-fold increase by 2030 in the above 60-year-old population with mental retardation. We have noted how children with mental retardation are more often abused, and issues relating to how such individuals function as parents and, at times, as perpetrators of crimes.

In contrast to these negatively-tinged issues, however, the picture has brightened considerably for persons with mental retardation within our society. Over the past 30–40 years, both children and adults with mental retardation are increasingly participating in all aspects of modern life. Whereas once many children and adults were institutionalized, we now see children attending integrated classes in regular schools. Most adults engage in some sort of work, and, although most still live at home with parents, our society at least acknowledges the living needs of adults with mental retardation. Even the problem areas addressed—aging, parenthood, abuse, and criminality—in some ways simply reflect the increased participation of individuals with mental retardation within our society.

We end this chapter, then, on a positive note. Without being too Polyannish or (again) predicting a Cinderella-period both for the field and for persons with mental retardation, the coming years appear promising. Using the past few decades as our guide to the future, advances seem clear in research, in treatment, and in society as a whole. If so, someday persons with mental retardation might even lose their status as one of our society's most unacknowledged, under-appreciated special groups.

REFERENCES

1. American Psychiatric Association. (2004). *Diagnostic and statistical manual of mental disorders* (4th ed., text revision). Washington, DC: Author.
2. Potter, H. W. (1927). Mental deficiency and the psychiatrist. *American Journal of Psychiatry, 83*, 691–700.
3. Tarjan, G. (1966). Cinderella and the prince: Mental retardation and community psychiatry. *American Journal of Psychiatry, 122*, 1057–1059.
4. King, B. H., State, M. W., Shah, B., Davanzo, P., & Dykens, E. M. (1997). Mental retardation: A review of the past 10 years. Part I. *Journal of the American Academy of Child and Adolescent Psychiatry, 36*, 1656–1663.
5. American Association on Mental Retardation (2002). *Mental retardation: Definition, classification, and systems of supports* (10th ed.). Washington, DC: Author.
6. Sparrow, S. S., Cicchetti, D. V., & Balla, D. A. (2005). *Vineland Adaptive Behavior Scales* (2nd ed.). Circle Pines, MN: AGS Publishing.

7. MacMillan, D. L., Gresham, F. M., & Siperstein, G. N. (1993). Conceptual and psychometric concerns about the 1992 AAMR definition of mental retardation. *American Journal on Mental Retardation, 98,* 325–335.

8. Larson, S. A., Lakin, K. C., Anderson, L., Kwak, N., Lee, J. H., & Anderson, D. (2001). Prevalence of mental retardation and developmental disabilities: Estimates from the 1994/1995 National Health Interview Survey Disability Supplements. *American Journal on Mental Retardation, 106,* 231–252.

9. Eyman, R. K., & Miller, C. A. (1978). A demographic overview of severe and profound mental retardation. In C. E. Meyers (Ed.), *Quality of life in severely and profoundly mentally retarded people.* Washington, DC: American Association on Mental Retardation.

10. Polloway, E. A., Smith, J. D., Chamberlain, J., Denning, C. B., & Smith, T. E. C. (1999). Levels of deficits or supports in the classification of mental retardation: Implementation practices. *Education and Training in Mental Retardation, 34,* 200–206.

11. Denning, C. B., Chamberlain, J. A., & Polloway, E. A. (2000). An evaluation of state guidelines for mental retardation: Focus on definition and classification practices. *Education and Training in Mental Retardation, 35,* 226–232.

12. Dykens, E. M. (1995). Measuring behavioral phenotypes: Provocations from the "New Genetics." *American Journal on Mental Retardation, 99,* 522–532.

13. Hodapp, R. M. (1997). Direct and indirect behavioral effects of different genetic disorders of mental retardation. *American Journal on Mental Retardation, 102,* 67–79.

14. Dykens, E. M., Hodapp, R. M., & Finucane, B. M. (2000). *Genetics and mental retardation syndromes: A new look at behavior and interventions.* Baltimore, MD: Paul H. Brookes.

15. Yang, Q., Rasmussen, S. A., & Friedman, J. M. (2002). Mortality associated with Down's syndrome in the USA from 1983 to 1997: A population-based study. *Lancet, 359,* 1019–1025.

16. Chapman, R. S., & Hesketh, L. J. (2000). Behavioral phenotype of individuals with Down syndrome. *Mental Retardation and Developmental Disabilities Research Reviews, 6,* 84–95.

17. Miller, J. F. (1999). Profiles of language development in children with Down syndrome. In J. F. Miller, M. Leddy, & L. A. Leavitt (Eds.), *Improving the communication of people with Down syndrome* (pp. 11–39). Baltimore, MD: Paul H. Brookes.

18. Leddy, M. (1999). The biological basis of speech in people with Down syndrome. In J. F. Miller, M. Leddy, & L. A. Leavitt (Eds.), *Improving the communication of people with Down syndrome* (pp. 61–80). Baltimore, MD: Paul H. Brookes.

19. Hodapp, R. M., Evans, D., & Gray, F. L. (1999). What we know about intellectual development in children with Down syndrome. In J. A. Rondal, J. Perera, & L. Nadel (Eds.), *Down's syndrome: A review of current knowledge* (pp. 124–132). London: Whurr Publishers Ltd.

20. Hodapp, R. M., & Zigler, E. F. (1990). Applying the developmental perspective to individuals with Down syndrome. In M. Beeghly & D. Cicchetti (Eds.), *Children*

with Down syndrome: A developmental perspective (pp.1–28). New York: Cambridge University Press.

21. Zigman, W. B., Silverman, W., & Wisniewski, H. M. (1996). Aging and Alzheimer's disease in Down syndrome: Clinical and pathological changes. *Mental Retardation and Developmental Disabilities Research Reviews, 2,* 73–79.

22. Whittington, J. E., Holland, A. J., Webb, T., Butler, J., Clarke, D., & Boer, H. (2001). Population prevalence and estimated birth incidence and mortality rate for people with Prader-Willi syndrome in one UK health region. *Journal of Medical Genetics, 38,* 792–798.

23. Dykens, E. M., Leckman, J. F., & Cassidy, S. (1996). Obsessions and compulsions in persons with Prader-Willi syndrome: A case-controlled study. *Journal of Child Psychology and Psychiatry, 37,* 995–1002.

24. Dykens, E. M., Hodapp, R. M., Walsh, K. K., & Nash, L. (1992). Profiles, correlates, and trajectories of intelligence in Prader-Willi syndrome. *Journal of the American Academy of Child and Adolescent Psychiatry, 31,* 1125–1130.

25. Dykens, E. M. (2002). Are jigsaw puzzles "spared" in persons with Prader-Willi syndrome? *Journal of Child Psychology and Psychiatry, 43,* 343–352.

26. Dykens, E. M., Hodapp, R. M., & Finucane, B. (2000). *Genetics and mental retardation syndromes: A new look at behavior and interventions.* Baltimore, MD: Paul H. Brookes.

27. Dykens, E. M., (2003). Anxiety, fears, and phobias in Williams syndrome. *Developmental Neuropsychology, 23,* 291–316.

28. Mervis, C. B., Robinson, B. F., Rowe, M. L., Becerra, A. M., & Klein-Tasman, B. P. (2003). Language abilities of individuals with Williams syndrome. *International Review of Research in Mental Retardation, 27,* 35–81.

29. Reiss, S., & Szyszko, J. (1983). Diagnostic overshadowing and professional experience with mentally retarded persons. *American Journal of Mental Deficiency, 87,* 396–402.

30. Moss, S. (1999). Assessment: Conceptual issues. In N. Bouras (Ed.), *Psychiatric and behavioural disorders in developmental disabilities and mental retardation* (pp.18–37). New York: Cambridge University Press.

31. Dykens, E. M. (2000). Annotation: Psychopathology in children with intellectual disability. *Journal of Child Psychology and Psychiatry, 41,* 407–417.

32. Koller, H., Richardson, S. A., & Katz, M. (1983). Behavior disturbance since childhood among a 5-year birth cohort of all mentally retarded young adults in a city. *American Journal on Mental Retardation, 87,* 386–395.

33. Gilberg, C., Persson, E., Grufman, M., & Themmer, U. (1986). Psychiatric disorders in mildly and severely mentally retarded urban children and adolescents: Epidemiological aspects. *British Journal of Psychiatry, 149,* 68–74.

34. Einfeld, S. L., & Tonge, B. J. (1996) Population prevalence of psychopathology in children and adolescents with intellectual disability: II epidemiological findings. *Journal of Intellectual Disability Research, 40,* 99–109.

35. Hodapp, R. M., & Dykens, E. M. (2001). Strengthening behavioral research on genetic mental retardation disorders. *American Journal on Mental Retardation, 106,* 4–15.

36. Moss, S., Emerson, E., Bouras, N., & Holland, A. (1997). Mental disorders and problematic behaviours in people with intellectual disability: Future directions for research. *Journal of Intellectual Disability Research, 41,* 440–447.

37. Dykens, E. M. (2000). Psychopathology in children with intellectual disability. *Journal of Child Psychology and Psychiatry, 41,* 407–417.

38. Rojahn, J., Matson, J. L., Naglieri, J. A. & Mayville, E. (2004). Relationships between psychiatric conditions and behavior problems among adults with mental retardation. *American Journal on Mental Retardation, 109,* 21–33.

39. Dekker, M., & Koot, H., (2003). DSM-IV disorders in children with borderline to moderate intellectual disability. I: Prevalence and impact. *Journal of the American Academy of Child and Adolescent Psychiatry, 42,* 915–922.

40. Dykens, E. M., Shah, B., Sagun, J., Beck, T., & King, B. H. (2002). Maladaptive behavior in children and adolescents with Down syndrome. *Journal of Intellectual Disability Research, 46,* 484–492.

41. Tonge, B. J., & Einfeld, S. L. (2003). Psychopathology and intellectual disability: The Australian child to adult longitudinal study. *International Review of Research in Mental Retardation, 26,* 61–93.

42. Shepperdson, B. (1995). Two longitudinal studies of the abilities of people with Down's syndrome. *Journal of Intellectual Disability Research, 39,* 419–431.

43. Kent, L., Evans, J., Paul, M., & Sharp, M. (1999). Comorbidity of autism spectrum disorders in children with Down syndrome. *Developmental Medicine and Child Neurology, 41,* 151–158.

44. Dykens, E. M. (1999). Prader-Willi syndrome. In H. Tager-Flusberg (Ed.), *Neurodevelopmental disorders* (pp. 137–154). Cambridge, MA: MIT Press.

45. Dimitropoulos, A., Feurer, I. D., Butler, M. G., & Thompson, T. (2001). Emergence of compulsive behavior and tantrums in children with Prader-Willi syndrome. *American Journal on Mental Retardation, 106,* 39–51.

46. Roof, E., Stone, W., MacLean, W., Feurer, I. D., Thompson, T., & Butler, M. G. (2000). Intellectual characteristics of Prader-Willi syndrome: comparison of genetic subtypes. *Journal of Intellectual Disability Research, 44,* 25- 30.

47. Dykens, E. M., Cassidy, S. B., & King, B. H. (1999). Maladaptive behavior differences in Prader-Willi syndrome due to paternal deletion versus maternal uniparental disomy. *American Journal on Mental Retardation, 104,* 67–77.

48. Vogels, A., De Hert, M., Descheemaeker, M. J., Govers, V., Devriendt, K., & Legius, E., et al. (2004). Psychotic disorders in Prader-Willi syndrome. *American Journal of Medical Genetics, 127,* 238–243.

49. Stavrakaki, C. & Klein, J. (1986). Psychotherapies with the mentally retarded. *Psychiatric Clinic of North America, 9,* 733–743.

50. Spreat, S., Conroy, J. W., & Jones, J. C. (1997). Use of psychotropic medication in Oklahoma: A statewide survey. *American Journal on Mental Retardation, 102,* 80–85.

51. Singh, N. N., Ellis, C. R., & Wechsler, H. (1997). Psychopharmacoepidemiology of mental retardation: 1966 to 1995. *Journal of Child and Adolescent Psychopharmacology, 7,* 255–266.

52. Ryan, R (1993). Response to psychiatric care of adults with developmental disabilities and mental illness in the community. *Community Mental Health Journal, 29*, 477–481.

53. McCarthy, J., & Boyd, J. (2002). Mental heath services and young people with intellectual disability: Is it time to do better? *Journal of Intellectual Disability Research, 46*, 250–256.

54. Solnit, A., & Stark, M. (1961). Mourning and the birth of a defective child. *The Psychoanalytic Study of the Child, 16*, 523–537.

55. Crnic, K., Friedrich, W., & Greenberg, M. (1983). Adaptation of families with mentally handicapped children: A model of stress, coping, and family ecology. *American Journal of Mental Deficiency, 88*, 125–138.

56. Hodapp, R. M., & Ly, T. M. (2005). Parenting children with developmental disabilities. In T. Luster & L. Okagaki (Eds.), *Parenting: An ecological perspective* (2nd ed., pp. 177–201). Mahwah, NJ: Erlbaum.

57. Seltzer, M. M., Greenberg, J. S., & Krauss, M. W. (1995). A comparison of coping strategies of aging mothers of adults with mental illness or mental retardation. *Psychology and Aging 10*, 64–75.

58. Fidler, D. J., Hodapp, R. M., & Dykens, E. M. (2000). Stress in families of young children with Down syndrome, Williams syndrome, and Smith-Magenis syndrome. *Early Education and Development, 11*, 395–406.

59. Stoneman, Z. (2005). Siblings of children with disabilities: Research themes. *Mental Retardation, 43*, 339–350.

60. Taunt, H. M., & Hastings, R. P. (2002). Positive impact of children with developmental disabilities on their families: A preliminary study. *Education and Training in Mental Retardation and Developmental Disabilities, 37*, 410—420.

61. Krauss, M. W., Seltzer, M. M., Gordon, & Friedman, D. H. (1996). Binding ties: The roles of adult siblings of persons with mental retardation. *Mental Retardation, 34*, 83–93.

62. Heller, T. (2000). Aging family caregivers: Needs and policy concerns. *Family support policy brief #3*. Portland, OR: National Center for Family Support.

63. Holburn, S., Perkins, T., & Vietze, P. (2001). The parent with mental retardation. In L. M. Glidden (Ed.), *International review of research in mental retardation* (Vol. 24, pp. 171–210). San Diego, CA: Academic Press.

64. Espe-Sherwindt, M., & Crable, S. (1993). Parents with mental retardation: Moving beyond the myths. *Topics in Early Childhood Special Education, 13*, 154–174.

65. Feldman, M. A., Towns, F., Betel, J., Case, L., Rincover, A., & Rubino, C. A. (1986). Parent education project II. Increasing stimulating interactions of developmentally handicapped mothers. *Journal of Applied Behavior Analysis, 19*, 23–37.

66. Tymchuk, A. J. (1990). Parents with mental retardation: A national strategy. *Journal of Disability Policy Studies, 1*, 43–55.

67. Perkins, T. S., Holburn, S., Deaux, K., Flory, M. J., & Vietze, P. M. (2002). Children of mothers with intellectual disability: Stigma, mother-child relationship and self-esteem. *Journal of Applied Research in Intellectual Disabilities, 15*, 297–313.

68. Ammerman, R. T. & Baladerian, N. J. (1993). *Maltreatment of children with disabilities.* Chicago, IL: National Committee to Prevent Child Abuse.

69. Sullivan, P. M. & Knutson, J. F. (2000). Maltreatment and disabilities: A population-based epidemiological study. *Child Abuse & Neglect, 24,* 1257–1273.

70. Sobsey, D. (2002). Exceptionality, education, and maltreatment. *Exceptionality, 10,* 29–46.

71. Janko, S. (1994). *Vulnerable children, vulnerable families: The social construction of child abuse.* New York: Teachers College Press.

72. Westcott, H. L., & Jones, D. P. H. (1999). Annotation: The abuse of disabled children. *Journal of Child Psychology and Psychiatry, 40,* 497–506.

73. Holland, T., Clare, C. H., & Mukhopadhyay, T. (2002). Prevalence of 'criminal offending' by men and women with intellectual disability and the characteristics of 'offenders': Implications for research and service development. *Journal of Intellectual Disability Research, 46,* 6–20.

74. Barron, P., Hassiotis, A., & Banes, J. (2004). Offenders with intellectual disability: A prospective comparative study. *Journal of Intellectual Disability Research, 48,* 69–76.

75. Perske, R. (2005). Search for persons with intellectual disabilities who confessed to serious crimes they did not commit. *Mental Retardation, 43,* 58–65.

76. Sellinger, M. H., Hodapp, R. M., & Dykens, E. M. (in press). Leisure activities of individuals with Prader-Willi, Williams, and Down syndromes. *Journal of Developmental and Physical Disabilities.*

77. Dykens, E. M. (in press). Music and anxiety in Williams syndrome: A harmonious or discordant relationship? *American Journal on Mental Retardation.*

Chapter 3

Autism Spectrum Disorders: A Crisis of Urgent Public Concern

Ruth E. Cook

Autism was once thought to be a rare disorder. In fact, it received little attention until 1943 when a psychiatrist, Leo Kanner, produced his case material identifying the unique features of this disorder in each of 11 children he observed at the Johns Hopkins Hospital in Baltimore.[1] Since this landmark paper, our knowledge of autism spectrum disorders (ASDs) has grown exponentially, especially recently. For example, we have learned that autism is not caused by cold, uncompassionate parents (refrigerator moms) as was once the commonly accepted speculation of causation. Today, alarmed by the explosion in the number of cases fof children and youth identified with ASD, advocacy groups are clamoring for more research into both the causes and potential educational treatments. As a result, major advances in understanding the biological bases of ASD are occurring, and more refined diagnostic practices and better educational and therapeutic interventions are becoming available.

Scientists, parents, teachers and therapists continue to be baffled at the apparent increase in prevalence of these pervasive developmental disorders. Research, however, is finding that early and intensive intervention can lead to improvement. Yet little is understood about the extent of the human tragedy that this illness imposes on children, families, and communities. When children with ASD become adults, the impact on society can only be imagined, for longitudinal research is scarce. In order to better understand the nature of the crisis, this chapter will present primary information about ASD including some of the promising educational/intervention techniques currently available.

AUTISM SPECTRUM DISORDERS: WHAT ARE THEY?

ASDs range from a severe form, called autistic disorder, to a milder form called Asperger syndrome (AS). No two individuals with ASD seem to have identical symptoms. A symptom may be mild in one person and severe in another. Persons classified with ASD vary widely in abilities. Some may demonstrate near- or above-average intellectual and communication abilities, while others may be severely developmentally delayed and totally lack spoken language skills. Therefore, the term autism spectrum disorders is used to refer to the broad range of subtypes and levels of severity that fall on this spectrum of pervasive developmental disorders (PDDs).

All PDDs are characterized by "severe and pervasive impairment in several areas of development: reciprocal social interaction skills, communication skills, or the presence of stereotyped behavior, interest, and activities" (p. 69).[2] Five PDDs are referred to as ASD. These include autistic disorder, childhood disintegrative disorder, Rett disorder, AS, and pervasive developmental disorders-not otherwise specified (PDD-NOS).[3] These PDDs range in severity, are usually diagnosed in childhood, are prevalent throughout life, and affect people from all socioeconomic and ethnic backgrounds throughout the world.

A Note about Terms

When reading the literature, it is important to remember that the term "autism" is often used either specifically to refer to autistic disorder or more generally to ASD. In addition, another term that is often used synonymously with ASD is PDD. This term is the diagnostic category heading under which the five specific diagnoses described briefly below are listed.

Autistic Disorder

The term autistic disorder refers to individuals, usually males, who exhibit these impairments prior to 36 months of age and are moderately to severely intellectually impaired. Diagnostic criteria for autistic disorder fall into three main categories: (1) qualitative social interaction impairments, (2) qualitative communication impairments, and (3) repetitive and restricted stereotyped patterns of behavior, activities, and interests.

As infants, these children show little interest in being held and may not be soothed by physical closeness with caregivers. They demonstrate significant limitations in eye contact, social smiling, and interactive play. As young children, they prefer to be alone and may not show anxiety when separated from family members. However, they may become anxious when there are changes to their environment or routine. They often repeat the words of others, demonstrate repetitive motor behavior, and have strong attachments to objects. Such children commonly demonstrate delays in or total lack of spoken language development. As they grow older, they rarely share pleasure or excitement with others and have limited social interactions. They develop few or no friendships and often exhibit persistent and repetitive, ritualistic speech or behaviors.

Childhood Disintegrative Disorder

According to the *Diagnostic and Statistical Manual of Mental Disorders*, Fourth Edition, Text Revision *(DSM–IV–TR)*,[2] children diagnosed with childhood disintegrative disorder (CDD) have behavior similar to those of children with autism disorder. However, children within this classification grow and develop normally for a period of time. They show typical social and communicative interactions and behavior for at least two years. Then, usually between three and four years of age, they begin to display "a clinically significant loss of previously acquired social skills or adaptive behavior, bowel or bladder control, play or motor skills" (p. 77).[2] These children, more often males, may have seizures and display very low intellectual functioning. While their disintegration is progressive, they do eventually stabilize and cease to deteriorate. Some do recover previously attained developmental skills. This disorder, fortunately, is very rare.

Rett's Disorder

Rett's disorder is another very rare disorder, occurring almost exclusively in females. After a period of apparently normal development, between six and twenty-four months, autism-like symptoms begin to appear. Head growth decelerates, motor skills deteriorate, stereotypic hand wringing and washing may begin, and she becomes socially and communicatively unresponsive. These individuals demonstrate severe impairments in language development as this disorder is usually associated with severe to profound mental retardation. Serious medical concerns include seizures, respiratory problems, and risk of sudden cardiac death.[2]

Asperger Syndrome

AS was named after Dr. Hans Asperger, a Viennese physician who first discussed it in 1944. The children described by Asperger had many of the same characteristics discussed by Kanner a year earlier. However, Asperger described children who were higher functioning and whose impairments were, primarily, within the area of social interaction. AS was generally ignored until the 1990s when the American Psychiatric Association added the syndrome to its list of pervasive developmental disorders.[4]

This disorder can be especially puzzling to parents and professionals as these children tend to exhibit average to above-average intelligence, and have few, if any, distinctive physical characteristics. These children, usually males, are often misunderstood, and their behavior is misinterpreted. It is extremely difficult to diagnose this syndrome. The characteristics of children and youth with AS are most easily seen in situations that are often missed in a medical setting. These include: (a) interactions with peers, (b) stressful situations, (c) environments where the schedule or routine is not predictable, (d) when sensory stressors are apparent, and (e) when these children or youth encounter new situations.[5] Medical professionals must rely on reports from caregivers who observe their young patients in a variety of settings over time.

Pervasive Developmental Disorder-Not Otherwise Specified

PDD-NOS is thought to be a somewhat vaguely defined diagnostic classification that includes children who demonstrate "severe and pervasive impairment in the development of reciprocal social interaction or verbal and nonverbal communication skills" (p. 77).[2] Children and youth within this category do not meet the criteria for the other categories and generally fall at the higher functioning end of the ASD continuum. Their impaired verbal and nonverbal communication skills and/or stereotyped behaviors or interests do interfere with development of social skills.

There is often confusion between AS and PDD-NOS. However, individuals with AS typically do not have language delays and may read precociously or have extraordinarily rich vocabularies. Nevertheless, children with AS still struggle with the social aspects of language and nonverbal communication. Individuals with either classification, whose behaviors are less of a determent to their daily lives, are often referred to as having "high functioning autism."

HOW PREVALENT ARE AUTISM SPECTRUM DISORDERS?

Precisely how many people have ASD today is currently unknown. To date, there have been few scientific, population-based studies. Therefore, there is little reliable information on the prevalence of ASD. In the past, only those with severe autistic characteristics were diagnosed with autism; others were categorized as mentally retarded or developmentally delayed. However, within the last two decades, diagnostic criteria have broadened dramatically. Clearly service providers are reporting dramatic increases in the numbers of children and families seeking services. To address the need for prevalence statistics with sound credibility, the Centers for Disease Control is launching the first integrated, multi-state, ASD prevalence investigation.[6] Hopefully, this cooperative alliance of researchers investigating the epidemiology of ASD in 18 states will yield accurate estimates of ASD and lead to widespread appreciation of ASD as a public health concern.

The Fastest Growing Developmental Disability

National organizations cite figures suggesting that, today, ASD is the fastest growing developmental disability. The National Center on Birth Defects and Developmental Disabilities estimates that using current criteria, up to 500,000 children and youth between birth and 21 years of age have an ASD. However, many are not diagnosed until school age or later, so their figures may underestimate actual prevalence.[7]

Autism is now at least the sixth most commonly classified disability in the educational system of the United States.[8] The most common disability classifications include specific learning disabilities, speech or language impairment, mental retardation, emotional disturbance, and other health impairments which often include children diagnosed with attention deficit/hyperactivity disorder (AD/HD). Between 1994 and 2003, the number of children being classified as having ASD increased six-fold from 22,664 to 141,022.[8] There is no doubt that more children are getting education services for ASD than ever before. However, it is necessary to remember that as the category of autism was only added in 1991, the growth in number of children classified may be, in part, due to the recent addition of this category.

Questions Continue

Extensive dialogue continues among professionals and parents as to whether or not the increase in demand for services is due to a true increase in prevalence or due to changes in how we identify and classify individuals with ASD. Recently, Laidler[9] made compelling arguments questioning prevalence data disseminated by the U.S. Department of Education. His contention is that the Department of Education figures are at odds with studies of the incidence of autism because the criteria used by school districts to categorize children as autistic are not rigorous or consistent from district to district or state to state. This is understandable as the diagnosis of autism is basically subjective. There are no objective findings, radiologic studies, or laboratory tests that are diagnostic of autism. There is also no distinct cutoff point between typical and autistic behavior. As federal law only allows 10 qualifying disabilities under the Individuals with Disabilities Education Act, assessment criteria tend to be broad in an effort to serve those who appear to need service.

Therefore, it is currently impossible to present reliable data on the prevalence of ASD within our society. There is no question that today education is serving significantly more children and youth under the category of autism than in past decades. However, scientifically based research is not yet available to determine what role broader eligibility criteria, enhanced availability of services, and increased public awareness play in increasing the numbers being classified as having an autistic spectrum disorder.

Whether or not ASD is the first or second most common serious developmental disability is irrelevant when one considers the immense impact on families of any devastating developmental disability. All PDDs are conditions that demand urgent public attention and mobilization of resources to alleviate the inevitable stress and waste of human potential.

WHAT CAUSES AUTISTIC SPECTRUM DISORDERS?

Experts do not know exactly what causes ASDs. In opposition to earlier theories of causation, currently experts as well as parents are thoroughly convinced that autism and related disabilities are not caused by cold and unresponsive caregivers (refrigerator mothers). Instead, family and twin studies suggest an underlying genetic vulnerability to ASD. Research involving families with at least one child with ASD indicate a higher incidence of recurrence in later births.[10] In addition, an increased frequency of occurrence is found in patients with genetic conditions such as fragile X syndrome and tuberous sclerosis.[11]

The basis of this vulnerability appears to be neurophysiological. There are differences in how the individual's central nervous system responds to and integrates incoming sensory information. A large number of studies have found that autistic individuals have a compromised immune system. One hypothesis is that the child's compromised immune system predisposes the child to ASD. Although the search for specific autism genes is under way, scientists believe that genetic inheritance is not the sole contributor to autism.

Immunizations

In recent years, concerns have been adamantly expressed that immunizations, particularly measles, mumps, and rubella (MMR) vaccine, may precipitate autism. The culprit is thought to be thimerosal, a mercury-based preservative used in MMR vaccine. Thimerosal has been removed in vaccines in the United States since 1999. However, many parents are still concerned as vaccines already disseminated were not recalled. Despite the media reports of anecdotal evidence from parents and members of the U.S. Congress blaming immunizations for the development of symptoms characteristic of ASD, there is currently not enough scientifically based evidence to support a causal link between autism and MMR or other vaccines used in immunizations.

Several large-scale studies concluded that there was no causal relationship between childhood vaccination and the development of ASD.[12] Given contradictory information and vocal concerns of such prominent experts in the field of autism as Dr. Bernard Rimland,[13] the controversy over immunizations continues. Therefore, a panel from the Institute of Medicine is now closely examining these studies as well as studies looking at exposure to lead and other heavy metals.[14] This is a very positive step as additional independent and unbiased clinical studies are urgently needed.

Emerging Diagnostic Approaches

Biological understanding of the basis of ASD is only beginning to move forward with the aid of modern technology and availability of both normal and autism tissue samples to perform postmortem studies. With the emergence of new brain imaging tools such as computerized tomography (CT), positron emission tomography (PET), and magnetic resonance imaging (MRI), study of the structure and function of the brain is possible. Postmortem and MRI studies indicate that several major brain structures are implicated in autism.[15] These include the cerebellum, cerebral cortex, limbic system, corpus callosum, basal ganglia, and the brain stem. Other research is focusing on the role of neurotransmitters such as serotonin, dopamine, and epinephrine.

Researchers are not only eager to find and eliminate the cause or causes of ASD, but they are also searching for ways to identify ASD as early as possible so that early intervention may be provided. The growth dysregulation hypothesis holds that the anatomical abnormalities seen in autism may be caused by genetic defects in brain growth factors.[16] During the first two years of life, brains of young children with autism experience brain growth spurts unlike those of typical children. If so, then it may be possible that sudden, rapid head growth in an infant may be a warning signal that can lead to early diagnosis and effective biological intervention or possible prevention of autism. Other causative or complicating factors being investigated include allergies to food and medicines, gastrointestinal abnormalities, maternal exposure to mercury, and lack of essential minerals.

Organizational Initiatives

While we wait eagerly for scientific breakthroughs that might determine the cause of ASD, it is imperative that parents quit blaming themselves. It is equally important that the general public continue to push for the resources needed to provide effective education of children and youth with ASD, support for their families, and the public services necessary for adults with ASD to live as normally as possible.

It is important to realize that, on both a national and an international level, communities are waking up to the need to address the crisis presented by the presence of ASDs. For example, The Children's Health Act of 2003 (SB 1951, Public Act 93-0495) created the Interagency Autism Coordinating Committee (IACC). This committee includes the directors of the National Institute of Mental Health, the National Institute of Neurological Disorders and Stroke, the National Institute on Deafness and Other Communication Disorders, the National Institute of Child Health and Human Development, and the National Institute of Environmental Health Sciences, as well as representatives from eight other national agencies. This committee was instructed by Congress to develop a 10-year agenda for autism research. Their plan was presented at the first Autism Summit Conference. Included in this plan was the establishment of eight network research centers that are conducting research in the fields of developmental neurobiology, genetics, and psychopharmacology. In addition, 10 Collaborative Programs of Excellence in Autism are studying the world's largest group of well-diagnosed individuals with autism.

What is truly significant about the results of the Children's Health Act of 2000 is that data from all of these entities will be analyzed through a data coordination center. Thus, we can soon expect significant progress in understanding the prevalence and causes of ASDs.

HOW ARE AUTISM SPECTRUM DISORDERS DIAGNOSED?

While the causes of what appears to be a dramatic rise in the number of children and youth with ASD are the subject of much debate and study, experts are in agreement on one thing: early diagnosis and intervention is crucial to the possibility of a good prognosis. However, it is not enough to agree that early identification is critical as the process of diagnosis is fraught with difficulty, making the goal of early intervention sometimes easier said than done.

As stated earlier, there is currently no single test to diagnose ASD. There are no definitive biological signs or symptoms of ASD. In fact, as the name "autism spectrum disorder" suggests, ASDs cover a wide range of behaviors and abilities. Children with ASD develop at different rates in different areas of growth. They might show lags in language, social, and cognitive skills, while their motor skills might be on target. Some children with ASD can learn a hard skill before they learn an easy one. Although they may be good at things like putting puzzle pieces together, they might have trouble with developing a skill that is easy for others, like talking with other children.

ASD is diagnosed through careful observation/assessment of behavior and knowledge of the individual's developmental history. Parents and pediatricians who suspect that a child might have a PDD are encouraged to seek further evaluation from qualified professionals such as neurologists and psychiatrists who are familiar with this group of disorders.

Early Clues

In infancy, signals for formal developmental evaluation include no babbling, pointing, or other gestures by 12 months of age; no single words by 16 months of age; and no two-word spontaneous phrases by 24 months of age. Loss of previously learned language or social skills is an important high risk signal at any age.

The American Academy of Neurology recommends a dual process of diagnosis: "(1) routine developmental surveillance and screening specifically for autism to be performed on all children to first identify those at risk for any type of atypical development, and to identify those specifically at risk for autism; and (2) to diagnose and evaluate autism, to differentiate autism from other developmental disorders."[17]

At level one, specialists are encouraged to look for the high risk signals noted above and to listen very carefully to parents, as they tend to be highly sensitive and specific in detecting global developmental deficits.[18] Diagnosis of ASD is a complex clinical process that is dependent on close observation and informed clinical opinions. Unfortunately, there are currently few places in the country where professionals are thoroughly trained in the diagnostic process. These procedures are not learned easily in workshops or sessions at a conference. To develop sophisticated clinical judgment, training, supervision and feedback from experts are required.

Behavioral Criteria

To receive a diagnosis of autism or a related disorder, children must meet a certain number of the behavioral criteria as described in the *DSM–IV–TR*.[2] As these criteria are more applicable to children around the age of three or older, diagnosis at an earlier age can be more difficult. In general, even though ASD involve a wide spectrum of symptoms, individuals do have three common areas of deficit: communication problems, impaired social relationships, and unusual patterns of behavior. Communication skills and social interactions are not simply delayed or similar to that of a younger child, instead they are often unusual or even bizarre. The behaviors and communication cues of children with ASD are frequently very difficult to interpret.

To identify conditions of ASD as soon as possible, Ozonoff, Rogers, and Hendren[19] urge screening in infancy. Clinicians should pay particular attention to young children who do not look at faces and avoid eye contact, who do not attempt to imitate others, who do not respond when called by their name, who do not attempt to show objects to others by pointing at things, and who do not, in general, show interest in others. In order to focus on such behavioral symptoms, collaboration with caregivers is essential. While language delays are the symptom that most commonly captures the attention of parents, problems in other areas of development hold the key to being able to recognize behavioral signs at earlier and earlier ages. As children become preschoolers, parents may notice that children line up toys rather than play with them and may become obsessive about watching and rewatching segments of a particular video or DVD. Older children who are verbal may obsess in talking about particular topics of interest.

Children with ASD can have other associated problems that include sleep disturbances, gastrointestinal problems, seizure disorders, and sensory and auditory processing disorders. Some may be extremely sensitive to touch, certain textures, or sounds. However, at the same time, they may appear to be extraordinarily gifted in music, memory, math, or drawing.

Once high risk signals have been recognized, children must be referred for more intensive screening that should include a formal audiological assessment and screening for lead poisoning. Specific screening for ASD may include formal tools such as the Checklist for Autism in Toddler (CHAT) for children from 18 months and the Autism Screening Questionnaire for children four years of age and older.[20]

Multidisciplinary Screening

A complete evaluation is a comprehensive multidisciplinary process, usually beginning with the pediatrician who insures that a thorough family history, medical, and neurological evaluation is completed. In addition to the pediatrician and audiologist, this multidisciplinary process can include one or more of the following professionals: psychologists, neurologists, speech-language pathologists, child psychiatrists, occupational therapists, and physical therapists, as well as special educators. Included below are some of the areas of concern to these specialists who must be clinically knowledgeable of the unique characteristics of ASDs.

Speech-Language and Communication Evaluations

Comprehensive assessment of both preverbal and verbal individuals should include assessment of both receptive and expressive language and communication, voice and speech production, and in verbal individuals, a collection and analysis of spontaneous language samples to augment scores on formal language tests. Specific attention will be paid to whether or not available speech and language skills are functional and appropriate.

Cognitive and Adaptive Behavior Evaluations

Cognitive instruments used by well-trained psychologists should provide a full range of standard scores that do not depend on social ability and should include independent measures of verbal and nonverbal abilities. A measure of adaptive functioning such as the Vineland Adaptive Behavior Scales should be included.[21]

Sensorimotor and Occupational Therapy Evaluations

Experienced occupational or physical therapists assess fine and gross motor development, sensory processing abilities, tactile sensitivity, unusual or stereotyped mannerisms, and the impact of these elements on the individual's life. Occupational therapists should be concerned with how well the individual can function given daily life requirements, including those of play or leisure activities, self-care, or work tasks.

Neuropsychological, Behavioral, and Academic Assessments

These assessments should be performed as needed and should include social skills and relationships, educational functioning, learning style, motivation and reinforcement, and self-regulation. Such assessment is absolutely necessary for an early intervention specialist and educators to assist in procuring services and planning intervention/instructional activities.

Family Assessment

When children are under the age of three, to determine eligibility for service, appropriately trained professionals are expected to collaborate with families in assessing their resources, concerns, and priorities. It is expected that they will guide the development of an Individualized Family Service plan that will determine the services to be publicly provided and the outcomes to be realized as a result of these services. After the age of three, Individual Program Plans are to be developed collaboratively by both parents and educators.[22]

A Final Word on Screening and Diagnosis

As young children with ASD can respond to their environment in both positive and negative ways, and with behavior that is inconsistent, a common mistake is often made. That mistake comes from the "wait and see" mentality. Because we have learned that early intervention can be effective, it is essential that professionals and parents do not fall into the wait and see mentality. Parents' concerns should not be dismissed because of the absence or presence of any one behavior. Instead, concentration should be on the bigger picture to look for patterns of behavior.

WHICH DISORDERS MOST COMMONLY ACCOMPANY ASD?

Accompanying or comorbid disorders often have medical implications and treatment needs separate from those for the general characteristics of ASD. For example, a high percentage of individuals with ASD have some form of sleeping disorder. Lack of sleep and the resulting fatigue can exacerbate symptoms. Then there is the impact of lack of sleep on caregivers that must be considered. It is important to be aware of the side effects of medications and the effect of the caffeine found in sodas and chocolate. A reliable bedtime schedule is essential, while daytime naps might be discontinued for older preschoolers who are not sleeping through the night.

A significant portion of children with ASD also suffer from a seizure disorder such as epilepsy. Even if seizures are not serious, they can increase anxiety and heighten communication difficulties. As there are medications that can control seizures, it is essential that medical assistance be acquired immediately when seizures present themselves. Other medical conditions that can co-occur with ASD are fragile X syndrome, neurofibromatosis, tuberous sclerosis, and phenylketonuria. Obviously, close collaboration with medical practitioners is essential to handle the conditions of comorbidity.

Although children with ASD have been found, as a group, to hear as well as other children, they may have auditory processing problems. Such processing problems may prevent them from understanding the meaning of sounds they hear or distinguishing sounds in the foreground from sounds in the background. These problems may have a negative impact on academic performance and should be considered when assigning seats in the classroom or setting up the environment for a child expected to complete his or her homework.

Children with autism disorder have a high rate of pica or the tendency to eat inappropriate substances such as soil, paint, and paint chips.[23] This tendency can lead to bowel obstruction and the possibility of overexposure to lead. Thus, the importance of tests for lead poisoning during screening and diagnosis is obvious. Other conditions of comorbdity to consider include depression and anxiety disorders, especially with AS. Gastrointestinal disorders, higher rates of food allergies, and problems with attention and concentration are often reported by parents. Surprisingly, whether a tendency toward AD/HD is a symptom of ASD or a separate disorder is yet to be determined.

Many autistic children have unusual sensitivities to sounds, sights, touch, tastes, and smells. High-pitched intermittent sounds, such as fire alarms or school bells, may be painful to autistic children. Sensitivity to tactile and auditory stimuli may be responsible for the child's withdrawal or avoidance of social interaction, as well as difficulty tolerating certain sounds and processing speech. This avoidance, in turn, can interfere with the processes of attachment and development of social skills, as well as with the development of communication skills. Thus many children with autism have very limited speech and language skills.

Putting together the comprehensive puzzle of causality and the implications of disorders as complicated as those of ASD is not easy. Nevertheless, researchers are detecting more correlations between ASD and other disorders. These discoveries may make it possible for clinicians to break these disorders into more discrete elements that lend themselves more readily to effective treatment.

WHAT EDUCATIONAL INTERVENTIONS AND STRATEGIES ARE AVAILABLE?

Even though every individual diagnosed with a spectrum disorder may be different, the families of these individuals all face the same overwhelming challenge. That is, the challenge of finding the best treatment or intervention for each complex condition. This means that parents not only have to deal with the emotional impact of a devastating diagnosis, but they also have no clear choice of educational intervention options. This dilemma was underscored by the National Research Council's report published in 2001[24] in which a committee of experts who were charged with the task of integrating the scientific, theoretical, and policy literature concluded "there are virtually no data on the relative merit of one model (of intervention) over another" (p. 171).

Nevertheless, there are a number of intervention approaches that are showing positive changes in children who receive intensive services from an early age. It is important to note that these interventions tend to focus on various aspects of the disorders and on different developmental domains. Because of the variability in the targeted skill areas, the underlying theoretical assumptions, and the strategies employed, the selection of a particular approach (or combination of approaches) should depend on the needs and characteristics of each individual with ASD, and the concerns and preferences of family members.

Research does suggest that children with ASD can improve considerably with certain kinds of interventions. Although research does not conclude that there is one best model of intervention, it does suggest that, "Several features shared by most efficacious treatments, regardless of model, philosophy, or type, have been identified: they begin early, are intensive (at least 25 hours a week), are individualized and developmentally appropriate, and are family centered, involving parents at every level" (p. 23).[25] The best programs are those that incorporate a variety of multidisciplinary best practices based on individual needs.

Features of Program Effectiveness

To promote scientifically validated methods of instruction for children and youth with ASD, The Committee on Educational Interventions for Children with Autism, Division of Behavioral and Social Sciences and Education, National Research Council provided a list of program features that the committee found to be critical to the effectiveness of the early intervention experience for young children.[26] These include:

- Entry into the program as soon after diagnosis as possible
- Active engagement in intensive instructional programming for the equivalent of a full school day, five days a week, with full-year participation available depending on age/developmental level
- Repeated, planned teaching opportunities organized around relatively brief periods of time
- Sufficient amounts of adult attention in one-to-one and small group settings to meet individualized goals
- Inclusion of a family education component
- Low student/teacher ratios (no more than two young children per adult)
- Strategies for ongoing program evaluation and assessment of individual children's progress, with program adjustments made accordingly.

The committee also prioritizes six foci of interventions. These include focus on functional, spontaneous communication; social instruction that is delivered throughout the day in various settings; the teaching of interactive play skills; instruction that facilitates the development and transfer of cognitive skills; positive, contextual behavioral support; and focus on functional academic skills.[27]

Evidence-Based Practices

The No Child Left Behind Act of 2001[27] repeatedly emphasizes the importance of utilizing instructional and intervention methods that have been subject to scrutiny and scientific evaluation. In an attempt to assist parents in recognizing when educational practices are linked to scientifically based research, Simpson and colleagues[3] recently published a critique of the most commonly used interventions and treatments for individuals with autism-related disabilities. Before discussing some of the interventions that have been found either to have evidence of significant and convincing empirical efficacy or are promising, it is important to note that while we have some knowledge about what may be effective treatment, research into the effectiveness of the vast array of available approaches is clearly just beginning.

Behavioral Strategies

Many behavioral techniques have been used as part of the intervention plan for individuals with ASD. Behavioral techniques include specific procedures aimed at teaching new skills and behaviors. These techniques include modeling, prompting, shaping, fading, task analysis, differential reinforcement, precise behavior quantification, and frequent measurement. They are not used in isolation, but in combination. Functional analysis of behavior involving ongoing monitoring of progress and modification of techniques as needed is critical to the success of behavioral interventions. Specific training of parents in techniques to reduce inappropriate behaviors and increase appropriate or adaptive behaviors is usually an essential component of such programs.

Discrete Trial Training

Traditional programs that follow Lovaas's discrete trial training (DTT) approach to behavior therapy are very intensive (from 20–40 hours per week) and involve one-on-one specific response training.[28] This is a highly structured training method that is frequently recommended. Skills are taught in distraction-free environments through repeated, structured presentations. The DTT format consists of (1) adult directions, input, and prompting, (2) child responding, (3) adult feedback [reinforcement] relative to that response, and (4) some method of tracking progress toward previously designated goals and objectives. In general, discrete trials are a set of acts that include a stimulus or antecedent, a behavior, and a consequence.

While the DTT approach is one of the most empirically validated interventions available, professionals urge caution in adopting this technique at the exclusion of all others, especially for extended periods of time. Unless specific techniques are used to train for generalization, skills demonstrated in the training context may not be demonstrated in different environments. Lovaas's 1987 claim[29] that DTT could lead children to recover from ASD sparked considerable controversy as follow-up studies have not fully supported this conclusion. Therefore, in an effort to improve the generalization of skills from teaching settings to daily use in the real world, traditional behavioral techniques are being modified to permit instruction in more natural environments such as the classroom or wherever social and communication behaviors typically occur.

Another controversy surrounds the number of hours of DTT recommended for children with ASD. While traditional DTT recommends 40 hours a week, others find equal effectiveness with 15 or more hours a week.[3] Another controversy addresses the significant costs involved in implementing discrete trial training. Costs vary depending on the location, the number and training of the interventions, the number of hours and duration of the interventions. Long-term studies are definitely needed to understand if such costs will result in significant savings over an individual's lifetime if individuals can learn to function independently. In the mean time, programs devoted to DTT must continuously find and train individuals to administer the intervention, plan carefully to coordinate and supervise these individuals, disrupt family functioning, and require expensive community resources to facilitate this approach.

Applied Behavior Analysis

The bulk of ASD intervention research has been conducted from the perspective of applied behavior analysis (ABA).[26] ABA procedures can be used to increase desired behaviors, decrease inappropriate behaviors, and teach new behaviors to individuals of all levels of functioning. Rather than being tied to specific procedures, ABA tends to include any method that changes behavior in systematic and measurable ways.

Initially, ABA procedures were reactive, focusing on consequences of behaviors after they occurred. There is now increasing emphasis on intervention procedures that focus on what to do before problem behaviors occur. ABA prevention strategies focus on antecedent conditions in the individual or the environment that set the stage for or trigger problem behaviors. Preventative interventions that involve changing schedules, modifying curricula, rearranging the physical environment or the social grouping have been shown to decrease the likelihood of inappropriate behaviors.[30]

Even though the focus is on prevention of problem behaviors, ABA generally takes the perspective that analysis of inappropriate behavior should consider two environmental features and one behavior or set of behaviors that have a temporal relationship. Functional analysis that follows the A-B-C model first considers the "A," antecedents (events or internal conditions) that occur before the individual exhibits "B," behavior. "C," consequences, are the events that follow the behavior that will increase or decrease the likelihood that the behavior will be repeated. For example, (A) the teacher tells the child it is time to sit in a circle when the child is hungry. The child runs to the other side of the room (B). The teacher laughingly chases after the child (C). In this situation, a functional analysis might hypothesize that the child enjoys the attention and activity involved in being chased and will repeat the behavior next time he is asked to join the circle. Or, the functional analysis reviews that the child did not eat his snack and may be hungry. Therefore, if (1) either circle time is changed, (2) eating of snack is more closely supervised, or (3) the child receives a firm "No" instead of being chased, there is a definite possibility that the inappropriate behavior might cease.

Experts do agree that behavioral approaches have the potential to produce positive outcomes and can be effective in teaching communication and social skills. However, there is no empirical evidence that behavioral approaches should be used to the exclusion of all other methods. Therefore, it is generally recommended that principles of ABA and behavioral intervention strategies be included as an important element in any intervention program.[31]

Naturalistic Behavioral Strategies

Naturalistic behavioral strategies are forms of DTT based on each individual's interests and motives. Two examples of naturalistic strategies are incidental teaching and pivotal response training. Incidental teaching consists of a chain of prespecified child-tutor interactions. These interactions involve materials preferred by the child and include prompting and shaping techniques within natural settings involving child-initiated interactions. Research has demonstrated the effectiveness of incidental teaching in the development of communication skills and interaction with peers.[32] Although the strategy was designed primarily for young children, it is being used successfully with a variety of individuals. This approach is also cost-effective and requires no specialized materials.

Pivotal response training (PRT) was designed to facilitate the inclusion of children with ASD into natural environments. It focuses on change in certain pivotal areas such as responsiveness to multiple cues, motivation, self-management, and initiation.[33] PRT uses the principles of ABA excluding negative interactions and reducing dependence on artificial prompts. Research supports the effectiveness of PRT showing that it increases motivation, improves play skills, and leads to improvements in language skills.[3] It is one of the more family-friendly approaches to intervention. There are a number of advantages to this approach as it considers individual motivation and promotes inclusion rather than one-on-one training.

Structured Teaching Strategies

The most well-known model of structured intervention program is Treatment and Education of Autistic and Related Communication Handicapped Children (TEACCH), headquartered at the University of North Carolina.[34] TEACCH is built on the principle of modifying the environment to accommodate the needs of individuals with ASD. Four main components are the focus of this approach: physical organization, visual schedules, work systems, and task organization. Physical organization refers to the layout of the area for teaching. Clear and specific boundaries are marked by visual information to direct children's activities in a predictable manner. Irrelevant visual and auditory stimuli are blocked. Visual schedules tell the children what activities are to take place and in what sequence. Their anxiety is lessened by being able to predict what will come next. These schedules are especially helpful in assisting individuals with ASD who often have deficits in attention and memory and time and organization. Schedules are individualized for each individual based on their need for concrete (objects) or abstract (drawings) representation. They may represent either short or long periods of time.

Work systems and task organization determine what work students will do independently. These systems tell students what activities are to be completed in their independent work areas. The purpose of the work systems is to visually specify what and how much work is to be completed to fulfill the obligations of the work session. Finally, task organization presents students with information on what needs to be done within a task. This approach emphasizes using individuals' relative strengths in the areas of visual processing, visual-spatial skills, and sensory-motor processing to overcome deficits in the areas of auditory processing, verbal expression, attention, organization, and generalization of skills.

Research on this structured teaching method has generally been promising, although few recent peer-reviewed studies exist. Parents and teachers tend to be very enthusiastic about this model, and school districts have been supporting the costs of training that can be substantial if interested individuals must travel to North Carolina to be trained. The trainer of trainers model has been utilized to increase the numbers of TEACCH programs throughout the country.

In some areas, parents are being trained in this model as well, and there is dated research to suggest the efficacy of this approach.[35]

Augmentative Communication

One of the most widely used augmentative communication programs is the Picture Exchange Communication System (PECS). It was designed for individuals with ASD and other disabilities who lack expressive language skills.[36] As children with ASD often have difficulty pointing using gestures, they can benefit from using gestures to make choices from an array of objects or visual symbols. PECS teaches individuals how to exchange symbols as a means of communication. It systematically uses behavioral steps to teach individuals how to initiate communicative requests by approaching the communication partner and exchanging a symbol for a desired object or action.

Thus, individuals are assisted in the development of functional communication as a social means of getting their needs met. PECS was not designed with speech as the ultimate goal. Its major benefit is that it increases the rate of spontaneous communicative interactions. Once individuals initiate exchanges 80 percent of the time, professionals are encouraged to begin introducing a pointing system or institute the use of a voice output communication device. It is encouraging to note that despite severe limitations in auditory processing and in oral (spoken) language, some children with autism can learn to use pictures and print in meaningful ways, and some become good readers.

To date, few studies have been published in peer-reviewed journals to demonstrate the efficacy of PECS. However, it is widely used with young children and anecdotally appears to be a promising approach. Hopefully, those who use this approach will become more involved in documenting the progress of their students and publishing their findings.

Relationship-Based Intervention

Though not yet substantiated by the scientific community, the Developmental, Individual-difference, Relationship-based (DIR) model (floor time) originated by Greenspan[36] is gaining in popularity. The basis of this approach is an intervention known as floor time. Greenspan's developmental theory guides the four primary goals associated with the child-directed play experience. These include: "(1) encouraging attention and intimacy, (2) two-way communication, (3) encouraging the expression and use of feelings and ideas, and (4) logical thought" (p. 125).[37]

Floor time is designed for use with young children. It is based on the premise that critical missed developmental milestones may be acquired through intensive child-directed play and positive interactions with caring adults. In contrast to other approaches, it addresses emotional development in a non-threatening approach. It focuses on the whole child and integrates across areas of development within 20-minute sessions. During these session, the caregiver or play partner take an active role in supporting spontaneous and fun activities directed by the child's interests and actions. It is crucial that the adult does not try to teach a particular skill at this time as the child is to be the leader in the activity.

The following five steps are involved in the floor time process: (1) the adult observes the child playing in order to determine how best to approach the child, (2) the adult approaches the child and joins the activity while trying to match the child's emotional tenor and interests, a circle of communication is opened, (3) the adult follows the child's lead as the child directs the interaction, (4) the adult expands on the child's play theme without being intrusive, and (5) the circle of communication is closed when the child expands on the adult's input and a new circle is begun.

Floor time is a popular and most appealing approach as it provides an opportunity for pleasant adult-child interactions and builds on activities natural to all children. However, the effectiveness of this approach has not been substantially documented. Given the potential of this approach for helping parents to engage their child in happier, more relaxed ways while fostering their relationships, it is hoped that researchers will conduct the studies needed to promote such a positive approach to intervention.

Transactional, Family-Centered Intervention

Prioritizing social communication, emotional regulation, and transactional support (SCERTS), the SCERTS model is new to the array of available educational intervention options.[38] This model is a much welcomed synthesis of developmental, relationship-based, and skill-based approaches to intervention. It has a theoretical and empirical base that reflects current and emerging recommended practices noted in the literature as discussed above. Goals include the enhancement of joint attention, symbol use, and self-regulation, while providing visual, interpersonal, professional, and family support. Individualized educational intervention is based on an understanding of each individual's strengths and weaknesses as guided by developmental research. Intervention strategies are derived from evidenced-based practice of contemporary behavioral and developmental approaches. This more integrated, comprehensive approach supports communication and socioemotional development in everyday activities and routines. Although the SCERTS model is built on evidence-based practices, effectiveness of the total model will be determined once the program is disseminated and developmental progress of participants is determined.

WHERE ARE WE NOW?

The increase of children and youth with ASDs who need and receive educational and medical services is well-documented. Currently, experts cannot agree on why there has been a substantial increase in numbers of individuals with autism or related disorders being served by our public service agencies. However, they can agree that we are experiencing both a human and an economic crisis:

+ A human crisis when one considers the toll on families and the individuals, themselves.
+ An economic crisis when we consider the costs to society in terms of lifelong public services, impact on families, recruitment and training of practitioners, lawsuits resulting from lack of knowledge about what interventions are the most effective, and lack of individual human productivity. Looking at education alone, the General Accounting Office found that during 1999–2000, the cost to educate a child with autism was $18,790, while it cost only $6,556 to educate a typical child.[39]

To diminish or minimize human devastation, it is urgent that funding be provided for the essential research necessary to understand the causes of this devastating phenomenon. By understanding the causes, we might begin to prevent future generations from facing these crises. Finally, it is absolutely critical that we involve the scientific community in longitudinal investigations to determine what medical treatments and educational interventions will most benefit those who are already afflicted. By increasing public knowledge about ASD, it is hoped that society will no longer tolerate the confusion and ignorance related to prevention and treatment of ASD that currently exists.

REFERENCES

1. Kanner, L. (1943). Autistic disturbances of affective contact. *The Nervous Child*, 2, 217–250. Reprinted in Donnellan, A. M. (Ed.), *Classic readings in autism* (pp. 11–53). New York: Teachers College Press.
2. American Psychiatric Association (2000). *Diagnostic and statistical manual of mental disorders* (4th ed., text revision) Washington, DC: Author.
3. Simpson, R. L., deBoer-Ott, S. R., Griswold, D. E., Myles, B.S., Byrd, S.E., & Ganz, J.B., et al. (2005). *Autism spectrum disorders*. Thousand Oaks, CA: Corwin Press.
4. American Psychiatric Association (1994). *Diagnostic and statistical manual of mental disorders* (4th ed.). Washington, DC: Author.

5. Myles, B. S. (2005). *Children and youth with asperger syndrome.* Thousand Oaks, CA: Corwin Press.

6. Autism Society of America. (2005, July 15). *How Do you Know? The Prevalence of Autism Spectrum Disorders.* Retrieved April 24, 2006, from http://asa.confex. com/asa/2005/techprogram/S1404.HTM.

7. Centers for Disease Control and Prevention. *About Autism.* Retrieved July 10, 2005, from http://www.cdc.gov/ncbddd/autism.htm.

8. Individuals with Disabilities Education Act (IDEA) Data. *Number of children served by disability and age group, 1994–2003.* Retrieved July 10, 2005, from http:// www.ideadata.org/arc_toc6.asp#partbcc.

9. Laidler, J. R. (2005). US Department of Education data on "Autism" are not reliable for tracking autism prevalence. *Pediatrics, 116,* 120–124.

10. Szatmari, P. (1999). Heterogeneity and the genetics of autism. *Journal of Psychiatry and Neuroscience, 24,* 159–165.

11. Baker, P., Piven, J., & Sato, Y. (1998). Autism and tuberous sclerosis complex: Prevalence and clinical features. *Journal of Autism and Developmental Disorders, 28,* 279–285.

12. Hviid, A., Stellfeld, M., Wohlfahrt, J., & Melbye, M. (2003). Association between thimerosal-containing vaccine and autism. *Journal of the American Medical Association, 290,* 1763–1766.

13. Rimland, B. (2001, July 19). *What I have learned: Four and a half decades as a parent and researcher.* Keynote address at the 36th Annual Conference of the Autism Society of America, San Diego, CA. Retrieved July 15, 2005, from http://www. vaccinationnews.com/DailyNews/January2002/WhatIHaveLearned.htm.

14. Strock, M. (2004, April). "Autism spectrum disorders." Athealth.com. Retrieved January 3, 2005, from http://www.athealth.com/consumer/disorders/autismpdd.html.

15. Akshoomoff, N., Pierce, K., & Courchesne, E. (2002). The neurobiological basis of autism from a developmental perspective. *Development and Psychopathology, 14,* 613–634.

16. Courchesne, E., Carper, R., & Akshoomoff, N. (2003). Evidence of brain overgrowth in the first year of life in autism. *Journal of the American Medical Association, 290,* 337–344.

17. American Academy of Neurology. (2000). *Practice parameter: Screening and diagnosis of autism.* St. Paul, MN: Author.

18. Glascoe, F. P., & Sandler, H. (1995). Value of parents' estimates of children's developmental ages. *Journal of Pediatrics, 127,* 831–835.

19. Ozonoff, S., Rogers, S. J., & Hendren, R. L. (2003). *Autism spectrum disorders: A research review for practitioners.* Washington, DC: American Psychiatric Publishing, Inc.

20. Berument, S. K., Rutter, M., Lord, C., Pickles, A., & Bailey, A. (1999). Autism screening questionnaire: Diagnostic validity. *The British Journal of Psychiatry, 175,* 444–451.

21. Sparrow, S., Balla, D., & Cicchetti, D. (1984). *Vineland Adaptive Behavior Scales.* Circle Pines, MN: AGS Publishing.

22. *The Education of the Handicapped Act Amendment of 1986*. Public Law 99-457. 99th Cong., 2nd sess., October 1986.

23. Tierney, E. (2004). Co-morbidity in autism. *The Exceptional Parent, 34*, 60–63.

24. Lord, C., & McGee, J. P. (2001). *Educating children with autism*. Washington, DC: National Academy Press.

25. Ozonoff, S., Rogers, S. J., & Hendren, R. L. (2003). *Autism spectrum disorders: A research review for practitioners*. Washington, DC: American Psychiatric Publishing, Inc.

26. Lord, C., & McGee, J. P. (2001). *Educating children with autism*. Washington, DC: National Academy Press.

27. *No Child Left Behind Act of 2001*. Public Law 107-111. 107th Cong., 2nd sess., 8 January 2002.

28. Lovaas, O. I. (1981). *Teaching developmentally disabled children*. Baltimore, MD: University Park Press.

29. Lovaas, O. I. (1987) Behavioral treatment and normal educational and intellectual functioning in young autistic children. *Journal of Consulting and Clinical Psychology, 55*, 3–9.

30. Carr, E. G., Levin, L., McConnachie, G., Carlson, J. I., Kemp, D. C., & Smith, C. E. (1994). *Communication-based interventions for problem behavior*. Baltimore, MD: Paul H. Brookes.

31. Scheuermann, B. & Webber, J. (2002). *Autism: Teaching does make a difference*. Belmont, CA: Wadsworth.

32. McGee, G. G., Morrier, M. J. & Daly, T. (1999). An incidental teaching approach to early intervention for toddlers with autism. *Journal of the Association for the Severely Handicapped, 24*, 133–146.

33. Koegel, L. K., Koegel, R. L., Harrower, J. K., & Carter, C. M. (1999). Pivotal response intervention I: Overview of approach. *Journal of the Association for the Severely Handicapped, 24*, 174–185.

34. Schopler, E., Mesibov, G. B., & Hearsey, K. (1995). Structured teaching in the TEACCH system. In E. Schopler & G. B. Mesibov (Eds.), *Learning and cognition in autism* (pp. 243–267). New York: Plenum.

35. Short, A. B. (1984). Short-term treatment outcome using parents as co-therapists for their own autistic children. *Journal of Child Psychiatry and Allied Disciplines, 25*, 443–458.

36. Frost, L .A., & Brody, A. S. (1994). *The picture exchange communication system training manual*. Cherry Hill, NJ: Pyramid Educational Consultants, Inc.

37. Greenspan, S. I., Wieder, S., & Simons, R. (1998). *The child with special needs: Encouraging intellectual and emotional growth*. Reading, MA: Addison Wesley.

38. Prizant, B. M., Wetherby, A. M., Rubin, E., & Laurent, A. C. (2003). The SCERTS Model: A transactional, family-centered approach to enhancing communication and socioemotional abilities of children with autism spectrum disorder. *Infants and Young Children, 16*, 296–316.

39. General Accounting Office (GAO). (2005). *Special education: Children with autism*. Washington, DC: Author.

Chapter 4

Frequently Asked Questions about Attention Deficit/Hyperactivity Disorder

Carolyn Pender and Bradley Smith

Attention-deficit/hyperactivity disorder (AD/HD) is a common, chronic, impairing disorder characterized by developmentally inappropriate levels of inattention and/or hyperactivity/impulsivity.[1] Despite the fact that it is one of the most heavily researched disorders in child psychiatry, there remains a great deal of controversy and misunderstanding regarding this disorder.[2] This chapter takes a unique approach in that it is written to accommodate individuals who are impatient, have short attention spans, or both. The brief question and answer format will allow the reader to avoid getting bogged down in detail. Instead, the interested reader can skip to the questions of greatest interest or personal relevance, gain information within a brief period of time, and have access to a chapter that, as a whole, leads to a comprehensive and contemporary understanding of the major issues related to AD/HD.

INTRODUCTION TO ATTENTION DEFICIT/ HYPERACTIVITY DISORDER

What Is AD/HD?

The answer to this question is complicated, so please be patient with our detailed answer. As the slash between the AD and HD in AD/HD implies, the set of symptoms defining AD/HD are best described as two disorders. One type of AD/HD is related to problems with regulating attention. The other type of AD/HD is associated with problems with impulsivity and hyperactivity. Not all individuals with AD/HD show the same symptoms, nor does each person experience symptoms of AD/HD to the same level of severity. Moreover, AD/HD related impairment can be inconsistent and unstable, with tremendous variability across and within settings (e.g., good in math, but not science class on Tuesday, and visa versa on Wednesday). Furthermore, symptoms may vary across the life span. In general, variability should be considered one of the hallmarks of AD/HD.

Before continuing, we should note that some people do not think that AD/HD is a "real" disorder. Like all mental health disorders, AD/HD is socially defined in the sense that there is no single medical test to define the disorder. Individuals with AD/HD or other mental health disorders such as depression or schizophrenia show symptoms that are extreme relative to other individuals in society. This concept is illustrated by a joke that depicts a hypothetical conversation between a mental patient and a psychiatrist. The joke starts with the patient saying, "Doctor, I am not crazy, all of the rest of the world is insane." To that the psychiatrist responds, "You may be correct, but we are the majority."

Unfortunately, because there is no simple, objective test for AD/HD, some have questioned the validity of AD/HD. To deal with the multitude of questions about AD/HD, the National Institutes of Health held a consensus forming conference in 1998.[3] One of the firm conclusions was that that AD/HD is a real disorder that can be reliably diagnosed and responds to some types of treatment. Based on this consensus forming conference and an overwhelming body of scientific evidence, saying that AD/HD is fake is the intellectual equivalent of saying the world is flat.

There is growing evidence that AD/HD is biologically based, and someday there may be an objective medical test for AD/HD.[2] This should not be confused with the notion that the only appropriate treatments for AD/HD are biological, such as the stimulant drug methylphenidate. If AD/HD is biologically based, then it is important to understand interactions between biology and environment. The complexity of the biology/environment interaction helps to explain why AD/HD is so variable across individuals, ages, and settings. Given the right fit with one's environment (e.g., the right job, spouse, or school), or with treatments that help one fit into the environment (e.g., stimulant medication and behavior contracts), people with AD/HD can lead very productive lives. Moreover, some have even argued the AD/HD can be a gift in some circumstances.[4] In most cases, however, AD/HD can be a real challenge for the individuals with the disorder as well as those who care for them (e.g., parents, teachers, and spouses).

How Is AD/HD Diagnosed?

A state-of-the-art diagnosis of AD/HD should be made based on the following five critical considerations: (1) there are developmentally inappropriate levels of AD/HD symptoms, (2) AD/HD symptoms are reported by multiple persons, (3) the AD/HD symptoms are responsible for clinically significant impairment in multiple settings, (4) the symptoms are chronic and have been present since an early age, and (5) other causes for clinically significant impairment have been ruled out.

A truly comprehensive AD/HD evaluation includes a thorough diagnostic interview, a medical examination, collection of information from independent sources such as parents, family members, or spouses, *Diagnostic and Statistical Manual of Mental Disorders*, Fourth Edition (*DSM–IV*)[1] symptom checklists completed by two different sources, standardized AD/HD behavior rating scales, and other types of psychometric testing selected by the clinician depending on the individual's presenting symptoms (e.g., screening for depression or anxiety). When appropriate, such as when there is conflicting information across sources, individuals should also be observed in various settings to discover sources of disagreement and rule out other common causes of inattention and hyperactivity/impulsivity. These include an inability to complete assigned work in school or problems in the workplace due to a lack of basic skills, an overly distracting or chaotic environment, and the presence of symptoms visible only in selected environments or situations (e.g., a so-called bad fit in only one classroom).

Unfortunately, most individuals do not undergo state-of-the-art evaluations for AD/HD.[2,12] Consequently, AD/HD is frequently misdiagnosed, and sloppy assessment has been partially responsible for adding to the controversial nature of this disorder. A minimally acceptable diagnosis of AD/HD should be based on the following information: (1) a count of clinically significant symptoms of AD/HD that is above an age-appropriate cutoff and/or ratings of AD/HD symptoms that show extreme levels compared to same age peers (e.g., in the 95th percentile or higher), (2) has input from multiple persons, (3) documents significant impairment in multiple settings, (4) shows that the symptoms have been present for a very long time, preferably since early childhood (e.g., before seven years of age), and (5) reasonably rules out competing explanations for the impairment, including medical and psychiatric conditions.[5] The issues of symptoms and multiple informants are discussed in greater detail below.

The most widely used sets of symptoms to describe AD/HD are found in the *DSM–IV*.[1] The *DSM* is widely regarded as the most up-to-date diagnostic manual; however, updates in the *DSM* can lead to changes and confusion regarding the list of symptoms or diagnostic criteria for AD/HD (for example, the reader is encouraged to refer to the following section on ADD versus AD/HD). For present purposes, the most current *DSM* criteria (i.e., *DSM–IV*) will be described here. Since children and adults typically show different symptoms of AD/HD (the reader is encouraged to read the section further on in this chapter that addresses the differences between child and adult displays of AD/HD symptoms), it is likely that subsequent versions of the *DSM* (e.g., *DSM–V*, which is currently being developed) may introduce new diagnostic considerations for adolescents and adults.

According to the *DSM–IV*,[1] children must display at least six symptoms of either inattentive behavior and/or hyperactive/impulsive behavior in order to meet AD/HD diagnostic criteria. The symptoms must be considered developmentally inappropriate, must be present in a minimum of two different settings (e.g., home and school), must have been present for at least six months, and must result in significant impairment in major life activities (e.g., school, social relationships, hobbies, home life). Also, symptoms must not be better explained by other disorders such as psychosis, bipolar disorder, pervasive developmental disorders, or mental retardation.

The *DSM–IV* inattention symptoms are as follows: (1) fails to give close attention to details, (2) shows difficulty sustaining attention, (3) does not seem to listen to when spoken to directly, (4) does not follow through on instructions, (5) has difficulty organizing tasks or activities, (6) avoids tasks that require sustained mental effort, (7) often loses things necessary for completion of tasks, (8) is easily distracted, and (9) is forgetful in daily activities.

The *DSM–IV* hyperactive/impulsive symptoms include: (1) fidgets with hands or feet or squirms in seat, (2) leaves seat in situations where it is considered inappropriate to do so, (3) runs about or climbs excessively, (4) has difficulty playing quietly, (5) is often "on the go" or acts as though "driven by a motor," (6) talks excessively, (7) blurts out answers before questions are completed, (8) has difficulty awaiting their turn, and (9) interrupts or intrudes on others.

After reading these symptoms, it is common to say something like "that sounds like me" or "that sounds like my child." This is because many people exhibit some of these symptoms, some of the time. To have AD/HD, however, most of these symptoms need to present most of the time, plus other criteria need to be met. Remember, the symptoms are only one-fifth of a decent assessment for AH/HD.[5]

Requesting multiple persons to document AD/HD symptoms and related-impairment is of critical importance in making an accurate AD/HD diagnosis and in developing the best possible treatment plan for the presenting symptoms. For example, individuals with AD/HD are known to have limited insight into their AD/HD symptoms. Consequently, if all data for an assessment of AD/HD is collected from only the person with AD/HD, then that assessment is likely to result in a false negative (i.e., saying the person does not have AD/HD when the person really does have AD/HD).[2] For example, this tendency was well-illustrated in a study of young adults with well-documented childhood histories of AD/HD.[6] When researchers asked individuals about their problems in functioning resulting from AD/HD, the diagnosis rate was approximately 5 percent of the sample. In contrast, when data from parents, spouses, or roommates were considered, the diagnosis rate was estimated to be about 65 percent.

In addition to being cautious about under-reporting of symptoms by someone with AD/HD, it is also critical to pay careful consideration to the functioning of other informants. For example, when a stressed or depressed parent provides all of the information for an assessment, it may be tainted by their biased perspective (e.g., bad mood or hopelessness). In such cases, rating data from another caregiver such as another person living in the home, as well as the child's teachers, is necessary to obtain a more accurate understanding of the child's current functioning.

What Is the Difference between ADD and AD/HD?

The labels attention-deficit disorder (ADD) and AD/HD are a source of confusion, and create a considerable quandary. On the one hand, the labels correctly convey the notion that AD/HD is at least two different types of conditions. On the other hand, the term ADD perpetuates an outdated conceptualization of what we now call AD/HD. To understand this situation, it may be helpful to review the history of the *DSM*.

In the *Diagnostic and Statistical Manual of Mental Disorders*, Second Edition (*DSM–II*),[7] there was a diagnosis called "Hyperkinetic Reaction of Childhood,"[2] however, the most prominent psychiatrists of the time began to theorize that the fundamental problem associated with this condition was inattention. The term ADD first appeared in the *Diagnostic and Statistical Manual of Mental Disorders*, Third Edition (*DSM–III*), published in 1980.[8] The ADD label reflected the *DSM* committee members' opinion that symptoms of inattention were the core of this disorder. The committee also acknowledged the presence of hyperactivity. Hence, the *DSM–III* specified two diagnoses: (1) ADD without hyperactivity (i.e., ADD) and (2) ADD with hyperactivity (ADD-H).

Subsequent research demonstrated that some individuals were hyperactive or impulsive without being inattentive. Hence, when the *DSM–III* was revised in 1987, the *DSM–III–R* introduced the term attention-deficit/hyperactivity disorder. This was a new name for a long-recognized problem (refer to the following section). A major criticism of the term AD/HD was that it was not specific enough, and that it lumped a diverse group of individuals under the same diagnostic label. Furthermore, research was growing to show that inattention and hyperactivity/impulsivity were separate but correlated sets of problems.

When the *DSM* was revised again in 1994,[1] the new *DSM–IV* criteria made clear distinctions between inattention and impulsivity. More specifically, three subtypes were introduced to more accurately describe the condition. These are described in more detail below.

The first *DSM–IV* category is AD/HD predominately inattentive subtype, which is very similar to the now obsolete (i.e., *DSM–III*) ADD without hyperactivity. Individuals diagnosed with this label show signs of poor attention regulation, but not any unusual difficulty with impulsivity or hyperactivity.

The second *DSM–IV* category is AD/HD predominantly hyperactive/impulsive subtype. Individuals with this subtype have problems with impulse or activity regulation, but function reasonably normally with regard to attention. This diagnostic category is one of the unique contributions of the *DSM–IV*, which states for the first time in the history of the *DSM* that some individuals experience problems solely related to hyperactivity/impulsivity.

The final *DSM–IV* category is AD/HD combined subtype, which is highly similar to the outdated (i.e., *DSM–III*) term ADD with hyperactivity. This term refers to individuals who show both difficulties with inattention as well as hyperactivity/impulsivity.

To summarize, using the terms ADD and AD/HD (a) creates confusion, (b) perpetuates old diagnostic criteria that do not fit with contemporary notions of AD/HD, and (c) fails to recognize cases in which problems are primarily due to hyperactivity/impulsivity The best way to avoid confusion is to use the *DSM–IV* terms "AD/HD predominately inattentive subtype", "AD/HD predominately hyperactive/impulsive subtype", or "AD/HD combined subtype".

Is AD/HD Something New?

The answer to this question is a resounding, "No!" and anyone who suggests that the diagnosis of AD/HD is some sort of modern invention is totally misguided. Admittedly, the term "AD/HD" is fairly new, as this disorder was only formally recognized by the APA in the mid-1980s[8]; however, the concept of AD/HD has been discussed by experts working with children for at least 100 years,[2] probably longer. Although AD/HD was almost certainly discussed prior to the first publications appearing on the disorder, the first formal description of what we now call AD/HD was by George Still who gave a series of three lectures to the Royal College of Physicians that were published in 1902. In this series, Dr. Still described these children as lacking moral control, which in the parlance of the times, apparently referred to developmentally high levels of impulsivity. His sample of children showed similar tendencies as children with

AD/HD today. For instance, Dr. Still suggested that males were three times more likely to show evidence of the condition, and that most children showed symptoms by eight years of age.

While Dr. Still made numerous contributions to the early understanding of the disorder we now call AD/HD, the conceptualization of AH/HD has evolved considerably since this time. For example, Still hypothesized that deficits in inhibitory volition, moral control, and sustained attention were casually related to each other and resulted from the same underlying neurological deficiency, supposedly some type of brain damage. Modern scientists and clinicians would not describe AD/HD as a sign of brain damage because years of research have failed to identify any gross neurological deficits. The causes of AD/HD are subtle and complex, and have been with us for a long time.

How Common Is AD/HD?

A good answer to this question is that AD/HD is common enough that we would expect every classroom in the United States to have at least one child with AD/HD (assuming equal distribution of AD/HD across classrooms and a class size of approximately 20 students). More technically, according to the *DSM–IV*,[1] between 3 percent and 5 percent of school aged children meet criteria for AD/HD in the United States. While the 3–5 percent prevalence rate is currently the most commonly cited range, other researchers have suggested rates ranging from as low as 1.6 percent to a high of 16 percent.[9] Reasons for such wide ranges in prevalence of AD/HD among children include different methods used to determine whether the child meets criteria for AD/HD, age and gender of the research sample, varying degree of stringency used in differentiating kids with AD/HD from those without the disorder, and differences in the nature of the population (e.g., urban versus rural samples).

Interestingly, males are three times more likely to receive a diagnosis of AD/HD than females.[2] In clinical samples (e.g., groups of children seen in a research setting), males tend to meet criteria for a diagnosis of AD/HD five–nine times more often than females. While popular media and press often claim this difference in frequency of diagnosis between males and females results from males naturally being more active, hyperactive, and aggressive than most females, researchers have only recently begun to study gender differences in AD/HD.

AD/HD is more common among children than adults, and is more likely to be seen in middle to lower-middle social classes. Further, there is increased diagnosis of AD/HD in population dense areas. To date, there is no evidence that AD/HD prevalence varies by ethnicity after social class and urban/rural lifestyle have been accounted for. As summarized by Barkley,[2] research has shown that AD/HD exists across the world, with children meeting *DSM–IV* diagnostic criteria in countries such as Germany, Japan, the Netherlands, New Zealand, and Canada, just to name a few.

If You Can Focus on Some Things but Not Others, Can You Still Have AD/HD?

The answer to this question is a resounding "Yes!" This is one of the great paradoxes of AD/HD. In many cases, persons with AD/HD can attend to intrinsically interesting activities (e.g., fishing or videogames) for extended periods of time, but rapidly lose interest in tedious work or school-related activities. Similarly, persons with AD/HD may attend well in novel situations, but rapidly lose interest over time. Thus, it may appear as though the ability to pay attention in some situations and not others is an issue of willpower or motivation. However, AD/HD should not be described as laziness.[5] Rather, AD/HD might be viewed as different levels of attention and/or impulse regulation that are associated with unique sensitivities to reinforcement. Figuring out how to deal with unique levels of inattention and/or impulsivity and related motivational difficulties is one of the greatest challenges of working with individuals with AD/HD.

What Are the Common Disorders That Might Be Confused with AD/HD?

The answer to this question is complicated, and due to the limited space for this chapter, our response is probably incomplete. We will discuss some disorders that are commonly confused with AD/HD, but will not list them all. Generally speaking, the disorders commonly confused with AD/HD fall into three categories. First, there are medical disorders that might be confused with AD/HD but can be ruled out medically, for example hyperthyroidism. Second, there are psychiatric disorders that can be confused with AD/HD that would take precedence over an AD/HD diagnosis, at least until the disorder is properly treated. Examples of these disorders are cases of psychosis or mania. Third, there are disorders that can be confused with AD/HD but can also co-occur with AD/HD. Indeed, Russell Barkley,[2] a leading expert in AD/HD research, has suggested that at least 80 percent of children with AD/HD show evidence of a second disorder, while 60 percent or more children have two or more comorbid disorders. Other estimates suggest a more conservative estimate of 60 percent of children showing evidence of another disorder.[10] Examples of commonly comorbid *DSM–IV* disorders include: oppositional defiant disorder (ODD), conduct disorder (CD), anxiety disorders, major depressive disorder (MDD), and tics and Tourette's syndrome. Each of these disorders will be discussed in more detail below.

ODD is characterized by a pattern of negativistic, hostile, and defiant behavior lasting at least six months with children showing behaviors such as losing their temper, arguing with adults, actively defying or refusing to comply with adult rules, and being angry and resentful.[1] In 40–70 percent of cases, children showed comorbid AD/HD and ODD, with AD/HD symptoms thought to contribute to ODD due to the many daily hassles created by AD/HD. Individuals with ODD only are primarily irritable rather then inattentive or impulsive.

CD is defined by repetitive and persistent patterns of behavior in which the basic rights of others or major age-appropriate societal rules or norms are violated with symptoms lasting for at least the previous six months. Examples of symptom clusters related to CD are (a) aggression to people or animals, (b) destruction of property, (c) deceitfulness or theft, and (d) serious violations of rules or laws.[1] In 20–56 percent of cases, children show comorbid AD/HD and CD. Due to the more serious nature of CD, children showing this comorbidity will often show greater impairment in general functioning as well as poorer long term outcomes. Individuals with CD only are planful and often unremorseful or uncaring about victims, whereas individuals with AD/HD may commit transgressions impulsively or accidentally and later regret their actions.

Anxiety disorders are characterized by excessive anxiety and worry occurring more days than not, for at least six months, and interfere with a number of events or activities such as work and school performance. There are many forms of anxiety and it is beyond the scope of this section to describe them all. Briefly, symptoms of an anxiety disorder that might be confused with AD/HD include restlessness or feeling keyed up or on edge, difficulty concentrating or mind going blank, irritability, muscle tension, and sleep disturbance (including difficulty falling asleep or staying asleep or restless sleep).[1] Between 10–14 percent of children with AD/HD also meet criteria for an anxiety disorder. Some researchers believe that anxiety among children with AD/HD results from poor emotion regulation as opposed to actual fear.[2] Comorbid anxiety is an important diagnostic consideration because children with AD/HD plus anxiety may receive less benefit from treatment with medication than do children with AD/HD who are not anxious.

MDD is characterized by depressed mood or a general loss of interest or pleasure in activities. Some of the symptoms of a major depressive episode that might be confused with AD/HD include impaired concentration, restlessness, overactivity, decreased sleep, and lack of interest in formerly pleasurable activities.[1] Estimates of the overlap between AD/HD and depression vary widely (i.e., 0–45% of children diagnosed with AD/HD meet criteria for MDD); however, it has been suggested that it is typical for one out of four individuals with AD/HD (25%) meet *DSM–IV* criteria for MDD by age 20. Depression can be a serious, life-threatening condition due to the elevated risk for suicide, and therefore should always be monitored when working with someone with AD/HD.

Tourette's syndrome is typically characterized by spontaneous vocalizations or movement, technically tics which are defined by sudden, rapid, recurrent, and nonrhythmic movements or vocalizations.[1] Recent reports suggest that approximately 7 percent of children with AD/HD have tics or Tourette's syndrome; however, 60 percent of individuals with Tourette's syndrome also have a diagnosis of AD/HD. In some cases, use of stimulant medication in the treatment of AD/HD may exaggerate Tourette's-like symptoms in some children. If this happens, families are encouraged to consult their child's prescribing physician to determine whether a lowering of dosage may serve to decrease the presence of tics. If necessary, doses of stimulants can be lowered, other medications can be tried instead of stimulants, or other medications may be administered in conjunction with stimulants to decrease or eliminate tics.

While mania can co-occur with AD/HD, it is rather infrequent in comparison to other disorders. For example, recent research findings suggest that between 6 and 10 percent of children with AD/HD also experience mania. Mania is characterized by a distinct period of abnormally and persistently elevated or irritable mood lasting at least a week. Mania also involves the individual showing inflated self-esteem, a decreased need for sleep, being more talkative than usual, having flights of ideas or high levels of distractibility, and showing increased goal-directed activity (e.g., working on "projects," hypersexuality, and other intrinsically motivated pursuits).[1] When treating a child showing signs of mania and AD/HD, it is of fundamental importance to manage the manic symptoms and possible bipolar disorder (sometimes called manic-depression) before addressing the AD/HD symptoms. In most cases, effective treatment involves polypharmaceutical management and intensive behavior therapy. Children displaying manic symptoms and AD/HD are at an increased risk for substance abuse and suicide as adolescents. These children also tend to show psychotic-like disturbances in thought, higher irritability, increased aggressiveness, and more violent behavior. These two conditions are more likely to co-occur in families where there is a history of bipolar disorder.

Similar to mania, psychosis may also co-occur with AD/HD, but the prevalence rate is considerably lower than that of other disorders. Psychosis involves the presence of one or more of the following symptoms: delusions, hallucinations, disorganized speech, and grossly disorganized behavior (e.g., difficulty with gross and fine motor coordination and movement).[1] The first generation of drugs used to treat psychosis, called typical antipsychotics, work in the opposite manner of stimulant drugs to treat AD/HD and often make attention symptoms worse. The new generation of anti-psychotic drugs, sometimes call atypical antipsychotics, treat psychosis without causing a lot of attention-related side effects. Thus, these new medicines are a promising option for individuals with a history of AD/HD. Regardless of the choice of medication, the combination of family or other highly structured social support, plus medication, is clearly the best treatment for schizophrenia.

Are Accommodations Appropriate for Individuals with AD/HD?

The appropriate accommodations are those that work, are fair and manageable, and do not inadvertently reinforce the problem behavior.[2] Furthermore, accommodations should be tailored to the individual, tested for effectiveness, and must be sustainable within the setting for extended periods of time. For instance, a student with AD/HD may find massed practice of arithmetic problems to be aversive and difficult to complete. If the student can demonstrate mastery of the arithmetic concept in a few problems, and do them with reasonable accuracy and fluency, there is no need for massed practice, especially if failing to complete lengthy practice assignments is the major reason for their failure to earn a good grade in class. In such a situation, an appropriate accommodation may be to give fewer arithmetic problems. However, the accommodation should be a two-way street. For example, if the student performs poorly on the reduced set of problems, the expectation should be something like completing extra arithmetic problems until they demonstrate adequate levels of accuracy and fluency. However, it cannot be stressed enough that simply doing more of the same (i.e., assigning more arithmetic problems) is not considered an appropriate accommodation for children with AD/HD. Extra practice of the skill may involve the student staying after school or arriving early before the school day begins to do the extra work under different conditions than the regular classroom.

In the past couple of years, a wide range of accommodations have been suggested by various AD/HD specialists. It is important to keep in mind that not all accommodations are created equal, and that some approaches are considered to be better than others. Since it is not possible to cover all forms of accommodations that are currently available in the treatment of this disorder, basic classroom considerations and other general academic accommodations will be covered in greatest detail since AD/HD-related accommodations are most commonly used with school-aged children.

Some accommodations are very simple. For example, in order to benefit fully from classroom instruction, children with AD/HD should be seated in close proximity of the teacher using a traditional desk configuration. Seating a child with AD/HD in the rear of the classroom with their back facing the teacher will drastically reduce participation in class and may impede skill mastery. Indeed, understimulating children with AD/HD can sometimes make problems worse. Excluding children with AD/HD is counterproductive and, in most cases, illegal.

With regards to class assignments, students with AD/HD often benefit from having tasks broken down into smaller steps. Instead of allowing the child more time to complete the whole assignment, breaking down the task into smaller tasks using the same total amount of time often helps promote task completion by keeping the student on task. Given that many children with AD/HD have trouble sustaining their attention over long periods of time, accommodations such as longer test taking time are potentially counterproductive. Moreover, giving more time to complete assignments puts increased demands on teachers or other school professionals, and can be more effectively dealt with by seating the student in the front of the room and providing brief and frequent checks on their progress toward clearly specified intermediate goals for the test or assignment.

Some accommodations deal with student's organizational skills or problems such as losing assignments. A related accommodation might be giving students with AD/HD weekly assignments rather than assigning homework on a daily basis. Decreasing the number of times students are expected to transport materials between home and school may be counterproductive. In some cases this accommodation may result in decreased loss of assignments, decreased chance of the student simply forgetting to turn in completed work, and increased likelihood of actual work completion. Unfortunately, giving weekly assignments only avoids dealing the problems related to organization and forgetfulness. Moreover, once a week assignments up the ante, so to speak, regarding forgetting (i.e., losing a weeks worth of work instead of one day). Therefore, we think it is better to work with the student, parents, and other involved individuals to develop better skills at transporting and tracking assignments on a daily basis.

To help children be as organized as possible, parents may want to invest in three ring binders or folders and to adopt a specific organization system facilitated by dividers or folders for each subject or for certain activities. For example, you might make divider sections or folders for each of the following tasks: notes, assignment log, homework I am working on, homework that is done, homework to be handed in, and returned assignments. Creating a specific section for all of the student's work often helps decrease messy lockers, disorganized school bags and bedrooms, and helps assure that the student does not forget to complete assignments or hand them in when they are due. Most students with AD/HD will greatly benefit from having organization checked and rewarded on a daily basis, including older students (e.g., in high school or college).

A low cost accommodation that can be effective with all students, but especially those with AD/HD, is to consider scheduling the most difficult subjects early in the morning as opposed to later in the day when fatigue may increase AD/HD symptoms. Likewise, medication can be adjusted so that the peak effects are timed to occur when medication is most needed. Teachers should also try and mix together less desirable activities with highly desirable activities to help sustain interest and encourage continued participation. Providing students with a daily schedule also helps to build a routine and informs students of what is required and expected of them at different times throughout the day each day of the week. Establishing a regular schedule early in the academic year can help boost work productivity and decrease behavior problems in the classroom.

General classroom instruction should be stimulating and rewarding for students. Therefore, teachers should be animated and use strategies to assure participation from all students. This may be achieved by having the teacher walk around the class while teaching and tap students' shoulders for responses to encourage them to pay attention and follow the lesson more closely. Teachers may also use computer programs to allow students with AD/HD to practice basic and applied skills. Books on tape and videos or DVDs are other tools that often result in greater acquisition of knowledge. Research has also shown that having students with AD/HD take notes during lessons results in higher test performance then simply having them sit and listen.[11] When reading, students with AD/HD should be periodically asked comprehension questions to assure they are processing the material they are reading. Note taking and writing summaries can often be very helpful. Such strategies will probably help the whole class, but may benefit students with AD/HD the most.

Since students with AD/HD often show difficulty with impulsivity, they should be discouraged from providing impulsive responses when answering the teacher. However, this creates a conflict between punishing impulsive responses and potentially inadvertently punishing participation. A good solution for this conflict is to have teachers ask students to write down their response on a write-on, wipe-off board or on a piece of paper before they have the chance to blurt out their response. The teachers can then check and reinforce participation without having students with AD/HD blurting out answers and aggravating other students.

To increase students' motivation to learn in the classroom or complete chores at home, teachers and parents may want to consider implementing a token reward system that is positively based and allows students to earn various privileges. Opportunity for reward should be frequent so that students with AD/HD do not lose motivation and revert to negative behavior. For information on how to implement a positive point system, readers are encouraged to consult Smith, Barkley, and Shapiro.[12] Another option for teachers and parents to manage behavior is to use a daily report card (DRC). This system encourages communication between the teacher and parent of a child with AD/HD by having the teacher rate the child's behavior in various areas on a five point scale each day. Examples of behaviors to be rated may include: participation, completed class assignments, followed class rules, followed teacher directions, and got along well with peers. The DRC may be used in conjunction with an at home plan which gives the child the opportunity to earn rewards from their parents for good behavior. By maintaining communication throughout the academic year, parents are less likely to receive any surprising news regarding their child's academic performance and behavior at report card time. Thus, a DRC can be low-cost and very effective accommodation for students with AD/HD.

Teachers should also pay attention to the frequency they praise their students and show appreciation. Unfortunately, many students with AD/HD have the majority of their interactions with teachers because they broke a rule or otherwise behaved inappropriately. This creates a situation such that attention from the teacher may actually inadvertently reinforce bad behavior. Whenever possible, teachers and parents should give much more attention to good behavior then bad behavior. Increasing the student's opportunities to earn positive praise from their teacher often results in a decrease in undesirable behavior. Indeed, the best way to decrease the frequency of an undesired behavior is to increase the frequency of a positive behavior that is incompatible with the negative behavior. For example, a student who bothers other children when they are supposed to be working can have this problem corrected by reinforcing the student for doing work at their seat. This is not really an accommodation, it is simply good behavior management. Hence, some so-called accommodations for students with AD/HD are simply good skills applied more often with this demanding population.

Most qualified school psychologists should be able to help with accommodations and behavioral interventions. If not, parents might pursue a behaviorally oriented psychologist for help. Behavioral methods are very powerful and should be a fundamental part of working with school-aged children with AD/HD. Remember, if we can get whales to jump through burning hoops, we can get kids with AD/HD to do what they are asked to do at school.

AD/HD ACROSS THE LIFE SPAN

Do Children Outgrow AD/HD?

Generally speaking, children diagnosed with AD/HD do not "outgrow" the symptoms of the disorder. Recently, scientists have discovered that AD/HD symptoms persist into adulthood in approximately 40–80 percent of cases.[2] Moreover, those who met criteria for AD/HD as children but no longer meet criteria as adults are typically much more impaired than their peers who were never diagnosed with AD/HD. Symptoms may be less obvious as individuals mature. This decline in obvious symptoms might explain why some experts used to think that children outgrew AD/HD. Instead, there is now a broad consensus that AD/HD is a chronic disorder that persists across the life span for the majority of individuals.[2,5,10,12,13]

A typical course of development would begin with a child showing excessively active, noncompliant, and difficult behavior as a toddler, which often results in delays in academic readiness skills. Throughout elementary school, difficult and mischievous behavior tends to continue, with parents experiencing increasing difficulty caring for the child. Throughout the teenage years, parents often report high levels of familial conflict and stress. Disagreements surrounding issues such as substance use, inappropriate conduct, academic difficulties, and reckless and dangerous driving are common among adolescents with AD/HD. As such, parents of teenagers with AD/HD often experience greater stress than parents of non-AD/HD teens. Recent research studies have suggested that teens with AD/HD are more likely to experience car accidents, receive more speeding tickets, are less likely to graduate from high school, and are at greater risk for teenage pregnancy.[2]

While the current body of knowledge of AD/HD among adults remains sparse, a couple of well-conducted longitudinal studies have found continuing problems for AD/HD into young adulthood. Specifically, the disorder has been linked to interpersonal problems, poor academic achievement, problems with traffic violations and accidents, and vocational difficulties.[2] Furthermore, AD/HD has been associated with an increased number of criminal convictions, antisocial behavior, and substance use problems. In many of these cases, comorbid conduct disorder develops into antisocial personality disorder, so that AD/HD alone does not account for severe antisocial or substance abuse problems. However, AD/HD is uniquely associated with risk for smoking, and thus persons with AD/HD may suffer the health consequences of smoking at a higher rate than the general population.[14]

A recent study of college students completed by the authors of this chapter found that college students showing elevated symptoms of inattention displayed different deficits in functioning than students with high levels of impulsivity.[13] Specifically, compared to those with lower levels of inattention symptoms, first year college students with high levels of inattention reported more difficulties with social relationships, more conduct problems, a greater number of alcohol-related problems, and more depression. In contrast, compared to those with lower levels of impulsivity, students who were impulsive showed greater deficits in academic performance, increased difficulties with social relationships, and a greater number of hours spent consuming alcohol. These findings support the idea that AD/HD is a set of disorders with different clusters of problems.

Are There Differences in Symptoms between Children and Adults with AD/HD?

The answer to this question is most definitely yes! Indeed, this is a major limitation of the current *DSM–IV* diagnostic criteria. The system used to diagnose AD/HD was developed for use with children, but is currently the same for children and adults. The major limitations of this system are related to (a) the developmental appropriateness of the list of symptoms, and (b) the requirement that AD/HD-related problems need to be documented prior to the age of seven.[2] The list of symptoms for inattention might work with both children and adults, but the symptoms for hyperactivity/impulsivity are problematic for use across the life span. For instance, most 30 year olds do not have problems with remaining seated or running and climbing excessively. Many adults with AD/HD report feeling restless, but the *DSM* does not ask for subjective feelings of hyperactivity even though psychiatrists ask about subjective feelings when assessing other disorders such as MDD. Due to the vast difference in symptom display between children and adults, some experts have suggested that a new set of symptoms should be developed and tested with adults. In fact, there are some new rating scales for adults to help diagnose AD/HD that might be more developmentally appropriate than using the usual *DSM–IV* criteria.

One way to cope with limitations of the *DSM–IV* system when working with older individuals is to "relax" the cutoffs or symptom criteria. As mentioned earlier, the *DSM–IV* currently requires an individual to display six out of nine possible symptoms in the broad areas of inattention and/or hyperactivity/impulsivity. However, many of the symptoms associated with AD/HD apply more to younger children than to adults (e.g., acts as though driven by a motor, climbs on things when it is inappropriate to do so). Thus, it is arguably easier for a child to receive a diagnosis of AD/HD than an adult. Accordingly, some have suggested that to diagnose an adult with AD/HD predominately inattentive subtype, you should only require five symptoms instead of six. Likewise, and perhaps more radically, some have suggested that a diagnosis of AD/HD predominately hyperactive/impulsive subtype should require only four symptoms from the *DSM–IV* list of nine. This recommendation is based, in part, on research showing that at five symptoms of inattention and four symptoms of hyperactivity/impulsivity are cutoffs at about the 95th percentile for adults.[2] Thus, the lower cutoffs would maintain the base rate of AD/HD at about 5 percent for both children and adults.

Another problem with the *DSM–IV* criteria for diagnosing AD/HD is the requirement that the age of onset must be established prior to seven years of age. When an older person presents for an evaluation for AD/HD, it is often very difficult to confidently establish that there were problems with AD/HD prior to age seven. Retrospective recall is extremely problematic and is likely to be strongly biased by whether or not the person thinks they have AD/HD. While comments in elementary school report cards can sometimes be used to infer difficulties related to AD/HD, it is very hard to meet the early onset criteria for *DSM–IV* in the absence of such data.

When early onset cannot be established objectively, or if the client just barely misses the cutoff for *DSM–IV* diagnosis of AD/HD, it is acceptable to diagnose them with AD/HD-NOS. Such a diagnosis carries the message that the clinician thinks the client has AD/HD, but the client does not strictly meet the *DSM–IV* criteria for AD/HD. Usually such a diagnosis is accompanied by an explanation why the NOS designation was used and the diagnosis should be considered just as valid as any other diagnosis of AD/HD.

How Do Problems Related To AD/HD Change across the Life Span?

Problems related to AD/HD change quite a bit across the life span, and unfortunately often grow worse as deficits accumulate and consequences for mistakes or misbehaviors become more serious. Although there are many anecdotes to the contrary, infants and toddlers who will eventually be diagnosed with AD/HD are not easily distinguished from their non-AD/HD peers because children of this age naturally exhibit such (and developmentally appropriate) high levels of inattention and impulsivity that AD/HD symptoms are often not noticeable.

Parents who argue that their child showed signs of AD/HD as an infant and toddler are probably heavily influenced by the bias of their current knowledge about the child. Most assuredly, some children are more difficult to manage than others, but the early emergence of management problems could be related to comorbid conditions such as ODD as much as to AD/HD. Thus, it is hard to determine if early problems are due to AD/HD or co-occurring conditions.

There is growing evidence that AD/HD can be reliably and validly diagnosed among preschoolers.[2] At this age, impulsive children run the risk of being rejected by peers due to inappropriate interpersonal behavior such as aggression and rule breaking (e.g., failing to wait their turn). Inattentive children who get lost in their own world may be neglected by their peers, but are not usually actively rejected. Mealtimes and chores may be more difficult with preschoolers with AD/HD. Parents may notice that these children become bored easily and need a lot more adult help than most kids to keep them occupied and safe or to complete tasks, such as getting dressed or cleaning up a room. Those who attend day care may present challenges to teachers, especially during quiet times and during group activities when peer relationship problems may surface. In some situations, behavior may be so severe that the child may even get expelled from a series of child care settings.

When children with AD/HD enter elementary school, they enter a nearly perfect environment for detecting AD/HD. These hyperactive and/or inattentive students are asked to sit still and pay attention for extended periods of time, which can be highly problematic for this group. Even "normal" students complain that school is boring. Imagine how a child with AD/HD feels?

The peak age for noticing AD/HD symptoms is during first grade, with the first referrals for help peaking around second or third grade. Presenting problems related to AD/HD at this age include academic difficulties, discipline problems at school, discipline problems at home, and conflict with peers. Elementary-age children with AD/HD often have very little insight into their problems and interventions need to be almost entirely implemented and managed by adults. Fortunately, insight and self-directed coping with AD/HD can start to improve during adolescence.

Although full consideration of the host of developmental changes that arise during the transition from childhood to adolescence is beyond the scope of this chapter, we consider five issues that are salient to adolescence that deserve consideration with respect to treatment. First, adolescence is typically marked by greater cognitive capacities that are characteristic of formal operations. These new capacities involve the ability to think more abstractly and the increased ability to solve problems in a systematic manner. Consequently, adolescents, as compared to children, are more self-conscious, better able to analyze their own performance, better able to predict their own behavior ahead of time, and better able to critically evaluate possible available strategies to achieve a goal.[15] These improved cognitive abilities and new social expectations might impact the effectiveness of available treatments for adolescents as compared to children. Second, adolescence is marked by a focus on identity formation and the establishment of greater independence. Related to this is the notion of adolescent "storm and stress" which is often manifested as increased oppositionality toward authority figures. Third, difficulties associated with increased independence and autonomy are typically met by a greater reliance on peers as intimate partners rather than simply friends with similar interests. Fourth, the transition from elementary to middle and high school results in a different daily routine. Adolescents routinely interact with up to six different teachers across the course of the day and are expected to have greater responsibility in keeping up with their materials, staying on task, and arriving on time, and so forth. Finally, physiological changes, such as growth and the development of secondary sexual characteristics, have major influences on social behavior and its consequences.[15] For example, aggression and defiance, which often accompany AD/HD, are more problematic with a six-foot-tall, 180-pound individual as compared to a four-foot-tall, 80-pound individual!

As the adolescent with AD/HD matures into adulthood, the problems associated with the disorder tend to get more varied and dire. Significant school problems include discipline or academic problems that may lead to expulsion or school failure. Unfortunately, AD/HD is clearly associated with elevated risk for failing to graduate from high school, and is probably associated with increased risk for failing to graduate from college. Most likely due to comorbid CD, many individuals with AD/HD engage in delinquent behavior and substance abuse and suffer the legal and health consequences of these risky behaviors. Interpersonal difficulties may lead to conflict at home and difficulty maintaining long-term relationships, either friendships or romantic relationships. Problems in the workplace may arise due to behaviors related to inattention and/or impulsivity, or due to poor social or learning skills. There is now fairly strong documentation that individuals with AD/HD are more likely to be involved in motor vehicle accidents than their non-AD/HD peers. It seems likely that there is an elevated risk for other accidents due to impulsivity and/or inattention. Another concern is risky sexual behavior and related consequences such a pregnancy and sexually transmitted diseases. Finally, as discussed in the comorbidity section, there is an elevated risk for depression and anxiety.

To summarize, individuals with AD/HD show a higher likelihood of experiencing psychiatric, medical, vocational, legal, interpersonal, and academic difficulties than persons without AD/HD.[2] It is important to note that many persons with AD/HD manage to avoid all of these problems and lead fairly normal lives. Others suffer transient problems, which they overcome or find accommodations for, and then function without great difficulty. Some, however, are so seriously impaired by AD/HD and related consequences that they lead troubled lives and may become a significant burden on family, friends, and society. Appropriate treatment could presumably prevent these negative outcomes and high costs to society.

TREATMENT FOR AD/HD

What Are the Essential Ingredients for Effective Treatment of AD/HD?

The most critical consideration when treating AD/HD is that the intervention needs to be active at the point of performance. Numerous studies have shown the effects of medication in the treatment of AD/HD are temporary and that behavior therapies and skills training techniques often employed to treat AD/HD do not generalize readily to other settings.[2,5,10,12] Thus, the medicines used to treat AD/HD need to be in the person's system when they are engaged in the activities the medicine is supposed to help. Likewise, behavioral interventions need to be active in all of the settings where behavioral support is needed. Skills and behavior management plans need to be actively supported at the point of performance to be effective.

A second essential ingredient is an individualized, evidence-based approach to determining what works. Too often, persons with AD/HD get the treatment of the week (e.g., they try the newest drug, the newest self-help routine, or the newest biofeedback technique) without careful consideration if that treatment works for them. A good starting place is to select evidence-based treatments that have a strong track record of effectiveness in the scientific literature (e.g., stimulant medication and behavioral interventions). It is prudent to stay away from treatments that do not have a strong evidence base (e.g., biofeedback) or have evidence that they do not work (e.g., dietary methods). Even when using a proven treatment, response to AD/HD treatment is highly idiosyncratic, so all treatments should be carefully studied using individual case study methods. If your doctor or psychologist does not take baseline measures (e.g., parent and teacher ratings) prior to making treatment changes (e.g., a different dose of medicine or new behavior plan), your treatment is not being properly evaluated.

What Are the Best Evidence-Based Treatments Currently Available for Reducing AD/HD Symptoms?

A multimodal approach to treatment of AD/HD symptoms is recommended as the best way to treat the disorder.[2,5,10,12] That is, in order to fully address all the symptoms characteristic of AD/HD, it is necessary to provide treatment in a variety of different ways. For example, a comprehensive treatment of the disorder should include a combination of medical, educational, behavioral, and psychological interventions. These interventions do not have to be administered by a single individual, but can be provided by a team of professionals.

What Are the Most Commonly Used Medicines for AD/HD?

Currently, most children are treated for AD/HD with stimulant medication.[10,12] Over the past 30 years, methylphenidate, which is the active ingredient in Ritalin, has been the most commonly prescribed drug for AD/HD. Many other stimulants are on the market and recently Adderall, which is a mixture of amphetamine salts, has been capturing a larger part of the market share. A promising new drug, Straterra, may achieve its effects in a method somewhat different than the stimulants. Most physicians agree that the stimulant drugs above, especially long-acting versions that are taken once a day (e.g., Concerta and Adderall XR) are the first choice medications for AD/HD.[2] Straterra is probably worth trying if methylphenidate or amphetamines do not work. Some physicians prescribe antidepressants and antihypertensives to treat AD/HD, but this is far less common than stimulants and Strattera and is probably not as safe and effective.

How Safe and Effective Are the Commonly Used Medicines for AD/HD?

The short answer is, pretty safe. This can be said with some authority because stimulant medication is probably the most heavily researched medicine in child psychiatry, and possibly in all of pediatric medicine. Probably the greatest safety concerns are slowed growth and the risk of developing motor tics. Fortunately, almost all stimulant side effects, which are rare, are dose-dependent, and remit with a lowered dose or discontinuation of the medicine.

The issue of effectiveness and practicality is a bit more complicated. For a detailed discussion of the efficacy, safety, and practicality of medications used to treat AD/HD, we recommend a recent review by Smith and colleagues.[12] For present purposes, we would like to note that stimulant medication has been shown to be effective over as long as five years if taken regularly, and that it works for children, adolescents, and adults. Current estimates of positive response rate of stimulant medication are around 82 percent.[2] Since the identification of AD/HD seems to be occurring earlier and earlier, it is worth mentioning that stimulants have been found to be safe and effective for children between the ages of four and five; however, very little is known about the safety of these drugs for children ages three and younger.

An important practicality consideration is that methylphenidate and amphetamines are considered rapid acting stimulants since they produce effects within 30–45 minutes following oral ingestion and peak in their effectiveness within two–four hours. These drugs lose effect after three to seven hours, so it is important to administer them frequently (often two or three times a day). A recent development in the treatment of AD/HD is the emergence of extended release forms of methylphenidate. While earlier versions of long term stimulants did not work for many children, newer versions such as Adderall XR and Concerta appear to be more effective. Benefits of these newer once a day delivery systems include decreased issues with medication compliance, more consistent release of medication into the system (less highs and lows of medication effectives), and no need for a midday booster dose to complete homework.

It is noteworthy that the safety and efficacy of drugs other than stimulants and Strattera is very limited. Some physicians prescribe antidepressants or other drugs (e.g., Clonadine) either alone or in combination with stimulants to treatment AD/HD. Such practices are not well-supported by research and should be very carefully monitored, if tried at all (see Smith et al).[12]

Can AD/HD Be Prevented?

Since the cause of the disorder has not yet been identified, it is not possible at this time to determine whether or not AD/HD can be prevented. While some groups of researchers and organizations claim that symptoms can be reduced using various techniques and strategies, there is currently no scientific proof that any of these techniques can be used to help prevent AD/HD.[2]

In terms of prevention, the best approach to take to AD/HD is analogous to taking care of your teeth. Some people are going to be more prone to cavities than others. Therefore, some may need more vigorous oral hygiene and more frequent checkups than others. Early and persistent intervention should prevent major problems from developing. Thus, like dental cavities, AD/HD might not be completely preventable. Nevertheless, good preventive care can prevent major problems (e.g., school problems akin to toothaches) and the need for major treatment (e.g., tutoring akin to root canals).

What Are Some of the Common Myths Regarding Treatment of AD/HD?

Taking about all of the myths related to treating AD/HD could fill more than an entire book. There is no way we can adequately address this complex and potentially emotional issue in this short section. However, we will offer a few broad comments.

First, not all treatments are equal. Treatments for AD/HD can be crudely categorized as evidence-based, untested, and disproven.[2] While experts researching the treatment and management of AD/HD have identified several empirically proven forms of treatment for the disorder, many organizations and specialists continue to promote untested or even disproven therapies in the treatment of AD/HD. Currently, many forms of treatment for AD/HD symptoms commonly suggested by the popular press and media are not evidence-based. Implementing non-evidence based treatment for AD/HD symptoms often results in a failure to reduce impairment. Moreover, in some circumstances, untested or disproven therapies may actually result in a worsening of symptoms than no treatment at all.

So-called treatments for AD/HD that are disproven include elimination diets (e.g., the removal of sugar, additives, or dyes from the individual's food intake), megavitamins and minerals, sensory integration training, chiropractic skull manipulation, play therapy, individual child psychotherapy, biofeedback, self-control therapies, and social skills therapies conducted in clinics.[2] Many other such treatments for AD/HD have not yet been adequately tested, and following testing might be added to the list of disproven attempted treatments.

Many people profess to know that one or more of the above treatments works. These beliefs are persistent and are often related to mistakes in causal thinking and ignorance or bias regarding good research. For example, many parents believe that sugar causes their child with AD/HD to be hyperactive. As evidence, they may cite some episodes of particularly bad behavior at a birthday or Halloween party. What they are missing in these cases is that many factors other than sugar can account for poor behavior at parties, such as unclear rules, excitement, and substances such as caffeine. For every complex problem (e.g., AD/HD), there is a simple solution (e.g., sugar restriction), and it is wrong.

Parents who believe that some interventions are effective (e.g., sugar restriction) might be correct about behavior change, but could be wrong about the cause. For instance, some parents are adept at paying close attention to their child and setting limits. Thus, good parenting rather than the diet itself must be considered as a cause of change, rather than less sugar. We should note, however, that even those parents who are adept in parenting may create stigma and unnecessary parenting stress through interventions such as restriction of sugar. For instance, consider the labeling that occurs when a school class or group of peers is told that a child cannot have candy, soda, or other sweets because the child has AD/HD. Given that dozens of studies have shown that restricting sugar has no positive effect, all of the risks of controlling sugar are done with no real benefit to the child. Thus, disproven interventions for AD/HD are a losing proposition for persons with AD/HD.

Some other myths about AD/HD are the so-called garage mechanic and magic bullet approaches to treatment. The garage mechanic approach is very appealing from an adult effort standpoint because it is akin to dropping the car off at the shop and getting it fixed. This does not work with AD/HD because, as noted elsewhere in this chapter, an essential element of effective treatment is that it is active at the point of performance. Play therapy with a therapist or biofeedback training is almost certainly not going to help AD/HD-related problems at home or in the classroom.

With regard to the magic bullet myth, this is akin to hoping that AD/HD can be cured by a single intervention. There is no known treatment that cures AD/HD. Therefore, we recommend a dental model approach to this disorder, with persistent day-to-day intervention, regular checkups, and occasionally some extensive professional help. Taking stimulant medication regularly and daily behavioral contingencies are akin to brushing and flossing one's teeth. Visits to the doctor are like regular checkups. Family therapy, tutoring, or school-based interventions are akin to getting braces. Sometimes some exceptional structure is needed that, following growth, maturation, and good care, can be relaxed or removed when good progress is made.

EDUCATION ABOUT AD/HD

What Have Been Some Major Developments in AD/HD Research in the Past Decade?

There have been numerous breakthroughs in the identification, diagnosis, treatment, and management of AD/HD within the past decade. For example, the shift in conceptualization published in the *DSM–IV* suggesting that AD/HD is a set of disorders as opposed to one condition has been central in shaping research development on the origins of the disorder as well as in ways to treat it. For example, we now know it is possible for someone to display difficulty with sustaining attention independently of difficulties with hyperactivity or impulsivity and vice versa. Also, it is possible for some people to show difficulty with a combination of both areas.

Other notable advances have been made in the treatment of AD/HD. Within the past decade, numerous treatments have been disproven in the management of AD/HD, while others have repeatedly been shown to be effective in the treatment of AD/HD. Also with regards to treatment, advances in medication delivery systems such as the creation of once daily delivery doses have helped many families to decrease side effects, boost productivity, and facilitate medication compliance.

While still a growing area of research, experts are beginning to develop a clearer picture of AD/HD among adolescents and adults. Though currently very little is known about AD/HD among adolescents and adults when compared to children, considerable advances have been made such as ascertaining that AD/HD is not merely a childhood disorder that individuals grow out of. Also, it is becoming increasingly clearer that children and adults do not always display the same classic AD/HD behaviors, and so identification and treatment for these two groups should differ to address the different needs of the groups.

What Are Some Major Unanswered Questions about AD/HD?

The answer to this question might depend on whom you ask. We think there are several pressing questions. These are listed below. First, the cause, or more likely causes, of AD/HD need to be better understood. This includes advances in the understanding of the genetics of AD/HD and the effect of exposing individuals with AD/HD tendencies to different environments that may shape the expression of this multiply determined disorder. Second, it would be helpful to be able to predict individual response to treatment in advance. Currently, finding which treatment works best for an individual is a matter of trial and error. Third, the long-term effects of treatment for AD/HD are currently very poorly understood. Most current data is for five years or less (usually much less). Data on various approaches to treatment with implications for long-term results, such as medication holidays when children are out of school, are almost completely unstudied. Another big question, which may be especially hard to answer, is why has there been such a big increase in awareness of AD/HD over the past couple of decades?

What Are Some Reputable Sources that Can Further Help Educate Me about AD/HD?

Within the past few years, AD/HD has been increasingly highlighted by the popular press and media, with countless television and radio shows addressing the issue both accurately and inaccurately. In addition, numerous books have been written on this disorder and literally thousands of Web sites dedicated to AD/HD are currently accessible to the general public. While considerable amounts of information are readily available to the public, it is important to note that the amount of misinformation on this condition is equal to or likely surpasses the amount of reputable information on this topic. Thus, consumers should be very wary when consulting sources about AD/HD.

A very good resource for parents is Children and Adults with Attention-Deficit/Hyperactivity Disorder (CHADD), which is a non-profit organization serving children and adults with AD/HD. Their Web site address is http://www.chadd.org/ and information is posted in both English and Spanish. CHADD offers AD/HD fact sheets, magazine subscriptions, contact numbers for popular organizations, information regarding cutting edge AD/HD research findings, education and employment for individuals with AD/HD, as well as numerous other helpful links and services. The information posted online is also available in hard copy form.

Families who are explicitly searching for information published on AD/HD in Spanish should consult J. J. Bauermeister's *Hiperactivo, impulsivo, distraido, Me conoces?* (New York: Guilford).

The National Institute for Mental Health (NIMH) also offers accurate and detailed information on AD/HD. Their Web site is http://www.nimh.nih.gov/healthinformation/adhdmenu.cfm. This site includes information on defining AD/HD, identifying the disorder accurately in children, a listing of appropriate treatment for the disorder, and identifying appropriate services for children with AD/HD.

College age students with AD/HD may benefit from consulting J. S. Bramer's *Succeeding in College with Attention-Deficit Hyperactivity Disorders: Issues and Strategies for Students, Counselors, and Educators* (Plantation, FL: Specialty Press, Inc).

Finally, other helpful Web sites include: ADDA Organization, http://www.add.org; National Information Center for Children and Youth with Disabilities, http://www.nichcy.org; ADD warehouse, http://www.addwarehouse.com; and the Council for Exceptional Children, http://www.cec.sped.org.

What Should I Do If after Reading This Chapter I Think I May Have AD/HD?

If after reading this chapter you suspect that you or someone close to you may have AD/HD, you should schedule an appointment with your primary care physician in order to learn more about the disorder. If the primary care physician suspects that the individual in question is experiencing symptoms characteristic of AD/HD, a comprehensive examination should be conducted. It is important to keep in mind that the diagnosis of AD/HD is a fairly complex and lengthy process, and that simple self-report questionnaires found online often fail to accurately identify AD/HD symptoms. Thus, it is the recommendation of the authors that individuals always seek professional advice in the diagnosis, treatment, and management of AD/HD.

REFERENCES

1. American Psychiatric Association. (1994). *Diagnostic and statistical manual of mental disorders* (4th ed.). Washington, DC: Author.
2. Barkley, R. A. (2006). *Attention deficit hyperactivity disorder* (3rd ed.). New York: Guilford.
3. The National Institutes of Health (NIH) Consensus Development Conference Statement. (1998, November 16–18). *Diagnosis and treatment of attention deficit hyperactivity disorder (ADHD)* (Vol. 16, Issue 2, pp. 1–37). Bethesda, MD: Author.
4. Hallowell, E. M., & Ratey, J. J. (1994). *Driven to distraction: Recognizing and coping with Attention Deficit Disorder from childhood through adulthood.* New York: Touchstone.
5. Children and Adults with Attention-Deficit/Hyperactivity Disorder (CHADD). (2004). About AD/HD: The disorder named AD/HD. Retrieved July 2005, from http://www.help4adhd.org/en/about/what/wwk1
6. Barkley, R. A., Gordon, M., & Goldstein, S. (2002). Research on comorbidity, adaptive functioning, and cognitive impairment in adults with AD/HD: Implications for a clinical practice. In S. Goldstein & A. T. Ellison (Eds.), *Clinician's Guide to Adult AD/HD: Assessment and Intervention* (pp. 46–71). San Diego, CA: Academic Press.
7. American Psychiatric Association. (1968). *Diagnostic and statistical manual of mental disorders* (2nd ed.). Washington, DC: Author.
8. American Psychiatric Association. (1980). *Diagnostic and statistical manual of mental disorders* (3rd ed.). Washington, DC: Author.
9. Goldman, L. S., Genel, M., Bezman, R. J., & Slanetz, P. J. (1998). Diagnosis and treatment of Attention-Deficit/Hyperactivity Disorder in children and adolescents. *Journal of the American Medical Association, 279,* 1100–1107.
10. The National Institute of Mental Health (NIMH). *Attention deficit hyperactivity disorder (ADHD).* Retrieved July 10, 2005, from http://www.nimh.nih.gov/healthinformation/adhdmenu.cfm
11. Smith, B. H., Waschbusch, D., Willoughby, M., & Evans, S. (2000). The efficacy, safety, and practicality of treatments for adolescents with attention-deficit/hyperactivity disorder (ADHD). *Clinical Child and Family Psychology Review, 3,* 243–267.
12. Smith, B., Barkley, R. & Shapiro, C. (in press). Attention-deficit/hyperactivity disorder. In E. J. Mash & R. A. Barkley (Eds.), *Treatment of childhood mental disorders* (3rd ed.). New York: Guilford.
13. Pender, C., Smith, B., & Dowd, H. (2005). *DSM–IV AD/HD dimensions of inattention and hyperactivity/impulsivity as predictors of functioning in first-year college students.* Unpublished master's thesis, University of South Carolina, Columbia, SC.
14. Smith, B. H., Molina, B. G., & Pelham, W. E., Jr. (2002). The clinically meaningful link between ADHD and alcohol. *Alcohol Research and Health, 26,* 122–129.
15. Teeter, P.A. (1998). *Interventions for ADHD treatment in developmental context.* New York: Guilford.

Chapter 5

Obsessive-Compulsive Disorder: Diagnostic, Treatment, Gender, and Cultural Issues

Rudy Nydegger and Michele Paludi

How can you diagnose someone with an obsessive-compulsive disorder, and then act like I have some choice about barging in here?
—Melvin Udall, *As Good as it Gets*

In the movie *As Good as it Gets*, Melvin Udall (played by Jack Nicholson) will not walk on lines in the sidewalk or on tiled floors. After he enters his apartment he locks the door five times and then proceeds to wash his hands. Udall's medicine cabinet is replete with soaps, and each time he washes his hands, he opens two new soaps, washes his hands in near boiling water and then discards the soaps. Udall describes his behavior as, "I've got this, what, ailment." The ailment to which he refers is obsessive-compulsive disorder (OCD). While the movie's director, James L. Brooks, tries to put a comedic slant to Udall's "ailment," in reality, OCD is no laughing matter.

OCD afflicts approximately 3.3 million American adults ages 18 to 54, or about 2.3 percent of people in this age group in a given year.[1] Research indicates that OCD typically begins during early childhood or adolescence and affects females and males equally,[2] although symptoms observed in children are more frequently observed in boys and those observed in adolescence are more common in girls. Individuals with OCD suffer from obsessions, which are repeated, intrusive, unwanted thoughts that cause distress and extreme anxiety.[1] In addition, these individuals may also suffer from compulsions, referred to as rituals (e.g., Udall's hand washing) that the person with the disorder goes through in an attempt to reduce his or her anxiety. Performing rituals, however, provides only temporary relief, and not performing them markedly increases anxiety. Individuals who have obsessions do not automatically have compulsive behaviors. Conversely, most people with compulsions do have obsessions, for example, thoughts of becoming infected by shaking hands with others.[1]

Characteristics of individuals with OCD involve issues of control, perfection, and orderliness.[3] Fears of loss of control over what might happen to them haunts these patients constantly, and thus they control the things that they feel that they can, even if that control is irrational, uncomfortable, embarrassing, and dysfunctional. Their need to accomplish everything right often interferes with their productivity. Individuals with OCD also set unreasonably high standards for themselves and others. They tend to be critical of others as well as themselves when they don't live up to these high standards.

In the workplace, individuals with OCD avoid working in teams since they believe coworkers are incompetent or careless. Furthermore, they avoid making decisions because they fear making mistakes. OCD sufferers are rarely generous with their time or money, and often have difficulty expressing emotion.[1]

Most people with OCD recognize that their behavior is odd and may even describe it as crazy, but clearly feel that they don't have the ability to change it or to avoid performing the rituals. Other patients actually seem to feel that there is nothing unusual about their behavior and believe that what they are doing is entirely reasonable. This lack of insight presents a slightly different twist on the understanding and treatment of OCD.

For many people suffering from OCD, the rituals are like severe superstitions. Patients may know that their behavior is not really necessary and even might understand that it is irrational, but so often fear unknown catastrophic outcomes that they feel that performing the ritual is good sense just in case. Maxmen and Ward[4] refer to this thought process as pathological doubting: "If I don't do this something terrible will happen."

Children, adolescents, and adults who suffer from this disorder may be reluctant to seek help because they are embarrassed or self-conscious about this complex disorder, or they fear having to give up the security of the compulsive rituals. Thus, they find ways to hide their behavior from others in such a way as to not draw attention to themselves. They are usually so concerned about how others will look at them that they often keep their problems a secret.[4] We note, however, that people of color may be reluctant to seek treatment because of cultural values associated with keeping personal, private issues within the family. We will discuss this further in a later part of this chapter.

OCD is sometimes accompanied by depression, eating disorders, substance abuse, attention-deficit/hyperactivity disorder (AD/HD), or other anxiety disorders.[5,6] While traditional theories about the causes of OCD included family problems or attitudes learned in early childhood (e.g., inordinate emphasis on cleanliness, or that certain thoughts are unacceptable), current evidence suggests OCD has a neurobiological basis. Thus, research now focuses on the interaction between neurobiological factors and environmental influences.[7]

In this chapter we will discuss the etiology of OCD, diagnostic issues, comorbidity, and pharmacological and psychotherapeutic approaches to dealing with this disorder. We also offer distinctions between OCD and obsessive-compulsive behaviors, for example, (1) childhood bedtime rituals, the goal of which is to learn mastery over one's environment and (2) thoughts (feelings of uncleanliness) and behaviors (repeatedly checking the locks in their home) common to sexual assault survivors who attempt to be in control in the present of what they feel they were not in control over in the past prior to the sexual assault.

We will also address the life-cycle developmental nature of OCD in this chapter. Gender and race comparisons will also be discussed, noting the bias that has typically existed in studying OCD in women and people of color as well as in the diagnosis and treatment of this disorder. We will conclude this chapter with a discussion of the quality of life issues of individuals with OCD.

We begin with a case study that illustrates the symptoms of OCD.

Charlie and His "Stuff"

Charlie's alarm clock went off at 4:30am, and he knew that he had to get up and get moving because he had to be to work before 9, and his boss was really fussy about lateness. He sat up, reached over with his right hand to turn off the alarm, and pushed the button down four times and then stood up and put his slippers on—right foot first of course. He straightened up the pillow, pulled up the sheet, brought the blanket up to the top of the sheet, and then realized that he hadn't turned the pillow over, so he took everything off of the bed and started to make it again. After several tries he got it right, and finished the bed.

Next, Charlie went into the bathroom and washed his hands four times, and then used the bathroom and washed his hands three times but couldn't remember if he had done it two or three times, so he started again and washed them four times this time. He started his shower and undressed, folding his bed clothes and putting them neatly in the clothes hamper. As he stepped into the shower he remembered that he hadn't said his morning prayers, so he stepped out of the shower, turned the water off, and began his morning prayer ritual. As he was saying The Lord's Prayer for the tenth (and hopefully final) time, he happened to think of the really cute girl in the next office at work, and he briefly thought of what she would look like naked. Oh no! He had an impure thought while trying to say his prayers so he had to start over again. He couldn't imagine what God would do to him if he couldn't say his prayers without impure thoughts. He had to go through all 10 prayers only thinking about God or Jesus (Mary was okay too), or he had to start over. However,

whenever that girl entered his thoughts it was really difficult to keep from thinking about her. Today it only took him 20 minutes to finish his prayers, so it wasn't
too bad.

After going through the elaborate washing and rinsing rituals he had to go
through in the shower, then brushing his teeth, combing his hair, putting on
deodorant and aftershave, and getting dressed—all in the proper order, he was
able to fix some breakfast and go to work. Today was going to be a good day. It
only took him three and one-half hours to get ready for work, and he was feeling
pretty good about it.

Charlie has OCD. However, he, like many people with this condition, has
not sought treatment. Why? He knows how crazy his behavior looks, and the
idea of having to tell someone about it is just too humiliating. Further, the idea
of giving up the rituals that seem to keep him safe is just too scary. Charlie has
few friends, no girlfriend, and spends most of his free time alone at home. This
is really the only place he feels safe, and the only place where he can openly
take care of the rituals that he feels that he must fulfill to avoid some awful
outcomes he can't even imagine—but he knows they would be terrible. The
real tragedy for Charlie is that he has a very treatable condition, with new and
effective ways to control and treat this very troublesome disorder. Most people
with this condition do not get adequate treatment, and thus they live a life of
quiet desperation, hiding their dysfunctional life from people who would laugh,
judge, berate, and abuse them.

SYMPTOMS

OCD is a disorder that seems to have its roots in childhood with over
two-thirds of patients reporting substantial symptoms before the age of
15, and almost all patients report having had some symptoms in childhood. OCD tends to be more common among patients who are more highly
educated and with higher socioeconomic status and higher IQ scores. The
lifetime prevalence rate is about 2.6 percent, and the rates between the
sexes is about equal, although boys/men tend to clinically manifest
the disorder about five years before girls/women.[4] This is consistent with
the finding that there are more boys than girls who suffer from the disorder
in childhood.

The onset of OCD is usually insidious, but it may also have an acute onset
usually following some stressful or traumatic event. OCD is recognized as
a chronic disorder although the symptoms tend to wax and wane.[4] According to the *Diagnostic and Statistical Manual of Mental Disorders*, Fourth
Edition (*DSM–IV*), OCD is characterized by recurrent obsessions and/or

compulsions that interfere considerably with a person's daily functioning.[8] Further, obsessions are, "persistent ideas, thoughts, impulses, or images that are experienced as intrusive and inappropriate and cause marked anxiety or distress" (p.418).[8] Compulsions are defined as being "repetitive behaviors . . . or mental acts . . . the goal of which is to prevent or reduce anxiety or distress" (p. 418).[8] Over 90 percent of patients suffering from OCD have both obsessions and behavioral rituals, and only 2 percent of the sample studied reported only obsessions when mental rituals were added.[9] It is generally assumed that compulsions are performed in order to reduce distress associated with obsessions.[1]

Interestingly, this view is consistent with Freud's early view of OCD, in which he described compulsions as being based on the defense of "undoing" which was intended to "undo" the symbolic harm done by the obsessive thoughts.[10] Psychoanalytic theory suggests that OCD develops in three phases: first, an internally perceived dangerous impulse is recognized; second, there is a threat perceived of what might happen if the impulse were acted upon; and, third, the person calls upon defenses to avert the feared threat.[4] A more recent study[9] found that 90 percent of patients stated that compulsions functioned to prevent harm associated with the obsessions or at least to reduce obsessional distress.

One of the major complicating factors with OCD is the frequent finding of comorbidity. That is, very often a person with OCD has at least one other diagnosable psychological condition. By far, depression is the most common complication, although there are several others as well. Although going insane, being totally incapacitated, or permanently incarcerated are common fears experienced by patients with OCD, these in fact rarely happen. Further, despite much suicidal thinking, less than 1 percent of patients with OCD actually commit suicide. There are also some more uncommon disorders that may coexist with OCD, but are not necessarily caused by it. These include anorexia and bulimia, trichotillomania, Tourette's syndrome, and body dysmorphic disorder.[4]

Since depression is the most common comorbid condition, it has been studied more often than some of the others identified above. Research suggest that there is direct evidence that disturbances in OCD are mediated by comorbid depressive symptoms.[11] Patients who scored high on the Hamilton Rating Scale for Depression (HRSD) performed significantly worse than controls and patients with low HRSD scores on several neuropsychological tests.[7] Further, patients with high HRSD scores showed deficits on a (creative) verbal fluency test. It has been found that patients often have difficulty with so-called executive functions, and it appears that this may be due in part at least to symptoms of depression.[11]

The relationship between OCD and post-traumatic stress disorder (PTSD) has also been discussed in the literature. Huppert et al.[12] concluded that the relationship between these two disorders may largely be accounted for by a combination of symptom overlap and comorbid depression in both conditions. Thus, the relationship between OCD and PTSD is based upon the fact that the two disorders share some similar symptoms, and that depression is a complicating factor for both problems.

One of the authors of this chapter (Nydegger) has treated a patient who had pre-existing OCD, and then due to a life-threatening emergency developed PTSD. Treating these conditions was very complicated, and it was often difficult to decide what was actually being treated. This was even more problematic because after the PTSD arose, the symptoms of OCD were exacerbated, and the patient became depressed as well. Fortunately, with very persistent and consistent treatment with cognitive-behavioral psychotherapy and psychotropic medications, the patient gradually began to improve and start to function more normally. However, this case clearly demonstrated how challenging treating OCD can be when complicated by a condition like PTSD. Clearly, in this case the OCD certainly didn't cause the PTSD, nor did the PTSD cause the OCD. However, the treatment of both problems was complicated by the presence of the other condition.

When dealing with complex diagnostic situations, care should be taken in making the appropriate formulation of the problem. For example, when making a differential diagnosis, OCD should not be diagnosed when the obsessions and the compulsions arise out of another disorder. For example, schizophrenic delusions are not the same thing as obsessions even though there may be an obsessive quality to them. Also, we find obsessive brooding and self-devaluing in major depressive disorder (MDD), and both MDD and OCD have episodic courses. However, this does not mean that MDD is OCD. In fact, OCD should only be diagnosed in this case if it precedes the MDD.[4]

It is often thought that patients with OCD understand that their disorder is irrational, and often this is the case. However, there are some patients who feel that their obsessions and the resultant compulsions are entirely real and that there is nothing irrational about them. This variant of OCD used to be called atypical, and these patients do not have a less favorable prognosis.[4] The present view of this issue is that there is a continuum of insight or strength of belief among patients with OCD, and that not all patients recognize the senselessness of their thoughts and behaviors. This view has become so predominant that it led to a revision of the *DSM–IV* definition of OCD, so that some patients may now be diagnosed as having OCD "with poor insight."[13]

One condition that is very similar to OCD is obsessive-compulsive personality disorder (OCPD). However, it is clear that these two disorders are not related other than the fact that there are similarities in symptom profile. Otherwise they are very different. For example, OCD is egodystonic and OCPD is egosyntonic. That is, people with OCD don't like the symptoms and find that they severely interfere with their lives. People with OCPD just find their behavior normal and don't see anything wrong with it. Further, OCPD doesn't involve true obsessions and true compulsions.[4]

OCD is often confused with other types of compulsive disorders like compulsive gambling, eating, and sexual behavior. People with OCD don't like having to do what they do, and they certainly don't enjoy the obsessive thinking that they often have to experience. However, people with these other compulsive disorders actually enjoy the compulsive activities, and they don't imagine some type of disaster if they don't complete the compulsive action. In fact, they may find the compulsive behavior as a distraction from unpleasant thoughts or feelings that may otherwise trouble them.[4]

Attempts have been made to categorize the symptom patterns of OCD. Typically, the groupings that are usually referred to are: washers; checkers; doubters and sinners; counters and arrangers; and hoarders.[4] Factor analytic studies have identified several factors. For example, Kloosterman, Antony, Richter, and Swinson[14] identified four factors that captured most of the symptoms: obsessions and checking; symmetry and ordering; contamination and cleaning; and hoarding. Subsequent analyses[14] also suggested that groupings based solely on overt behavior may be inadequate, and future analyses might look for other relevant factors as well. Mataix-Cols, do Rosario-Campos, and Lechman[15] found five very similar factors: symmetry; ordering and hoarding; contamination; cleaning and obsessions; and checking. They suggest that OCD might best be understood as a spectrum of potentially overlapping syndromes with similar symptom patterns.

EXPLANATIONS FOR OCD

Research on OCD has suggested a biological basis for this disorder. Psychopathology in general and obsessions in particular tend to run in the families of people who suffer from OCD. Further, concordance rates for OCD are 70 percent for monozygotic twins and 50 percent for dizygotics.[4] This certainly suggests some type of genetic mechanism as well as environmental factors. However, we note that an individual with OCD has a 25 percent chance of a first degree relative having it as well.[4]

The biological research in general indicates abnormalities in the frontal lobes, basal ganglia, and cingulus areas of patients with OCD. In fact, as we will discuss later, in extreme cases cingulotomy has improved or even cured OCD. Further, it is known that the basal ganglia is involved in over-learned routine behaviors such as grooming, and the prefrontal areas in planning and organizing behaviors. It is also assumed that since the drugs that seem to help OCD are serontonergic that the serotonin system is somehow involved with OCD as well.[16]

Another interesting line of biological research on OCD found that patients with a compulsive hoarding type of OCD had significantly lower glucose metabolism in the posterior cingulate gyrus and cuneus. This is a different pattern of cerebral glucose metabolism than is found in non-hoarding OCD patients or in non-OCD controls. This research suggests that "OCD hoarding may be a neurobiologically distinct subgroup or variant of OCD whose symptoms and poor response to anti-obsessional treatment are mediated by lower activity in the cingulate cortex" (p.549).[7]

One final biological approach to the understanding of OCD comes from studying infectious disease. It has been found that children who suffer from group A streptococcal infections can develop an acute form of OCD.[17] This is referred to as pediatric autoimmune neuropsychiatric disorder associated with group A streptococcal infection (PANDAS). Other studies[18] have found that infections with group A beta-hemolytic streptococci, among others, can trigger autoimmune responses that might exacerbate some cases of childhood-onset OCD, and can also impact or cause tic disorders including Tourette's syndrome. These studies, too, imply a neurophysiological basis for OCD, and even suggest a mechanism for how it might develop. We will explore some of the treatment implications of this later in the chapter.

In addition to the biological views of OCD, there are cognitive and neuro-psychological components of OCD as well. For example, people with OCD have poor memory function and cognitive organizational deficits.[19] They are more likely to suffer rigidity in thought[19] and have an apparent diminished ability to selectively ignore competing external (sensory) and internal (cognitive) stimuli, especially intrusive thoughts.[20]

One interesting memory study[21] found that OCD patients showed a better memory for contaminated objects than for clean ones. This pattern was not found in normal controls. Thus, for these patients it wasn't just a general deficit in memory, because objects that were related to their obsessions were more easily remembered; or at least this is what appears to be happening.

Szechtman and Woody[22] suggest that people with OCD don't get a "feeling of knowing" that a task or activity is complete. Thus, if a person is motivated to do something that will make them feel more secure and they don't get a sense of closure that would terminate the security motivation system, then they will continue to feel that this need still required fulfillment. Thus, patients with OCD do not have this terminator emotion to the same extent as do normal people.

In another series of cognitive studies on OCD Savage et al.[23] found that non-verbal memory problems in OCD are mediated by impaired strategic processing.

While this line of cognitive research implies psychological factors as well as biological ones, there is nothing in this research that is inconsistent with a biological etiology, and in fact some of the cognitive researchers have even suggested neurobiological mechanisms that might be implicated, or at least have speculated that there might be some underlying biological basis to the cognitive disturbances.[22]

DEVELOPMENTAL CONSIDERATIONS

As we discussed in the introduction, OCD typically begins or at least has its origins in early childhood or adolescence.[24] Symptoms that are observed in children are more frequently observed in boys; those seen in adolescence are more common in girls. About 1 percent of children have OCD.[24] It is recommended that it is best to treat OCD early because the longer OCD goes untreated, the more generalized the symptoms become, thus making it more difficult to treat.[24]

OCD may follow children into adulthood, and even with treatment during childhood some children may have no or minimal symptoms as adults. Some children go into remission, only to have symptoms return during adulthood. Symptoms experienced as a child are likely to be different from those experienced as an adult.[1] It has also been hypothesized that hormones and stress may cause changes in an individual's biological makeup, thus affecting OCD symptomatology as well.[2]

Some researchers are pursuing lines of research that suggest that there may be different variants of OCD that affect children and adults differently. For example, one series of studies conducted in India found gender differences, symptom pattern differences, and onset differences between juvenile OCD, juvenile-onset adult OCD, and adult-onset OCD. This suggests that juvenile OCD could be a developmental subtype of ODC, and may not be the same disorder that we see in adults.[25]

Young people with OCD had higher scores on inflated responsibility, thought-action fusion, and one aspect of perfectionism (e.g., concern over mistakes) than did other individuals. In fact, an inflated sense of responsibility predicted symptom severity in children. While there is some evidence that there is a downward extension of cognitive appraisals by adults in childhood OCD, there is also evidence of developmental shifts in cognitive appraisal as well.[26]

In order to meet the criteria for OCD as outlined in the *DSM–IV*, individuals must have either obsessions or compulsions or both. Most children and adolescents do have both, as do most adults.[2] In screening for OCD in childhood, questions about obsessions and compulsions are asked of children, for example:

> Do you have to check things over and over again?
> Do you count to a certain number or do things a certain number of times?
> Do you have to wash your hands a lot, more than most children?
> Are there things you have to do before you go to bed?

The majority of children and adolescents answer "yes" to these questions. Simply answering "yes" does not necessarily indicate OCD. In fact, children exhibit normative, developmentally appropriate behaviors and rituals that do not constitute a diagnosis of OCD.[2] These behaviors (e.g., routines at mealtime, bathing, and bedtime) are likely to be exhibited between the ages of two and eight years. Children may insist on bedtime rituals, collect sports cards, comic books, and/or dolls. Game playing in middle and later childhood frequently becomes highly ritualized and rule-bound. These behaviors are a direct response to children's need to control and master their environment and their anxiety. As children gain mastery, they become increasingly independent and therefore enhance their confidence and self-esteem.[27]

In addition, children often exhibit superstitions, a form of magical thinking in which they believe in the power of their thoughts or behavior to control events in their world.[27] This kind of magical thinking is often found in children and may be found in adolescents as well.[28] Rhymes such as "step on a crack, break your Momma's back," also assist children in developing mastery. These rituals help children develop new competencies and define their world, although most of these ritualistic behaviors disappear on their own during middle childhood.[2] In adolescence, rituals may subside but obsessive preoccupation with an activity, a singer, or a sports idol is common. All of these behaviors are considered normative; part of children's and adolescents' identity development.[29]

Normative compulsive behaviors are distinguished from OCD on the basis of timing of behaviors, content of obsessions, and the severity of the symptoms. Unlike the childhood and adolescent rituals that produce competence and mastery, OCD produces dysfunction.[26] Therefore, children's responses to questions listed above are not the sole information collected by a psychologist in diagnosing children with OCD. In childhood OCD, a family history of OCD is more frequent than in adult onset OCD, suggesting that genetic factors may play more of a role in childhood OCD. Thus, a family history of all psychological conditions including OCD must be obtained when conducting a clinical interview and/or history. Information about motor and vocal tic disorders is important to obtain as well[30] since childhood-onset OCD may have a higher rate of comorbidity with Tourette's syndrome, PANDAS and

AD/HD.[31] OCD can make daily life difficult for children and adolescents. OCD behaviors consume a great deal of time and energy, making it more difficult for children to complete tasks, for example, homework or chores, and have a well-rounded life that involves varied activities and time with friends. Children and adolescents with OCD commonly feel pressured because they don't have enough time to do everything. They might become irritable because they have to stay awake late into the night or miss an event in order to complete their rituals. At school, children with OCD have difficulties with attention or concentration because of their intrusive thoughts.[32] In addition to feeling frustrated or guilty for not being able to control their own thoughts or actions, children with OCD experience anxiety and low self-esteem as a consequence of shame or embarrassment.[2]

Research suggests that common obsessions for children and adolescents include fear of germs, preoccupation with bodily wastes, lucky and unlucky numbers, intrusive sounds or words, and preoccupation with household appliances.[2] The most common compulsive behaviors identified in research include grooming rituals (e.g., hand washing, showering), repeating rituals (e.g., checking to ensure that an appliance is off, checking homework), rituals to undo contact with a "contaminated" object or person, hoarding things. Children with OCD also have an excessive fear of harm to self or others, and especially to their parents.[2]

Furthermore, children and adolescents with OCD frequently have obsessions and compulsions regarding food. They engage in abnormal eating habits (e.g., only eating one kind of food or never eating a type of food that might be good for them). This behavior could pose a serious threat to their nutrition, including the possibility of becoming anorexic.[5] In fact it has been demonstrated that there is higher than expected prevalence of OCD in young women with anorexia nervosa.[33]

WOMEN AND OCD

While there is not much difference in the incidence rates between men and women with respect to OCD, and the types of treatments that are offered are not gender specific it is misleadingly easy to assume that there are no relevant gender issues in OCD. However, it is clear that there are relevant gender issues, though there has not been as much research in this area as there should be. For example, a study on Turkish women with OCD found that patients suffering from this disorder were more sexually nonsensual, avoidant, and anorgasmic than women with generalized anxiety disorder.[34] Another study found that women with panic disorder or OCD had lower sexual desire and lower frequency of sexual contact than controls. Further, OCD patients reported more sexual dysfunction in total and were less satisfied with their sex lives than were patients with panic disorder or controls.[35] These are just two examples of how OCD can affect women differently than men (there are no studies demonstrating these problems with men patients with OCD). In addition, women victims of sexual assault and pregnant women frequently exhibit obsessive-compulsive behaviors. We discuss these two issues in the next section. Of course the following discussion on sexual assault may offer some explanation for the above findings.[34]

Earlier in this chapter we made a distinction between OCD and obsessive-compulsive behaviors. We illustrated this distinction by discussing obsessive-compulsive behaviors that are developmentally normative in children who are learning to gain mastery and control over their environment.

Obsessive-compulsive behaviors have also been observed in women survivors of sexual victimization (i.e., child sexual abuse, rape, battering, and sexual harassment). The incidence rates of sexual victimization are alarming. Thirty percent of all women are battered at least once in their adult lives.[36] Incidence of sexual harassment among undergraduate women ranges between 30 and 85 percent each year.[37] The incidence is even higher for women in graduate school and in the workforce.[38] At least 20 percent of women have been a victim of incest.[39] Further, between 8 and 15 percent of college women have disclosed they were raped, at least one-third of battered women have been raped by the batterer.[36] The enormity of the incidence rates becomes more staggering when we note the untold numbers of children under 12 year of age who are victims of sexual assault.[40]

Several studies have documented the high cost of sexual victimization to women.[41] For example, rape survivors exhibit very high distress levels within the first week.[42] Their distress peaks in severity three weeks following the victimization, continues at a high level for one month, and then starts to improve three months post-rape. One-fourth of women who are raped continue to experience negative effects several years post-victimization. Similar findings have been reported for sexual harassment, incest, and battered women.[43]

As another example, adult women who were survivors of incest had identifiable degrees of impairment when compared with non-victims. For example, 17 percent of adult women who survived incest as children were clinically depressed, and 18 percent were considered severely psychoneurotic. In their lifetimes, survivors were more likely than non-victims to have had problems with depression, alcohol and other drug abuse, panic, and obsessive-compulsive behaviors.

With respect to engaging in obsessive-compulsive behaviors, survivors of sexual victimization report feelings of being unclean, even after repeated showering or bathing. In addition, survivors commonly check locks, check under their beds and behind shower curtains, repeatedly check the back seat and under the car before getting in, and repeatedly phone family and/or friends along the route they are taking to return to their home to alert them where they will be and when they expect to return.[42] Some survivors carve or cut themselves to be rid of skin the perpetrator touched.[44] The goal of these behaviors is to defend the survivor against pain and to maintain control over their lives. These obsessions and compulsions are an attempt for the woman to be in control in the present of what they perceive they were not in control in their past before the victimization. This does not mean to imply that women survivors of sexual assault are responsible for the victimization and/or preventing it.

We note that these obsessive and compulsive behaviors are not only engaged in by survivors of sexual victimization but also by most adolescent and adult women in their daily lives. Women report feeling safer and more in control by using these obsessive and compulsive behaviors. These behaviors are coping mechanisms and safety strategies women develop from childhood to reduce fear and increase perceived safety. It is a normative part of female development, especially in a culture that enables sexual victimization against girls and women to go unpunished and blames women for their victimization.

Keeping these facts and examples in mind, one needs to be careful in diagnosing OCD in a girl or woman (and boy or man) who has been abused and/or assaulted sexually. Further, some types of obsessive worrying in women may not only be normal, but may be healthy and safe. For example, would one diagnose a woman as having OCD because she very frequently worries about being attacked, but lives in a high crime area and has to walk home from work at night? Or, would we think it pathological for a woman who lives alone to have a routine where she checks her apartment or home when she comes in, and checks the windows and doors before retiring at night?

Clearly, some obsessive and compulsive features may actually be secondary to a primary problem. When this appears to be the case, we should look at the sequence of events and when symptoms appear. If an individual has no OCD types of characteristics until *after* she or he has been victimized, then the symptoms are not likely to be OCD, but rather attempts at coping with the fears and powerlessness that comes from being a victim of violence. Similarly, when an individual's obsessions and/or compulsions are entirely rational and functional given her or his specific circumstances, then it makes no sense to pathologize them by labeling them as OCD.

Pregnancy has been frequently recognized as a major risk factor in precipitating OCD.[45] Since obsessions and compulsions can appear separately or with a comorbid anxiety or mood disorder, the incidence of OCD in women during pregnancy or postpartum is not known.[46] Two studies have provided some insight into prevalence rates. One reported that pregnancy was associated with onset of OCD in 39 percent of patients[47]; another reported 13 percent among their patients.[48] Williams and Koran[73] also reported OCD occurring in primigravida in 52 percent of the patients studied. Signs of postpartum OCD typically begin in women four to six weeks after giving birth.

Women are at greater risk for OCD during pregnancy and postpartum if they have a previous history and/or family history of OCD. It has been found that in pregnancy, OCD may worsen due to hormonal changes.[49] In addition, during pregnancy, women who have OCD are twice as likely to experience postpartum depression. Obsessional thoughts and compulsive behaviors related to women in the postpartum period include: obsessional fears about the baby's bottles being contaminated resulting in compulsively sterilizing the bottles, and obsessive fears about the baby drowning during bath time. In addition, postpartum women may frequently check on the baby because they fear something bad will happen. Some mothers worry obsessively about harming their baby, or about being an unfit mother.

RACE AND ETHNIC COMPARISONS

Relatively few empirical studies have been conducted concerning OCD in people of color.[50] The paucity of research on people of color is characteristic of research on all anxiety disorders.[51] Epidemiological data suggest that the prevalence of OCD among racial and ethnic minorities is equal to that of white individuals and that the core features of OCD are independent of cultural variations.

However, although the prevalence rates may be similar, racial differences in help-seeking and symptom presentation may result in underreporting and misdiagnosis.[52] Fontenelle, Mendlowicz, Marques, and Versiani[53] reported that the content of obsessions is related to culture. They reported more aggressive and religious obsessions among Brazilian and Middle Eastern individuals than individuals from North America and Europe. In addition, Neal-Barnett[50] has identified that there are barriers to people of color seeking treatment for OCD. For example, African Americans and American Indians believe that psychological research has been offered to support the belief of inferiority among minorities and, therefore, they often refuse treatment. In addition, Asian Americans believe problems should be handled within the family and obtaining therapy is discouraged by many Asian American families.

Thus, while there is little data that demonstrates racial or ethnic differences in OCD, it would be shortsighted and irresponsible to conclude that there are no differences or relevant issues related to race or ethnicity. Probably the most telling fact is that there is so little research done on this topic at all. Obviously this is an area that needs further study.

TREATMENT AND PROGNOSIS

OCD has been discussed in the professional and popular literature for centuries. However, OCD was frequently met with therapeutic pessimism, and patients were often un- or under-treated because of the lack of effective therapies. For many years OCD was seen as a basically treatment-resistant condition for which there was little that could be done. It is only in the last three decades that we have seen the development and use of effective psychological and pharmacological treatments.[9]

Fortunately, in recent years, effective treatments have been developed that have provided very good outcomes, and as we mentioned earlier in this chapter, about 70 percent of OCD patients that receive treatment show some degree of improvement in their condition.[1] Typically, a combination of antidepressant medications and cognitive-behavioral psychotherapy (CBT) is recommended. Exposure/response prevention (ERP) techniques are the most widely used CBT methods.[4] March[54] concluded that CBT alone or with pharmacotherapy is effective treatment for OCD in children and adolescents.

Franklin, Abramowitz, Bux, Zoellner, and Feeny[55] looked at treatment results for patients treated with CBT, half of whom were also receiving medication for the condition, while half did not. They found that both treatment groups improved, and that there was no difference between the treatment outcomes for the groups who had CBT with medication or CBT without medication. They thus concluded that OCD can be treated effectively by CBT alone.

Some patients have only obsessions but no compulsions, and these patients have traditionally been difficult to treat. However, Freeston et al.[56] found that CBT was effective with this group of patients as well. Thus, for many OCD patients with both obsessions and compulsions and for those with obsessions alone, CBT is usually seen as the treatment of choice. However, staying in this type of treatment can be difficult for some patients. If patients do continue with this treatment, they can expect sustained improvement. Reid[57] suggested that response prevention that keeps the patient in the situation where they are experiencing anxiety for at least 30 minutes can effectively eliminate compulsive rituals, but he too finds that this is very difficult for some patients to tolerate. Part of the CBT treatment also involves exposure to situations that may be anxiety provoking, and Ito, Marks, de Araujo, and Hemsley[58] found that *in vivo* exposure is usually preferred, and is superior to imaginal techniques. They also reported that the imaginal techniques did not add much to the *in vivo* methods. Further, Franklin et al.[55] also found that CBT was very effective as a treatment, and relied primarily on ERP, but they also determined that attempts to shorten treatment or space out the sessions had a diminished effect on treatment success.

In another study looking at the intensity and timing of treatment,[59] results indicated that both intensive treatment (daily for three weeks) and twice-weekly treatment (for eight weeks) were both effective. There was a moderate trend favoring intensive treatment immediately following therapy, but there was no difference in the treatment groups on follow-up. There was some evidence of relapse with intensive treatment, but not with the twice-weekly group.

While much of the psychotherapy research in the treatment of OCD has focused on CBT, there has been some research looking at the effects of other forms of psychotherapy as well. One study found that cognitive psychotherapy was as effective as exposure in treating OCD.[60] However, other research suggested that cognitive therapy alone is not usually effective nor does it add much to other psychological or medical therapies. Most authors agree that the primary role of dynamic and supportive psychotherapy is limited to consolidating gains from other treatment methods, helping with compliance with treatment, and helping with the treatment of comorbid conditions.[73] Thus, it seems clear that CBT is the preferred form of psychological treatment for OCD, and that other types of psychotherapy (e.g., cognitive or psychodynamic) might be secondary or supportive, but should rarely be the treatment of first choice for this condition.

Some of the early breakthroughs in the treatment of OCD came from the discovery of therapeutic efficacy of certain of the antidepressant medications. Today, the drugs of choice are the selective serotonin reuptake inhibitors (SSRIs), clomipramine (Anafranil), and newer antidepressants.[57] Clomipramine was the first OCD-specific medication, and has been the treatment of choice for many providers. This drug is a tricyclic antidepressant, but unlike the other tricyclics, it is a potent serotonin reuptake inhibitor as well. It has also been found that the other tricyclic drugs had little effect on OCD. The benzodiazepines (Valium, Xanax, Klonipin, Ativan, etc.) were used for many years in the absence of other more effective drugs, and their antianxiety effects might have had some minimal benefit, but they have largely been replaced by the newer and more effective drugs and are rarely the drugs of first choice for the treatment of OCD any longer.[57]

Other drugs have been found to be helpful adjunctive therapies for treatment-refractory OCD patients. For example, potent neuroleptics in low doses, clonazepam, and the monoamine oxidase inhibitors are common choices for this purpose.[57] Olanzapine (Zyprexa) was found by Petrikis, Andreou, Bozikas, and Karavatos[61] to be helpful in treating OCD patients who had comorbid bipolar disorder. Shapira et al.[62] also found that olanzapine was helpful in treating some OCD patients who did not respond to other medications. Reid[57] pointed out that some medications can decrease compulsions and anxiety in behavioral programs, but other drugs like the benzodiazepines can actually interfere with the learning and the conditioning process with CBT. Thus, while medications might be helpful with some patients, there are some (specifically the antianxiety drugs) that might actually interfere with treatment. This, of course, suggests that in order to treat this condition, the patient probably needs to be in touch with at least some of the anxiety that is generated by the treatment methods or the anxiety response will not extinguish.

In sum, about 60 percent of patients will respond favorably to an adequate dose of SSRI medication or clomipramine within about nine–ten weeks.[63] As Rivas-Vasquez[64] pointed out, SSRIs and atypical antidepressants have equal or superior efficacy and a better side effect profile than their predecessors, but they are not without their side effects. The most common for these drugs are nausea, diarrhea, insomnia, headaches, sexual dysfunction, sedation, and weight gain. Maxmen and Ward[4] also concur that the SSRIs and clomipramine are the first-line treatments today, and point out that they may need higher dosage levels than used for other disorders. They report that about 70 percent of patients will receive some benefit, but also suggest that most will have some residual symptoms. Approximately 10–15 percent of patients will have a complete and full remission, and even the partial responders will have about a 40 percent reduction in symptoms. Most OCD patients will need to stay on the medication chronically since 85 percent relapse after a month or two after stopping the medication has been reported. We caution this finding since this study did not include patients who were also receiving CBT.

When taking these medications for the treatment of OCD the typical reasons why they are not effective are that patients terminate the medication prematurely[4] or that the drug is not taken at an adequate dosage level.

In one study done in India,[25] juvenile OCD patients were followed for two–nine years (mean = 5 years); nearly 75 percent of patients were adequately treated with medication. About 21 percent were seen as having clinical OCD on follow-up, and around 48 percent were in true remission. They found that an earlier age at onset was associated with a better course and outcome for the disorder.

As we mentioned earlier, some researchers have related OCD and OCD-like symptoms to PANDAS. Allen, Leonard, and Swedo[18] treated a group of children who fit the PANDAS profile with immunosuppressant drugs. All of the patients in this sample improved with this type of treatment. This is a minority of patients who actually fit the PANDAS profile, and unless they fit the profile and have not responded to another form of treatment, trying something like this would not be a likely first-line treatment because of the risks and side effects. However, this finding is intriguing and suggestive, and may provide some insights into additional treatment methods.

Treatment of OCD during pregnancy must take into account pharmacological effects of drugs on the development of the fetus.[65] For example, it has
been found that there are several symptoms of withdrawal, including tremors
and seizures, in infants born to women taking clomipramine for OCD. If medication is necessary, SSRIs are safer than clomipramine for use during pregnancy.[45] In addition, the impact of untreated OCD during pregnancy versus
the effects of the drug on the fetus must be weighed when deciding to discontinue medication. OCD can be treated successfully using psychotherapy alone,
and when a mother is breast-feeding, this option should be kept in mind. Anti-
obsessional medications are all secreted in breast milk, although some transfer at higher rates than others. Studies indicate that breast-fed babies become
hyperirritable when the mothers were taking these medications for OCD.[45]
For a more detailed discussion of postpartum depression and its treatment, see
Nydegger, this volume.

For the most severely disabled OCD patients who have not responded to
any other types of treatment, they may be candidates for one of several different types of stereotactic neurosurgery with acceptable to excellent results
in 30–45 percent of the most difficult to treat patients.[57] Researchers[4] found
that 25–30 percent of patients would benefit from a cingulotomy. Baer et al.[66]
found that 28 percent of 18 previously unresponsive OCD patients were virtually symptom free after more than two years, and another 17 percent were
partial responders following a cingulotomy. Hodchkiss, Malizia, Bartlett, and
Bridges[67] found similar results. Baer et al.[66] also report that serious adverse
effects of the surgery are very rare.

These results lend credence to the theories of the etiology and pathology of
OCD. Second, they provide a treatment alternative for those patients who have
a serious and disabling form of OCD and who have not responded to any other
type of therapy. While the success of biological treatments (drugs and surgery
both) may imply some relationship with treatment response, Thienemann and
Koran[68] found no correlation between treatment outcomes and either neurologic soft signs or neuropsychological test results. Also, these successful biological treatments do not necessarily indicate a physical etiology for this disorder.
However, it is our belief that OCD may actually be a group of related disorders
with different etiologies and different courses, and that some of the causal factors may be genetic or neurophysiological, but some of them may be entirely
psychological or environmental.

Adults seek treatment for OCD because they recognize that this disorder is
interfering with their lives. Children, however, don't typically realize that they
have a problem with obsessions and compulsions. Toddlers, preschool, and

early school age children do not have the cognitive capacity to understand the nature of the obsessions or compulsions. Children are often brought to their physician when their parents believe they are exhibiting unacceptable behavior and are having difficulty in school. A major distinction in the *DSM–IV* criteria for children and adults is the criterion of insight. While most, but not all, adults are aware of the illogic and dysfunctional nature of their symptoms, this is rarely true of children.

The treatment of OCD in children is much the same as that for adults, and usually includes medication and CBT.[69] When dealing with children who have OCD, it is important that the disorder be explained to them with consideration of their stage of cognitive development (e.g., concrete operations, formal operations). The child's cognitive development thus necessitates changes in the psychotherapeutic approach that might be used.[70] When children understand the biological basis of OCD, they typically find it easier to externalize the symptoms and to not blame themselves for the disorder. Thus, therapeutic approaches with children must focus on concrete models and concepts.[70]

When discussing treatment, it is important to also discuss the role of the family in OCD. There is no evidence that family problems cause OCD, but clearly they can exacerbate it. More importantly, families can't cure OCD either, but family support and involvement can certainly help the treatment effort. It is important for the family members of an OCD patient to be involved with treatment for many reasons. First, OCD is the type of problem that will affect everyone in the family in one way or another. Thus, family members should get involved and ask questions of the providers as well; they need to understand the disorder and their role in helping. They should also be aware of the fact that negative comments and behaviors can actually make the condition worse by driving it underground and encouraging the patient to hide the symptoms and to deny the need for help.

Family members can also work with clinicians, schools, and so forth, to help implement the types of treatment strategies that will support the goals of therapy. We also encourage family members to find and get involved with support groups to help them deal with the impact of this disorder. Finally, we always strongly recommend that family members, and especially parents, not get so wrapped up in caring for the OCD patient that they neglect their own needs. Taking care of oneself is vitally important in the big picture of managing the impact of OCD on a family.

Prognostically, OCD is usually considered to be a chronic, although sometimes episodic, condition.[57] Thomsen[71] reported that 17 percent of one pretreatment cohort were receiving psychiatric disability payments as adults, regardless of the age of onset or social background. This certainly suggests that, for many patients, the outcomes of this disorder can affect them throughout their entire adult life. There are, however, findings that do help us understand some of the factors that will impact the outcomes of OCD in different ways. For example, Thomsen[71] found that severe obsessive-compulsive syndromes in childhood or adolescence do predict severe adult problems. Maxmen and Ward[4] pointed out that treatment outcomes are not related to the content of obsessions, and that patients with milder symptoms, no compulsions, a briefer duration of clinical symptoms, and higher premorbid functioning do have a better prognosis. Similarly, researchers also found that age of onset, symptom severity, and symptom duration were all correlated with treatment response.[72]

Hiss, Foa, and Kozak[73] put two groups of patients who had been through a treatment program in one of two post-treatment groups. One group received intensive relapse prevention (RP) and the other received attention control (AC) treatment. While both groups improved immediately after the post-treatment activity, only the RP group maintained the gains over time, and the AC group showed a return of the symptoms for most patients. Thus, in addition to treatment, there is good evidence that a relapse prevention program will probably bolster and consolidate the effects of even the best treatment programs. This fact also will positively impact the findings of the apparent chronicity of OCD, and will help deliver even better treatment outcomes.

SUMMARY

As we have discussed in this chapter, OCD is a complex and complicated disorder that severely impacts the lives of patients and families. The etiological picture is a confusing one because of the findings that suggest a genetic basis for the disorder and/or a neurophysiological cause as well. However, there are other researchers and theorists that hold to a primarily psychological and/or environmental cause for ODD. Clearly there is a physiological component for some patients with OCD, but this is not as clear with other patients. OCD is a complex disorder that may have a number of different variants that probably have different causes and different pathologies as well. As we learn more about this disorder, we will probably find that there are clear and distinct differences between the different types of OCD, and hopefully this will aid in improved treatments and perhaps even prevention of this serious disorder.

The good news for this problem appears to be the development and use of effective treatment methods. As mentioned by March,[74] CBT with or without medication is an effective treatment for children and adolescents. This is also true for adults. We have also found that there is an increasingly large arsenal of effective medications that can be very helpful as well. While there are differences of opinion as to whether medication is a necessary component of treatment, there is little question of the fact that certain medications (e.g., the SSRIs and clomipramine, as well as some newer atypical antidepressants) can be very helpful. Other medications or medical procedures have also proven effective for patients who do not respond to the more conventional treatments. Suffice it to say, the large majority of patients with OCD—children, adolescents, or adults—can be helped with treatment, and the involvement and support of families and the use of response prevention programs can improve these outcomes as well.

RECOMMENDED READINGS

Abramowitz J., Schwartz S., Moore K., & Luenzmann K. (2003). Obsessive-compulsive symptoms in pregnancy and the puerperium: A review of the literature. *Journal of Anxiety Disorders, 17,* 461–478.

Adams, G., & Burke, R. (1999). Children and adolescents with obsessive-compulsive disorder: A primer for teachers. *Childhood Education, 76,* 2–7.

Flament, M., & Cohen, D. (2001). OCD in children and adolescents. In N. Fineberg, D. Marazziti, & D. Stein (Eds.), *Obsessive-compulsive disorder: A practical guide* (pp. 153–166). London: Martin Dunitz Publishers.

Jenike M., Baer L., & Minichiello W. (1998). An overview of obsessive-compulsive disorder. In M. Jenike, L. Baer, & W. Minichiello (Eds.), *Obsessive-compulsive disorders: Practical management* (pp. 3–11). St. Louis, MO: Mosby.

March, J., & Mulle, K. (1998). *OCD in children and adolescents, A cognitive-behavioral treatment manual.* New York: Guilford.

Steketee, G., Pigott, T., & Schemmel, T. (2002). *Obsessive-compulsive disorder: The latest assessment and treatment strategies.* New York: Compact Clinicals.

RESOURCES

Anxiety Disorders Association of America
11900 Parklawn Drive
Suite 100
Rockville MD 20852–2624
301.231.9350

OC Foundation

676 State Street

New Haven, CT 06511

203.401.2070

info@ocfoundation.org

OC Information Center

Madison Institute of Medicine

7617 Mineral Point Road, Suite 300

Madison, WI 53717

608.827.2470

mim@miminc.org

National Institute of Mental Health

C/O Research on OCD

Building 10, Room 3D4110 Center Drive MSC 1264

Bethesda, MD 20892

301.496.3421

Pediatrics and Developmental Neuropsychiatry Branch

National Institute of Mental Health

Building 10, Room 4N 208

Bethesda MD 20892–1255

301.496.5323

REFERENCES

1. Steketee, G., Pigott, T., & Schemmel, T. (2002). *Obsessive-compulsive disorder: The latest assessment and treatment strategies*. New York: Compact Clinicals.
2. Flament, M., & Cohen, D. (2001). OCD in children and adolescents. In N. Fineberg, D. Marazziti, & D. Stein (Eds.), *Obsessive-compulsive disorder: A practical guide* (pp 153–166). London: Martin Dunitz Publishers.
3. Stein, D., Fineberg, N., & Harvey, B. (2001). Unusual symptoms of OCD. In N. Fineberg, D. Marazziti, & D. Stein (Eds.), *Obsessive-compulsive disorder: A practical guide* (pp. 37–50). London: Martin Dunitz Publishers.
4. Maxmen, J. & Ward, N. (1995). *Essential psychopathology and its treatment* (2nd ed., rev. for *DSM–IV*). New York: W. W. Norton.
5. Grilo, C. (2004). Factor structure of DSM–IV criteria for obsessive compulsive personality disorder in patients with binge eating disorder. *Acta Psychiatrica Scandinavica, 109*, 64–69.
6. Peterson, B., Pine, D., Cohen, P., & Brook, J. (2001). Prospective, longitudinal study of tic, obsessive-compulsive, and attention-deficit/hyperactivity disorders in an epidemiological sample. *Journal of the American Academy of Child and Adolescent Psychiatry, 40*, 685–695.

7. Lucey, J. (2001). The neuroanatomy of OCD. In N. Fineberg, D. Marazziti, & D. Stein (Eds.), *Obsessive-compulsive disorder: A practical guide* (pp. 77–88). London: Martin Dunitz Publishers.

8. American Psychiatric Association. (1994). *Diagnostic and statistical manual of mental disorders* (4th ed.). Washington, DC: Author.

9. Foa, E., Kozak, M., Goodman, W., Hollander, E., Jenike, M., & Rasmussen, S. (1995). DSM–IV field trial: Obsessive-compulsive disorder. *American Journal of Psychiatry, 152,* 90–94.

10. Freud, S. (1959). Notes upon a case of obsessional neurosis. In A. Strachey & J. Strachey (Eds. & Trans.), *Sigmund Freud: Collected papers* (Vol. 3, pp. 296–390). New York: Basic Books. (Original work published 1909)

11. Moritz, S., Brikner, C., Kloss, M., Jacobsen, D., Fricke, S., & Bothern, A., et al. (2001). Impact of comorbid depressive symptoms on neuropsychological performance in obsessive-compulsive disorder. *Journal of Abnormal Psychology, 110,* 653–657.

12. Huppert, J. D., Moser, J., Gershuny, B., Riggs, D., Spokas, M., Filip, J., et al. (2005). The relationship between obsessive-compulsive and post-traumatic stress symptoms in clinical and non-clinical samples. *Journal of Anxiety Disorders, 19,* 127–136.

13. Kozak, M., & Foa, E. (1994). Obsessions, overvalued ideas, and delusions in obsessive-compulsive disorder. *Behavior Research and Therapy, 32,* 343–353.

14. Kloosterman, P., Antony, M., Richter, M., & Swinson, R. (2004). The relationship between miscellaneous symptoms and major symptom factors in obsessive-compulsive disorder. *Behavior Research and Therapy, 42,* 1453–1467.

15. Mataix-Cols, D., do Rosario-Campos, M., & Lechman, J. (2005). A multidimensional model of obsessive-compulsive disorder. *American Journal of Psychiatry, 162,* 228–238.

16. Jenike, M., Baer, L., Ballantine, T., Martuza, R., Buttolf, L., & Kassem, N. Cingulogomy for refractory obsessive-compulsive disorder. *Archives of General Psychiatry, 48,* 548–554.

17. Murphy, M., & Pichichero, M. (2002). Prospective identification and treatment of children with pediatric autoimmune neuropsychiatric disorders associated with group A streptococcal infection (PANDAS). *Archives of Pediatric and Adolescent Medicine, 56,* 356–361.

18. Allen, A., Leonard, H., & Swedo, S. (1995). Case study: A new infection-triggered, autoimmune subtype of pediatric OCD and Tourette's Syndrome. *Journal of the American Academy of Child and Adolescent Psychiatry, 34,* 307–311.

19. Shin, M., Park, S., Kim, M., Lee, Y., Ha, T., & Swon, J. (2004). Deficits of organizational strategy and visual-memory in obsessive-compulsive disorder. *Neuropsychology, 18,* 665–671.

20. Clayton, I. C., Richards, J., & Edwards, C. (1999). Selective attention for obsessive compulsive disorder. *Journal of Abnormal Psychology, 108,* 171–175.

21. Radomsky, A., & Rachman, S. (1999). Memory bias in obsessive-compulsive disorder (OCD). *Behavior Research and Therapy, 37,* 605–615.

22. Szechtman, H., & Woody, E. (2004). Obsessive-compulsive disorder as a disturbance of security motivation. *Psychological Review, 111,* 111–127.

23. Savage, C., Dechersbach, T., Wilhelm, S., Rauch, S., Baer, L., Reid, T., et al. (2000). Strategic processing and episodic memory impairment in obsessive-compulsive disorder. *Neuropsychology, 14*, 141–151.

24. Adams, G., & Burke, R. (1999). Children and adolescents with obsessive-compulsive disorder: A primer for teachers. *Childhood Education, 76*, 2–7.

25. Reddy, Y., Srinath, S., Prakash, A., Girimaji, S., Sheshadri, S., Khanna, S., et al. (2003). A follow-up study of juvenile obsessive-compulsive disorder from India. *Acta Psychiatrica Scandinavica, 107*, 457–464.

26. Libby, S., Renolds, S., Derisley, J., & Clark, S. (2004). Cognitive appraisals in young people with obsessive-compulsive disorder. *Journal of Child Psychology and Psychiatry, 45*, 1076–1085.

27. Santrock, J. (2003). *Child development.* New York: McGraw Hill.

28. Bolton, D., Dearsley, P., Madronal-Luque, R., & Baron-Cohen, S. (2002). Magical thinking in childhood and adolescence. *British Journal of Developmental Psychology, 20*, 479–494.

29. Kroger, J. (2000). *Identity development: Adolescence through adulthood.* Thousand Oaks, CA: Sage.

30. Swedo S., Leonard H., & Mittleman B. (1997). Identification of children with pediatric autoimmune neuropsychiatric disorders associated with streptococcal infections by a marker associated with rheumatic fever. *American Journal of Psychiatry, 154*, 110–112.

31. Snider, L., & Swedo, S. (2003). Childhood onset obsessive-compulsive disorder and tic disorders: Case report and literature review. *Journal of Child and Adolescent Psychopharmocology, 13*, 81–88.

32. Watkins, C. (2001, January). *Obsessive-compulsive disorder in children and adolescents.* HealthyPlace.com. Retrieved April 24, 2006 from www.healthyplace.com/communities/anxiety/children_ocd.asp.

33. Joyce, P., Carter, F., Horn, J., McIntosh, V., Luty, S., McKenzie, J., et al. (2003). Anxiety and psychoactive substance use disorder comorbidity in anorexia nervosa or depression. *International Journal of Eating Disorders, 43*, 211–219.

34. Aksaray, G., Yelken, B., Kaptanoglu, C., Oflu, S., & Ozaltin, M. (2001). Sexuality in women with obsessive-compulsive disorder. *Journal of Sex and Marital Therapy, 27*, 273–277.

35. Minnen, A., & Kampman, M. (2000). The interaction between anxiety and sexual functioning: A controlled study of sexual functioning in women with anxiety disorders. *Sexual and Relationship Therapy, 15*, 47–57.

36. Stahly, G. (2000). Battered women: Why don't they just leave? In J. Chrisler, C. Golden, & P. Rozee (Eds.), *Lectures on the psychology of women* (3rd ed.). New York: McGraw Hill.

37. Dziech, B. W. (2003). Sexual harassment on college campuses. In M. Paludi, & C. Paludi (Eds.), *Academic and workplace sexual harassment: A handbook of cultural, social science, management and legal perspectives* (pp. 148–171). Westport, CT: Praeger.

38. Gruber, J. (2003). Sexual harassment in the public sector. In M. Paludi, & C. Paludi (Eds.), *Academic and workplace sexual harassment: A handbook of*

cultural, social science, management and legal perspectives (pp. 49–75). Westport, CT: Praeger.

39. Courtois, C. (2000). *Healing the incest wound.* New York: Norton.

40. Finkelhor, D., & Dziuba-Leatherman, J. (1994). Children as victims of violence: A national survey. *Pediatrics, 94,* 413–420.

41. Lundberg-Love, P., & Marmion, S. (2003). Sexual harassment in the private sector. In M. Paludi, & C. Paludi (Eds.), *Academic and workplace sexual harassment: A handbook of cultural, social science, management and legal perspectives* (pp. 78–101). Westport, CT: Praeger.

42. Koss, M. (1993). Rape: Scope, impact, interventions and public policy. *American Psychologist, 48,* 1062–1069.

43. Foa, E., & Rothbaum, B. (2001). *Treating the trauma of rape: Cognitive-behavioral therapy for PTSD.* New York: Guilford Press.

44. Cavanaugh, R. (2002). Symptom complex, prevalence of traumatic body images of psychiatric patients with self-injurious behavior. *Journal of Pediatric Adolescent Gynecology, 15,* 97–100.

45. Kalra, H., Tandon, R., Trivedi, J.K., & Janca, A. (2005). Pregnancy-induced obsessive compulsive disorder: A case report. *Annals of General Psychiatry, 4,* 12.

46. Mania, G., Albert, U., Bogetto, F., Vaschetto, P., & Ravizza, L. (1999). Recent life events and obsessive-compulsive disorder: The role of pregnancy/delivery. *Psychiatry Research, 89,* 49–58.

47. Neziroglu, F., Anemone, R., & Yaryura-Tobias, J. (1992). Onset of obsessive-compulsive disorder in pregnancy. *American Journal of Psychiatry, 149,* 947–950.

48. Williams, K., & Koran, L. (1997). Obsessive-compulsive disorder in pregnancy, the puerperium, and the premenstrual. *Journal of Clinical Psychiatry, 58,* 330–334.

49. Goodman, R., & Gurian, A. (2001). *About obsessive-compulsive disorder.* New York: New York University Child Study Center. Retrieved April 24, 2006 from www.aboutourkids.org/aboutour/articles/about_ocd.html.

50. Neal-Barnett, A. M. (1999,July). *Multi-cultural issues in OCD.* Workshop presented at the Annual Membership Conference of the OC Foundation, Arlington, Virginia.

51. Gorman, J., Shear, K., Cowley, D., Cross, C.D., March, J., Roth, W., et al. (1998). *Practice guideline for the treatment of patients with panic disorder.* Washington, DC: American Psychiatric Association.

52. Wang, P. (2005). Long delays common between age of onset and first treatment of mental disorders in the U.S. *Archives of General Psychiatry, 62,* 603–613.

53. Fontenelle, L., Mendlowicz, M., Marques, C., & Versiani, M. (2004). Transcultural aspects of obsessive-compulsive disorder: A description of a Brazilian sample and a systematic review of international clinical studies. *Journal of Psychiatric Research, 38,* 403–411.

54. March, J. (1995). Cognitive-behavioral psychotherapy for children and adolescents with OCD: A review and recommendation for treatment. *Journal of the American Academy of Child and Adolescent Psychiatry, 43,* 7–18.

55. Franklin, M., Abramowitz, J., Bux, D., Jr., Zoellner, L., & Feeny, N. (2002). Cognitive-behavioral therapy with and without medication in the treatment

of obsessive-compulsive disorder. *Professional Psychology: Research and Practice, 33*, 162–168.

56. Freeston, M., Ladouceur, R., Gagnon, F., Thibodeau, N., Rhéaume, J., Letarte, H., et al. Cognitive-behavioral treatment of obsessive thoughts: A controlled study. *Journal of Consulting & Clinical Psychology, 65*, 405–413.

57. Reid, W. (1997). Anxiety disorders. In W. Reid, B. Balis, & B. Sutton (Eds.), *The treatment of psychiatric disorders,*(pp. 239–262). Bristol, PA: Bruner/Mazel.

58. Ito, L. M., Marks, I. M, de Araujo, L. A., & Hemsley, D. (1995). Does imagined exposure to the consequences of not ritualising enhance live exposure for OCD? A controlled study. II. Effect on behavioural v. subjective concordance of improvement. *British Journal of Psychiatry, 167*, 71–75.

59. Abramowitz, J., Schwartz, S., Moore, K., & Luenzmann, K. (2003). Obsessive-compulsive symptoms in pregnancy and the puerperium: A review of the literature. *Journal of Anxiety Disorders, 17*, 461–478.

60. van Oppen, P., de Haan, E., van Balkom, A. J., Spinhoven, P., Hoogduin, K., & van Dyck, R. Cognitive therapy and exposure in vivo in the treatment of obsessive-compulsive disorder. *Behavior Research and Therapy, 33*, 379–390.

61. Petrikis, P., Andreou, C., Bozikas, V., & Karavatos, A. (2004). Effective use of olanzapine for obsessive-compulsive symptoms in a patient with bipolar disorder. *Canadian Journal of Psychiatry, 49*, 572–573.

62. Shapira, N., Ward, H., Mandoki, M., Murphy, T., Yang, M., Blier, P., et al. (2004). A double-blind, placebo-controlled trial of olanzapine addition in fluoxetine-refractory obsessive-compulsive disorder. *Biological Psychiatry. 55*, 553–555.

63. Ravizza, L., Barzega, G., Bellino, S., Bogetto, F., & Maina, G. (1995). Predictors of drug treatment response in obsessive-compulsive disorder. *Journal of Clinical Psychiatry, 56*, 368–373.

64. Rivas-Vasquez, R. (2001). Antidepressants as first-line agents in the current pharmacotherapy of anxiety disorders. *Professional Psychology: Research & Practice, 32*, 101–104.

65. Zisook, S., & Burt, V. (2003). Psychiatric disorders during pregnancy. *Psychiatric Times, 20*, 1.

66. Baer, L., Rauch, S., Ballentine, H., Jr., Martuzza, R., Cosgrove, R., Cassem, E., et al. (1995). Cingulotomy for intractable obsessive-compulsive disorder. Prospective long-term follow-up of 18 patients. *Archives of General Psychiatry, 52*, 384–392.

67. Hodgkiss, A. D., Malizia, A. L., Bartlett, J. R., & Bridges, P. K. (1995). Outcome after psychosurgical operation of stereotactic subcaudate tractotomy, 1979–1991. *Journal of Neuropsychiatry and Clinical Neuroscience, 7*, 230–234.

68. Thienemann, M., & Koran, L. (1995). Do soft signs predict treatment outcomes in obsessive-compulsive disorder? *Journal of Neuropsychiatry and Clinical Neuroscience, 7*, 218–222.

69. March, J., & Mulle, K. (1998). *OCD in children and adolescents, A cognitive-behavioral treatment manual.* New York: Guilford.

70. Morrison, J., & Anders, T. (2001). *Interviewing children and adolescents: Skills and strategies for effective DSM–IV diagnosis.* New York: Guilford.

71. Thomsen, P. (1995). Obsessive-compulsive disorder in children and adolescents: A 6–22 year follow-up study of social outcome. *Child and Adolescent Psychiatry, 4,* 112–122.

72. Keijsers, G., Hoogduin, C., & Schaap, C. (1994). Predictors of treatment outcome in the behavioral treatment of obsessive-compulsive disorder. *British Journal of Psychiatry, 165,* 781–786.

73. Hiss, H., Foa, E., & Kozak, M. (1994). Relapse prevention program for treatment of obsessive-compulsive disorder. *Journal of Consulting & Clinical Psychology, 62,* 801–808.

74. March, J. (1995). Cognitive-behavioral psychotherapy for children and adolescents with OCD: A review and recommendation for treatment. *Journal of the American Academy of Child and Adolescent Psychiatry, 43,* 7–18.

Chapter 6

Eating Disorders: Anorexia Nervosa, Bulimia Nervosa, and Binge Eating Disorder

Jennifer Couturier and James Lock

Eating disorders are often glamorized in Hollywood, and attract enormous media attention when they afflict famous people. Well-known examples of celebrities who have suffered from eating disorders include: Karen Carpenter who eventually died from anorexia nervosa (AN), Tracey Gold from TV's *Growing Pains*, and more recently, Mary-Kate Olsen, whose eating disorder landed her on the cover of *People* magazine.[1] In an article titled "Mary-Kate's Private Battle," her battle was private no longer. Despite the intrigue and curiosity that eating disorders emote, they are illnesses that have devastating effects on individuals and their families. They are common conditions often occurring in young women, but eating disorders also occur in young men, and can actually begin at any age. This chapter will review descriptions of eating disorders, and then explore their history to gain a fuller understanding of the evolution of these disorders over time. We will then describe the prevalence of eating disorders, and then discuss some proposed causes, risk factors, and treatments for these disorders. We will end with a discussion of the impact of eating disorders on our society, along with potential new areas of research.

WHAT ARE EATING DISORDERS?

Eating disorders are often variously defined as social, cultural, biological, psychological, medical, psychiatric, or behavioral problems depending on the perspective that is taken. According to the *Diagnostic and Statistical Manual of*

Mental Disorders, Fourth Edition-Text Revision *(DSM–IV–TR)*,[2] eating disorders are divided into three main categories consisting of AN, bulimia nervosa (BN), and eating disorder not otherwise specified (EDNOS). The diagnostic symptoms of these disorders are presented in Table 6.1. Generally speaking, AN requires a low body weight, whereas BN affects individuals of normal weight who have eating problems such as binge eating (eating large amounts of food in an uncontrolled way) and purging (vomiting, or using laxatives, or other means). Both disorders involve a restriction in food intake to various degrees, and a preoccupation with shape and weight. In AN, there is a requirement that menstrual cycles have ceased for a period of three months.

The third category, EDNOS, is reserved for those individuals who do not exactly fit into either of the other two diagnostic categories, but still have significant problems pertaining to eating and their thoughts or feelings about weight

Table 6.1
Diagnostic Criteria for Eating Disorders

Anorexia Nervosa (AN)	Bulimia Nervosa (BN)	Eating Disorder Not Otherwise Specified
• Refusal to maintain body weight at or above a minimally normal weight for age and height • Intense fear of gaining weight or becoming fat • Body image disturbance, undue influence of weight or shape on self-evaluation, or denial of the seriousness of the current low body weight • Amenorrhea	• Recurrent episodes of binge eating, characterized by eating a large amount of food, and a sense of lack of control • Compensatory behavior to prevent weight gain (vomiting, laxatives, diuretics, fasting, exercise) • Binge eating and compensatory behaviors both occur about twice a week for 3 months • Self-evaluation is unduly influenced by shape or weight	• All of the criteria for AN are met, except for amenorrhea • All of the criteria for AN are met, except weight that despite significant weight loss, is in the normal range • All of the criteria for BN are met, except for the frequency and/or duration • Regular use of compensatory behavior after eating small amounts of food, when there is a normal body weight • Repeatedly chewing and spitting out food • Binge eating disorder: recurrent episodes of binge eating which are not accompanied by compensatory behaviors
Specifications: Restricting or binge-eating/Purging type	Specifications: Purging or Nonpurging type	

Source: Adapted from the *DSM–IV–TR*[2]

and shape. Often, children and adolescents fit into this category because they have been identified early and do not manifest all of the symptoms required, or they do not meet the duration of illness requirement for certain criteria for the diagnosis of AN (three months of amenorrhea) or BN (three months of binge eating and purging). One type of eating disorder within the EDNOS category has been gaining attention and research interest as a separate disorder. It has been labeled binge eating disorder (BED), and a set of research criteria are presently available in the *DSM–IV–TR*.[2] BED involves binge eating without the compensatory behaviors that are typically seen in BN (vomiting, laxatives, etc.). In order for BED to be diagnosed, the sufferer must experience marked distress about the binge eating, and it must occur on average at least two days per week for a period of six months. In addition, the binge eating must be associated with certain characteristics, such as eating rapidly, eating until uncomfortably full, eating large amounts when not physically hungry, eating alone, and feeling disgusted, depressed, or very guilty afterwards.

In addition to behavioral symptoms, eating disorders have medical complications. Due to the effects of starvation in AN, there can be problems with the heart, bones, and hormonal and fluid systems within the body, just to list a few examples.[3] All muscles, including the heart muscle, can become weakened, causing the heart to beat irregularly or to fail completely. This can be a cause of death in AN. Due to starvation, menstrual cycles stop, and because of this, not enough calcium is deposited into the bones. This can lead to osteoporosis, a condition most often associated with older women who no longer menstruate. Future fertility can also be impacted by these hormonal changes. Fluid systems can be disrupted by dehydration, which can also cause death. Even the brain can be affected by starvation since not enough nutrients are taken in to nourish the brain. Brain scans have shown brain shrinkage during the illness. In children and adolescents, growth can be halted as there are not enough nutrients present to build muscle, bone, and tissue needed for growth. The mortality rate for AN is the highest of all psychiatric illnesses, and death is largely attributed to these medical complications and to suicide.[4]

Anorexia Nervosa

Brittany was 14 years old when her mother became concerned about her significant weight loss and progressively diminishing variety of food choices. Over a period of only six months, Brittany had gone from being a socially active and engaging teenage girl with many friends to isolating herself in her bedroom. She refused to eat meals with the family and focused almost exclusively on homework. She had also taken an interest in running on the treadmill in order to be "more healthy." When Brittany's mother or father would try to get her to eat more, they were met with much resistance and decided they would just stop nagging her. When she was brought by her mother to see a doctor, Brittany had lost almost 30 pounds and was now about 75 percent of her normal weight. She was feeling faint at times, and had not had a menstrual period in four months. Her hair was falling out of her head, but a fine hair growth had appeared on her back. She was cold a lot of the time. Even though underweight, she told the doctor that she believed she was overweight and needed to lose a few more pounds. Although Brittany's mother was quite concerned about her, Brittany did not see any problem with her current low weight and could not understand why everyone was making such a big deal of it. The doctor did some tests and determined that Brittany's heart rate was very low and that she required admission to the hospital.

For BN, medical complications can be just as severe. These complications arise not due to starvation, but due to binge eating and purging which disrupt the delicate balance of chemicals in the body. For example, levels of potassium and sodium become out of balance. Since the heart relies on these elements to pump blood through the body, this leads to an inability of the heart to regulate its rhythm. As in AN, this can be a cause of death in BN. In addition, there can be severe damage to the teeth and esophagus due to vomiting. Tears can occur in the esophagus causing bleeding that can be very dangerous. Binge eating also has its dangers with the potential to cause the stomach to dilate and even rupture.[3] BED has also been associated with obesity, which has a multitude of medical risks as well, including diabetes, high blood pressure, and heart disease.

Bulimia Nervosa

Allison was 30 years old when she decided she needed help to overcome her eating disorder. Although she had suffered for many years, she was tired of hiding the binge eating and purging from her family. When Allison was a teenager, she was always worried about her weight even though it was average for her height. She began trying to lose weight by trying not to eat during the day. Each day by the evening, she would be ravenously hungry and would eat whatever she could find in the cupboards at home. At times she would eat a whole gallon of ice cream in a short period of time. She would feel very guilty after eating, and would vomit in order to get rid of what she had just consumed. Although her weight did not really change much, Allison continued on with this pattern of eating, on and off, for several years. As she became an adult, she began to have more insight into her pattern of eating, and discovered that fights with her boyfriend appeared to trigger binge eating and purging. She often turned to food to soothe an emotional upset. Allison eventually got married and had children, but found that keeping this secret from her family was very difficult. One day she went for an appointment to her dentist who noticed that her teeth were deteriorating and asked if Allison had a problem with vomiting. The following week, Allison fainted at work, and when brought to the emergency department, she was told that her potassium was critically low. Allison was treated with intravenous potassium, and at that point, she decided that she needed some professional help for her illness. She also decided that a first step in getting help would be to tell her husband about her long struggle with bulimia.

In terms of the outcome or prognosis of eating disorders, there is still much to learn. Generally, for AN, outcome appears to be good in about 50–70 percent of patients, with the others developing a more chronic illness that lasts many years or leads to death. The course of AN is highly variable, with some individuals recovering fully after a single episode, others experiencing many relapses and remissions, and still others chronically deteriorating over many years.[2] Estimated mortality rates are around 5–10 percent, however, there is an approximate 1 percent of increased mortality risk with each year the illness persists.[2,5] Outcome appears to be better for younger patients, for example, those who receive help for their illness in their teen years. Although many patients with AN recover in terms of weight restoration, enduring preoccupations about food and weight are common. In addition, of those initially diagnosed with AN, up to 40 percent go on to develop bulimic symptoms, and other psychological symptoms can persist including anxiety and depression. We know less about the long term prognosis of BN. The overall success rate for patients receiving treatment is between 50–70 percent, although relapse rates are high (30–50%).[4] Within clinic samples of patients with BN, symptoms appear to persist for at least several years. Often patients are reluctant to seek treatment due to shame and embarrassment, and may go untreated for many years. In any event, both AN and BN carry serious medical complications, and a significant proportion of individuals experience a chronic and debilitating course of illness.

A HISTORICAL VIEW OF ANOREXIA NERVOSA

AN and BN are very different in terms of their history. Agreement exists in the literature that AN was first described clearly by Gull in England and Lasegue in France almost simultaneously in the late 19th century.[6,7] BN first became clearly described a century later, by Russell in 1979.[8] We will first describe the historical significance of AN, and then turn to the more recent evolution of BN.

William Gull first coined the term anorexia nervosa, but Lasegue's description was similar, and he labeled the disorder *l'anorexie hysterique*. In Gull's earliest descriptions, AN involved significant weight loss, slowing of the pulse, skin changes, and loss of menstruation. He described so-called perversions of the ego as the cause of the disorder. Similarly, Lasegue described the cause as a morbid mental state, and felt that psychological distress was converted into food refusal. Both commented that no physical cause could be found for these illnesses, and Gull advised feeding these patients despite their protests. Interestingly, neither author commented on concerns about body image.

Although agreement exists as to the first clear descriptions of AN by Gull and Lasegue, there is much debate over the presence of earlier cases.[9] Cases of self-starvation have been documented as early as the 5th and 6th centuries, but were attributed to demonic possession and treated with exorcism. Following these cases, self-starvation was documented in accounts of sainthood. In 1380, Saint Catherine of Siena began starving herself at age 16 and died in her early thirties. At the time of her death she was refusing food and water. Saint Catherine believed she could not eat, and prayed that God would help her. In the 1700s, Saint Veronica was also afflicted at age 18 (perhaps even earlier, at age 15), and is documented to have been in a competition to show that she loved God the most. Saint Veronica was often seen by other nuns sneaking into the kitchen to binge on large amounts of food. She was treated in the infirmary by force-feeding, and ultimately recovered, living until the age of 67. Bell[10] reviewed the lives of 271 saints who lived in Italy from 1200 A.D., and deemed that about one-third of them suffered from holy anorexia. This condition involved food refusal and emaciation which was motivated by the belief that one possessed the ability to live without food, and thus reflected divine intervention. In the 17th and 18th centuries, several girls between the ages of 14 and 20 were labeled miraculous maids, engaging in self-starvation, and modeling themselves on saints. And, in the 18th–19th centuries, cases of so-called fasting girls are documented. These girls abruptly refused to eat, and drew much attention and fame. At this point, psychiatrists began attributing these disorders to a nervous condition rather than a religious or divine miracle.

Much of the disagreement surrounding the diagnosis of these earlier cases comes about from the unknown motivation behind the self-starvation. Those who do not believe that these early cases are cases of AN point to the lack of weight or shape concerns present in these individuals which would be necessary to meet the diagnostic criteria in the *DSM–IV–TR*. However, it is unclear from the documentation whether these concerns were present. Others would say that religious preoccupations do not preclude the presence of body image concerns, and that these may indeed be the earliest cases of AN. Strength is added to this position by looking at different cultural expressions of AN. A recent study from Hong Kong found that in 70 cases of AN, 59 percent did not describe any weight concerns, reporting digestive discomfort as the most common reason for being unable to eat.[11] This suggests that cultural factors may bring about body image concerns, but that these concerns are not necessary for induction of self-starvation or for a broader definition of AN. Keel and Klump[12] point out that the uniting factor between fasting saints and modern day AN is the paradox that the starvation is *both* deliberate *and* nonvolitional, meaning that the process may initially be self-initiated, or even maintained, but there is also an inability to stop the behavior. This differentiates AN from other processes of deliberate self-starvation, such as in a protest situation in which individuals are able to return to eating once the protest is over.

A HISTORICAL VIEW OF BULIMIA NERVOSA

In contrast to the long history of AN, BN has only recently been recognized as a diagnosis. Many contend it is not just a new diagnosis, but is truly a new disorder.[13] It was first called "bulimia" in the *DSM–III*[14] in 1980, but this description only included binge eating. In 1987 in the *DSM–III–R*,[15] it acquired the name "bulimia nervosa," and required binge eating and vomiting or other compensatory behavior to be present for the diagnosis. In ancient Egypt, Rome, Greece, and Arabia, there are reports of induced vomiting in order to cleanse the body, and by the 17th century, purgation was a popular remedy prescribed by physicians. There are famous stories about the vomitorium in ancient Rome where people used emetics (chemicals ingested to cause vomiting) in order to eat more. However, these ancient accounts were not likely to be the first cases of BN, as there is no evidence of a desire for a thin body shape, and the purpose of the vomiting is well described as improving health, or increasing intake, not for purposes of weight loss. Russell[13] also describes cases of bulimic behavior in several saints, but states that these more likely fit a picture of AN associated with some binge eating and purging, rather than BN. There are a few questionable cases that might be considered to be BN from the early 20th century, but most reliable descriptions of BN appear during the 1970s in which Russell compiled a series of 30 patients who exhibited binge eating, along with vomiting and an intense fear of becoming fat.[8]

Therefore, it appears that overeating or binge eating has existed since antiquity, but the disorder BN was identified in the 1970s. It is possible that BN existed before, but was never identified. However, Russell believes that cases must have been much fewer in number prior to the 1970s, and that the first cases occurred between the 1940s and 1960s.[13] The identification of BN in the 1970s provides a partial explanation for its relatively recent rise in prevalence, as does a recent emphasis on the thin body ideal in our society which is thought to be a potential cause of the illness. BN was initially described as being closely associated with AN, but has become a more distinctive disorder over time with studies of personality traits demonstrating a very different type of person that develops BN (more impulsive, extroverted, and emotional) compared to one who develops AN (obsessive, introverted, perfectionistic).

HOW COMMON ARE EATING DISORDERS AND IS THE PREVALENCE OF EATING DISORDERS INCREASING?

Both AN and BN are much more common in females compared to males, with over 90 percent of cases occurring in women for both disorders. AN typically begins in mid- to late adolescence (14 to 18 years of age), and although it may onset at potentially any age, it rarely has an onset in women over 40 years of age.[2] The average prevalence rate for AN is 0.3 to 0.5 percent for young females, and the incidence rate (number of new cases per year) is at least 8 per 100,000 people per year.[2,16] There has been much debate over whether the incidence and prevalence of AN is increasing. In their review, Hoek and van Hoeken[16] state that the incidence rate of AN in 15- to 24-year-old females definitely increased over the past century, until the 1970s. In their extensive and careful review, Keel and Klump[12] suggest a modest increase in incidence in AN, after controlling for factors such as population size changes, female proportion of the population, and method of ascertainment of diagnosis.

BN has a slightly later age of onset compared to AN, first occurring in late adolescence or early adulthood. The prevalence rate for BN is 1–3 percent, and the incidence rate is at least 12 per 100,000 people per year.[2,16] Keel and Klump[12] found that BN has been dramatically increasing in incidence since 1970, and concluded that there are actually no reports of BN prior to 1960. However, there is always a possibility that BN existed prior to 1960 in a hidden form of illness. In terms of the prevalence of the eating disorders in other areas of the world, AN appears to be just as prevalent in Western and non-Western nations, if the criterion of weight concerns is not required.[12] However, cases of BN appear only to occur in individuals who have had some kind of exposure to Western ideals. As a result of this, Keel and Klump[12] postulate that there may be an association between Westernization, body image disturbance, and BN, and concluded that AN does not appear to be a culture-bound syndrome, but that weight concerns and BN may be culturally bound phenomena.

BED is different from AN and BN in that the ratio of affected males to females is more equal. Compared to ratios of nine females for each male affected in AN and BN, about one and one-half females are affected for every male in BED. The overall prevalence in community samples ranges between 0.7 percent and 4 percent, however in samples of the population drawn from weight loss programs, 15 to 50 percent meet criteria for BED.[2] The illness often begins in late adolescence or early adulthood after significant weight loss from dieting, and appears to have a chronic course.

WHY ARE WOMEN MORE COMMONLY AFFECTED? DO EATING DISORDERS AFFECT MEN TOO?

It is unclear why women are more commonly affected by eating disorders than men. It has been postulated that there is more media attention devoted to the thin female ideal and that this exerts societal pressure for women to diet and rebel against their natural body weight. In more recent years, the ideal body shape for men has also changed, with more pressure for men to bulk up. Male action figure dimensions have changed over the past 30 years, becoming increasingly muscular beyond that which is humanly possible.[17] In addition, men's magazines often focus on gaining muscle mass and shaping up.

Whatever the media pressure, it is clear that eating disorders affect males too. Often the same types of symptoms are present in males with eating disorders as females. There can be some subtle differences. Boys are more likely to exercise than diet as compared with girls. In addition, their reasons for wanting to lose weight may be different from girls, as boys often begin dieting because they are overweight, or they want to avoid medical complications of obesity that affected their parent, or they want to improve sports performance.[18] Boys want to increase their upper torso while also getting rid of fat.[19] It has been suggested that there is a higher rate of eating disorders in males who express a homosexual or bisexual orientation, but the data available are not conclusive[20] Males with AN appear to have similar outcomes compared to girls with AN, although they require a substantially greater number of calories to gain weight. In addition, males with AN can experience the same medical complications as girls, with similar degrees of osteopenia and brain shrinkage. For males with BN, very little is known about their response to treatment or outcome. It is possible that fewer boys with BN seek treatment compared to girls, perhaps due to greater shame and feelings of isolation. But, there is some evidence that the number of boys seeking treatment for eating disorders is increasing in more recent years.[21]

WHAT ARE SOME CAUSES AND RISK FACTORS FOR EATING DISORDERS?

There has been much debate over the causes of eating disorders with many theories proposed, including: dysfunctional families, the media's emphasis on appearance and the thin ideal, low self-esteem, depression, and anxiety, to name just a few. The bottom line is that we do not know what causes eating disorders. However, researchers have been studying risk factors, which are factors associated with the illness that are present before the illness develops, in an effort to determine some potential causes of eating disorders. It is very difficult to prove that a factor causes a disorder due to the scientific rigor needed to prove causation, thus it is more prudent to discuss risk factors in eating disorders. In order to be labeled a risk factor, the characteristic in question must be present before the illness develops and the study must be conducted in such a fashion that people are studied longitudinally, over long periods of time, even before they have developed the illness. This is often hard to examine in research studies because patients only come to the attention of researchers once they are already ill. In order to be certain about the timing of risk factors, longitudinal studies that begin to study subjects before they are ill are essential. However, these studies are very costly as they require researchers to study large groups of the population over a period of several years or decades in order to capture a few individuals who eventually develop eating disorders. Some factors are fixed, however, in that we can assume they were present before the illness. An example of a fixed factor would be gender. If a factor has not been studied in a longitudinal way (before the illness), but is studied at the time the patient is already ill, and factors are reported on by the patient or family to have occurred in the past or present, the factor would be labeled as a correlate of the disorder rather than a risk factor.[22]

In a thorough review of the literature by Jacobi, Hayward, de Zwaan, Kraemer, and Agras,[2,20] several risk factors for eating disorders were described. They report that gender is one of the most significant risk factors for eating disorders given that there is a much higher prevalence of eating disorders in females compared to males. This ratio is estimated to be 9–10:1, with 9–10 females diagnosed with either AN or BN (the ratio is the same for both disorders) for every male. This ratio appears to be consistent in almost all studies looking at the prevalence of eating disorders, adding certainty to the claim that gender is a risk factor. Age appears to be another risk factor as the peak incidence of eating disorders is in adolescence and young adulthood. As in the case of gender, this finding is consistent across studies, and both age and gender are considered nonspecific risk factors because adolescence/young adulthood and female gender are also related to other psychiatric disorders including mood and anxiety disorders.

In terms of ethnicity, there are conflicting theories. Caucasian females were historically thought to be more at risk for eating disorders compared to other ethnic groups, but more recent studies have suggested that Hispanics have equal rates of eating disturbances, and Native Americans have higher rates, with blacks and Asians having lower rates. There is also some evidence that blacks in the United States have higher rates of binge eating behavior than Caucasians. Thus, the issue of ethnicity as a risk factor is a complex one, and simple conclusions cannot be made as of yet.[22] Similarly, acculturation has not been well-studied. It is thought that those who are more acculturated to Western cultures have more eating disturbances, as do those in more industrialized countries. Keel and Klump[12] present an argument in their review that rates of BN appear to be influenced by proximity to Western culture, whereas rates of AN do not vary according to cultural milieu. This suggests that BN is a culture-bound syndrome whereas AN is not. They add support to their argument by outlining the historical stability of AN throughout time, and the more recent emergence of BN with the heightening of media attention to the thin ideal. More evidence of the effect of the media on eating disorder symptoms was obtained in a naturalistic experiment in Fiji.[23] On this rather isolated island which has a very low prevalence of eating disorders, Becker, Burwell, Gilman, Herzog, and Hamburg[23] reported that after the introduction of television in 1995 the percentage of the population scoring in the high range on a psychological measure of disturbed eating attitudes was significantly increased. In addition, the percentage reporting self-induced vomiting to control weight was significantly higher. There was no evidence of anyone having AN, and rates of binge eating were no different. This study provided some evidence that television could have an impact on eating-related attitudes and behaviors, particularly in the domain of BN.

Dieting has long been associated with the development of eating disturbances and disorders. The evidence behind this theory comes from two sources. The first line of evidence is that patients who seek treatment for an eating disorder often report that dieting preceded the onset of their disorder, and the second comes from laboratory studies in which imposed dieting and restrained eating were related to the development of binge eating behavior. The relationship between dieting and eating disorders appears to be the strongest for people who binge eat, so this would include those with BN, BED, and AN binge-eating/purging type. The relationship is not as strong for those with AN restricting type. Of course, those who diet can be assumed to have weight or shape concerns that predate the onset of dieting, so perhaps weight and shape concerns and negative feelings about one's body are actually the true precursors to eating disorders rather than dieting itself. But, this would not explain the laboratory findings of imposed dieting leading to binge eating. In any case, considered altogether, weight concerns, negative body image, and dieting seem to be very strong and specific risk factors for eating disorders.[22] Childhood obesity and parental obesity appear to be specifically correlated with eating disorders, as are childhood feeding difficulties and digestive problems. It appears that childhood and parental obesity are more related to BN and binge eating, whereas picky eating is related to subsequent anorexic symptoms. Teasing by peers that is weight-related has been thought to increase the risk for eating disorders, however, this requires more study. It was once thought that certain types of athletes such as gymnasts, swimmers, jockeys, wrestlers, and dancers were at increased risk. Due to a lack of longitudinal studies, these sports cannot be labeled risk factors, however they do appear to be correlated with subclinical eating disorder symptoms. The evidence is not as strong for full syndrome eating disorders.

Disturbances in emotionality and general psychological problems have also been associated with the development of eating disorders. Disorders in mood, such as depression, have thought to be an underlying cause of BN in particular, whereas obsessive-compulsive disorders (OCDs) have been thought to underlie AN. However, it is often very difficult to determine whether these psychological problems existed prior to the onset of the eating disorder, or are current manifestations of the eating disturbance. An important study in distinguishing cause from effect was that done in 1950 by Ancel Keys.[24] This researcher and his colleagues studied 36 men who volunteered for a "starvation study" rather than perform military duties. For the first three months of the study the men were allowed to eat normally, and for the following six months they were restricted to 50 percent of their usual caloric intake. What these researchers observed was that in the state of starvation, these men developed increases in food preoccupations, and could not concentrate on their usual activities. They would talk about food, read about food, and daydream about food. Many developed an interest in cookbooks, and menus. They also developed odd eating behaviors, cutting up food into tiny pieces, prolonging their meals into two hour affairs, and gaining pleasure from watching others eat. Several developed binge eating if allowed access to food, periods in which their eating was out of control, and large quantities were eaten. There were also personality changes with increases in irritability, anger, depression, and even elation at times. Many became more obsessive, hoarding recipes, cookbooks, kitchen utensils, and even some items not related to food such as books and clothes. All of these behaviors are often seen in individuals with AN, and this study suggests that they may be consequences of starvation rather than causes of the disorder.

Given the requirement that the psychological disturbance was present before the eating disorder, it does appear that obsessive-compulsive personality disorder occurs more frequently in patients with AN compared to healthy people. In addition, psychiatric illness appears to be a nonspecific risk factor for eating disorders. A similar role has been found for prior sexual abuse. The rates of past sexual abuse appears to be similar in groups with eating disorders when compared to patients with other psychiatric illnesses.[22] Due to the nature of the studies done, past sexual abuse has been correlated with eating disorders, but cannot be called a risk factor since longitudinal studies have not been completed. A similar situation exists for adverse life events (e.g., death of a loved one) which appear to be correlated with psychiatric illness in general. There is also some evidence from longitudinal studies that low self-esteem can precede the onset of an eating disorder and thus low self-esteem can be classified as a risk factor, but more research needs to be done in order to determine its specificity to eating disorders. Perfectionistic traits also appear to be correlated with eating disorders.

Historically, family dysfunction has been targeted as a cause of eating disorders. Families have been described as having poor structure and boundaries, being too close, too critical and conflictual, or too chaotic. However, in many of these studies, the timing of the family dysfunction in relation to the onset of the eating disorder has not been considered. It is now thought that these familial patterns of behavior might be a consequence of the presence of the illness rather than a cause. There are currently no longitudinal studies to determine the role of families as risk factors for eating disorders, and until these studies are completed, family dysfunction can be considered to be related to eating disorders, just as family dysfunction is related to many other types of chronic illnesses.[22] In addition, there is some evidence that rates of eating disorders, mood disorders, and anxiety disorders are higher in relatives of people with eating disorders;, however, the timing of onset of these disorders has not been well-delineated, and these disorders might have emerged in the relative after the target patient was identified as having an eating disorder.

Biological factors may also be important in predisposing an individual to eating disorders. Although no genes have been identified as causative factors for eating disorders, it is thought that genetic vulnerability interacts with factors in the environment to culminate in an eating disorder. It is also thought that not only one gene is involved, but that many genes contribute to the development of an eating disorder. We know that genes must be important in contributing to eating disorders because rates of eating disorders are higher in identical twins than in fraternal twins. Since identical twins share all of their genetic information and fraternal twins only share half, we would expect identical twins to have higher rates of eating disorders if genetics were important, and this is the case in AN and BN. However, the degree of importance of genetics is not yet clear. For AN, the genetic contribution to the illness ranges between 58 percent and 88 percent, whereas in BN it ranges from 28 percent to 83 percent in various studies.[22] A chemical found within the brain called serotonin has also been implicated as a potential causal factor in eating disorders. Serotonin abnormalities have been found in those patients currently ill with AN and BN, and in those recovered from these illnesses. However, the time precedence of the serotonin abnormality has not been established, and it still remains unclear whether a serotonin abnormality was present before the illness developed. Other possible biological factors include preterm birth and pregnancy complications. Preterm birth appears to be associated with AN, and pregnancy complications with both AN and BN.[22]

From this discussion on risk factors it is clear that much more research needs to be done in this area. Many factors can only be considered to be correlated with eating disorders because longitudinal studies have not been completed. It appears that the evidence for age and gender as risk factors is the strongest, although these factors are nonspecific. In addition, weight concerns and dieting have an evidence base to support them as strong and specific risk factors for eating disorders. Due to the difficulties inherent in longitudinal risk factor research, it may be a long time before we know what risk factors are important in the development of eating disorders, and even longer before we know what actually causes these disorders.

WHAT TREATMENTS ARE CURRENTLY AVAILABLE AND EFFECTIVE?

One of the difficulties in treating individuals with eating disorders is that very little research has been conducted, and there is only a small evidence base of treatment studies. Generally, there are two broad types of treatments that can be used: talking therapy, otherwise known as psychotherapy, and medication treatment, otherwise known as pharmacotherapy. There are also different types of settings in which these treatments are delivered: inpatient (in the hospital), outpatient (outside the hospital), and day treatment (partial hospitalization). In addition to the psychiatric aspect of treatment which will be discussed below, there is also a need for medical monitoring by a general practitioner, pediatrician, or other type of medical doctor experienced in the treatment of eating disorders. Some patients may also opt to see a nutritionist, although the evidence base for nutritional counseling is sparse. The largest role for nutritional counseling is likely in the inpatient setting. There are several sets of guidelines that help professionals in making treatment decisions, two examples of these are the Practice Guidelines for the Treatment of Patients with Eating Disorders (revision) developed in the United States,[4] and the National Institute for Clinical Excellence Guidelines developed in the United Kingdom.[25]

For adults with AN, there is actually very little data from randomized con-trolled trials (the most rigorous kind of clinical research) that provide clear support for any effective treatment. There is a slightly larger evidence base for treating adolescents with AN. A major problem in doing research on this pop-ulation of patients is that dropout rates and treatment noncompliance are quite high. Another obstacle to research on AN is that the disorder is relatively rare, and thus it is difficult to gather a large enough group of patients at one research centre. In addition, there can be medical complications that result in patients being withdrawn from treatment studies.[26]

There is some evidence that specific types of psychotherapy can be effective in producing significantly greater amounts of weight gain when compared to routine treatment for adults with AN.[27] These types of therapy shown to be effective by Dare, Eisler, Russell, Treasure, and Doge[27] are: (1) focal psychoan-alytic psychotherapy which is a nondirective therapy addressing the conscious and unconscious meaning of the eating disorder symptoms, and the effects of the symptoms in relationships with others including the therapist, and (2) family therapy in which the eating disorder is recognized as affecting all family members, and the focus is on eliminating the eating disorder from its controlling role in the family. However, at the end of one year of treatment, only one-third of the adults in this study no longer met the criteria for AN, indicat-ing that a significant proportion were still ill even after treatment with the spe-cialized therapies. There is also some data to suggest that cognitive behavior therapy (CBT) may be marginally helpful in those who have had AN, but are now at a normal weight. This therapy aims to challenge distorted beliefs about weight and shape, modify negative thoughts and dysfunctional assumptions, and establish healthy eating behavior in patients with AN. When compared to those receiving nutritional counseling, those receiving CBT remained in treatment significantly longer without relapsing.[29] Dropout and relapse rates were significantly higher in the nutritional counseling group compared to the CBT group (73% vs. 22%). A recent randomized trial compared CBT alone, fluoxetine alone, and the combination of the two in patients who had met the criteria for AN within the prior 12 months.[26] Only 37 percent of those randomly assigned to treatment actually completed the study, with comple-tion rates of 27 percent in the medication alone group, 43 percent in the CBT alone group, and 38 percent in the combination group. The authors concluded that medication alone cannot be an effective treatment for AN given that the majority of patients do not find this treatment acceptable.

In contrast to studies involving adults, studies involving adolescents with AN are slightly more encouraging. Russell, Szmukler, Dare, and Eisler[30] found that adolescents who had been ill for less than three years with AN gained more weight with family therapy than with individual therapy. These benefits of family therapy were still apparent at the five-year follow-up point.[31] The type of family therapy used in this study, called Maudsley family therapy or family-based treatment,[32] views the parents as capable of refeeding their affected child and it also involves the siblings. This therapy goes against prior psychotherapeutic views of AN in which parents were viewed as too controlling and pathological, but instead views the parents as the best resource for the ill child. The evidence base for family-based treatment for children and adolescents with AN is definitely growing, and this type of treatment has now been shown to be effective in several studies.[33,34] There is also one type of individual treatment that focuses on improving self-esteem and self-confidence that has been shown to be effective for adolescents with AN in one small study.[33]

In terms of medication treatment for AN, no rigorous clinical studies have shown medication to be of benefit in the acutely ill phase of AN. One study found that an antidepressant drug called fluoxetine appeared to be effective in maintaining weight once patients were already weight-restored.[35] Those who remained on fluoxetine for one year did better in terms of weight and symptoms of depression, anxiety, obsessions and compulsions, and core eating disorder symptoms compared to those who did not complete the year of treatment and compared to those who were on placebo. However, this was a very small study and the dropout rates were extremely high (6/16 in the fluoxetine group, and 16/19 in the placebo group) making the interpretation of the results quite difficult. No other medications have clearly shown a benefit in treating AN in controlled clinical trials. Some of the newer antipsychotics, such as olanzapine and risperidone have demonstrated weight gain in some preliminary reports. Medications should not be used as the primary treatment for AN given the lack of evidence and high nonacceptance rate, and are usually only used to treat other illnesses co-occurring with AN, such as OCD or major depression. Fluoxetine for preventing relapse and the newer antipsychotics for the acute phase of AN may prove to be helpful, but definitive studies are currently lacking. In terms of the treatment setting, guidelines suggest that management of patients with AN should be attempted on an outpatient basis unless there is medical instability necessitating admission to hospital.

For patients suffering from BN, the first line of treatment with the most evidence is outpatient psychotherapy, with CBT specifically modified for patients with BN.[36] Another type of psychotherapy called interpersonal psychotherapy (IPT) has also been shown to be effective in patients with BN, but it may take longer to notice beneficial effects compared to CBT.[37] Whereas CBT focuses on cognitions or thoughts related to binge eating and purging, IPT focuses on relationships and feelings and their association with the eating disorder. In addition to the confirmation of CBT and IPT as treatments of choice for BN, a recent review also concluded that self-help approaches that used CBT manuals were promising and merit further study.[38]

In terms of medication for BN, many studies have confirmed that antidepressants reduce binge frequency.[39,40] The Food and Drug Administration has approved the antidepressant fluoxetine for treating BN, as it has the most evidence for reducing the frequency of binge eating.[41] One antidepressant (bupropion) is contraindicated for treating BN due to the increased risk of seizures. In terms of treatment setting, the vast majority of patients with BN can be treated on an outpatient basis, but hospitalization might be necessary if patients become suicidal or if medical complications arise. There are no treatment studies involving adolescents with BN, but preliminary literature has been published on adapting family treatment typically used for AN to adolescents with BN.[42] In addition, there are some preliminary studies examining a modified version of CBT for adolescent patients with BN so that it is appropriate for their developmental level.[43–45]

The most effective treatments for BED are similar to those effective for BN. CBT and IPT have been modified for BED and have been found to be effective.[46] CBT generally has the most evidence to support its use, and CBT-based self-help manuals may be even more effective in those suffering from BED compared to those with BN.[38] IPT is also recommended as an alternate treatment for BED.[25] Another type of psychotherapy called dialectical behavior therapy (DBT) modified for BED has been shown to be effective as well.[47] It teaches patients a variety of skills focusing on mindful meditation, distress tolerance, and emotion regulation. Although there are no large studies of these therapies involving children and adolescents, guidelines suggest that these psychotherapies should be offered to this population.

In terms of medication for BED, three major classes have been studied: antidepressants, antiobesity drugs, and anticonvulsant drugs. The antidepressants, including the selective serotonin reuptake inhibitors (SSRIs) such as fluoxetine, have been shown to be effective in reducing binge eating in patients with BED.[48] Several randomized controlled trials (RCTs) have confirmed the efficacy of several different SSRIs in this regard. The drug sibutramine demonstrated reduction of binge frequency and weight loss in obese patients with BED in an RCT, and the anticonvulsant topiramate produced similar results, also in rigorous clinical trials. Although all of these drugs appear to be effective in treating BED, the SSRIs are easy to administer and have fewer side effects than the other drugs, making them the first-line treatment in terms of medication for BED. These medications have not been studied in children and adolescents with BED, and trials are needed.

WHAT ARE THE COSTS OF EATING DISORDERS TO INDIVIDUALS, FAMILIES, AND SOCIETY?

The comprehensive costs of eating disorders to individuals, families, and society are difficult to summarize as costs are not just captured by the monetary cost of treatment, but also encompass the years of productive life lost and the burden of illness to individuals and their families. In terms of treatment costs, AN is just as costly or even more costly when compared with schizophrenia. This is largely attributable to the use of hospitalization. In terms of societal burden, there is the cost to the health care system of hospitalization, along with medical and psychiatric care. There is also the loss of productive years of life when patients are too ill to work or study and from the elevated rates of premature death. With the advent of managed care in the United States and the lack of empirically supported treatments for AN, treatment coverage has become difficult.[49] This increases the financial and emotional burden on families already struggling to manage.

In addition to the medical and psychiatric morbidity that individuals with eating disorders face, there are social and vocational consequences as well for those chronically affected by eating disorders.[50] Social isolation, with dependent relationships on family members, are common in these chronic illnesses, as are limited friendships, decreased probability of marriage, and problems with sexual fulfillment. The isolation produced by eating disorders, particularly AN, in the critical developmental stages of adolescence can result in delays in development of social skills, identity formation, and autonomy. In terms of long-term outcome, many former eating-disordered patients do not reach vocational expectations given their abilities and background. Although there has been limited research on quality of life in eating disorders, it is likely to be reduced in many areas in those suffering from chronic eating disorders.

In terms of the burden of illness on family members, it is great. Very few normal family functions remain after living with an eating-disordered person for a year or more.[51] Mealtimes often become a battleground filled with tension and conflict. Usual family routines and roles become disrupted, and individual roles within the family are disorganized. Siblings are also affected, and are often confused, distressed, and resentful of the attention devoted to their ill brother or sister. The family's social life often stops, as parents are filled with shame and guilt about their potential role in causing the illness. Parents may feel completely isolated and alone, and may delay treatment due to their shame of having a child suffering from a mental illness and their imagined role in causing it. More research needs to be done on how to help families in seeking treatment earlier in the course of these illnesses and in supporting them once treatment is initiated.

WHERE IS RESEARCH ON EATING DISORDERS HEADED?

Much more research is needed in the field of eating disorders. We currently know little about the causes of eating disorders. Longitudinal studies might aid in answering these questions, however they are expensive to carry out and likely will not change the evolution of these disorders as many risk factors are not modifiable. Much of the research currently being done with patients with eating disorders is focusing on possible genetic links by studying families with two or more patients with eating disorders. It is hoped that common genes can be found. In addition, imaging studies looking at the structure and function of the brains of ill and recovered patients is providing new information about the neurochemistry involved in eating disorders. Although these studies are important, as with research on risk factors, genetic and biological factors are likely to be nonspecific and not modifiable. Studies trying to prevent eating disorders may not be the most helpful either, as we cannot predict who might develop an eating disorder, and we do not yet know enough about how to prevent eating disorders.

Studies focusing on those already ill within the early stages of the illness in adolescence appear most promising. When the illness becomes more chronic in adulthood, treatment compliance is even more problematic and prognosis is poor. Our best chance of intervention appears to be in adolescence when the illness is developing and parents can have more of an impact in getting their child help. In addition, studies targeting adolescents with eating disorders are most needed because early intervention is thought to be important in modifying the course of the illness and improving prognosis. Currently, studies on adolescent patients with eating disorders are scarce. More clinical trials studying medications and psychotherapy would be most helpful in determining effective treatments for AN, BN, and BED. These studies all cost money to complete, and in order for researchers to carry them out, the government must be willing to provide funding for eating disorders research. Public pressure on government can make a difference. Often patients themselves, or family members of patients, are critical in persuading government agencies to fund research on eating disorders.

REFERENCES

1. Tauber, M. (2004, June 29). Mary-Kate's Private Battle. *People, 61,* 54–58.
2. American Psychiatric Association. (2000). *Diagnostic and statistical manual of mental disorders* (4th ed., text rev.). Washington, DC: Author.
3. Rome, E. S., & Ammerman, S. (2003). Medical complications of eating disorders: An update. *Journal of Adolescent Health, 33,* 418–426.

4. American Psychiatric Association Work Group on Eating Disorders. (2000). Practice guideline for the treatment of patients with eating disorders (revision). *American Journal of Psychiatry, 157,* 1–39.

5. Steinhausen, H. C. (2002). The outcome of anorexia nervosa in the 20th century. *American Journal of Psychiatry, 159,* 1284–1293.

6. Gull, W. (1874). Anorexia nervosa (apepsia hysterica, anorexia hysterica). *Transactions of the Clinical Society of London, 7,* 222–228.

7. Lasegue, E. (1883). De l'anorexie hysterique. *Archives Generales De Medecine, 21,* 384–403.

8. Russell, G. (1979). Bulimia nervosa: an ominous variant of anorexia nervosa. *Psycholigcal Medicine, 9,* 429–448.

9. Silverman, J. (1997). Anorexia nervosa: Historical perspective on treatment. In D. M. Garner and P. E. Garfinkel (Eds.), *Handbook of Treatment for Eating Disorders* (pp. 3–10). New York: Guilford.

10. Bell, R. M. (1985). *Holy Anorexia* Chicago: University of Chicago Press.

11. Lee, S., Ho, T. P., & Hsu, L. K. (1993). Fat phobic and non-fat phobic anorexia nervosa: A comparative study of 70 Chinese patients in Hong Kong. *Psychological Medicine, 23,* 999–1017.

12. Keel, P. K., & Klump, K. L. (2003). Are eating disorders culture-bound syndromes? Implications for conceptualizing their etiology. *Psychological Bulletin, 129,* 747–769.

13. Russell, G. (1997). The history of bulimia nervosa. In D. M. Garner & P. E. Garfinkel (Eds.), *Handbook of Treatment for Eating Disorders* (pp. 11–24). New York: Guilford.

14. American Psychiatric Association. (1980). *Diagnostic and statistical manual of mental disorders* (3rd ed.). Washington, DC: Author.

15. American Psychiatric Association. (1987). *Diagnostic and statistical manual of mental disorders* (3rd ed., rev.). Washington, DC: Author.

16. Hoek, H. W., & van Hoeken, D. (2003). Review of the prevalence and incidence of eating disorders. *International Journal of Eating Disorders, 34,* 383–396.

17. Pope, H. G., Jr., Olivardia, R., Gruber, A., & Borowiecki, J. (1999). Evolving ideals of male body image as seen through action toys. *International Journal of Eating Disorders, 26,* 65–72.

18. Anderson, A. (1990). Diagnosis and treatment of males with eating disorders. In A. Anderson (Ed.), *Males with eating disorders* (pp. 133–162). New York: Brunner/Mazel.

19. Andersen, A. E., & Holman, J. E. (1997). Males with eating disorders: Challenges for treatment and research. *Psychopharmacology Bulletin, 33,* 391–397.

20. Robb, A., & Dadson, M. (2002). Eating disorders in males. *Child and Adolescent Psychiatric Clinics of North America, 11,* 399–418.

21. Braun, D. L., Sunday, S. R., Huang, A., & Halmi, K. A. (1999). More males seek treatment for eating disorders. *International Journal of Eating Disorders, 25,* 415–424.

22. Jacobi, C., Hayward, C., de Zwaan, M., Kraemer, H. C., & Agras, W. S. (2004). Coming to terms with risk factors for eating disorders: application of risk terminology and suggestions for a general taxonomy. *Psychological Bulletin, 130,* 19–65.

23. Becker, A. E., Burwell, R. A., Gilman, S. E., Herzog, D. B., & Hamburg, P. (2002). Eating behaviours and attitudes following prolonged exposure to television among ethnic Fijian adolescent girls. *British Journal of Psychiatry, 180,* 509–514.

24. Keys, A., Brozek, J., Henschel, A., Mickelsen, O., & Taylor, H. (1950). *The biology of human starvation.* Minneapolis, MN: University of Minnesota Press.

25. National Collaborating Centre for Mental Health. (2004). *National Institute for Clinical Excellence Guidelines.* London, Author.

26. Halmi, K. A., Agras, S., Crow, S., Mitchell, J., Wilson, T., Bryson, S. W., et al. (2005). Predictors of treatment acceptance and completion in anorexia nervosa: Implications for future study designs. *Archives of General Psychiatry, 62,* 776–781.

27. Dare, C., Eisler, I., Russell, G., Treasure, J., & Dodge, L. (2001). Psychological therapies for adults with anorexia nervosa: Randomised controlled trial of outpatient treatments. *British Journal of Psychiatry, 178,* 216–221.

28. Franko, D. L., Blais, M. A., Becker, A. E., Delinsky, S. S., Greenwood, D. N., Flores, A. T., et al. (2001). Pregnancy complications and neonatal outcomes in women with eating disorders. *American Journal of Psychiatry, 158,* 1461–1466.

29. Pike, K. M., Walsh, B. T., Vitousek, K., Wilson, G. T., & Bauer, J. (2003). Cognitive behavior therapy in the posthospitalization treatment of anorexia nervosa. *American Journal of Psychiatry, 160,* 2046–2049.

30. Russell, G. F., Szmukler, G. I., Dare, C., & Eisler, I. (1987). An evaluation of family therapy in anorexia nervosa and bulimia nervosa. *Archives of General Psychiatry, 44,* 1047–1056.

31. Eisler, I., Dare, C., Russell, G.F.M., Szmukler, G., le Grange, D., & Dodge, E. (1997). Family and individual therapy in anorexia nervosa. A 5-year follow-up. *Archives of General Psychiatry, 54,* 1025–1030.

32. Lock, J., le Grange, D., Agras, S., & Dare, C. (2001). *Treatment manual for anorexia nervosa: A family-based approach.* New York: Guilford.

33. Robin, A. L., Siegel, P. T., Moye, A. W., Gilroy, M., Dennis, A. B., & Sikand, A. (1999). A controlled comparison of family versus individual therapy for adolescents with anorexia nervosa. *Journal of the American Academy of Child and Adolescent Psychiatry, 38,* 1482–1489.

34. Lock, J., Agras, W. S., Bryson, S., & Kraemer, H. C. (2005). A comparison of short- and long-term family therapy for adolescent anorexia nervosa. *Journal of the American Academy of Child and Adolescent Psychiatry, 44,* 632–639.

35. Kaye, W. H., Nagata, T., Weltzin, T. E., Hsu, L. K., Sokol, M. S., McConaha, C., et al. (2001). Double-blind placebo-controlled administration of fluoxetine in restricting- and restricting-purging-type anorexia nervosa. *Biological Psychiatry, 49,* 644–652.

36. Fairburn, C. G., Marcus, M. D., & Wilson, G. T. (1993). Cognitive behavior therapy for binge eating and bulimia nervosa: A comprehensive treatment manual.

In C. G. Fairburn & G. T. Wilson (Eds.), *Binge eating: Nature, assessment, and treatment* (pp. 361–404). New York: Guilford.

37. Agras, W. S., Walsh, T., Fairburn, C. G., Wilson, G. T., & Kraemer, H. C. (2000). A multicenter comparison of cognitive-behavioral therapy and interpersonal psychotherapy for bulimia nervosa. *Archives of General Psychiatry, 57*, 459–466.

38. Hay, P. J., Bacaltchuk, J. & Stefano, S. (2004). Psychotherapy for bulimia nervosa and binging. *Cochrane Database Syst Rev,* CD000562 (2004).

39. Walsh, B. T., & Klein, D. A. (2003). Eating disorders. *International Review of Psychiatry, 15*, 205–216.

40. Zhu, A. J., & Walsh, B. T. (2002). Pharmacologic treatment of eating disorders. *Canadian Journal of Psychiatry, 47*, 227–234.

41. Fluoxetine in the treatment of bulimia nervosa. A multicenter, placebo-controlled, double-blind trial. Fluoxetine Bulimia Nervosa Collaborative Study Group. (1992). *Archives of General Psychiatry, 49*, 139–147.

42. le Grange, D., Lock, J., & Dymek, M. (2003). Family-based therapy for adolescents with bulimia nervosa. *American Journal of Psychotherapy, 57*, 237–251.

43. Schapman, A., Lock, J., & Couturier, J. (in press). Cognitive-behavioral therapy for adolescents with bulimia: A case series. *International Journal of Eating Disorders.*

44. Lock, J. (2002). Treating adolescents with eating disorders in the family context. Empirical and theoretical considerations. *Child and Adolescent Psychiatric Clinics of North America, 11*, 331–342.

45. Lock, J. (in press). Adjusting CBT for adolescent bulimia nervosa: A report of a case series. *American Journal of Psychotherapy.*

46. Agras, W. S., Telch, C. F., Arnow, B., Eldredge, K., Detzer, M. J., Henderson, J., et al. (1995). Does interpersonal therapy help patients with binge eating disorder who fail to respond to cognitive-behavioral therapy? *Journal of Consulting and Clinical Psychology, 63*, 356–360.

47. Telch, C. F., Agras, W. S., & Linehan, M. M. (2001). Dialectical behavior therapy for binge eating disorder. *Journal of Consulting and Clinical Psychology, 69*, 1061–1065.

48. Carter, W. P., Hudson, J. I., Lalonde, J. K., Pindyck, L., McElroy, S. L., Pope, H. G., et al. (2003). Pharmacologic treatment of binge eating disorder. *International Journal of Eating Disorders, 34*(Suppl. S), 74–88.

49. Striegel-Moore, R. H., Leslie, D., Petrill, S. A., Garvin, V., & Rosenheck, R. A. (2000). One-year use and cost of inpatient and outpatient services among female and male patients with an eating disorder: Evidence from a national database of health insurance claims. *International Journal of Eating Disorders, 27*, 381–389.

50. Lock, J. (2003). A health service perspective on Anorexia Nervosa. *Eating Disorders, 11*, 197–207.

51. Nielsen, S., & Bara-Carril, N. (2003). Family burden of care and social consequences. In J. Treasure, U. Schmidt, & E. van Furth (Eds.), *Handbook of Eating Disorders* (pp. 75–90). West Sussex, UK: John Wiley & Sons, Ltd.

Chapter 7

Body Dysmorphic Disorder: When Does Concern about Appearance Become Pathological?

Shauna L. Shapiro and Angela Gavin

To varying degrees, most people spend time attending to their appearance. Many are concerned with their level of physical attractiveness. However, for some, this normal concern turns into an extreme fixation and causes tremendous suffering. Body dysmorphic disorder (BDD) is a mental disorder defined as a preoccupation with a perceived defect in one's appearance.[1] The concern over one's perceived defect is markedly excessive, and this preoccupation causes significant distress or impairment in one's functioning.[2] An Italian doctor, Morselli,[2] first coined the term dysmorphophobia in 1886 from *dysmorph*, a Greek word meaning misshapen. It was introduced at this time to describe a pathological concern for one's appearance, and subsequently renamed BDD in 1987 by the American Psychiatric Association classification.[3]

This diagnosis can be traced back to Freud who referred to one of his patients with the classic symptoms of BDD as "wolf man" (p. 67).[4] Freud's patient believed his nose was ugly and avoided all public life and work. Recently, people have referred to BDD as "the distress of imagined ugliness" (p. 688).[6] This label is particularly upsetting to the patient who is genuinely concerned with his/her appearance. The level of shame that accompanies this disorder can be significant, and many overlook the poignant symptoms associated with BDD. This leads to severe under diagnosis of BDD in most clinical settings.[7]

DIAGNOSIS

The *Diagnostic and Statistical Manual of Mental Disorders*, Fourth Edition, Text Revision *(DSM–IV–TR)*[8] classifies BDD as a somatoform disorder. There are two main diagnostic criteria that need to be met in order to receive the diagnosis of BDD. The first is a preoccupation with an imagined defect in appearance. Even when a slight physical anomaly is present, the person's concern is markedly excessive. The second criterion is that the person's preoccupation causes clinically significant distress or impairment in social, occupational, or other important areas of functioning.[8]

To a certain degree, many people, at one time or another, have worried about some aspect of their appearance. For the person with BDD, any external representation of their physical appearance can trigger their obsession and BDD related behaviors and thoughts. Their internal representation of themselves is full of negative cognitions, and this perpetuates the dysmorphic anxiety.[9]

To obtain a diagnosis of BDD, it is assumed that the preoccupation, in one way or another, handicaps their social, school, or occupational life. There are varying degrees of how this disorder can handicap a person. Some may be aware that their perception is skewed, whereas others are firmly convinced a defect exists and can become delusional. Although the degree of insight varies, the skewed perceptions lead to significant negative consequences for persons with BDD.

It is common for someone with BDD to be unemployed, single, or separated. People with BDD are extremely preoccupied with their perceived flaw and find it difficult to control their preoccupation, often feeling self-conscious in the presence of others. A person with BDD frequently believes they are unworthy, undesirable, and unlovable, which leads to further isolation. They often avoid a variety of social and public situations because they are so uncomfortable with themselves, or if they do attend these events, they are accompanied by feelings of anxiety and self-doubt.

Further, the isolation and hopelessness that stem from this disorder often leads to significant depression and even suicide. Arthur and Monnell[10] report that 29 percent of BDD sufferers attempt suicide. The significant number of harmful consequences, including even suicide and death, signals the need for a thorough assessment procedure to diagnosis and treat BDD.

Anthony was a 24-year-old biology graduate student. He had been concerned about his appearance since his freshman year in high school. His greatest concern was his nose. He believed the small bump on his nose caused him to look ugly and disformed. By his senior year, he convinced his parents to give him the money for rhinoplasty. However, after the surgery, he was still dissatisfied with his nose. He stopped going out with his friends and had difficlty looking people directly in the eyes. Although he continued to be successful in his academic study, his social life dwindled until his only social contact was a weekly dinner with his mother.

ASSESSMENT

Often persons with BDD have felt their concerns are discounted and overlooked. There are several important questions to ask a person when determining if he or she has BDD. An assessment includes an investigation of several different aspects of a person's life. Phillips[11] presents several questions to help diagnose BDD, including the following:

> Are you worried about your appearance in any way? What is your concern? Does this concern preoccupy you? Do you think about it a lot and wish you could worry about it less? If you add up all the time you spend thinking about your appearance each day, how much tome do you think it would be? What effect has this preoccupation with your appearance had on your life? Has it interfered with your job, schoolwork, your relationships or social life, other activities or other aspects of your life? Have your appearance concerns caused you a lot of distress? Have your appearance concerns affected your family and friends? (p. 945)

These questions can be a helpful guide to facilitating both understanding and diagnosis. A thorough assessment is essential and provides a frame of reference when interacting with a person who may have BDD. In addition to asking questions, it is important to observe behavioral clues such as exhibited anxiety or depression, social isolation, self-consciousness, and delusional thoughts. These are all significant features to consider when trying to determine if a person has BDD.

In addition, three measurements have been developed to help with assessment of BDD. These include the Body Dysmorphic Questionnaire, the Body Dysmorphic Disorder Examination, and the Yale-Brown Obsessive-Compulsive Scale Modified for BDD (BDD-YBOCS).[9] All three measures are self-report instruments typically used for research purposes. However, Sarwer[9] suggests that they might be useful in a clinical setting to guide therapy and treatment. With the rise of persons with BDD, health professionals could clearly benefit from having a reliable and valid clinical assessment tool. Thorough assessment and diagnosis will help facilitate the recovery process.

SYMPTOMS

People with BDD commonly engage in a variety of behaviors that have become symptomatic of this disorder. Some camouflage themselves to hide their perceived defect. This may involve wearing heavy makeup, brushing their hair a certain way, growing a beard, changing their posture, or wearing certain clothes and accessories that conceal any perceived flaws. Behaviors include checking one's appearance either directly or in reflective surface, often referred to as mirror-gazing. Another tendency of persons with BDD is to engage in excessive grooming by removing, cutting, or combing their hair.

Also, it is common for some to pick at their skin to make it smooth or to remove any perceived ugliness. They often compare themselves to models in magazines or television. Some behaviors involve dieting, excessive exercise, and/or weight lifting. In addition, people with BDD often spend excessive amounts of time alone, unwilling to allow others to see their perceived defects. In fact, some persons with BDD become housebound.[11]

BDD and its associated symptoms and behaviors can arise gradually or can involve an abrupt onset of symptoms. Regardless of how quickly the symptoms manifest themselves in the patient's life, it is important to be aware of the range of severity. BDD patients display an extended continuum of symptoms. Some are able to maintain relationships, a job, and a social life, while others fall on the opposite end of the spectrum and are completely incapacitated.[9] No matter the level of severity, it is always crucial to assess for suicidal ideation and to never underestimate the seriousness of BDD.

Jannette is a 21-year-old college student. She spends two hours each morning preparing to go to class. Her routine involves an extensive facial and makeup application to cover the pores of her skin which she believes are excessively large and make her very ugly. In her bathroom are over 50 recent glamour magazines, with photos of beautiful flawless models. She points to their skin, noting that you cannot see any pores, and that the color is even and beautiful. She sighs, "Why is my skin so horrible. . . ." When it is explained that these photos have been airbrushed and these people do not look this flawless in real life, she sighs again and says, "I wish I could airbrush my face before going out in public."

COMMON CONCERNS

There are several common complaints that emerge regarding the imagined or slight flaws that accompany BDD. The three areas that receive a majority of the complaints are the skin, hair, and nose.[10] Veale[1] asserts the most common area of obsession involves some aspect of the face and/or head. It is common that many of the obsessions concern features of the face or head, such as thinning hair, acne, wrinkles, scars, vascular markings, paleness, redness of the complexion, swelling, facial asymmetry, or the lack of or excessive facial hair. Other common preoccupations include the shape, size, or some other aspect of the nose, eyes, eyelids, eyebrows, ears, mouth, lips, teeth, jaw, chin, cheeks, or head. Any body part can be an area of concern, such as the breasts, hips, genitals, buttocks, arms, hands, feet, legs, hips, shoulders, spine, or abdomen. Someone with BDD can also obsess over his or her overall body size, body build, or muscularity. This preoccupation can involve a single body part or several body parts. Sometimes their complaint can be vague, such as "saggy eyes," or it can be specific, such as "excessive facial hair."

What transpires is a discrepancy between what they see in the mirror and what an objective observer sees. If they become delusional, they hold a false belief about their appearance despite contradictory evidence. Nearly half of all BDD patients suffer from appearance beliefs that are delusional.[13] Delusional patients can receive both the diagnoses of BDD and delusional disorder.[14] What they view in the mirror, over time, is a construct of these fabricated thoughts and beliefs about their appearance, not the actual reflection. The image they perceive affects their mood, behaviors, and serves to perpetuate the obsessive-compulsive tendencies.

Sarah was a 31-year-old mother of two. She was concerned that her body was covered in cellulite, and that no matter how much she exercised and dieted, it would not go away. She spent significant amounts of money on creams and invested three hours each day to specific toning exercises to reduce her cellulite. She no longer wore shorts or skirts in an attempt to cover her body, and refused to go swimming because she did not want her body exposed. She thought about her cellulite constantly and found it was difficult to concentrate on her children or her husband. She spent the majority of her time online exploring the various new treatments for cellulite. She shared that she woke up each morning and went directly into the bathroom to look in the mirror at her cellulite. She secretly hoped it would be gone each morning, and when she saw it there, she felt the weight of depression envelop her.

PREVALENCE

There has been some controversy regarding how prevalent BDD is in the United States, as no controlled studies have been conducted. It is estimated that 1–2 percent of the U.S. population may suffer from BDD,[6,10,15] and that 6–15 percent of dermatologic and cosmetic surgery patients are afflicted with this disorder.[5,7] An important direction for future research is to accurately assess the pervasiveness of this disorder because it often goes misdiagnosed as obsessive-compulsive disorder (OCD), depression, or other psychological disorders. It is thought to be underdiagnosed because it is a relatively new disorder in the bible of psychological disorders, the *DSM*, and because people are often reluctant to reveal their concern due to deep feelings of embarrassment or shame.[11]

There is also conflicting information regarding the prevalence of BDD in both males and females. Clinical samples exhibit a fairly even distribution among the sexes,[6] however some researchers argue that BDD is more prevalent in females. No empirical studies have confirmed this. However, there have been noticeable differences in the type of preoccupations that males and females report. Women are more likely to become preoccupied with their breasts, hips, legs, and body size, whereas men report being more concerned with their genitals, height, body hair, and body build.[5]

BDD is so often under or misdiagnosed that it is difficult to assert a common age for its onset. Veale[1] points out that it is common for BDD to go undiagnosed for 10 to 15 years. Even years after the onset of this disorder, it appears that many patients are able to recall an event that triggered their concern with their appearance. Their concerns proceeded to develop into hyper-vigilance around their perceived flaw. Some reports indicate that BDD commonly arises in adolescence or the early twenties; a time when looks are emphasized and people are the most sensitive to appearance-related remarks.[6,9,12,16]

DUAL DIAGNOSIS

Persons with BDD have often have more than one psychological disorder. Due to this frequent comorbidity, psychiatric settings often overlook the diagnosis of BDD and focus on the other psychological disorder.[10] Major depressive disorder (MDD) is the most common disorder associated with BDD. Between 54 percent and 69 percent of patients have a diagnosis of MDD in addition to BDD.[9] However, it is important to note that typically dysmorphic thoughts predate a person's depressed mood, and BDD typically precedes MDD.[9] Therefore, it is important to focus on BDD as its own disorder in need of treatment, instead of focusing only on treating the depression which is often done.

Social phobia is another common condition associated with BDD. Sarwer[9] reports that approximately one-third of BDD patients have been diagnosed with social phobia, defined as a fear of being in social situations. People with BDD have developed an extremely negative view of themselves, which exacerbates their feelings of anxiety and fear of social situations.

Another common comorbid disorder is OCD, which involves disturbing thoughts, images, or impulses (obsessions) that occur over and over again and are often followed by compulsive behavior to alleviate the obsessions. Between 30 percent and 78 percent of persons with BDD are also given a lifetime diagnosis of OCD.[9] Many similarities exist between the two diagnoses. Commonly, BDD is referred to as an OCD-spectrum disorder because of their overlap.[13,17,18,19,20] In both disorders, persons experience obsessive thoughts and images that are out of their control. The person does not want to have these ideas and finds them disturbing and intrusive. These obsessions skew the way the person sees themselves and the world. It becomes difficult to distinguish what is reality and what is delusional thinking, leaving the patient lost in a sea of confusion and isolation. Both disorders lead to negative consequences, such as harmful behaviors, social isolation, and impairment of work and relationships.

In addition, patients with OCD and BDD present many similarities in age, sex, employment status, areas of impairment, and comorbid disorders. Studies of the brain suggest the dysfunction in the frontal-striatal system found in BDD is also found in OCD.[11] A study by Hanes[21] discovered a similar impairment in the executive functioning of BDD and OCD. Symptoms are also similar, such that patients with OCD and BDD report similarities in their pattern of compulsive behaviors, such as mirror-checking and camouflaging.[22] Despite their comparable features, significant differences clarify the need for separate diagnoses and treatment. Many people who are diagnosed with OCD engage in certain behaviors in order to relieve their anxiety. This is in contrast to a person with BDD who experiences an increase in anxiety when engaging in various rituals. Phillips, Gunderson, Mallya, McElroy, and Carter[23] conducted a BDD-OCD comparison study which revealed numerous differences. Persons with BDD were more likely to have suicidal ideation, to have attempted suicide, and also to be unemployed. They were also less likely to be married.[22] Further, patients diagnosed with BDD reported higher rates of depression, social phobias, and psychotic symptoms. People with BDD had more delusions of reference and poorer insight. Overall, the quality of life of someone with BDD may be worse than someone with OCD. It appears that BDD is not a scientific alternative of OCD.

Although BDD clearly has relationships with other disorders such as social phobia, depression, and OCD, its increasing prevalence demonstrates the necessity for a separate diagnosis.[22] These obvious distinctions are important to mention to reduce the large number of misdiagnoses. Therefore, it is important that we understand BDD in relation to other disorders. Assessing for dual diagnosis informs professionals of the severity of the disorder and how it interferes with general functioning. If it is needed, dual diagnosis can assist the therapeutic process and guide treatment interventions.

ETIOLOGY

There have been multiple factors associated with the etiology of BDD. Unfortunately, the results are inconclusive because there has been limited research conducted on BDD.[1,17] The specific etiology of BDD remains unknown.[9] It is apparent there is more than one single cause for this disorder. Biology, genetic predisposition, psychological factors, and sociocultural experiences all impact the etiology of this specific disorder.

Veale[1] highlights specific risk factors including: a genetic predisposition; a shy, anxious temperament; people who struggle with perfectionism; childhood adversity, such as teasing or bullying; a history of dermatological or other physical stigmata as an adolescent; and being more aesthetically sensitive. Clearly, our environment and the culture we live in affect our thoughts, behaviors, and frames of reference. We are currently living in a culture obsessed with appearance and physical attractiveness. Turning on the television and picking up a magazine sends us a clear message that physical attractiveness is highly valued. Our cultural standards are constantly becoming more and more difficult and impossible to attain. This leads to unrealistic expectations and significant anxiety derived from trying to meet the current beauty ideal.

Biby[17] suggests that comparison targets are a common source of body dissatisfaction. People compare themselves to airbrushed models and celebrities, and this unrealistic quest sets people up for body image disturbances. It is not surprising that researchers declare the prevalence of this disorder to be increasing as our society places a greater emphasis on appearance. These cultural norms which focus on the value of external appearance and qualities can lead people to have a distorted view of what is important and what leads to happiness.

People begin to link their self-worth and self-esteem to their appearance and become unaware of more intrinsic and internal qualities that are valuable. They begin to equate attractiveness with happiness, status, and attention. This preoccupation with appearance is culturally supported and can develop into obsession and even a mental disorder such as BDD. The media projects specific norms related to appearance about which people strive to attain. Individuals compare themselves to unrealistic standards and perceived norms. People strive to reach unattainable appearance-related goals.

One's previous life experiences can also trigger the onset of BDD. Slaughter and Sun[24] list low self-esteem, critical parents and significant others, early childhood trauma, and unconscious displacement of emotional conflict as predisposing factors for BDD. Another predictor is being teased about appearance or bullied.[17] Family characteristics have also been suggested in the etiology of BDD. For example, those who had unpleasant childhood experiences or dissonant family backgrounds are at greater risk for developing BDD. Also, those who have been physically or sexually assaulted or abused have a greater risk for developing BDD. Such a difficult experience can trigger a person to question his or her self-worth and physical appearance and develop low levels of self-esteem and self-acceptance.[11]

Other factors that may predispose someone to developing BDD are having poor social support and peer relationships, as well as being socially isolated.

In addition, a person's temperaments can predispose him or her to developing BDD. Veale[1] has observed specific temperaments in BDD sufferers: shy, anxious, and perfectionistic. A person who has a tendency towards perfectionism may strive to attain impossible ideals regarding his or her appearance. They place excessive demands on themselves to achieve a certain ideal of perfectionism, and have a heightened perception to every imperfection that may exist. Their quest to be perfect may involve spending excessive time and attention on their appearance. A heightened sensitivity develops as a result of their obsessive nature. Buhlman, McNally, Wilhelm, and Florin[25] say BDD patients are already vulnerable towards being distracted by emotional cues. These perpetual behaviors and thoughts can lead to altered perceptions and ultimately to delusions.

Biology may also account for the development of BDD. Biby[15] suggests possible neurological defects in a person with BDD. Studies have found that there may be temporal lobe disturbance which contributes to a person's distorted thinking process.[17] The positive outcomes of selective serotonin reuptake inhibitors (SSRIs) treatment for persons with BDD leads researchers to speculate that the etiology of BDD could be related to poor regulation and depletion of serotonin. It is unclear whether or not altered levels of serotonin are an indicator or a consequence of the disorder.[24]

TREATMENT

Empirically validated treatment options are limited at this time due to few clinical studies. It is not uncommon for persons with BDD to first seek help from a dermatologist or plastic surgeon. In fact, Veale[1] indicates about 5–15 percent of people who receive cosmetic surgery have BDD. Veale[1] reports that in 82.6 percent of people who sought cosmetic surgery, the symptoms remained or worsened. Surgery is a poor treatment option since most patients with BDD turn to new complaints once the original perceived defect has been removed. Since the patient's perception of him or herself is already skewed, the results of any surgical procedure may range from dissatisfaction to aggression.[4] Fortunately, persons with BDD are not limited to surgical procedures to improve their quality of life.

The two main treatment options that have been researched and studied in BDD are the use of medication, specifically SSRIs, and cognitive-behavioral therapy (CBT). Indeed, treatment studies demonstrate a reduction in the distress and impairment associated with BDD after the use of SSRIs and CBT.[26] The Food and Drug Administration has not officially approved any medications for the treatment of BDD.[14] Yet, available data indicates that persons with

BDD respond best to SSRIs compared to other forms of medication, including non-SSRI antidepressants.[11,12,14]

In response to SSRIs, most patients report a decreased preoccupation with their perceived defect. They also experience a greater ability to control BDD related thoughts and behaviors, and an improvement in their mood, suicidal thinking, and general functioning.[14] Phillips and Rasmussen[27] discovered a remarkable improvement in BDD patients through a controlled study involving treatment with fluoxetine (an SSRI). There was a direct correlation between fluoxetine use and improvements in the overall functioning and quality of life of BDD patients. A mental health subscale revealed positive developments after a 12-week use of fluoxetine.

In addition, Slaughter and Sun[24] highlight the clinical efficacy of SSRIs for the treatment of persons with BDD. Results demonstrated a decreased preoccupation with the perceived flaw, a decrease in compulsive behaviors, improved insight, and improvements in overall functioning. Several studies have noted that higher doses of SSRIs are required for BDD than needed for depression, OCD, or eating disorders. Rather than discontinue the use of SSRIs, it is more effective to increase the dosage or try another type of SSRI medication.[5,14] A doctor must consider the patient's tolerability and preference when increasing the dose of any medication. Usually BDD patients respond within 6–16 weeks to a prescribed SSRI.[14] Phillips[11] recommends the patient use the maximum dose recommended if the previous dose was ineffective and the patient can tolerate the increase. If after 16 weeks there is no response to the SSRI, it is suggested that the medication be changed and another SSRI be given. A doctor should closely monitor a patient because the risk for relapse and suicide increase when switching a medication. Phillips[11] also recommends using the SSRI for a minimum of one year before discontinuing use to decrease the likelihood of relapse. Like many other medications, it is extremely important to slowly taper the patient off of SSRIs. The most important thing to do is to tailor the treatment to each individual patient since so little research has been done on treating BDD with medication.[14]

CBT is a structured form of psychotherapy that involves challenging maladaptive thoughts (cognitions) and increasing the recognition of a link between cognitions, emotions, and behaviors. A treatment plan usually includes techniques such as self-monitoring exposure, cognitive restructuring, and relapse prevention.[9] Self-monitoring involves tracking one's obsessive thoughts throughout the day and noting accompanying emotions and behaviors. Exposure involves exposing the patient to their feared thought or situation and helping them acknowledge, understand, and learn ways to cope with it. Behavioral interventions seek to lessen, and eventually eliminate, the compulsive behaviors of those with BDD by gradually exposing patients to anxiety-provoking situations that lead to BDD behaviors. Through these experiences, they learn to tolerate the discomfort. Cognitive restructuring is a technique which helps the person reframe (restructure) thoughts by viewing them in a different light and from a different perspective. Finally, relapse prevention includes identifying specific situations and potential triggers that might be associated with a setback. The patient then proactively thinks of ways to cope with these situations and thereby prevent, or at least reduce, the risk of relapse.

In summary, CBT helps people recognize their repetitive thoughts and unconscious behaviors and begin to confront their fears and anxieties. This increased awareness helps patients to witness their maladaptive thought patterns and incorporate more adaptive cognitions, which can lead to significant improvement. CBT proves to be effective in dealing with the irrational beliefs of those with BDD. This type of psychotherapy challenges their false beliefs and obsessive behaviors. Through therapy, the patient begins to expand his self-concept to include more dimensions than appearance. The behavioral interventions used in this form of psychotherapy target the tendency towards social isolation and anxiety.[24] Slaughter and Sun[24] report that CBT leads to increased comfort, relaxation, and joy, and more time socially interacting with others.

Rosen, Reiter, and Orosan[12] conducted a promising controlled study of CBT for persons with BDD. This study provided evidence that CBT is an effective method of treatment for BDD. Specific techniques used included modifying intrusive thoughts of body dissatisfaction, adjusting overvalued beliefs about physical appearance, exposure to avoided body image situations, and eliminating body checking. The treatment group demonstrated improvements in self-esteem, appearance preoccupations, and body dissatisfaction, as well as overall functioning. This controlled study demonstrated the value of using CBT to treat persons with BDD. Phillips[11] and Anderson and Black[5] argue that CBT should be used as a first-line approach for mild BDD and in combination with medication for severe BDD. The associated risks of this disorder, such as suicide, reinforce the need for frequent sessions and an intensive treatment program.[4,12]

An important factor to consider regarding treatment is that persons with BDD are often resistant and hesitant to enter treatment. They are often reluctant to share their thoughts and behaviors with others due to shame and embarrassment. Educating the patient with BDD about their disorder can help address their resistance. Many may believe they are alone in their suffering and that there is no escaping their present lifestyle. Normalizing the condition and educating them about the number of other people who experience similar symptoms is crucial. In addition, it is important to affirm the possibility of treatment and improved functioning. If it appears appropriate for the patient, his or her family and close friends might help facilitate the treatment process. Much is unknown about BDD and its effective treatment methods. A crucial direction for future research is to examine alternative treatments for BDD.

FUTURE DIRECTIONS: MINDFULNESS-BASED INTERVENTION FOR BDD

Current theories about the etiology and maintenance of BDD suggest that mindfulness training may be helpful for this problem. Mindfulness-based interventions are attracting increasing attention, and the recent empirical literature suggests that they may be effective for a variety of disorders.[28] Future research could benefit from exploring the potential applications of mindfulness to the treatment of BDD. Below we introduce mindfulness and put forth its possible benefit for the treatment of BDD.

Mindfulness meditation, although derived from a 2,500-year-old Buddhist practice, has been incorporated into Western medicine as a universally applicable and culture-free intervention. It was initially incorporated as the central component of the Mindfulness-Based Stress Reduction Program (MBSR) developed Kabat-Zinn and colleagues,[29] and has since expanded into numerous interventions, including dialectical therapy for borderline personality disorder,[30] mindfulness-based cognitive therapy for prevention of relapse of MDD,[31] and mindfulness-based eating awareness therapy (MB-EAT) for eating disorders.[32] Twenty years of research on mindfulness interventions has demonstrated its effectiveness across a wide range of clinical disorders, including stress, anxiety, and depression in both clinical and non-clinical populations.[33,34]

Further, research suggests that mindfulness is an effective intervention for prevention of relapse of MDD.[31] Evidence also suggests that MBSR may be an effective intervention for psoriasis,[35] chronic pain,[29,36] and fibromyalgia.[37] Finally, and most specifically related to BDD, mindfulness has been associated with improvements in anxiety-related disorders,[38] eating disorders,[32] and OCDs.[39]

Mindfulness is defined as nonjudgmental awareness of the present moment.[29] It is often conceived of as a skill[40] which can be developed through formal meditation practice. During mindfulness practice, participants learn to regulate their attention by focusing nonjudgmentally on stimuli, including bodily sensations, cognitions, and emotions. As the skill of mindfulness develops, participants are able to observe thoughts, emotions, and sensations "without evaluating their truth, importance, or value, and without trying to escape, avoid or change them."[41] Mindfulness is believed to increase self-awareness and self-acceptance, and to reduce emotional reactivity. The cultivation of greater awareness and clarity allows one to make conscious choices instead of automatically reacting to difficult and stressful situations. Numerous models[40,41] have been presented on the mechanisms and pathways through which mindfulness effects change.

Meditation is often simplistically and naively represented as a so-called relaxation technique; however, it is better understood as a means for promoting self-awareness and self-regulation. Mindfulness allows one to gain insight into affective, cognitive, and behavioral aspects of human functioning. In fact, mindfulness meditation is often referred to as insight meditation. The word mindfulness is translated as *to see with discernment* or to see clearly (pp. 19–20). This ability to see one's self and one's life with greater clarity seems to be of potential benefit in the treatment of BDD. For example, as discussed above, BDD is comprised of automatic negative thoughts and compulsive behaviors that arise do to a perceived defect. Typically, the person with BDD does not see reality clearly and is consumed with thoughts about the perceived flaw and emotions of worthlessness. These cognitions and emotions translate into a dysfunctional way of being in the world, which is limiting on many levels, and leads to numerous deleterious consequences. Through mindfulness intervention, inaccurate cognitions could be recognized and seen as thoughts and not absolute truths. Emotional states could be noted and observed as opposed to reacted to, and compulsive urges to behave in unhealthy ways could be identified instead of enacted.

It is interesting that mindfulness interventions have been successfully adapted for the treatment of OCD, anxiety disorders, and eating disorders, which are all highly related to BDD. It has been suggested that one of the underlying mechanisms of mindfulness is acceptance.[42] Clearly, one dimension of BDD involves a fundamental lack of acceptance of oneself. Mindfulness intervention serves the dual role of increasing one's awareness of maladaptive thoughts, feelings, and behaviors, as well as helping one to cultivate an acceptance for the way things are. This ability to see oneself clearly and accept all aspects is at the heart of mindfulness practice. For persons with BDD, this seems a valuable, if not essential tool. We suggest that future research could benefit greatly from exploring the applications of mindfulness-based interventions for the treatment and prevention of BDD.

CONCLUSION

BDD has become an increasingly prevalent disorder that results in significant deleterious consequences for persons who suffer from it. This disorder is an insidious one, as it falls along a continuum that is becoming more and more normal in American culture: an obsession with appearance. However, it is crucial that this disorder be rigorously explored and taken seriously by current psychological theory, research, and practice. Although research is beginning to examine symptomology, etiology, and treatment for BDD, this research is still in its infancy. Well-designed and controlled studies are needed to add to the growing body of literature. Further, creative and innovative interventions need to be developed. Finally, and most importantly, psychologists need to be aware of the prevalence of BDD and of its debilitating consequences if left untreated. Current abnormal psychology needs to draw the line in discerning when *concern about appearance becomes pathological.*

REFERENCES

1. Veale, D. (2004). Body dysmorphic disorder. *Postgraduate Medical Journal, 80,* 67–71.
2. Fava, G. A. (1992). Morselli's legacy: Dysmorphophobia. *Psychotherapy and Psychosomatics, 58,* 117–118.
3. American Psychiatric Association. (1987). *Diagnostic and statistical manual of mental disorders* (3rd ed., rev.). Washington, DC: Author.
4. Leavy, D. (2004). Body dismorphic disorder. *Postgraduate medicine, 50,* 67–71.
5. Anderson, R. C., & Black, J. (2003). Body dysmorphic disorder: Recognition and treatment. *Plastic Surgical Nursing, 23,* 125–130.
6. Patterson, W. M., Bienvenu, O. J., Chodynicki, M. P., Janniger, C. K., & Schwatrz, R. A. (2001). Body dysmorphic disorder. *International Journal of Dermatology, 40,* 688–691.
7. Wilson, J. B., & Arpey, C. J. (2004). Body dysmorphic disorder: Suggestions for detection and treatment in a surgical dermatology practice. *Dermatologic Surgery, 30,* 1391–1399.
8. American Psychiatric Association. (2000). *Diagnostic and statistical manual of mental disorders* (4th ed., text rev.). Washington, DC: Author.
9. Sarwer, D. B., Gibbons, L. M., & Creand, C. E. (2004). Treating body dysmorphic disorder with cognitive-behavioral therapy. *Psychiatric Annals, 34,* 934–941.
10. Arthur, G. K., & Monnell, K. (2004). *Body dysmorphic disorder.* Retrieved April 25, 2006 from http://www.emedicine.com/med/topics3124.htm
11. Phillips, K. A. (2000). Body dysmorphic disorder controversies and treatment challenges. *Bulletin of the Menninger Clinic, 64,* 18–36.
12. Rosen, J. C., Reiter, J., & Orosan, P. (1995). Cognitive-behavioral body image therapy for body dysmorphic disorder. *Journal of Consulting and Clinical Psychology, 63,* 263–269.
13. Phillips, K. A. (1998). Body dysmorphic disorder: Clinical aspects and treatment strategies. *Bulletin of the Menninger Clinic, 62,* 33–48.
14. Phillips, K. A. (2004). Treating body dysmorphic disorder using medication. *Psychiatric Annals, 34,* 945–953.

15. Cotterill, J. A. (1996). Body dysmorphic disorder. *Dermatologic Clinics, 14,* 457–463.

16. Marshall, C., Mandell, P., & Minkel, W. (2003). Body dysmorphic disorder. *School Library Journal, 49,* 63–72.

17. Biby, E. L. (1998). The relationship between body dysmorphic disorder and depression, self-esteem, somatization and obsessive-compulsive disorder. *Journal of Clinical Psychology, 54,* 489–500.

18. Hollander, E., Cohen, L. J., & Simeon, D. (1993). Body dysmorphic disorder. *Psychiatric Annals, 23,* 359–364.

19. Hollander, E., & Phillips, K. A. (1993). Body image and experience disorders: Body dysmorphic and depersonalization disorders. In E. Hollander (Ed.), *Obsessive compulsive-related disorders* (pp. 17–48). Washington, DC: American Psychiatric Press.

20. McElroy, S. L., Phillips, K. A., & Keck, P. E., Jr. (1994). Obsessive-compulsive spectrum disorder. *Journal of Clinical Psychiatry, 55*(Suppl.), 33–51.

21. Hanes, K. R. (1998). Neuropsychological performance in body dysmorphic disorder. *Journal of the International Neuropsychological Society, 4,* 167–171.

22. Frare, F., Perugi, G., Ruffolo, G., & Toni, C. (2004). Obsessive-compulsive disorder and body dysmorphic disorder: A comparison of clinical features. *European Psychiatry, 19,* 292–298.

23. Phillips, K. A., Gunderson, C. G., Mallya, G., McElroy, S. L, & Carter, W. (1998). A comparison study of body dysmorphic disorder and obsessive-compulsive disorder. *Journal of Clinical Psychiatry, 59,* 568–575.

24. Slaughter, J. R., & Sun, A. M. (1999). In pursuit of perfection: A primary care physician's guide to body dysmorphic disorder. *American Family Physician, 60,* 56–69.

25. Buhlman, U., McNally, R. J., Wilhelm, S., & Florin, I. (2002). Selective processing of emotional information in body dysmorphic disorder. *Journal of Anxiety Disorders, 16,* 289–298.

26. Jefferys, D. E., & Castle, D. J. (2003). Body dysmorphic disorder- a fear of imagined ugliness. *Austin Family Physician, 32,* 722–725.

27. Phillips, K. A., & Rasmussen, S. A. (2004). Change in psychosocial functioning and quality of life in patients with body dysmorphic disorder treated with Fluoxetine: A placebo-controlled study. *Psychosomatics, 45,* 438–444.

28. Baer, R. A. (2003). Mindfulness training as a clinical intervention: A conceptual and empirical review. *Clinical Psychology: Science and Practice, 10,* 125–143.

29. Kabat-Zinn, J. (1990). *Full catastrophe living.* New York: Delacorte Press.

30. Linehan, M. M. (1993). *Cognitive-behavioral treatment of borderline personality disorder.* New York: Guilford.

31. Teasdale, J. D., Segal, Z. V., Williams, J. M. G., Ridgeway, V. A., Sousby, J. M., & Lau, M. A. (2000). Prevention of relapse/recurrence in major depression by mindfulness-based cognitive therapy. *Journal of Consulting and Clinical Psychology, 69,* 615–623.

32. Kristeller, J. L., & Hallett, B. (1999). Effects of a meditation-based intervention in the treatment of binge eating. *Journal of Health Psychology, 4,* 357–363.

33. Miller, J. J., Fletcher, K., & Kabat-Zinn, J. (1995). Three-year follow-up and clinical implications of a mindfulness meditation-based stress reduction

intervention in the treatment of anxiety disorders. *General Hospital Psychiatry, 17*, 192–200.

34. Shapiro, S. L., Schwartz, G. E., & Bonner, G. (1998). Effects of mindfulness-based stress reduction on medical and premedical students. *Journal of Behavioral Medicine, 21*, 581–599.

35. Kabat-Zinn, J., Wheeler, E., & Light, T. (1998). Influence of a mindfulness meditation-based stress reduction intervention on rates of skin clearing in patients with moderate to severe psoriasis undergoing phototherapy (UVB) and photochemotherapy (PUVA). *Psychosomatic Medicine, 60*, 625–632.

36. Kabat-Zinn, J., Lipworth, L., & Burney, R. (1985). The clinical use of mindfulness meditation for the self-regulation of chronic pain. *Journal of Behavioral Medicine, 8*, 163–190.

37. Kaplan, K., Goldberg, D., & Galvin-Nadeau, M. (1993). The impact of a meditation-based stress reduction program on fibromyalgia. *General Hospital Psychiatry, 15*, 284–289.

38. Craske, M. G., & Hazlett, S. H. (2002). Facilitating symptom reduction and behavior change in GAD: The issue of control. *Clinical Psychology: Science and Practice, 9*, 69–75.

39. Singh, N., Wahler R., Winton, A., & Adkins A. (2004). A mindfulness-based treatment of obsessive-compulsive disorder. *Clinical Case Studies, 3*, 275–287.

40. Bishop, S. R., Lau, M., Shapiro, S., Carlson, L., Anderson, N. D., Carmody, J., et al. (2004). Mindfulness: A proposed operational definition. *Clinical Psychology: Science and Practice, 11*, 230–241.

41. Baer, R., Fischer, S., & Huss, D. (in press). Mindfulness-based cognitive therapy applied to binge eating: A case study. *Cognitive and Behavioral Practice.*

42. Austin, J. H. (1999). *Zen and the brain.* Cambridge, MA: The MIT Press.

43. Shapiro, S. L., & Astin, J. (2004). Meditation and transformation: The role of reperceiving. *Biofeedback, 32*, 37–40.

44. Hayes, A. M. & Feldman, G. (2004). Clarifying the construct of mindfulness in the context of emotion regulation and the process of change in therapy. *Clinical Psychology, Science, and Practice, 11*, 255–262.

Chapter 8

Munchausen by Proxy

Catherine C. Ayoub

"Well, Mrs. Gregory (mother) we've got good news. The Holter monitor shows no significant findings that lead us to believe that Julie has a heart condition requiring further tests. Nothing outside a normal parameter." The hospital doctor is following the zigzags on my chart, showing us what he can't find. Mom slaps her leg.

"What? What do you mean, you can't find anything?" She counts on her fingers the number of things leading up to this moment. "Dr. Kate called you, she told you this kid had a racing heart, was out of breath all the time. She told me we were going to get helped here, that we'd finally be able to get to the bottom of things. What are you trying to tell me here, that this kid is normal? That I'm making this up?

From Julie Gregory's autobiography *Sickened:*
The Memoir of a Munchausen by Proxy Childhood[1]

In 1977, Roy Meadows, a British pediatrician, coined the term Munchausen by Proxy (MBP) to describe illness-producing behavior in a child that is exaggerated, fabricated, or induced by a parent. Meadows adapted the term used by Dr. Asher in 1951 for adult Munchausen syndrome to describe use of the child as a proxy. Adult Munchausen syndrome is a psychiatric disorder in which an adult intentionally induces or feigns symptoms of physical or psychiatric illness in order to assume the sick role. Both conditions were named for the infamous 18th-century Baron Karl Friedrich Freiherr von Munchausen, a military mercenary who told fantastic stories of his exploits. Hence, the term Munchausen became known in the mid-20th century as a psychiatric condition that centrally involved deception, or what Marc Feldman[2] describes as "disorders of simulation."

In the last 15 years, a growing body of literature on MBP supports the assertion that it is a separate disorder from Munchausen syndrome, with specific characteristics, etiology, and prognosis. At the same time both MBP and Munchausen syndrome are members of this group of disorders that involve willful medical or emotional deception.

MBP is described as both a pediatric and a psychiatric disorder. These terms capture the interaction that leads to abuse of the child by a mentally ill parent perpetrator. The form of child abuse resulting from MBP is now called *abuse by pediatric illness or condition falsification*. The psychiatric diagnosis for the perpetrator is called *factitious disorder by proxy*.[3] As a consequence, work in the field focuses on the child's victimization as well as on the parent's psychiatric disorder; the literature includes perspectives from pediatrics, psychology, social work, psychiatry, education, law, and ethics. Many authors expand the discussion to include not only the interaction between the parent (usually mother) and the child, but also the relationships among the mother and the various health care providers. MBP is also characterized as a disorder involving family dysfunction and transgenerational effects, as well as powerful marital relationship dysfunction, all combining to perpetuate the abuse of the child.

The medical and psychological literature is now replete with articles and more than a dozen books dedicated to the topic. Major pediatric and child psychiatric texts contain descriptions of MBP. Definitional constructs have been synthesized by several groups in an effort to reach a multidisciplinary consensus in the field. The disorder has been widely recognized as a legitimate and quite dangerous form of child abuse in most juvenile and family courts around the country.[4]

DEFINITIONAL ISSUES IN MUNCHAUSEN BY PROXY

MBP is described as "the intentional production or feigning of physical or psychological signs or symptoms in another person who is under the individual's care for the purpose of indirectly assuming the sick role" (p. 475) in the *Diagnostic and Statistical Manual of Mental Disorders*, Fourth Edition *(DSM–IV)*.[5] However, a great deal has been written on the disorder since this limited description was provided in 1994. A clearer way to understand the nature of the child's victimization is to consider how illness is systematically exaggerated, fabricated, and/or induced by a parent or caregiver.

Children are victimized by a variety of means, limited only by the imagination of the perpetrator. They are often inappropriately placed in the sick role, and subjected to unnecessary hospitalizations, tests, procedures, and treatment for physical, psychological, or educational conditions (e.g., attention-deficit/hyperactivity disorder (AD/HD) and learning problems). The second component of MBP is the psychiatric condition of the perpetrator that helps explain the motivation, willfulness, and clinical presentation of the caregiver. Caregivers intentionally falsify history, signs, and/or symptoms in their children to meet their own self-serving psychological needs.

According to the current literature, between 77 percent and 98 percent of perpetrators are women; the vast majority of them are the child's biological mothers.[6] Some fathers have also been identified as perpetrators, as have other caregivers such as foster mothers. Another form of MBP involves adult victims, most often patients abused by their nurse caregivers. It remains a fact that factitious disorder by proxy is for the most part a disorder of women and a misuse of so-called mothering.

The prevalence of MBP continues to be debated and is a difficult issue to assess given the convincing deception that is the core of the disorder. There is likely underreporting of the problems and underestimation of its prevalence. One careful, conservative British study[7] estimated that the combined annual incidence of MBP in the form of nonaccidental poisoning and nonaccidental suffocation was at least 2.8/100,000 in children aged less than a year. However, given these estimates and the wide spectrum of pediatric conditions that have been known to be feigned in both young and older children, the problem is far from rare. Furthermore, experts now agree that many MBP cases are likely to go undetected because of the covert nature of their presentation, the striking ability of the perpetrators to fool those around them, and the many obstacles to the identification of these cases by professionals.

CHARACTERISTICS OF CHILD VICTIMS OF MUNCHAUSEN BY PROXY

In order to illustrate some of the salient characteristics of MBP, we present our current prospective study of 30 child victims and their families in which MBP was confirmed through court findings. Of the 30 children, 27 percent were infants, 33 percent were toddlers or preschoolers, 23 percent were elementary school age, and 17 percent were teenagers. This is consistent with the literature that finds that the majority of victims of MBP are less than six years of age, but also documents serious MBP with older children and adolescents. Boys and girls were equally affected, and over three-fourths of the children were Caucasian in our study; this as well is consistent with the findings of others.

The number of illness presentations of the children in our study was quite varied. Many children had multiple symptoms and multiple organ systems involved in their physical or emotional illnesses, and many were repeatedly subjected to serious and potentially life-threatening situations in the name of their illness and its treatment. While Mary Sheridan, in her meta-analysis of 451 cases of MBP, found that 6 percent of the child victims and 25 percent of their siblings died,[6] in our study, which included identified victims and their siblings, 17 percent of the children died, the majority as victims of suffocatory abuse or apnea.

Although the children presented with a wide variety of symptoms, some symptom groups predominated; these findings are consistent with others in the literature, but in no way encompass the vast number of illnesses that are feigned. Most children had multiple symptoms in at least three and as many as seven different organ systems. A typical medical history included many office visits, often to a variety of specialists, and a number of major and minor surgical procedures to relieve symptoms that were exaggerated, fabricated, or induced.

In 23 percent of the cases, children had gastrointestinal symptoms including vomiting, failure to thrive or grow, reflux, esophagitis, chronic secretory diarrhea, neurologic intestinal pseudo-obstruction, and chronic abdominal pain. Many of these children had had a number of procedures to assist their ability to maintain adequate nutrition, including feeding tubes in their stomachs (gastrostomy) and/or intestines (jejunostomy), and nutritional supplementation directly into their veins (TPN). Once children had direct lines into their blood streams, they often experienced an extraordinary number of infections of these lines—up to 300 to 400 times the expected rates for infection. Children with gastrointestinal problems were likely to have had complaints since the first year of life and tended to become more and more debilitated as time went on.

A second group of children (30%) were reported to have recurrent seizures. A third group of children experienced repeated episodes of apnea (20%). These children would reportedly stop breathing and often required resuscitation. Three children in this group died. This is consistent with the findings of a number of authors.[8,9] Another group of children (13%) experienced abnormal serum insulin levels, either as uncontrolled diabetes or as unexplained low blood sugar (hypoglycemia). Yet another group of children were diagnosed with rare autoimmune or genetic disorders (10%), while others had unexplained exacerbation of their asthma (10%), the most common of chronic childhood conditions. One child was poisoned, and two had blood or bleeding difficulties (7%). The final group of children had psychiatric or learning disabilities that were exaggerated, fabricated, or induced. Their problems included AD/HD, bipolar disorder, and psychosis (10%).

The child's medical care occurs in a context of a caregiving relationship in which the medical management of the child is posed as maternal care. Some of the perpetration occurs in forms difficult for a child to detect or understand as victimization, such as misadministration of medication or misrepresentation of medical history. A failure to detect or appreciate the perpetration prevents children from developing the more explicitly traumatized worldview of children victimized in more direct forms of maltreatment, but also has made it easier for them to misapprehend, deny, or compartmentalize their victimization. In the face of persistent fabrication, children risk potential serious physical injury due to exposure to unnecessary procedures, and almost universally suffer serious and long-lasting psychological trauma. Judith Libow[10] found that adult survivors frequently reported that abuse continued not only throughout childhood, but extended well into adulthood. Schreier and Libow[11] note that often children are at serious physical risk even while in state custody, since some parents may attempt to increase their harm to the child or attempt abduction as they are confronted.

MANAGEMENT OF ABUSE BY PEDIATRIC CONDITION FALSIFICATION

Safety is the first and primary management issue for the MBP child victim. This often means removal of the child from the home with no, or at most, closely supervised contact with the perpetrating parent. Placement with another family member may be appropriate if the relative appreciates the meaning and seriousness of the MBP diagnosis. Long-term management should include monitoring, team-based treatment, and case oversight by the court. Many children recover dramatically from their physical illnesses when they are separated from their mothers.

A number of authors have proposed MBP protocols for hospitals and health care facilities. Kinscherff and Ayoub[4] recommend protocols for health care providers, schools, and psychiatric facilities that include:

+ prompt case consultation with relevant medical specialties and a consultant knowledgeable about MBP
+ prompt notification and consultation with hospital legal staff familiar with the protocol and state child protection and criminal procedure law
+ provisions for ensuring the safety of the child, including: (1) intensive monitoring or temporary suspension of parent-child contact pending more definitive diagnosis and/or the involvement of child protection authorities; (2) a procedure by which a preemptive court order barring removal of the child by parents might be secured prior to informing parents of the allegations of MBP; or (3) a protocol permitted under state law by which a physician might place a "hold" upon discharge pending notification of the court
+ statements of conditions under which covert staff or electronic surveillance would be initiated as a routine element of the protocol, as well as specification of who has the authority to initiate covert staff or electronic surveillance

- description of how the mandated reporting requirement will be accomplished, including designation of a specific person to make the mandated report and the content of the report to be made to state child protection authorities
- indication of the steps to be followed in the event a parent attempts to remove a child against medical advice, including the role to be played by hospital security
- provision for designation of a single source of information to whom the family or others with an interest in the case can turn for reliable information regarding the situation and the condition of the child
- designation of persons responsible for assessing the reactions of hospital staff, including the need for staff meetings to resolve differences regarding case management or involvement of child protection authorities.

Optimally, the MBP protocol pulls together a clinical management team that has access to professional consultation regarding clinical care, child protection, documentation, and legal case management. Hospital child maltreatment or psychiatric consultation liaison teams should be specifically trained about MBP and promptly contacted when medical or psychiatric units raise concerns about a case.

Implementing an MBP hospital protocol not only reduces the likelihood that individuals or units will make legal errors in managing suspected cases, but it also provides documentation of parental informed consent, execution of mandated legal duties, and evidence of a process of thoughtful professional judgment that is the best defense in the event of formal complaints against professional licenses or malpractice lawsuit. Use of a protocol reduces the number of false allegations, and makes it more likely that genuine MBP cases are identified, and that the level of clinical risk to the child is accurately assessed. This, in turn, makes it more likely that cases requiring a response from state authorities will result in the temporary placement of the child out of the home, or in the appointment of a guardian to make medical decisions pending the outcome of further investigation.

CHARACTERISTICS OF THE PERPETRATORS AND FAMILIES IN MUNCHAUSEN BY PROXY

If there is reasonable suspicion of pediatric illness falsification abuse, then it is important to consider whether there is information in the record consistent with clinical indicators of factitious disorder by proxy in the children's mother or primary caregiver. These features would include

- the presence of impostering for the purpose of actively relating to and controlling individuals seen as powerful, most often, but not limited to, physicians. These relationships are not necessarily serial and may be multiple. In a number of instances, once cases become public and/or the power over the child is shifted from medical personnel to the court, the focus of the mother's relationships and controls also shifts. Impostering is often seen in MBP mothers beyond the scope of their interactions with health care personnel, and those relationships should be assessed as well. Characterological traits of lying are incorporated into the parent's need to gain control and attention by impostering the "good mother" and often other roles as well, such as the dedicated child advocate, the well-to-do volunteer, or the committed health educator. Since monetary gain is another route to power, the deception may well extend to financial and other status realms.

+ Relationships between the mother and child often present as intense. Mothers may be overbearing and their need to be recognized may escalate symptoms just as the child's health begins to improve. At the same time, MBP mothers may be unable to describe their children as three-dimensional individuals, and may express little distress in separation from them.

+ Mothers are often quite knowledgeable about medical concerns and techniques. Many have or aspire to jobs in medically related environments and/or have access to medical information or individuals with such knowledge.

+ The majority of women diagnosed with MBP have underlying characterological disorders of a mixed type and frequently experienced a childhood trauma such as a serious illness, separation, or death. They often describe their childhood histories as either idyllic or severely abusive. Sexual abuse is another common finding in the childhood histories of these mothers. They are usually highly organized in their emotional functioning, but on psychological testing reveal poor perceptual accuracy and reality testing, anger, and narcissistic traits.

In our study we found mothers to be the perpetrators in all of the 30 cases. In each case they "impostered" to present as good and caring mothers. The psychological motivation for their actions was to receive status-enhancing praise and acknowledgement for their self-sacrificing, competent care of their children. Although mothers were extremely convincing in their roles, discovery often illustrated the deliberate and planful nature of the deception. Many mothers worked to subtly manipulate people that they perceived as powerful— usually physicians, but also their child's nurses, therapists, or consultants. A number of mothers used their children's illness to seek notoriety for themselves by requesting special services from foundations like "Make a Wish" and by contacting celebrities to publicize their child's plight. In each case the child was used as the object or vehicle to direct admiring attention to the mother's parenting. The child's needs as perceived by the mother often changed as her status-seeking behavior varied or escalated. The central organizing feature of maternal behavior was playing the role of the caring parent rather than concern for the genuine needs of the child.

Mothers in our study ranged from 17–41 years of age. In many cases they had been groomed for the part within their own families of origin. They were often closely held, but not protected, by their own mothers. Many mothers had very ambivalent relationships with their own mothers. Although families of origin were often presented publicly as flawless, typical maternal histories included sexual abuse, physical assault, and marital conflict and neglect. In 65 percent of the cases, mothers induced illness in their children; evidence of exaggeration and fabrication was present in every case in our study.

All of the mothers were very knowledgeable about their children's conditions. Some gained their knowledge from formal careers as health care professionals (nurses, nurse's aides, pharmacy assistants, medical office managers), while another group were being trained as medical assistants or special education advocates at the time of the abuse. About half of the women in the study had some formal education relating to the physical health, psychological, or educational issues of their children.

Mothers also had a higher than expected rate of substance use, which in all cases included narcotics obtained from physicians for multiple physical or psychological complaints. More than half of the women showed some evidence of fabricating, exaggerating, or inducing symptoms of their own. Several had lengthy histories of physical complaints, many of which were not evident until evaluators asked about maternal medical histories. In the cases in which mothers and their children each had multiple symptoms, the exacerbation of symptoms seemed to alternate between mother and child. In some cases, fathers also had symptoms of illness that were identified by their spouses, who often accompanied them for their own assessment and treatment. In our study three fathers with multiple psychiatric diagnoses had those diagnoses rescinded when they were reevaluated by their original diagnosticians out of the presence of their wives.

Marital situations varied across the families. About a third of the fathers in our study had some history of drug and alcohol abuse. Marital conflict and domestic violence were prevalent in a number of cases, often leading to divorce. In one group of two-parent families, husbands strongly supported their wives in spite of clear evidence and legal findings of MBP abuse of their children. These fathers often served as messengers between their wives and their children, and frequently coerced their children into increased contact.

Other fathers, involved only sporadically in the lives of their children, essentially enabled the abuse either through their passivity or collusion with and support of the perpetrator prior to detection. These fathers were the most likely to continue to support their perpetrator wives after detection, making them unreliable protectors of the child. (This is also the case for any potential caregivers, family members, or professionals, who ally with the perpetrator and disavow any risk to the child.) Some fathers not only supported their partners, but became more actively engaged in a variant of the maternal impostering behaviors. In follow-up, we found that little could be done to change a father's position about his wife if he was strongly allied with the MBP mother at the time of disclosure. In at least three of our cases, fathers initially followed the court's suggestion to separate from their wives in order to reunite with their children, only to return to their wives and clearly articulate their belief that the abuse had not occurred.

A second group of fathers appear estranged at the time of the abuse. They may be separated or divorced; their wives often claim no knowledge of the father's whereabouts. With some limited detective work, these fathers are usually located and discovered to have been in contact with their ex-spouse, especially through child support agreements. These fathers have been systematically shut out of their children's lives and are often willing to become reinvolved with their children if they have some state protection from their wives. Extended family, particularly paternal relatives, are also often estranged and may be positive resources for care of the children.

Although 55 percent of the study fathers acknowledged the allegations of MBP as opposed to only 10 percent of mothers, a majority of fathers equivocated about the veracity of the allegations for a considerable period of time. Some hesitated to get involved because their wives strongly opposed any increased contact with their children. Some fathers who are able to separate both physically and emotionally from mothers, restructure the family system to acknowledge MBP, and actively work to protect the child, have been able to safely parent following a lengthy intervention period. Safe and secure parenting is also contingent upon the father's ability to function as the primary caregiver, a role for which many MBP fathers are poorly equipped. Once fathers clearly separate from the MBP mother's influence and engage in productive treatment, an extended assessment of their parenting capacity is recommended.

Careful evaluation of family members and relatives is strongly recommended before any contact with the child victims is permitted. MBP is a family system disorder that frequently is transgenerational and in which extended family may serve as enablers strongly supporting the mother's continued denial and impostering. For these reasons, family placements are viewed with considerable skepticism in most MBP cases. However, in our study, placements with paternal relatives were some of the most successful from the child's perspective. Regardless of the relationship between the child and the caregiver, the caregiver must fully understand the nature of the disorder, be willing to acknowledge the diagnosis, and demonstrate both ability and desire to protect the child. Second, relative placements tend to be stressed by the intense and often unrelenting pressure placed on relative custodians by the immediate family, especially by mothers and their advocates. Active attempts to increase contact with the child and to manipulate any approved contact often escalate and make such placements quite difficult. The court, child protective services, and providers should be actively involved in providing support and protection for relative caregivers.

IMPACT ON CHILD VICTIMS IN MUNCHAUSEN BY PROXY

The extent and longevity of emotional symptoms vary in part based on the developmental age of the child, the extent and intensity of their abuse exposure, and their current situational protection and support. Of the 30 children in our study, 43 percent were placed in foster care. One was returned to his mother, who did not receive any treatment. The remaining 24 percent of children were placed with a relative. In most cases, mothers visited regularly, anywhere from once a month to every day.

All of the children in our study were physically healthy upon leaving their biological homes, and all remained healthy except for the child returned to his mother. According to third-hand reports, that child has had recurrent physical symptoms. One child with factitious psychological symptoms did have some baseline disturbances that recurred while he was placed with his father.

Most of the child victims presented with significant emotional difficulties, the most common being oppositional-defiant disorder, posttraumatic stress disorder, and attentional disturbances. All of the children with significant exposure to falsification of symptoms had serious psychological sequelae with the potential for long-term impairment. Major psychiatric symptoms seen in a majority of the children are listed in Table 8.1.

Only the children removed very early in their victimization process and protected from subsequent maternal contact were free of major psychiatric symptoms. Children fared the best psychologically when they were removed from their biological homes at a young age, placed in permanent safe alternative homes as soon as possible, and had little or no contact with mother or her proxies.

The exception to this rule was the two situations in which mothers fully admitted their perpetration early and were sincere and committed in their work to change their behavior. An integrative treatment process lasting from five to seven years included all of the treatment providers for the child and family, child protective services, and a court-designated expert in MBP.

Table 8.1
Characteristics of 30 Children Victimized by Pediatric
Condition /Illness Falsification

1. Hyperarousal/attentional and concentration difficulties

2. Oppositional behavior, including oppositional defiant disorder

3. Lack of perspective taking

4. Driven by appearance

5. Attachment disordered — clingy, unable to play alone, demanding of attention, unable to establish and maintain relationships with adults or peers

6. Sense of entitlement and exclusion from adherence to basic rules of interaction

7. Illness complaint prone

8. Lying, impostering, manipulation to gain attention and meet needs covertly

9. Sexualized behavior/seductive behavior

10. Boundary confusion and issues with appropriate boundaries

11. Controlling (either through caregiving or aggressive/sadistic styles)

12. Body image issues, including view of self as ill or incapable

13. Aggressive/destructive behavior, especially with younger or weaker children or animals as targets

14. Self-mutilation, self-harm, especially in children as they enter adolescence

15. Anxious sadness and/or depression

16. View of the environment as either "the best" or "the worst" — no ability to see the nuances in behavior

17. Simplistic processing, compartmentalization of events and emotions through time

18. Distorted reality testing

19. Disturbed eating and sleeping patterns

Children did worse from a psychiatric point of view when their victimization lasted more than two years before exposure, when they were returned to their mothers with little or no insight-oriented treatment for the perpetrator, and when they were exposed to their mothers for a considerable length of time without maternal progress in MBP-focused treatment. Children with unsupervised contact with their mothers or their mother's proxies also fared poorly, as did children whose fathers were unable to care for them due to dependency on mothers for structure. Finally, children whose permanent placement was delayed or never completed also experienced serious psychiatric symptoms.

The psychological impact of victimization through MBP is significant and chronic. Basic problems with attachment, relationship-building, and social interaction, as well as attention and concentration, are common in these children. The presence of oppositional disorders in these victims is significant, as are patterns of reality distortion, poor self-esteem, and attachment difficulties with adults and peers. Although these children can present as socially skilled and superficially well-adjusted, they often struggle with the basic relationships. Lying is a common finding, as is some sadistic behavior toward other children.

Children with stable, long-term placements in which they were protected from their mothers and supported in their move toward health had fewer long-term difficulties than children who had more exposure to their mothers and less stable placements. Even after an extended recovery, many of these children remain trauma-reactive and are vulnerable to cyclical anger, depression, and oppositionality. The implications for intervention are numerous. Several of the most salient are listed in Table 8.2.

FORENSIC ASSESSMENT OF MUNCHAUSEN BY PROXY

An evaluation to address issues of parenting capacity and the best interests of the child in light of allegations of exaggeration, fabrication, and/or inducement

Table 8.2
Interventions to Consider with Children Abused by Pediactric Condition/ Illness Falsification

1. Placement in a home that has expertise with emotionally disturbed children from the outset reduces the child's distress and decreases the likelihood of multiple placements.

2. Structure and external limit setting is critical to meeting the child's safety and care needs.

3. Careful supervision should be in place when placing Munchausen by Proxy victims with small children or animals.

4. School assessment is needed as early as possible. Any children are identified as having attention -deficity hyperactivity disorder when they are really trauma reactive.

5. If visits with mother are required, then limited, structured visits under careful professional supervision are strongly suggested in order to avoid further victimization.

6. Careful boundaries should be articulated to the child, and clear reinforcement of those boundaries should be enforced regularly.

7. Limit or end mother's visits if child's behavior escalates or remains distressed.

8. Insist on continuity of caregiving and limited respite care. Long-term placements should be sought from the beginning to reduce attachment difficulties.

Caregivers must be actively aware of the child's victimization and of the need for active protection.

of illness in a child by a parent is a complex process. When juvenile courts are involved, such evaluation is strongly recommended in order to inform and expedite decision making. In such situations, the focus of the assessment is on the interactional patterns between the caregiver(s) and each child, with attention to:

+ the child's illness experience and functioning (the child as alleged victim of child abuse by condition or illness falsification), and
+ the parent's psychological functioning with attention to differentiating factitious disorders by proxy (factitious disorder not otherwise specified (NOS) in the *DSM–IV*[5]) and other possible psychological etiologies of the parent's behavior, attitudes, and beliefs toward the child.[3]

The process of evaluation typically includes the following:

+ Comprehensive record review and contacts with collaterals is a central component of any evaluation in which MBP is raised as an issue. Collateral contacts include both professional and lay persons, including other family members, who might be able to shed light on the current situation.
+ The emotional and physical functioning of each parent or primary caregiver, both in the past and in the present, is explored through a series of clinical interviews and through psychological testing. In a number of cases, maternal grandparents are also interviewed either initially or as follow-up. Fathers and their family members, if they are in a position to have contact with the child, should also be evaluated, as should any other relative with interests in having contact with the children.
+ A review of the child's past and present physical and emotional functioning, including, but not limited to, information about past and current daily routines, symptoms, and behaviors is obtained through observations, record review, and interviews with past and current caregivers.[13]

Although such an evaluation is extensive, the complexity of the MBP situation usually requires such comprehensiveness in order for juvenile and family courts to proceed with findings and dispositional issues that focus on the child's best interests. Such an evaluation, ordered by the court, provides the evaluators with the neutrality as well as the court's authority to work with all parties and to request the court's support in gaining access to individuals and records.

VISITATION ISSUES IN MUNCHAUSEN BY PROXY

Visitation should be considered very carefully in cases of alleged MBP. The child's victimization is typically significant and chronic. Current literature indicates that victimization is likely to continue to occur with few exceptions, even in the light of treatment. Children have been revictimized by their mothers even during highly structured and well-supervised visits. In addition to the physical danger, visitation can offer enormous potential for psychological harm. Child victims of MBP tend to have long-term and serious sequelae to their abuse that are impacted by visitation. A number of experts recommend that there be no direct or indirect contact between child and mother (or other family members who might serve as proxies for mother) until the evaluation is complete, a treatment plan for the family is in place, and mother has made significant progress. If visitation is to be instituted after all these contingencies are satisfied, the following general guidelines are recommended:

- Visits should be regular; it is important for the child to know in advance when visits will take place. Visits should be scheduled to minimize disruption in the child's regular routine. For example, visits should not be scheduled during the school or day care hours. It is quite important for younger children especially that visits be held on the same day each week for the same length of time; it is equally important for the child's mental health that visits not be rescheduled or cancelled except for significant emergencies. In order to achieve this goal, a system of back up visitation supervisors is strongly recommended. In cases where there is considerable danger of physical or emotional distress to the child, visits should be discontinued. Reduction or discontinuation of visits is strongly recommended when, over time, mothers are unable to acknowledge perpetration, unless special circumstances warrant visitation in order to meet the child's best interests. Some therapists recommend that visitation with the perpetrating parent, spouse, and the child be postponed until the MBP mother has successfully participated in treatment for a year or more. The first visits are usually scheduled at long intervals, with frequency increasing if therapy progresses successfully.
- A consistent, professional supervisor who is fully informed about the details of the case should supervise all visits. This supervisor may be a trained clinician from the Department of Social Services or another agency. Relatives or any other partial parties should not attend or supervise visits until they are approved by both the child's and mother's therapists and found to be appropriate by the court. The supervisor must be able to observe and hear the child and mother at all times during the visitation process.
- Visits should be held in a neutral setting. They should not be held at the biological home or at the foster home, or at the home of relatives. Mutually agreed upon neutral sites can be explored with the understanding that the child does need some predictability in his surroundings and sites should not be changed frequently.
- During the visits, parents and/or other relatives should be engaged with the child or free to focus on him or her at his or her request. Conversations about the child, including information pertaining to his or her general health and well-being, as well as discussions about visitation and legal issues, should not

be allowed during visits. The supervisor/child protective worker and the parents are encouraged to set up a regular contact time outside of the visits to discuss such matters; this may take place either by phone or in person and should precede the weekly visits. Such exchanges should be scheduled at a routine, consistent time, and offered to one or both parents.

- The child's medical or psychological condition should not be discussed in his or her presence, nor should he or she be asked medically related questions except when an acute illness presents during the visit. The visitation supervisor/child protective worker should continue to relay current general information pertaining to the child during the scheduled encounters with the parents. All information about the child's condition should be relayed only through the designated professionals and not by relatives.
- Food should not be brought to the visits, nor should the child be asked to eat during this time except as mutually prearranged, especially in cases in which inducement was an issue. Exceptions can be made for special occasions such as birthdays with approval from therapists and the team. All food available at visits must be purchased and presented in the original store packaging. More permissive policies with regard to food should be made contingent on mother's progress in treatment.
- Visits may include parents and, in some cases, siblings. Other relatives who wish to visit under supervision may be included, if mutually agreed upon by the parties, following an evaluation of their interests and perspective on the child's victimization. No unsupervised visitation should take place with relatives unless those individuals are fully cognizant of and able to accept the child's victimization as described by the court findings and can abide by the agreements about information sharing developed by the supervisor with assistance from the treatment team.
- Exchange of gifts during visits is strongly discouraged. Exceptions may be prearranged for given holidays such as birthdays and Christmas; all gifts should be prescreened by child protection and/or the Guardian ad Litem. Parents should be encouraged to provide the visitation supervisor with a list of holidays on which they routinely exchange gifts so that such practices can be prearranged to the mutual benefit of all involved.
- In general, all electronic or photographic recording of visitation should be discouraged. Any such recording during visits should be collected and maintained by child protection or a designee of the court and made available to all parties. No unilateral photography or electronic records should be made. All electronic recording should be maintained with primary attention to maintenance of the child's privacy. The use of such material should be carefully agreed upon before any data is collected.
- Other forms of direct communication between parent(s) and the child such as telephone calls are strongly discouraged as they cannot be monitored as safely as face-to-face or written communication. If they are to occur, they should be

scheduled at regular intervals and should be monitored. Optimal monitoring includes audio recording for the protection of all involved. Expansion of contact to telephone calls should proceed with mother's progress in the latter stages of therapy.

PLACEMENT, INTEGRATIVE MANAGEMENT, AND REUNIFICATION

The presence of credible deception on the part of mothers in MBP makes it critical to use multidisciplinary teams to assist in the identification and management of MBP. One of the basic roles of the team is to assure the transparency and verification of the factual information pertaining to the family. After identification, professionals providing medical and psychological services to the child and family should form a team and work together to share information and coordinate treatment goals. Teams should at a minimum have one expert in MBP. The MBP team serves not only to improve the accuracy of the diagnosis, but also as a clinical and legal risk management mechanism.

Attempting to implement medical, child protection, mental health, and risk management measures without close coordination is ineffective and may result in the polarization of professionals and harm to the child. The treatment team is most effective when organized around the consultation and coordination of a court-appointed MBP expert (representing the child's best interests) and the oversight of the court; this expert can also serve as the liaison for reporting to the juvenile or family court. Continued juvenile court oversight is a central requirement for the success of this treatment process. The fragmentation of treatment goals is an ever present danger in the absence of a communication mechanism and requirement for providers.

In our study, 43 percent of children were initially placed in foster care, 10 percent of children were placed with fathers, 24 percent of children were placed with grandparents or aunts and uncles, and 10 percent either remained or were returned to their mothers who did not receive treatment. After five years of follow-up, 7 percent of the children remained with their fathers, 13 percent were returned to their fathers after foster care placements, 7 percent moved from the grandparents' home to their parents' after mother and father received intensive treatment, and 30 percent were released for adoption by relatives or foster parents. Most children continued to struggle with the psychological impact of their abuse, and many remained in mental health treatment for lengthy periods of time.

Any potential caregiver who persists in denying the child's abuse by the parent perpetrator when confronted with a finding by the court can justifiably be

denied contact with or placement of the child. If denial continues, then termination of parental rights with fathers as well as mothers is often recommended.[13]
Depending upon the situation, closely supervised visitation may continue with
selected family members, if found to be in the child's best interests.

Mental health treatment for the child typically includes developing safety
and social skills, reducing self-blame, embracing wellness/releasing illness
script, improving attachment relationships and reducing oppositionality, developing autonomy, reducing dissociation and compartmentalization of thinking
and feeling, maintaining appropriate boundaries, understanding and managing family conflicts and loyalties, and reframing positive peer relationships. By
early adolescence, most of the children were encouraged to consider and rework
their understanding of MBP victimization. Young teens who were unable to
work through their victimization had more difficulty negotiating adolescence
than those who were able to reorganize their experiences in such a way as to
reduce their sense of blame and confusion. Children who received little or no
treatment directed at their victimization were more likely to struggle with acting out and oppositionality, as well as depression and self-harm issues during
adolescence.

Treatment for mothers (perpetrators) is based on three prerequisites:
genuine acknowledgement of perpetration, psychiatric stability in daily life,
and successful treatment for substance abuse. The first phase of treatment for
maternal perpetrators following acknowledgement is typically identification
and exploration of their own victimization and its relationship to their attitudes and actions toward their children. Understanding her own victimization
in the context of her patterns of victimizing her child, and bringing these two
traumatic series of events into consciousness so that their relationship can be
understood, is central to the mother's treatment progress.

This integrative process also serves to reduce isolation and diminish the cognitive distortions that these mothers tend to develop in social relationships.
They learn to rely on the perceptions of trusted care providers with whom they
can check out, and if necessary, correct, their initial impressions of other people.
This integration of emotion, cognition, and action, combined with reduction of
cognitive distortion, forms the basis for treatment of MBP perpetrators, and is
also critical to general trauma treatment.

A third critical component of the first phase of treatment is to explore how the
marital relationship contributed to and perpetuated the child's abuse. Couples
who stay together must rework marital relationships so that there is a more active
system of checks and balances around their communication, and in turn their
actions related to the safety of the children. Each parent is accountable to the
other for this process, which requires that partners actively acknowledge their

enabling roles in the child's victimization. This relational reframing is made easier when other family members support the need to ensure the children's safety.

The second phase of the treatment is the reworking of the relationship of the child to the family, with the mother-child relationship as a central focus of this process. The elements to be addressed during this phase include maternal recognition of the child as a unique individual rather than the vehicle for maternal need gratification. This recognition must be followed by a significant period of redefinition of the attachment relationships within the family and a reframing of the child's identity from one encompassing illness to one that embraces wellness. Safety issues for parent and child should be addressed continuously along the way. Some mothers, for example, do not want to assume any caretaking responsibility when the child is legitimately ill. Fathers and other relatives may have specific roles as active participants if this occurs.

Communication between perpetrator and victim about the MBP abuse is another critical part of the healing process. Mothers in our small treatment group were able to tell their children about their abuse and were responsive to questions from their children about the factual basis of their recollection. This process also greatly enhanced the child's ability to differentiate reality from perceptions distorted by their self-blame or denial. Finally, marital communication, which was reframed in phase I, was actively supported and reinforced through both marital and family therapy as the children continued to develop and new challenges arose.

Treatment for fathers remains a central component to the success of intervention with mothers. Fathers continuing to support the denial of MBP abuse significantly reduced the odds for successful treatment of mothers. Fathers in the study were required to maintain an active presence in their families, a role that they often had abdicated. They were expected to actively parent and were clearly charged with responsibility for protecting and nurturing the child. It was difficult for many fathers to participate in therapy for themselves and to take on the role of client. They tended to prefer avoiding or denying their role in enabling their spouse's MBP actions, even when they were able to acknowledge the abuse of their children. However, fathers often worked on understanding the meaning of anger and control issues and grew in developing a more psychological mode of thinking through individual therapy. A number of fathers had abdicated basic parenting responsibility to their wives. As a result, many fathers required help with basic parenting skills. All of these strategies with fathers were aimed at reducing paternal rigidity and the propensity for denial that fueled the MBP abuse.

If fathers have problems with drugs, alcohol, or domestic violence, or if they have been regarded by their partners as ill, these issues as well must be addressed before primary responsibility of the children is placed with them. These additional problems found in a number of fathers reduce the likelihood that they will be able to assume primary responsibility for parenting their children. In two cases in our study, fathers initially took custody of their children but were not able to cope with the responsibility in the long-term.

LEGAL ISSUES IN MUNCHAUSEN BY PROXY

The conduct associated with MBP has a wide range of legal implications that can match the magnitude of the medical and psychosocial challenges. Attorneys and courts must deal with MBP cases in criminal prosecutions, child protection proceedings, and/or divorce actions. Health care providers working with suspected MBP cases should be aware of the legal considerations that arise when MBP is suspected. Not only are the means by which health care professionals detect and document an alleged case of MBP crucial to legal proceedings, but their conduct is also subject to scrutiny on issues including professional standards of care for diagnosis and treatment, informed consent for covert video surveillance or medical diagnostic procedures, and compliance with mandated reporting child abuse statutes. Both the child and family are best served by knowledgeable medical, mental health, social service, and legal personnel.

Unfortunately, the courtroom can become the extended battleground for mothers who are unable or unwilling to enter treatment. We have identified two groups of mothers. The first group of mothers fight against admission of MBP up until trial but then are unable to face the witnesses who describe their abusive actions. These women often attempt to settle their cases rather than to endure a court proceeding. In contrast, a second group of women appear to use the legal process to further their attention-seeking behaviors and to vigorously defend their cherished, carefully constructed identities as heroically loving caregivers to their children. These women seem to enjoy their roles on the stage of the courtroom, and often threaten professionals involved with extended litigation. They often take an active role in trying their own cases and may have hired and fired multiple attorneys in an effort to advance and control the promotion of their cause. This characteristic of never giving up is a hallmark of many of the maternal perpetrators. Many of them wait until their children are 18 to actively renew contact, even if their legal rights have been terminated.

In summary, MBP is a disorder that includes the significant and repeated abuse of a child, most often by the child's mother, who exaggerates, fabricates, and/or induces illness in the child. The physical danger to the child is considerable, and the psychological consequences to the child based on the violation of trust by the parent are tremendously powerful and enduring. Because perpetrators are so skilled at portraying good and caring mothers, they are often convincing, even if the underlying evidence of abuse is evident.

This disorder also has important implications for our perceptions of women, particularly the role of mothers in our society. It challenges the notion that good mothering is an innate quality of all women. It makes clear the ways in which women harm their own children to meet their own needs. Although a number of attributes of women have been challenged by modern feminists, the sentimental vision of Mother remains intact well into the 21st century. Juries today are more likely to act on behalf of child victims, but they remain least likely to act when the perpetrator is the victim's mother. This fact alone behooves child advocates to carefully document and stand firm when confronted with this most difficult and complex disorder that places the appearance of women against the rights of the child. It also requires that we work ever harder to understand the difficult life circumstances of the women that lead them to harm their own children.

REFERENCES

1. Gregory, J. (2003). *Sickened: The memoir of a Munchausen by Proxy childhood*. New York: Bantam Books.
2. Feldman, M. (2004). *Playing sick?* New York: Brunner-Routledge.
3. Ayoub, C., Alexander, R., Beck, D., Bursch, B., Feldman, K., Libow, J., et al. (2002). Position paper: Definitional issues in Munchausen by Proxy. *Child Maltreatment, 7*, 105–112.
4. Kinscherff, R., & Ayoub, C. (2000). Legal aspects in Munchausen by Proxy. In R. Reece (Ed.), *The treatment of child abuse: Common ground for mental* (pp. 242–270). Baltimore, MD: The Johns Hopkins University Press.
5. American Psychiatric Association. (1994). *Diagnostic and statistical manual of mental disorders* (4th ed.). Washington DC: Author.
6. Sheridan, M. (2003). The deceit continues: An updated literature review of Munchausen Syndrome by Proxy. *Child Abuse & Neglect, 27*, 431–451.
7. McClure, R. J., Davis, P. M., Meadow, S. R., & Sibert, J. R. (1996). Epidemiology of Munchausen syndrome by proxy, non-accidental poisoning, and non-accidental suffocation. *Archives of Disease in Childhood, 75*, 57–61.
8. Alexander, R., Smith, W., & Stevenson, R. (1990). Serial Munchausen by proxy. *Pediatrics, 86*, 581–585.
9. Lasher, L. & Sheridan, M. (2004). Munchausen by proxy: Identification, intervention, and case management. New York: Harworth Press.
10. Libow, J. (1995). Munchausen by proxy syndrome victims in adulthood: A first look. *Child Abuse & Neglect, 19*, 1131–1142.
11. Schreier, H. A., & Libow, J. A. (1993). *Hurting for love: Munchausen by Proxy Syndrome*. New York: Guilford.

12. Sanders, M., & Bursch, B. (2002). Forensic assessment of illness falsification, Munchausen by Proxy, and factitious disorder, NOS. *Child Maltreatment, 7,* 112–124.

13. Kinscherff, R., & Famularo, R. (1991). Extreme Munchausen Syndrome by Proxy: The case for termination of parental rights. *Juvenile & Family Court Journal, 5,* 41–53.

Chapter 9

Alzheimer's Disease: New Concepts in Diagnosis, Treatment, and Management

James E. Soukup

Alzheimer's disease (AD) is identified as one form of dementia in the *Diagnostic and Statistical Manual of Mental Disorders*, Fourth Edition *(DSM–IV)*[1] published by the American Psychiatric Association. This publication is the most current guide to the diagnosis of mental illness and clinical practice.

Dementia is defined as multiple cognitive deficits due to the physiological impact of a general medical condition, the effects of a substance, or due to other etiologies. Cognitive deficits include memory impairment and at least one other cognitive impairment including aphasia, apraxia, agnosia, or a disturbance of executive functioning. These deficits must be great enough to cause significant or occupational dysfunction.[1]

AD includes symptoms of the other dementias, including memory impairment; one or more of the cognitive disturbances (language, motor activity, failure to recognize or identify objects, and disturbed executive functioning); and significant functional disability. However, with Alzheimer's type dementia, the onset is gradual with a pervasive and progressive increase in disability. Dementias, especially Alzheimer's type, tend to increase with aging, although dementia is not a part of the normal aging process.

AD is an organic brain disorder that can be diagnosed by ruling out cognitive deficits due to other central nervous system conditions such as cerebrovascular disease, head trauma, Huntington's disease, Parkinson's disease, subdural hematoma, brain tumor, normal pressure hydrocephalus, and Creutzfeldt-Jakob disease. Other systemic conditions to be eliminated in the diagnosis are vitamin B12 or folic acid deficiency, niacin deficiency, hypothyroidism, hypercalcemia, neurosyphilis, and HIV infection. Emotion disorders such as depression, anxiety, and schizophrenia can present symptoms of dementia, as can general medical conditions and substances, including medications for emotional and physical disorders.

AD is divided into early onset (before age 65) and late onset (after age 65). The majority of patients develop the disease after 85. With the aging of the American population, the percent of those who develop AD will greatly increase. Costs of care, as well as the emotional trauma, both to the patient and the patient's family, will be significant. This is why understanding the disorder and providing an accurate diagnosis is important. Without an accurate diagnosis, appropriate treatment and care cannot be provided. Currently there is no cure for AD or treatments known to impede or reverse the cognitive impairments of the disease. However, many of the other forms of dementia that are often confused with AD are treatable and reversible.

The Alzheimer's Association supports the necessity of a comprehensive and complete diagnostic work up when AD is suspected. The components of a comprehensive evaluation should include a medical evaluation with laboratory work to rule out systemic and general medical problems, a neurological evaluation to rule out neurological factors, a neuropsychological assessment, a pharmacological review, and an evaluation of cultural and education factors and functional ability. Unfortunately, few patients suspected of having AD are provided with such an assessment. Often, the diagnosis is made after a 15-minute visit with the family and a 5-minute evaluation of the subject's cognitive ability with a physician. Misdiagnosis is thus not unusual, with failure to treat the treatable and reversible causes of the symptoms of dementia which are not AD.

The Alzheimer's Association estimates that 4.5 million Americans suffer from AD. This number has doubled since 1980.[1] Figures on the total number of AD sufferers could well be distorted because of lack of adequate diagnostic methods, with a tendency to designate all forms or other forms of dementia as AD. However, even with these inaccuracies and distortions the impact on our aging population and their loved ones is enormous. By the year 2050, the Association forecasts that between 11.3 and 16 million people will have AD. Increasing life span increases the risk of developing dementias of all types. It is estimated that from five–seven percent of all individuals over 65 suffer from AD. The probability of developing the disorder doubles every five years after age 65.

It is estimated that at age 85 nearly 50 percent of the population has AD.[1] (Incidentally, *DSM–IV* has a diagnostic category "Age-Related Cognitive

Decline."[1] The criteria is an objectively identified decline in cognitive functioning related to the aging process within normal age limits. This presents another diagnostic argument—what is the normal cognitive ability decline for any age? This illustrates clinical and professional diagnostic problems related to accuracy and reliability.)

The Alzheimer's Association states that an individual with AD will live an average of eight years after the onset of the symptoms as estimated by caregivers (again diagnostic confusion). The Association states that annual costs for caring for individuals with AD is close to $100 billion. These estimates are supported by the National Institute on Aging. The disease reportedly costs American businesses $61 billion, which includes Alzheimer's health care and lost productivity of caretakers. Of the millions of people suffering from AD, 70 percent live at home, with about 75 percent of the care provided by family and friends. Average nursing home costs per year run from $42,000–$70,000.[2] Recently, special care facilities for those with impaired memory have been developed. These special care units provide programs that tend to meet the needs of patients with AD and are becoming more and more popular and in demand. In 2000, Medicare costs for AD patients was $31.9 billion. In 2010, the cost is estimated to be $49.3 billion. Medicaid residential costs will go from $18.2 billion in 2000 to $33 billion in 2010.[3] AD creates a real crisis for the nation now and will increase in costs with the aging of the baby boomer generation.

DIAGNOSTIC UPDATE

Probably the most promising and significant event in the identification and treatment of AD is a change in the approach to the diagnosis of dementia. In the past, the process of diagnosing AD consisted of a brief interview with the patient and the patient's family members. Family members were asked to identify particular memory loss situations, such as misplacing car keys, as well as such problems as word finding and orientation confusion. Often, family members reported different levels of impairment.

The identified patient was then administered some type of memory and cognition test. This was usually the mini mental status exam (MMSE).[4] The MMSE is at best an inexact and limited measure of cognitive ability. Administration time takes about five minutes and consists of questions about date and place, an auditory immediate memory test, a task to measure attention and calculation ability, questions and tasks to assess language ability, and a visual-motor integrity test. This test is the most commonly used instrument to evaluate cognitive abilities, and was developed primarily as a screening device. A total of 30 points is possible. The test has norms for age and education level;

however, often these are not used. A score of 24–30 indicates intact cognitive abilities. A score of 20–23 suggests mild impairment, 16–19 moderate impairment, and 15 and below severe impairment.

However, test norms do not consider physical disability that may make task completion difficult, sensory disability, emotional state, sociocultural differences, and a variety of other factors, which often result in false positives. Individuals who do poorly on the MMSE and other similar instruments do not necessarily suffer from dementia. However, in the past, a brief interaction with the family and one with the identified patient resulted in the diagnosis of AD. False positives based on an inadequate diagnosis not only result in the true problems or causal factor of symptoms not being treated, but also have a tendency to be a self-fulfilling prophecy. The individual and family members tend to be devastated. The result often is depression and failure to provide an environment for intellectual stimulation and well-being.

Placement in daycare or permanent living facility is common based on the conception that indeed the person has AD and will only get worse. A limited evaluation fails to differentiate between treatable forms of dementia and irreversible AD. The question arises, "Why would a professional health provider rely on limited data when comprehensive diagnostic testing is possible?" There are a number of reasons.

One reason is limited time. The primary care physician is expected to provide a wide range of diagnostic opinions and treatment for a variety of health problems. Time is not available to conduct a comprehensive diagnostic evaluation for AD. A second reason is limited knowledge and ability to provide such an evaluation. Physicians are specialists. A cardiologist does not diagnose or treat cancer. It would be rare to find a physician who has the training and experience to conduct a neuropsychological evaluation, a comprehensive and complete pharmacological review, an evaluation of functional abilities, and a diagnostic work up of mental abilities, and also emotional and mental illnesses which may result in dementia.

A third reason is the fact that medical doctors tend to hesitate to refer outside of the profession. AD is a progressive physical (organic) disorder. Initially, AD was considered a normal aging process or a weakness of old age. However, research as far back as the 1970s suggested structural pathology with neuronal plaques and neurofibrillary tangles.[5] The proteins ACT and ApoE4 were suspected to be related to these conditions. (More information will be discussed in the chapter section on recent research and treatment.) A deficit in the neurotransmitter choline acetyltransferace was also suggested, as was brain atrophy.

It would seem that because AD is indeed an organic brain syndrome, laboratory tests would be available to diagnose the disorder. Neurologists certainly do play an important role in the diagnostic process to rule out other causes, such as brain injury or tumors. However, diagnosis can only be made on a behavioral basis, just as schizophrenia and chemical imbalance depression are diagnosed using clinical observation and behavioral tests, not medical tests.

The hesitation of physicians to utilize other professionals in a multidisciplinary approach may be related to lack of awareness that accurate and reliable objective tests and measures are available, problems in linkage with other professionals, and possibly an attitude that is common in our society—the attitude or belief that nothing can be done about dementia and that it is a symptom and part of aging. Baby boomers will not stand for this and will insist on more comprehensive and complete diagnostic processes and care. Another reason for an incomplete diagnosis and evaluation of dementia is lack of availability and training in the related professional fields. Geriatric neuropsychologists are rare. Doctors of pharmacology, until recently, have not been involved in the diagnosis and treatment of geriatric patients specifically. Case workers to monitor response to treatment and supervise care programs are scarce. Another reason is cost. A comprehensive evaluation involves a number of specialists. Not only must arrangements be made for appointments, but the compilation of data into a meaningful whole with a treatment plan must be arranged. While Medicare and Medicaid pay for many of these services, these services require a physician's referral. Billing is also complicated.

DIAGNOSTIC SPECIFICS

This section will discuss the role of each of the specialists in the diagnostic process and specifics as to areas of attention.

The physician's involvement in the diagnosis, treatment, and care of AD is key and critical. Usually the first contact for an evaluation is made with the primary care doctor. The American Psychological Association, in *Guidelines for the Evaluation of Dementia and Age Related Cognitive Decline*[6] published in February 1998, states that psychologists performing cognitive decline evaluations should inform the referring physician as to findings. In the case of the first contact being with the psychologist, it is important that a contact be made with a medical professional to evaluate and discover any medical disorder or reversible medical cause for dementia. The guidelines stress the importance of a multidisciplinary effort, cooperation, and respect.

The Alzheimer's Association guidelines suggest physicians use available diagnostic data from appropriate specialists in such fields as neurology, psychiatry, and neuropsychology to diagnose dementia. The Association states that data should include a medical history and evaluation of mental status, communication ability, and tests of memory, reasoning, visual-motor skills, and language skills. A physical exam including nutrition, blood pressure and pulse, and the evaluation of functions of the nervous system is suggested, along with laboratory tests to provide information on other medical problems, as well as an assessment of emotional status.

Over 50 physical illnesses and conditions present symptoms of dementia. Some of these include: anoxia, anemia, congestive heart failure, vitamin deficiencies, stroke, head trauma, acquired immune deficiency syndrome, other infections, neoplasm, cerebral vasculitis, multiple sclerosis, Cushing's syndrome, hyperthyroidism, hypothyroidism, dehydration, Huntington's syndrome, and Parkinson's disease. This list emphasizes the need for a complete medical evaluation. If the symptoms observed are motor problems, problems with gait, disinhibited behavior, depression, anxiety, patchy or focal neuropathy with intact language and memory, maintained ability to learn, orientation and intact executive functions, a diagnosis other than AD is probable.

Forms of dementia other than AD tend to present specific laboratory findings which help in a differential diagnosis. For example, vascular dementia presents focal neurological signs and symptoms. Magnetic resonance imaging (MRI) and computed temography (CT) usually demonstrate multiple vascular lesions of the cerebral cortex and subcortical structures.

DSM–IV[1] gives extensive information as to the determination of whether the dementia is due to general medical conditions. Of course, the physician is the appropriate health provider to make this determination. A pharmacological consult is usually of benefit as part of the diagnostic process and in planning treatment and care. Clinical evidence suggests that the elderly are often overmedicated. Confusion problems with memory disorientation and problems with functioning can be long-term side effects of both medical and psychotropic drugs. The withdrawal from the market of a number of prescription drugs because of increased risks has become more frequent. Consumer advocate groups claim that pharmaceutical companies withhold negative research results, and that the manufacturer's finance of studies related to the efficacy and safety of new drugs create doubt as to consumer safety and welfare. Escalating prices of prescription drugs well above the level of inflation also creates concern, especially when low-income families have to choose between food and medication.

The fact that many prescription drugs sold to the American public are significantly more expensive than those sold in Canada and other countries also appears to have raised resentment and concern. In April 2005, AARP's annual "Rx Watchdog Report"[7] stated that brand name prescription drugs in 2004 increased an average of 7.1 percent in price. This was the largest price increase in five years. The price increase was more than double the national rate of inflation for 2004. In 2003, the price increase was 7 percent. Since 1999, the price of over 150 popular brand name drugs increased 35.1 percent, nearly three times the inflation rate of 13.5 for this five-year period. Research published in the February 2005 *Journal of the American Geriatric Society*,[8] based on data of 175,000 adults enrolled in health maintenance organizations (HMOs), indicated that 28 percent of elderly individuals were prescribed at least 1 of 33 medications considered inappropriate.

Pharmaceutical companies claim that an increase in longevity is related to pharmacological intervention. Other research studies relate this to earlier diagnosis of medical problems and improved lifestyle. Studies have suggested that, indeed, exercise, good nutritional habits, intellectual involvement and stimulation, not smoking, and limiting alcohol intake does decrease the risk of developing dementia. This appears to be related to maintaining good health and a good attitude so the body functions in a healthy way. Prevention based on a healthy lifestyle, rather than intervention and medication seems to make sense.

When prescribing drugs for the elderly, distribution, metabolism and excretion differences, as related to the aging process, must be considered. Distribution of drugs is altered primarily by loss of body water and lean body mass. Metabolism varies between individuals. Monitoring of the process and drug impact is best done on an individual basis. Body weight, general health, and liver problems are some of the factors affecting drug reactions. Excretion is related to kidney functioning, with documented reduction in the glomerular filtration rate with age.

Other concerns and risk factors related to the elderly have to do with memory problems and proper dosage, time of medication, and taking the wrong medication. Lack of monitoring of side effects is common with the elderly patient, either failing to identify side effects or failing to inform others of negative side effects. Lack of monitoring and supervision is common, not only among individuals living independently, but also in nursing homes and other facilities such as assisted living homes.

Failure to contact medical caregivers on a regular basis can result in prescription drug misuse. In institutional settings, there is often a lack of consistency of medical care with visits by different physicians throughout one's stay. It is not uncommon for drugs once prescribed for a particular illness or symptom to be continued when no longer needed. Abuse of drugs, including pain medication, sedatives, and alcohol is a danger with the elderly. One study[3] suggests alcohol abuse by 2.8 percent of the general public over age 65. This is probably an underestimation.

All medications have side effects. Drugs which present symptoms of dementia include antihypertensives, corticosteroids, digitalis, opiates and synthetic narcotics, and psychoactive agents with anticholinergic properties. Side effects of antidepressant drugs can include sedation, hypotension, and anticholinergic impact. Neuroleptic drugs also can cause these side effects, plus extrapyramidal symptoms. Liver disease concern is related to certain anticholestral drugs, as well as medication for bipolar disorder. Antianxiety medication can be addictive. Weight gain is associated with many antidepressants, as well as some neuroleptic medications.

In a perfect world, monitoring of side effects, supervision to provide medical compliance, and the prescription of proper medication would be standard. Some facilities do provide pharmacological review on a regular basis, but generally drug misuse and abuse is common with the elderly. This is one reason that a pharmacological consult is recommended as part of the diagnostic process when evaluating symptoms of dementia. While a review of medication is important, it is just as important for family members of individuals with functional problems and/or dementia to monitor medication taken. Questions to ask one's physician include:

1. Why is this medication prescribed?
2. What are the desired effects? How are the effects monitored and by whom?
3. Are there other forms of treatment?
4. What are the risks and side effects?
5. What are the interactions with other medications being used?
6. How will changes in health and physical conditions change the effectiveness and the side effects?
7. How long will this medication be used, and how often will its use be reviewed?
8. What will be the cost of the drugs? Are there generic forms of the drug available, and are there cheaper sources for the medication?

Family members can also be of help to the physician in prescribing proper medication by reporting any history of drug abuse or dependency by the individual family member being evaluated. Hoarding of drugs, uncontrolled dose escalation, or obtaining drugs from multiple physicians should also be reported.

NEUROPSYCHOLOGICAL EVALUATIONS

As an aid in evaluating dementia and AD in particular, psychological and neurological evaluations are suggested not only by the Alzheimer's Association, but also by the American Psychological Association[6] and in *DSM–IV.*[1] This evaluation should include information as to intellectual abilities, cognitive abilities, emotional state, and functional level. This data is vital in arriving at an accurate diagnosis, as well as in making determinations as to treatment, management, and care. In most cases of diagnosis, brief mental status evaluations are inadequate instruments. False positives are common. Little data as to status of intellectual, cognitive, emotional, and functional ability and impairment is derived.

AD is an organic brain disease and requires tests for a wide range of multiple cognitive domains, including memory, attention, motor and perceptual skills, abstract and pragmatic reasoning, visual-spatial abilities, problem solving, and executive functioning. Too often diagnosis procedures are limited and performed by individuals with little training or background and experience in evaluating dementias.

Although research is being carried on at this time, there are no conclusive biological tests or markers short of autopsy to diagnose AD. Neuropsychological evaluations allow for differentiation between the forms of dementia, discriminating between dementias that are age-related, due to general medical conditions including other central nervous system conditions, systemic conditions that cause dementia, persisting effects of a substance, or emotional disorders such as depression which causes cognitive problems.

With the development of biological markers in the diagnosis of AD, a neuropsychological evaluation will still be important to assess pre-morbid abilities, onset of dementia, the functional aspects of the disease and level of impairment, a prognosis for the future, and identification of spared resources and abilities to provide for treatment and care.

Neuropsychological evaluations are based on standardized, reliable, valid tests and procedures, rather than a cursory examination and subjective diagnosis. The data obtained from a comprehensive evaluation provides the physician with data to make an accurate diagnosis, as well as information for treatment planning and care.

The use of psychometric tests is limited to those with extensive training and experience by licensing law. Guidelines for training and practice have been developed by the American Psychological Association.[6] One of the guidelines is that psychologists gain specialized competence. Competence in administering, scoring, and interpreting psychological and neuropsychological instruments in performing clinical interviews, determining which tests are best suited to the particular situation, and communicating the findings of the evaluation in a clear and comprehensible manner are all important. Advanced continuing education, training, and experience in the areas of gerontology, neuropsychology, and rehabilitation psychology are often pursued in order to maintain a level of competency and clinical ability. Education of other health care professionals about the limitation of brief screening devices and the need for more comprehensive evaluations is also suggested in the guidelines. These guidelines facilitate the achievement of the purpose of a neuropsychological evaluation, which is to aid in diagnosis, establish baseline performance, estimate the prognosis, and develop a treatment plan.

Areas of consideration in a neuropsychological evaluation usually include an estimation of pre-morbid intellectual abilities and current ability. Cognitive ability, resources, and limitation data include:

- Orientation
- Attention span and concentration
- Memory abilities

  Immediate memory
  Short-term memory
  Long-term memory
  Working memory

- Incremental learning ability
- Thought processes

  Psychosis
  Delusional thinking
  Abstract reasoning
  Pragmatic reasoning
  Problem-solving ability
  Ability to comprehend rational explanations

- Executive functioning

  Organization ability
  Planning ability
  Sequencing

- Expressive language ability

  Productive language
  Aphasia
  Agnosia
  Oral language
  Written language

- Receptive language

  Comprehension
  Perception

- Emotional state

Another area of evaluation, which is helpful in the diagnosis and care planning, is functional ability related to daily living skills. Some of this information can be obtained from family members. Meeting with the family is important in obtaining family history, as well as information about cognitive ability and impairment and functional ability. Information often differs from one family member to another and must be analyzed and considered for validity.

Functional ability evaluation include:

- Self-maintenance

  Physical functioning
  Personal care and hygiene
  Dressing and grooming
  Nutrition
  Speech and language ability
  Eating habits
  Maintenance of personal possessions
  Ability to use medications
  Health maintenance

- Social functioning

  Interaction with family
  Social skills
  Relationship with friends
  Peer group involvement
  Leisure and recreational involvement
  Use of alcohol and mood altering drugs

- Community living activities

  Homemaking skills
  Use of transportation
  Ability to shop for self
  Independent travel skills
  Ability to avoid common dangers
  Use of community services

The results of all types of psychological and neuropsychological tests are impacted by a variety of factors which must be taken into consideration in scoring and in determining validity and accuracy. This is especially true in evaluating the elderly. Factors include visual acuity, auditory acuity, gross and fine motor skill and ability, illnesses which interfere with test performance, emotional state at the time of testing, cultural and native language differences, and other conditions and environmental situations that have not been mentioned. In order to obtain an accurate evaluation, the examiner should consider confabulating factors and provide for a test experience which will allow the subject the fullest opportunity to succeed.

Specific parts of a neuropsychological evaluation usually include identifying data, tests and procedures used, any unusual or disturbing testing factors, referral and background information, mental status and behavioral observations, the diagnostic interview, a family interview, assessment results, a diagnosis, and recommendations. The form and specific tests of a neuropsychological evaluation vary with the examiner. However, the goal is to provide data as to intellectual, cognitive, and functional state, as well as emotional status to aid in diagnosis, treatment, and care.

A final consideration in the diagnostic procedure and follow-up using a multidisciplinary approach is to include a case manager. Treatment and care often require the services of a trained specialist such as a social worker, therapist, counselor, or psychiatric nurse. This need will be discussed in treatment and care.

Earlier in this chapter it was mentioned that a major breakthrough in the diagnosis of dementia (and AD in particular) has been the development and implementation of a multidisciplinary evaluation approach. AD continues to be an overdiagnosed and misdiagnosed disease because of the use of inaccurate and invalid assessment and evaluation techniques by many practitioners. Progress; however, is being made. This is evident from the development of facilities (especially at teaching hospitals) which use the approach, methods, and procedures discussed in this chapter. This trend will continue and result in better diagnostic methods, treatment, and care.

A sample of a neuropsychological assessment follows:

Neuropsychological Assessment

    Name:
    DOB:
    Date of Evaluation:
    Evaluator:
    Referral:

Tests and Procedures

    Chart Review
    Staff Interview
    Interview with Family
    Mental Status and Behavioral Observations
    Guilford Physical Complaints Checklist
    Guilford Self-Rating Symptom Checklist
    Geriatric Depression Scale
    WAIS-III

        Digit Span Test
        Comprehension Test

Bender Gestalt Test—Partial
Boston Naming Tests
Boston Aphasia Tests

    Visual Confrontation Test
    Sentence Reading and Comprehension Test
    Expressive Language Test
    Categories Test
    Comprehensive Language Test

Fairfield Geriatric Rating Scale
Blessed Dementia Test

REFERRAL DATA

The subject is a 76-year-old white female who was admitted to _____ Memory Impaired unit on January 30, 2003. Prior to that time, she had been living at home with her husband. The husband reported that about two years ago his wife began to develop signs of dementia, including problems with memory, disorientation, confusion, and impaired executive functions. The husband cared for the wife until January of this year, when it was determined that she would benefit from placement. A neuropsychological assessment was ordered because the onset and progression of the patient's dementia appeared to be atypical. As will be discussed in depth, the symptoms, behaviors, and functional disability are very severe and significant for one who, according to the husband's reports, was fairly functional a few years ago.

At the time of testing, the patient was described as agitated, restless, and irritable. Reportedly, she is confused and disoriented. Often, when wanting to relieve herself, she takes off her clothes in the hallway. Allegedly, she has become physically assaultive with staff.

At the time of testing, the patient was taking Aricept and Zyprexia, which reportedly have been of benefit. The husband stated that until two or three years ago, his wife still worked, was socially involved, and functional. He was vague about specifics, but stated that prior to the patient's deterioration, she had some visual problems with her left eye. The patient's recent medical history is unclear; however, it is possible that her problems are related, at least in part, to cardiovascular insult or injury and/or organic brain syndrome.

Mental Status and Behavioral Observations

The patient is a large woman who appears as her stated age. She was assessed at the facility. During the evaluation, the husband was present. The patient tended to rely on him for information; however, she was instructed to answer the questions initially on her own. His presence was helpful to verify the responses. The patient was unable to answer simple questions or provide much accurate information. She has significant problems with word finding and oral and written expression, which leads this examiner to suspect a transient ischemic attack (TIA) or stroke and/or organicity. She also has problems with receptive language. Questions had to be repeated and explained. Often, she lost track of instructions. She was unable to complete sequential tasks or understand simple instructions or explanations. There were signs of perceveration as well as frustration when she could not complete a task. She became especially agitated when unable to put into words her thoughts or find words. However, she was cooperative. It is important in interactions with her to be patient and not rush her. Under pressure, she decompensates. This is why she at times acts out. She is confused, disoriented, and frustrated. Directions and instructions will have to be repeated because of problems with memory and comprehension.

Diagnostic Interview

The patient did not know her age, the date, or the other specific information, including how many children she had. Her husband said that often she does not know who he is. She said that she thought she had four or five sons and one daughter. She did not know how many siblings she had. When asked, she said, "Just about all of us."

She said that she "felt good" and that the food was "good." When asked about her daily activities, she said that she was "just here." She does not appear to be depressed, but more agitated and restless. This is common in late-stage dementia.

Test Results

The patient obtained a score of five out of 30 on the Folstein, which suggests severe dementia. Same age-education cohort score is 27, with 25 the 25th percentile score. She is disoriented as to time, place, and person. She had significant problems with completing test tasks because of problems with comprehension, as well as focus and attention. She is easily distracted; however, when given cues and with repetition of instructions, she performed more adequately. Immediate, short-term, long-term, and working memory impairments are significant. She is unable to learn and retain new information, which makes behavioral management difficult. It is important to make sure that the patient understands by looking directly at her and being specific and direct in communication. Because she displays significant problems with receptive language, even simple explanations are often not understood. Repeating instructions and directions in basic terms is suggested.

The patient appears to be suffering from agnosia and has problems with written communication, both reading and writing. She can read simple words and knows letters and numbers, but does not understand the meaning of what she reads. Visual motor integrity problems, as well as language problems, suggest organicity. She scored significantly below average on the WAIS tests that measure memory and common sense. She has problems with executive functions, such as planning, organizing, and completing sequential tasks. Her score on the Blessed Dementia Rating Scale suggests severe functional disability. She has significant problems with memory and performance of every day activities and needs direction and help. Poor performance on the Boston Aphasia and Naming Tests support the diagnosis of severe cognitive impairment.

Diagnosis

294.8 Dementia Not Otherwise Specified (NOS)[1]

The patient's dementia is atypical, although there are symptoms of disorientation, impaired memory, aphaisa, apraxia, agnosia, impaired expressive and receptive language ability, problems with attention and focus and executive functions, and problems with self care. She does not appear to be depressed, but more accurately agitated, and at times aggressive because she is confused, disoriented, and frustrated. Because of the rapid deterioration of the patient's abilities and rather sudden onset, organicity is suspected, with possible cardiovascular insult or injury or structural brain damage.

Recommendations

The medication reportedly is of some benefit to the patient. Of course, all medical decisions must be made by the patient's physician. Behavior interventions include realization that she tends to decompensate under stress or pressure. She requires a calm environment, without being pushed beyond her capacities. She also is bored. Activities, such as looking at magazines or pictures, seem to interest her. During the neuropsychological assessment, she appeared to like to have a pen in her hand and write or draw on the paper. Do not expect her to interact as she did in the past. Just sitting with her and touching her can be helpful, or even just being with her in the same room. A complete medical exam, including a consult with a neurologist, is suggested.

TREATMENT: BASIC CONCEPTS AND RECENT RESEARCH

The *DSM–IV*[1] differentiates between forms of reversible and irreversible dementia. The irreversible dementia includes AD, vascular dementia and dementia due to HIV disease, head trauma, Parkinson's disease, Huntington's disease, Pick's disease, and Creutzfeldt-Jakob disease.

In the case of diagnosis of vascular dementia, there must be evidence of cerebrovascular disease. Symptoms are usually very specific and focal. Treatment of hypertension and vascular disease are very important in preventing further trauma and injury. The involvement of a neurologist and the use of CT or MRI examinations are important. Causal factors usually include multiple strokes with multiple lesions.

Dementia due to HIV disease is characterized by memory, thought, and problem solving ability impairment. Anoxia and motor problems are related symptoms, with depression common. Great gains in treatment have been made over the past years utilizing pharmacological and psychological intervention strategies for HIV disease. Head trauma dementia varies in impairment and dementia symptomotology, depending on the type and extent of injury. Amnesia, aphaisa, anxiety, mood lability, and problems with attention and concentration are common. The dementia is usually not progressive as it is with AD, and some abilities, such as language skills often return during the first six months following an injury. Again, the skills of a neurologist are important in determining the extent and type of structural injury. Treatment using physical, occupational, and language therapists is common.

Parkinson's disease is a neurological disorder that is progressive with tremor, rigidity, and balance problems. Symptoms of dementia, especially in elderly patients, are frequent with executive function impairment and problems with memory. Depression tends to coexist. Huntington's disease is inherited. The disease presents with problems in judgment, memory, and executive functions with disorganized speech and irritability common in late stages. Like AD, the disorder is progressively debilitating. Genetic testing and family history are used for a differential diagnosis, in that 50 percent of the children of individuals with Huntington's develop the disease.[1]

Pick's disease is a degenerative brain disease. Problems with memory, attention, and language are primary cognitive symptoms. While the differentiation between AD and Pick's is difficult, a neurological examination tends to discover frontal and temporal lobe damage most significant. Creutzfeld-Jakob disease is an insidious infectious disease with rapid progress. It too is irreversible. Extrapyramidal signs tend to appear with burst suppression electroencephalogram activity and myoclonia.

The importance of the involvement of a neurologist in the evaluation of dementia is illustrated above. However, it must be pointed out that in the normal aging process some brain atrophy and neuronal plaques and tangles are present. Extensive research is exploring this condition in an attempt to differentiate between AD, other dementias, and general medical conditions that present with symptoms of dementia.

The question may arise, "Why is a differentiation diagnosis necessary?" The answer is that many diseases and disorders can be treated. As of this date, there is no treatment for AD. An accurate diagnosis is important to obtain treatment for reversible dementias and disorders presenting with AD symptoms. Diagnosing AD also allows for care and management, as well as for research in the areas of prevention, treatment, and care.

Identification and treatment of dementias due to other general medical conditions (see previous text discussion), substance-induced persisting dementias, and medical/physical diseases and disorders presenting dementia symptoms relies on the medical practitioner and professional. As has been emphasized, ruling out these diseases and disorders is the basis for identifying AD. AD misdiagnosed leads to failure to treat. A medical exam alone fails to provide data for diagnosis of AD as well as identify impaired versus spared abilities and resources which can be used and built on to improve the quality of life for the patient with AD.

Psychological and emotional disorders or problems are often coexistent with AD, can present symptoms of dementia, or can interfere with the diagnosis of dementia. A psychological evaluation can be a part of a neuropsychological evaluation or performed by a psychiatrist or psychologist at a different time and setting.

A patient who suffers from anxiety can have problems with an evaluation. Problems with attention and focus, decompensation, and confusion because of stress often result in significantly poorer performance than if the subject is not suffering from anxiety. This is one reason why it is important to establish rapport with the subject. A clinical interview when conducted in a compassionate, unhurried, supportive manner can produce an atmosphere conducive to testing and allows the subject an opportunity to do well. Research has documented that memory and performance problems tend to develop when the individual is rushed, under stress, or anxious. Elderly individuals often need more time for recall. This is one reason that simple screening tests such as the MMSE are often inaccurate.

The individual tested tends to feel pressure. Also, in many cases, major life situation decisions are made based on the results of a 15-minute evaluation. These include decisions as to driving rights, competency, and living arrangements or placement. Those with AD tend to be anxious and agitated based on the fact that they are confused and disoriented. Inability to understand what is happening, problems with following directions, and problems completing tasks lead to frustrations and often agitation. Not only is agitation common when asked to perform a task in testing, but agitation and anxiety also tend to be a primary emotion with AD. Managing agitation is one of the main concerns in care taking and will be discussed later in this chapter, as will be suggestions on how to communicate with a patient with AD.

It is estimated that 16 to 20 million Americans suffer from depression.[3] An even larger number of people live with anxiety disorders. The elderly tend to have more emotional problems, particularly with anxiety and depression, than younger individuals. This is due to elements of loss related to physical impairments and disability, health concerns, physical problems, and loss of prestige, role, loved ones, and support systems. Diagnosticians must be aware of a subject's mental and emotional state. Because depression presents many symptoms of dementia, the disorder is often called pseudodementia. Problems with memory, attention, concentration, and orientation are common in depression.

Anxiety and depression are sometimes preexisting or coexisting with AD, and must be treated separately, either pharmacologically, psychologically, or both. Side effects of the drugs must be considered. Antidepressants can cause sedation, hypotension, cardiotoxicity, and anticholinergic side effects. Antianxiety medications tend to be counterindicated, especially in dementia, because they often cloud sensorium, can be addictive, and cause ataxia and impaired memory.

A trial and error study of use of medication with the elderly population, without experience in geriatric pharmacology and without an effective system in place for monitoring impact and side effects, can lead to detrimental results. Paranoia is fairly common with the elderly. Sensory loss (visual and auditory) and social isolation and withdrawal increase the risk for developing symptoms. It has been estimated that 20 percent of the individuals with AD suffer from paranoid symptoms.[3]

Alcoholism and drug abuse often increase with aging due to depression and anxiety, isolation, boredom, and lack of social involvement. Preexisting personality problems and disorders tend to become more severe. The elderly seem to be less willing to seek psychiatric help than younger individuals. There is also a tendency for mental health professionals to prefer intervention with younger and physically healthy individuals. Hopefully this will change.

RESEARCH

Exciting news is available in the area of research. For the fiscal year 2003, the federal government estimates that over $640 million was spent on research for AD.[5] Since 1982, the Alzheimer's Association has awarded $165 million in research grants. In a research update as of January 2005 by the Canadian Alzheimer's Association,[5] it is reported that there is no cure for AD and that the symptoms are irreversible. Also, there are no biological/physiological methods of diagnosing AD. As has been stressed, the process is one of ruling out causes of dementia that are related to other medical, systemic, substance induced, and emotional disorders. However, behavioral observations, scientific testing, and measurement of impairment are utilized, once the above-mentioned conditions are ruled out, to diagnose and manage AD.

Risk factors for AD include genetic disposition, age, previous head injury, Down syndrome, evidence of brain inflammation, and diabetes. Recent terminology includes the phrase mild cognitive impairment (MCI) as a condition that may lead to the development of AD. It is unclear as to whether MCI is actually early stage dementia or a disorder in and of itself.

Early stage AD is difficult to diagnose and differentiate from other forms of dementia or the disorder identified in *DSM–IV*,[1] being age-related cognitive impairment. Many claims for the treatment and cure of AD have been made; however, it is suggested that because AD is often misdiagnosed, the improvements in cognitive level and functional level are due to the successful treatment of a general medical condition that is actually not AD.

This same factor may apply in the focus on so-called ways to delay the onset of the disease. Healthy lifestyle factors indeed may result in physical and mental good health, but, again, there are problems in determining whether or not this delays AD. It most likely lessens the risk of developing disorders which cause cognitive decline. Intellectual stimulation and social involvement tend to create a healthier and better quality of life, but there lacks documentation that this reduces the risk of developing AD.

In the past, the primary cause of AD was suggested to be a deficit in the neurotransmitter acetylcholine which is important in memory and other cognitive processes. The Food and Drug Administration (FDA) has approved two classes of drugs called cholinesterase inhibitors to treat the cognitive loss symptoms of AD. Donepezzil (Aricept), rivastigmine (Exelon), and tacrine (Cognex) are available in prescription form to improve the maintenance of the level of acetycholine in the brain. Tacrine, however, is not as commonly prescribed because of risks of liver damage. Modest improvements for a short period of time have been reported, but no significant long-term benefit is documented.

These drugs are expensive, and like all medication, have side effects. However, it has been my clinical experience that many families are so devastated at having a member diagnosed with AD that any possible postponement of severity is considered to be of benefit. There is also the possibility that modest short-term improvement is a faction of wish fulfillment, and that any positive response is the focus of family attention.

More recently, research as to the cause of AD has focused on brain cell abnormalities and damage. In the healthy brain, a protein named beta-amyloid is split from a larger protein called APP. In the brain of those with AD, the enzymes that separate beta-amyloid from APP produce too much beta-amyloid, which results in high deposits of amyloid plaques. These plaques supposedly destroy nerve cells. Research is taking place to find inhibiting drugs to prevent beta-amyloid from splitting, to prevent amyloid deposits and to eliminate amyloid plaques. Clinical trials are now taking place. Success would be a real breakthrough, although there is still the question of the impact of plaques as a causal factor in AD. Research is also exploring how tangles of fibers inside nerve cells impact on dementia. Healthy nerve cells have tangles and plaques. The question is how these conditions affect the brain in those who develop AD. Another drug currently being researched is Alzhemed, which is claimed to prevent the soluble form of beta-amyloid from forming insoluble plaques. Clioquinal is another drug in research to test the hypothesis that copper, iron, and other metals in foods cause AD. The drug's purpose is to eliminate these from the body. At one time, aluminum deposits were thought to cause AD; however, this premise has pretty much been discounted. The herbal supplement Ginkgo biloba is also in clinical trial with the possibility that the product may delay AD onset.

Researchers are also involved in studies to combine cholinesterase inhibitors with other drugs like Memantine. Memantine is a drug which has been developed to eliminate toxic levels of glutamate. Glutamate is a chemical that is necessary for impulses to transmit across the junction (synapse) between cells. Glutamate leakage multiplies the risk of brain cell damage. Memantine was approved by the FDA in 2003 to treat advanced AD. Reducing beta-amyloid in the brain by injecting antibodies has been attempted; however, clinical trials have been discontinued because of the development of lethal brain inflammation in some participants. More recent studies have used naturally occurring immunoglobulin antibodies. Some improvement in cognitive functioning and a reduction of beta-amyloids have been reported.

Statins to slow the progress of AD is also being researched. Another trial is focused on a decrease in the abnormal level of beta-amyloids through the short-term use of statins. Anti-inflammatory medicine has been in research as an agent to treat AD; however, it has not been documented that taking anti-inflammatory medicine actually reduces the risk of AD or has any benefit in treatment. Stem cell research is also in progress.

A new test called biobarcode assay, which detects proteins in spinal fluid, is the focus of research as a possible biochemical indicator of early stage AD. The researchers claim that a protein called amyloid-beta-derived diffusible ligand (ADDL) is detected in all patients; however, that those with AD have increases in the level of ADDL as the disease progresses. This research is in early stage, with a sample population of only 30 in the initial sample. The proponents of this test admit that more tests with larger samples are needed over time and that at this time there is no evidence that high levels of ADDL exist only in AD patients and not patients with other forms of dementia.[9]

This section on research is included to give hope and suggest that money and effort are being expended to develop biochemical ways of diagnosing, treating, and managing AD.

MANAGEMENT AND CARE

A comprehensive diagnostic process, including health professionals such as physicians (general practice, neurology, psychiatry), a pharmacologist, a neuropsychologist, and a mental health specialist in the field of social psychology will provide information in order for an accurate diagnosis of AD to be made.

Medical tests allow for the differentiation of general medical conditions which present symptoms of AD. These conditions can be treated. Emotional disorders and substance abuse or use can be identified and treated. Disorders that cannot be reversed such as vascular dementia and dementia from head trauma can be managed and attempts made to control further damage. Dementias due to multiple etiologies other than AD can be identified and treated or managed. In the case of AD, an accurate and comprehensive diagnosis can provide direction for management and care based on the development of a plan to provide the best quality of life for both the patient and loved ones. This plan should be based on spared, as well as impaired, abilities.

Research related to the situation and needs of those with AD and caretakers is proceeding to allow for ways to improve care and provide for the family in the process. Two particular areas of change and significance are related to in-home professional services, and in the event that in-home services are not possible, residential placement in facilities that focus on the special needs of the patient with AD and the family. Developing a cure and treatment program must be based on the individual's problems and impairments, as well as strengths. In order to determine the level of functioning, an evaluation as to daily living skills is necessary. Various formats for the evaluation of these skills are available.

An evaluation should include skills in personal hygiene, eating, and dressing. Other areas include skills in performing household tasks, coping with finances, shopping, driving, ability to find one's way in familiar settings and familiar streets, and the ability to grasp explanations.

The neuropsychological evaluation provides data for care and management based on the quantitative, objective test results. Information should include data on orientation, attention and focus, memory, learning capacity, thought processes, executive functions, expressive and perceptive language abilities, and emotional state.

AD is a progressive degenerative disorder. Understanding the stage of degeneration and the related impairments will provide data as to current needs, as well as projected future condition and needs. From the time of diagnosis, the average life span of the individual is about eight years.

The stages of AD are:

Stage 1: No Cognitive Decline
Stage 2: Very Mild Cognitive Decline

> Complaints of forgetfulness
> Forgets names
> Loses items
> No objective deficits in employment or social situations
> Patient displays appropriate concern

Stage 3: Mild Cognitive Decline

> May remember little of passage read from a book
> Decreased performance in demanding employment and social situations
> Coworkers become aware of patient's relatively poor performance
> Difficulty finding words and names
> May get lost when traveling to unfamiliar locations
> Anxiety is common
> Denial is likely

Stage 4: Moderate Cognitive Decline

> Clear-cut deficits
> Concentration deficits
> Decreased knowledge of recent events in their lives and current events
> Difficulties traveling alone and in handling personal finances
> Recognizes familiar persons and faces
> Can still travel to familiar locations (e.g., corner drugstore)
> Withdrawal from challenging situations
> Denial becomes dominant defense

Stage 5: Moderately Severe Cognitive Decline

> Patient can no longer survive without some assistance
> May forget address or telephone number and names of close family members (e.g., grandchildren)
> Frequently disoriented to time or place
> Remembers own name and names of spouse and children
> May clothe themselves improperly (e.g., shoe on wrong foot)
> Needs no assistance with eating or toileting

Stage 6: Severe Cognitive Decline

Occasionally forgets spouse's name
Largely unaware of all recent events and experiences in his or her life
Retains some sketchy knowledge of his or her past life
Unaware of surroundings, season, or year
Sleep patterns frequently disturbed
Personality and emotional changes frequent (often occur at earlier stages)

   a. delusions (e.g., spouse is an impostor, imaginary visitors, talks to own
      reflection in mirror)
   b. repetitive behaviors—continual cleaning, raking leaves, or lawn mowing
   c. anxiety, agitation, occasional violent behavior
   d. loss of initiative, abulia, apathy

Stage 7: Very Severe Cognitive Decline

Inability to communicate, grunting
Incontinent
Needs assistance with toileting and eating
May be unable to walk
Focal neurological signs and symptoms common

Other factors important in care plan development and management relate to the patient's loved ones and their resources as well as needs. Caring for an individual with AD has a tremendous impact on family members, not only emotionally but financially, as well as in areas such as time involved, other family responsibilities, and interpersonal relationships. How each family member is affected depends on not only the individual's relationship with the patient, but the individual member's own situation, resources, and vulnerabilities. Often unsettled interpersonal problems exist not only within the family, but also with each family member and the person suffering from AD. These issues tend to become more obvious and stressful with the diagnosis of dementia.

The emotional responses of family members tend to parallel the patient's response during the stages of AD. They start with denial. This can be because of fear and lack of understanding. Denial tends to delay evaluation and care. The sooner a comprehensive evaluation is made, the sooner a diagnosis and treatment and care plan can be developed. The hope is that symptoms are not as extreme as suspected and that the condition is treatable and reversible. Confusion and anxiety also tend to be emotional responses of both the subject and the family. Symptoms of dementia can vary in intensity and duration during the course of the disorder. It is not uncommon for various family members to report different degrees of impairment and functional disability. Anger is another response, as is depression. The decisions related to care can result in feelings of guilt. While in-home health care and services are more and more available to the family, the stress of caring for an individual with AD is often overwhelming. Indeed, the caretaker's day is a 36-hour day.

The family must consider what living arrangement is best not only for the patient, but also for the family. These decisions must be based on an accurate diagnosis of needs, abilities, and resources. This is where a trained professional case manager can help. Possible living arrangements include:

+ Living at home independently
+ Living with family independently
+ Independent living at a facility
+ Assisted living at home with family or in a facility
+ Nursing home living
+ Memory impaired facility living

Many services are available to allow the patient suffering from AD to continue living in the least restrictive setting. Home care services have been mentioned. Day care facilities are available, as is respite care to allow caretakers some relief. Visiting volunteer programs from such organizations as Meals on Wheels, local churches, and other groups have developed. The Canadian Alzheimer's Association is researching the significance to an individual in losing their driving privileges and how to provide people in this situation with transportation. Support groups, educational classes, and counseling are available to caregivers, often through local Alzheimer's Association chapters.

Because it is difficult for a caretaker to research costs, availability, and needs while fulfilling the role of primary caretaker, professionals such as counselors and case managers are often available. Their initial involvement and ongoing availability should be a part of the diagnostic, treatment, and management/care process and program. Again the good news is that such comprehensive help is becoming more and more available.

TECHNIQUES TO COPE WITH ALZHEIMER'S DISEASE IN THE FAMILY

The following coping techniques for family members and caretakers is included to give guidance, and in an attempt to help deal with stress and related emotional factors:

1. Become educated as to the nature, course, and treatment possibilities.
2. Seek expert advice—a complete physical and behavioral assessment might be necessary.
3. Be involved with the individual and treatment. Provide love and support.
4. Consider joining a support group.
5. Become aware of the behaviors in the family due to Alzheimer's and of your own feelings and responses.

6. Stay involved, but not too involved—use creative detachment.
7. Develop your own interests and activities away from home.
8. Eliminate feelings of guilt.
9. Use a stress management plan.
10. Change unhealthy rules, roles, and rituals such as codependency, covering up rather than seeking an assessment or help, or not allowing the individual to discuss their feelings and concerns.
11. Test reality. This means overcoming denial and planning for the future.
12. Deal with feelings of loss and grief. Individual counseling might be of benefit.
13. Open up communication with other family members regarding care, financial matters, and expectations.
14. Have faith. Twelve-step mottos such as *Let Go, Let God* and *One Day at a Time* might apply.

COMMUNICATING WITH ALZHEIMER'S PATIENTS

Care and management interactions and processes depend on communications between caretaker and the individual suffering from AD. Recognition that the Alzheimer's patient suffers from language, comprehension, and reasoning impairment is the first step in developing ways of communicating. The degree and type of impairment differs from individual to individual, not only initially, but as the disease progresses. Physical problems such as auditory impairment, dysphonia, and visual disability complicate communication. Failure to be aware of not only physical disabilities, but organicity related to the disease, tends to result in problems related to care and management, and complicates diagnosis and treatment.

During the early stages of AD, the patient often recognizes expressive language problems, especially word finding and being able to complete the thought process. This leads to frustration, anxiety, and depression in many cases. There is a tendency to withdraw and become reclusive. Caretakers are not to become frustrated. Having to repeat information and dealing with the individual's inability to comprehend simple directions and carry out simple tasks often leads to impatience and anger. It must be realized that inability to understand and comply, not intentional opposition, are the causes of these behaviors and communication problems.

Improving communication benefits both the caretaker and the patient. Even as the disability increases, there are basic techniques that can be used. Suggestions include:

1. Improving those impairments such as auditory disability and visual problems.
2. The identity of specific language and thought processing problems. Give the individual time to find words and cues to finish incomplete thoughts and sentences.

3. Be patient and nonconfrontational. Arguing about misinformation or inaccurate beliefs such as that a deceased spouse is still alive only creates more problems. Discuss past happy events and occasions.

4. Treat the individual suffering from AD with respect and allow for dignity. Persuade instead of giving orders. In times of anger or agitation, distract the individual rather than confrontation.

5. Find a quiet place in which to communicate.

6. Look directly at the individual and be sure that you have their attention.

7. Be specific and concrete. Individuals with significant cognitive and comprehension problems do not usually understand humor.

8. When giving direction, keep it simple. Use cues and break tasks into steps. Repeat and give step-by-step help.

9. Do not over estimate skills and ask a patient to perform tasks beyond ability, but do allow the individual to experience success by completing tasks within their scope of ability.

10. Consider the person's ability to tolerate environmental stimulation. Too many visitors at one time, task demands, or noise and confusion in the environment can result in decompensation which leads to agitation or aggression.

11. Individuals in a state of decompensation usually do not respond to reasoning. Removal from the area of conflict or confusion or a simple command such as "stop that" can help.

12. Use nonverbal methods of communicating such as demonstration or role playing when verbal methods are not understood.

13. Gentle, caring body contact such as a hug or a hand or one's arm are often understood and beneficial. Just sitting with a late stage Alzheimer's patient can have a calming effect, or talking softly or singing. Remember someone is at home even in a vegetative state. Treating that person with respect and love helps the patient as well as the caregiver.

DEALING WITH DIFFICULT BEHAVIORS

Developing communication skills and techniques is a start in dealing with inappropriate, dysfunctional, or dangerous behaviors and emotional states and responses that tend to be associated with AD. These behaviors and emotions include agitation, aggression, wandering, overdependency, inappropriate sexual acts, paranoia, depression, and anxiety.

There are a number of causal factors for problematic behavior. One is related to health factors. The side effects of medication can cause agitation, as well as such things as confusion, ataxia, and depression. This is one reason that medication should be reviewed by a specialist in pharmacology, as well as monitoring the efficacy of the drug and long-term maintenance dosage impact.

Impaired vision and hearing can result in confusion and disorientation. Interpersonal interactions and relationships are made difficult.

Acute illness not only causes physical problems, but also emotional ones such as depression, anxiety, lack of motivation, and withdrawal. Pain management is important, but can lead to sedation and an altered state of consciousness, as well as cognitive disability. Chronic illnesses have similar effects. Dehydration and constipation can impact on behavior as well as cognitive ability. Once these health factors have been identified, steps can be taken to treat the problem.

Environmental facts affect behavior and functional ability. Great advances have been made in providing surroundings that are not overwhelming, with cues for orientation. More and more facilities built to house those with memory impairments have therapy and activity programs to keep the patient settled and calm as well as occupied.

The environmental factors that lead to acting out are those that contribute to confusion, anxiety, and disorientation. An environment may be too large, cluttered, noisy, and disruptive. Environments with excessive stimulation result in patient decompensation. A structured and familiar environment does not cause the individual as much stress in that there is less need to act in new ways. Cognitive limitations make adaptation to unknown and unfamiliar situations difficult.

Another factor that contributes to behavioral problems and decompensation is presenting the patient with too difficult a task. Knowing the individual's abilities will allow for challenges which engage the patient, but do not overwhelm. Tasks can be too complicated and beyond cognitive ability, too involved with too many sequential steps, or not modified for physical disabilities and impairments. Communication problems have been discussed. The identification of the causal factors or triggers, and managing and controlling these factors so they do not occur or cause problems, can result in behavioral control.

Wandering is common among those suffering from AD. Causal factors include boredom, lack of exercise, and lack of goal-directed activity. Management includes planned security, exercise and activity, medication, reduced stress (noise, crowding, isolation), anticipation of needs and need provision, and the elimination of fear. Other specific actions that can be taken include recognizing hazards; secure the living area; notify staff; and prepare an individual patient management program, or if at home, notify neighbors and police, have a photo of the individual available, and secure car keys.

Agitation and acting out aggressively can take place in a locked facility;, as well as in situations of home care. Causal factors include confusion and overload with a catastrophic response, emotional factors or organicity. Management suggestions include remaining calm, maintaining eye contact, redirection and rechanneling, reassurance, distraction rather than confrontation, removal of the stressors, and removal of the patient from the environment.

Medication may be necessary. Neuroleptic drugs were the drug of choice for managing agitation and aggression in elderly patients with AD rather than antianxiety medication. The newer medications tend to have fewer extrapyramidal side effects than the older class of antipsychotic drugs, but there can still be significant drug-related problems when using them. In May 2005, the FDA requested that manufacturers of atypical antipsychotics include warnings as to use of these medications with elderly patients suffering from dementia. These warnings include increased risk of death.

Overdependency, especially on one or more family members, is common in AD patients, and understandably so. The causal factors include fear, insecurity, confusion, and regression. It is often difficult to leave a loved one in the care of others. Daily twice daily visits and long stays ease one's feeling of guilt and concern, but may interfere with an individual's adaptation to a residential facility. Because the individual's memory and sense of time tend to be impaired, unfounded accusations of abandonment and neglect are common, causing family members or loved one's pain.

Management techniques include assurance as much as possible, realizing that rational arguments are often not understood or accepted. Limit responses to demands. Caretaker burnout can result in resentment for the caretaker, as well as development of health problems. If the individual is living at home, look into daycare programs. Respite care is available in many communities. Some churches and other organizations provide visiting volunteers. If the overly dependent individual is in a residential facility, provide them with security objects such as family pictures and items they can touch and hold. Pats and hugs from staff and attention help.

Inappropriate sexual behaviors can be related to continuing need for affection and intimacy or response to taclite stimulation. Common responses to being bathed or during toileting are anger, resistance, and agitation. These particular situations tend to be interpreted as intrusion. What appears to be a sexual behavior is not always sexual in nature. Tight underclothing can result in pulling, tugging, and touching oneself. Removal of clothing is usually not sexual, but due to discomfort of the clothes or just something to do. Understanding the intent in situations such as this allows for interventions such as use of other clothing that is loose and difficult to remove. Providing the individual with a pillow to hold and carry or stuffed toys sometimes help. In cases where the intent is indeed sexual, care must be taken, especially if another patient or staff member is approached. Correction and positive reinforcement of appropriate behavior might help. Monitoring the individual will possibly be necessary in an ongoing manner.

Paranoia and suspicion are related to disorientation, confusion, memory impairment, fear that needs will not be met, and preexisting personality traits exaggerated by age and cognitive impairment. Symptoms include isolation, accusations of staff, family, and others, hiding belongings, and anxiety. It is difficult to reassure such an individual or rationalize with them. Distraction sometimes works; however, the person tends to return to the subject and accusations as an obsession. Listening for a short time, but setting limits, is one intervention. Such behavior is irritating, but usually not dangerous.

Depression in aging, and especially with AD, is related to life-stage situation, as well as physical disability, pain, and chronic or acute illnesses. Other causes include cognitive impairment, with the realization that these impairments are significant and possibly progressive. Age-related losses, such as loss of the ability to drive, decreased physical stamina, loss of role and status, and loss of friends and loved ones exacerbate depression, as does concern about the future and financial status. In some situations, depression is a preexisting condition. Aging seems to exacerbate these emotional problems. A review of past psychiatric treatment and psychological functioning can provide data in order to properly treat these preexisting emotional problems. Management techniques of emotional problems might include increased involvement, physical activity, socialization, providing positive interaction with family and staff, attention, and love.

IN-HOME CARE OR PLACEMENT

A major decision faces every family concerning how to best care for the patient with AD as the disorder progresses. As was presented, AD is a progressive physical/organic illness, which is insidious and causes increasingly more significant impairment and disability as time goes by. These disabilities are those of impaired intellectual, cognitive, emotional, and functional capacity.

Initially, the disability will be minor, with problems in memory, orientation, and functioning. As the disease progresses, the disability becomes more severe, with the final stage one of vegetativeness. In the early stages, care focuses on quality of life issues and how to use spared resources and abilities, but in the late stages, care relates to hygiene and maintenance. At first, a family member or members and other loved ones may decide to care for the patient at home. Services are available to facilitate this; however, once the needs are evaluated and resources for care explored, the caretakers must decide who provides the care and how, when, and where.

A great deal of progress has been made in the last decade in providing in-home care. Long-term health insurance coverage in most cases allows for in-home care.

From a financial standpoint, as well as related to quality of life issues, it is beneficial to provide care in the least expensive and least restrictive setting. Outpatient services, such as the provision of psychological and psychiatric services, a neuropsychological assessment, and treatment planning can be coordinated with the AD patient at home, as can some medical services such as nursing care and therapy. Other services like companion care, shopping, food preparation, and cleaning help the patient live at home more independently. Some of these services are paid for by Medicare, Medicaid, or third-party service providers.

Individual communities, counties, and states offer benefit programs. A local case manager should have information on these services and can help the family research options and make care arrangements. Not-for-profit organizations also offer help. The Alzheimer's Association is a network of chapters providing educational services, support groups, and in some cases, programs including respite care. The Alzheimer's Association can be contacted by calling 1-800-272-3900 for a local chapter. The National Stroke Association deals with stroke victims and their families. The Area Agency on Aging and Aging Information Office provides services to senior citizens, including information on community resources. A great deal of information is available on the internet about AD, research, and services available.

Day care for individuals with AD is more readily available than a decade ago. These programs give the caretaker relief and also provide structured activities and a somewhat stimulating environment. A hot meal, social interaction, and activity programs are a part of most day care services. Because the needs and capacities of each individual with AD vary, it is important that the facility has an appropriate program and environment. Some individuals with AD will not be able to adapt to a day care program.

Respite care is short-term care, either on an inpatient basis or as an outpatient. Care is often available through a nursing home, in a hospital-related program, or as part of a residential care facility program. Medicare limits coverage to eighty hours a year.

Companionship care at home is another option which can be contracted for with a private agency. Quality of care and the training of in-home companions as well as costs vary widely. Researching and monitoring services is vital, as it is in all cases, not only of in-home services, but throughout one's stay at a residential facility. Quality of care is not necessarily guaranteed by an agency referral. The care is often better when a family member is available to observe and monitor services. Changes in patient ability and needs vary over the course of the disease and flexibility and changes in the care program will have to be made.

A patient with AD may require treatment or care in a hospital or nursing home if there are coexisting medical problems. However, in many cases, those with AD can live in assisted living facilities or facilities for those with significant cognitive and functional problems, but having no need for medical care. More and more individuals live at home with family or a live-in caretaker until the end. At home, around the clock care may be necessary. Even in some residential facilities, a companion may be necessary. Most residential settings will not allow an unattended patient who is agitated with a risk of acting out.

A recent trend in facility housing has been care for the individual in a home-like setting. The emphasis is to provide for quality of life care. Living in such a setting will not slow down the process of AD, but will allow family, as well as the patient, the benefit of a program that recognizes the dignity and value of the individual. Cost, of course, can be an important factor in making decisions as to residential care and management.

SUMMARY

While AD is not reversible and there is no cure for the disorder, there have been significant gains in the diagnosis, treatment, and care of patients with the disorder. The diagnostic process has become more accurate and reliable, based on increasing realization that in the past, AD has been overdiagnosed and misdiagnosed. A multidisciplinary approach can identify medical, physical, emotional disorders, and problems that present symptoms of AD; however, there are in fact other forms of dementia that can be treated and often reversed.

A comprehensive approach to diagnosis, treatment, and management requires the involvement of professionals from such disciplines as medicine (especially psychiatrists and neurologists), the behavioral sciences (including neuropsychologists), pharmacologists, social science professionals, and health care case workers. An accurate diagnosis not only provides for treatment of other forms of dementia, but also provides data for the development of a care and management plan for the patient and information for the family.

A second area of progress is in the area of research, with the focus on prevention and possible reversal or cure of symptoms of AD. Third, quality of life issues have become more significant in care and management with in-home services often more available, as well as the provision of education and support for caregivers, through such wonderful organization as the Alzheimer's Association. Residential care facility options have grown, with an emphasis in home-like environment, socialization, and activities that allow for the patient's maximum utilization of resources and spared abilities. Staff training programs have become more sophisticated and available.

These are recent and significant changes, especially in the areas of diagnosis and research. Hopefully, progress will continue to be made.

REFERENCES

1. American Psychiatric Association. (1994). *Diagnostic and statistical manual of mental disorders* (4th ed.). Washington, DC: Author.
2. Rice, D. P., Fox, P. J., Max, W., Webber, P. A., Lindeman, D. A., Hauck, W. W., et al. (1993). The economic burden of Alzheimer's disease care. *Health Affairs, 12,* 164–176.
3. Spar, J. E., & LaRue, A. (2005). *Geriatric psychiatry* (2nd ed.). American Psychiatric Press.
4. Folstein, M. F., Folstein, S. E., & McHugh, P. R. (2005). *Mini-mental status examination.* Lutz, FL: Psychological Assessment Resources.
5. Alzheimer Society of Canada. (2006). *What is Alzheimer's disease?* Retrieved April 28, 2006 from www.alzheimer.ca/english/disease/whatisit-intro.htm.
6. American Psychological Association. (1998). *Guidelines for the evaluation of dementia and age related cognitive decline.* Washington, DC: Author.
7. American Association of Retired Persons (AARP). (2005, April). *Affordable prescription drugs.* Retrieved April 25, 2006 from www.aarp.org/health/affordable_drugs/a2004-10-25-watchdog-archives.html.
8. Simon, S. R., Chan, K. A., Sournerai, S. B., Wagner, A. K., Andrade, S. E., & Feldstein, A. C. (2005). Potentially inappropriate medications use by elderly persons in U.S. health maintenance organizations, 2000–2001. *Journal of the American Geriatrics Society, 532,* 227–232.
9. BioInvestorForum. (2005). *Complete company profiles: BioInvestorForum 2005.* Retrieved April 28, 2006 from www.investorforum.bio.org/bif/2005/handbook.pdf.

Chapter 10

The Scientific Foundations of Gender Identity Disorders

Leslie M. Lothstein

In this chapter I will explore the phenomenon of gender identity within the context of the current dilemmas facing clinicians in evaluating and "treating" gender "disorders." It was the medicalization of the concept of gender that led to the view that variant gender identities were not normative, but aspects of an underlying mental illness. This conclusion was not based on psychological science but on conjecture, and has led, in some circumstances, to increased suffering of individuals with normative variant gender identities who were classified as mentally ill. Concurrently, other individuals who identified as transsexuals supported the diagnosis of mental illness so they could qualify for insurance reimbursement for sex reassignment surgery. Over time, the controversy has changed both with medicine's acceptance of the concept of transsexualism as a psychiatric diagnosis (as evidenced in the *Diagnostic and Statistical Manual of Mental Disorders*, Third Edition (*DSM–III*)[1] in 1980 and the *Diagnostic and Statistical Manual of Mental Disorders, Third Edition, Revised (DSM–III–R)*[2] in 1984), and a retraction of that diagnosis in the *Diagnostic and Statistical Manual of Mental Disorders*, Fourth Edition (*DSM– IV*)[3] in 1994. With the emergence of the phenomenon of transgenderism, the rules have further changed. The controversy reflected the lack of real science in understanding gender-related phenomena, coupled with a challenge to the prevailing viewpoint that there were only two sexes and two genders (the gender binary hypothesis).

GENDER DYSPHORIA: THE EVOLUTION OF DIAGNOSIS AND THE MEDICALIZATION OF GENDER IDENTITY/ ROLE

Since 1980, the American Psychiatric Association's manual on psychiatric diagnosis (*DSM–III*,[1] *DSM–III–R*,[2] *DSM–IV*,[3] and the *Diagnostic and Statistical Manual of Mental Disorders*, Fourth Edition, Text Revision (*DSM–IV–TR*)[4]) has listed gender identity disorder (GID) as an axis I psychiatric disorder, or mental illness.

In 1980, *DSM–III*[1] first identified the sexual diagnoses separately from the personality disorders. The current version, *DSM–IV–TR*,[4] published in 2000, defined GID as follows:

I. Having a strong and persistent cross-gender identification (not merely a desire for any perceived cultural advantages of being the other sex).

In children, the disturbance is manifested by four or more of the following:

1. repeatedly stated desire to be, or insistence that he or she is, the other sex
2. in boys, preference for cross-dressing or simulating female attire; in girls, insistence on wearing only stereotypical masculine clothing
3. strong and persistent preferences for cross-sex roles in make believe play or persistent fantasies of being the other sex
4. intense desire to participate in the stereotypical games and pastimes of the other sex
5. strong preference for playmates of the other sex

In adolescents or adults, the disturbance was viewed as manifested by symptoms such as a stated desire to be the other sex, frequent passing as the other sex, desire to live or be treated as the other sex, or the conviction that he or she has the typical feelings and reactions of the other sex.

II. Having persistent discomfort with his or her sex or sense of appropriateness in the gender role of that sex.

In children the disturbance is manifested by any of the following: in boys, assertion that the penis or testes are disgusting or will disappear, or the assertion that it would be better not to have a penis, or aversion towards rough and tumble play and rejection of male stereotypical toys, games, and activities; in girls, rejection of urinating in a sitting position, assertion that she has or will grow a penis, or assertion that she does not want to grow breasts or menstruate, or marked aversion towards normative feminine clothing.

In adolescents and adults, the disturbance is manifested by symptoms such as preoccupation of getting rid of primary and secondary sex characteristics (e.g., request for hormones, surgery, or other procedures to physically alter sexual characteristics to simulate the other sex) or belief that he or she was born the wrong sex.

III. The disturbance is not concurrent with a physical intersex condition.

IV. The disturbance causes clinically significant distress or impairments in social, occupational, or other important areas of functioning.

GIDs were further characterized in terms of sexual attraction to males, females, both, or neither. While DSM–IV[3] lists the prevalence as 1/30,000 for males and 1/100,000 for females seeking sex reassignment surgery to change their bodies to match their subjective feeling of gender, these statistics have been called into question by Roughgarden[5] and Conway[6] who reanalyzed the available sex reassignment data and estimated that 1 of every 500 men and women are gender dysphoric. They view the DSM–IV statistics as incorrect and misleading. DSM–IV does not view intersex conditions with accompanying gender dysphoria (GD), transient stress related cross-dressing behavior, or persistent preoccupation with castration or penectomy without a desire to acquire the sex characteristics of the other sex as qualifying for a diagnosis of GID.

CHALLENGES TO THE *DSM–IV*

The core issue in the DSM–IV[3] diagnosis of GID is that it is a mental illness with impairments in social-emotional functioning, and having symptoms and beliefs that are abnormal. As a mental disorder, individuals with GID are labeled as emotionally ill and in need of treatment.

The prevailing view of GID as a mental illness was challenged from multiple scientific, cultural, political, neuroscientific, sociological, and psychological perspectives. Richard Green[7] provided scientific data suggesting that some childhood cross-dressing may actually be a marker for later homosexuality, which is not a mental illness. Gender research supports the view that gender exists along a continuum and is not a binary phenomenon, and that the term gender variant best describes the actual way in which individuals experience their gender. The illness model for GID as expressed in DSM–IV[3] needs to be reexamined as new scientific evidence surfaces. Indeed, there is a movement to eliminate GID as a psychiatric diagnosis in the *Diagnostic and Statistical Manual of Statistical Disorders*, Fifth Edition *(DSM–V)* which is soon to be published. Currently, some mental health professionals and members of the gay, lesbian, bisexual, and transgender (GLBT) communities have argued that it is time to rid *DSM–IV* of the diagnosis of GID because there is no hard evidence that it is a mental disorder. The arguments are scientifically persuasive. However, such a decision would also have serious social policy and economic implications for those gender variant individuals who seek psychological consultation or those self-identified transsexuals who want insurance companies or state and federal agencies to pay for their so-called illnesses.

The scientific literature on gender, however, has also noted a subset of individuals diagnosed with GID who do experience a persistent and chronic dysphoria about their gender. Those individuals were seen as at high risk for also having a major affective disorder (e.g., depression, anxiety, and bipolar disorder), suicidal thoughts and plans, and seeking ways to have hormones and surgery prescribed in order to change their body to fit their psychological feelings of gender.[8] In most cases, the dysphoria may be iatrogenic of the interface between their basic brain circuitry and society's phobia directed towards transgendered behavior, which in some cases has led to violence against transgendered individuals.

THEORIES OF GENDER IDENTITY FORMATION

There are many theories to explain normative gender development. For purposes of this introduction I will summarize some of the main findings in order to introduce the clinical issues to be presented later. This review is not meant to be all-inclusive.

While our current views of gender owe their roots to Freud's clinical insights on bisexuality,[9] the scientific foundations of our contemporary clinical understanding of gender identity phenomena relates to insights from child development, biology, the neurosciences, psychoanalysis, and family process all within the context of one's culture. The classical binary construct of gender that people are either male or female is being challenged by the above disciplines as gender identity is now viewed along a continuum with gender variance being the norm, not the exception. As we explore the new findings on the scientific underpinnings of sexuality, specifically gender, the argument will be compelling to reject the label of mental illness when referring to gender variant behavior.

Historically, the origins of gender identify is traced to Freud's notion of bisexuality, which challenged the then current social mores that maleness and femaleness were fixed traits, and challenged a simplistic binary theory of gender.[9] "The idea," he says, "that everyone is a mixture of male and female qualities was a revolutionary and liberating insight in a society committed to sexual purity and a rigid separation of the sexes, a society that was quite threatened by any mixing or blurring of sex roles" (p. 82). Freud's unfinished journey was that he failed to understand the meaning of his own insights that one's gender was not fixed but instead fluid. As a result, Freud became stuck in his culture's patriarchal view of sex and gender, and never really understood how rigid adherence to a male/female gender role damaged the self and could lead to psychosis.

BIOLOGICAL THEORIES

Sexual Circuitry Hormones and the Brain

The default sex for humans is female. Unless testosterone is added and the male hormone receptors are working, all fetuses will have a female phenotype. Chromosomal sex (46XX female and 46XY male) is only one factor determining what our bodies will look like. If male hormone receptors are not working, then men will develop female bodies (without ovaries or a uterus). However, their brains will remain male. This process is also true for women but in reverse.

Scientific studies have documented the structural differences between male and female brains, called sexual dimorphisms. LeVay[10] summarized the recent neuroscientific findings focusing on differences in sex and gender related to the following: the size of the brain; and structural differences in certain nuclei ("a cluster of cells that can be reliably identified on the basis of its size and position; and the appearance of the nerve cells forming it" [p. 132]) in the hypothalamus (the sexually dimorphic nucleus of the preoptic area identifying a cell group that is "structurally different in the two sexes" [p. 139] caused by circulating male hormone differences during the critical phase of intrauterine development). Moreover, the past two decades have produced a wealth of studies relating genetics, familial traits, fetal brain development (as a result of intrauterine neurohormomal processes), and other hypotheses regarding the scientific foundations of gender as based in the brain's neurocircuitry, involving both hardware and software. Functional magnetic resonance imaging (fMRI) and other neuroimaging studies have corroborated specific brain nuclei in the brain (the size of a grain of sand) as responsible for specific brain differences between males and female and within each group.[11]

The role of the hypothalamus (a small structure in the base of the brain) has been identified as critical in sex and gender development, including sexual arousal, gender, sexual orientation, and love relationships. Injuries or changes in specific hypothalamic nuclei provide access to understanding variations in behavior.[12]

Some of the recent findings include the following: the size of the INAH3 (the third interstitial nucleus of the anterior hypothalamus) seems to be involved in sexual differences and varies both with sex and with sexual orientation; male typical behavior has been associated with the size and structural/functional differences in the medial preoptic area; and female typical behavior is related to differences in the ventromedial nucleus. These nuclei in males and females, according to LeVay,[10] "seemed to be key sites of actions of the hormones" (p. 132). Other nuclei that appear to be implicated in sexuality and gender are deeper brain structures such as the amygdala, the septal area, the bed nucleus of the stria terminalis, and the periaqueductal grey area (all of these nuclei are different in size, structure, and function for the two sexes). Other findings include the following: the anteroventral periventricular nucleus in females regulates the ovarian cycle and is larger in females; and the corpus callosum (responsible for social and interhemispheric communication) is larger in females. Additional studies that have focused on the sexual nuclei in the brain suggested that the medial preoptic nuclei in the hypothalamus was larger in males, and that male transsexuals and male homosexual brains are similar to females in certain structures. The ventromedial nucleus was viewed as larger in females and the anteroventral periventricular nucleus was responsible for the ovarian cycle. It is only within the past 20 years that a testes determining substance was discovered, called the HY antigen factor.[12,13]

Researchers have also pointed out the importance of the intrauterine milieu for fetal brain development related to later sex and gender. Subtle and overt differences in the fetal position in the uterus, temperature, and the site of implementation of the embryo or placenta blood supply can affect sex determination, arousal, sexual orientation, love relationships, and gender identity.[13] During each trimester of pregnancy, the brain's circuitry for arousal, sex, and gender are uniquely developed and patterned as part of the later software and hardware of the brain.[14] It is widely believed that it is within the intrauterine environment that the specifics of how gender and sexuality is organized are first established. The evolving brain circuitry and software/hardware development underlying sex and gender depends on the complex orchestration of the nuances of the individual fetus's intrauterine environment, bioavailability of sex appropriate hormones, chromosomal variances, and any subtle or gross effects of the environment (both internal and external) on behavior.

There are a number of neurohormonal syndromes that lead to atypical or variant gender behavior. The most notable are the following: congenital adrenal hypoplasia or androgen insensitivity syndrome (this disorder is what makes some men like Kim Novak, the actress, appear female, though they are chromosomal males; that is she has a 46XY male Karyotype, but her body was unable to use the androgen circulating in her blood); Turner's syndrome (girls with short stature, male appearing bodies and masculine behavior); and Kleinfelter's syndrome (men with quasi-female appearing bodies). All of these syndromes exist on a continuum with the individual's behavior ranging from phenotypically normative with regards to a general population to very atypical in terms of gender-sex appearance.[15]

Researchers are also looking at the effects of neurotransmitters on gender identity development. In one study on the effects of drugs on the intrauterine milieu and fetal brain development, Ehrhardt and Meyer-Bahlburg[12] concluded that girl children born to mothers who took diethylstilbestrol were more likely than not to be identified as tomboys during latency. None of these girls had sexual orientation or severe gender role problems as teenagers. They were very masculine females during latency.

In 1968, Baker and Stoller[15] evaluated six male to female transsexuals who were found to have a variety of biological conditions hidden by psychological forces. In 1979, Stoller[16] reported on a female transsexual who was treated for a psychological disorder when it turned out that she had a rare enzyme defect, 17 B hydroxy deficiency disorder, that caused anatomic hemaphroditism and psychological distress. There are also cases of gender identity disorders that are related to genetically determined deficiency of the enzyme delta steroid 5 alpha reductase. In one study,[17] 38 children from the Dominican Republic who were raised as females became males when they entered adolescence, as the genes that trigger sexual differentiation were set into motion and their bodies masculinized with the onset of puberty. All of these girls knew they were boys (that is, they had male brains) and were not surprised by the transformation that took place during their teen years.

Sexual Orientation and the Brain

In males and females the nuclei of anterior hypothalamus seems to be critical in terms of sexual orientation.[18] Hamer and Copeland[11] now feel with 99 percent confidence that there is a little segment on X chromosome called Q28 which influences the sexual orientation of men and is a lot different than the same segment in women.

Many studies on sexual orientation have focused on the prenatal sexual differentiation of the brain and the influences during critical development of the intrauterine environment. Some researchers such as Cochran, Ewald, and Cochran[19] have implicated viruses as the possible culprit for sexual orientation during prenatal development. LeVay[10] concluded, "When future research has delineated the entirety of the sexually dimorphic circuitry within the human brain and has established which parts are not, it will be possible to form a more educated hypothesis about the brain basis of sexual orientation" (p. 132).

Arousal and the Brain

Sexual arousal has been associated with temperament, affective level of excitement, and neurobiological processes associated with brain development. All baseline sexual arousal is dependent on circulating testosterone in males and females, and the availability of the male and female hormone receptors to utilize the available male (testosterone) and female (estrogen) hormones.

Androgen receptor genes are viewed as responsible for the level and state of sexual arousal. The way the brain is structured, androgen receptors align on the midline of the brain, suggesting they are part of the very old and primitive building blocks of the human species. If we lower androgen levels in males from the normative levels of 300–1000 nanograms per deciliter of blood to prepubescent levels (less than 100 nanograms per deciliter, or what is normal for females), men begin to loose their sex drive. For men who are hypersexual, the introduction of an antiandrogen agent that blocks androgen uptake at the receptor level may lead to a sharp decline in arousal. This procedure is often used to control hypersexuality in sex offenders.[20]

Women who use steroids for body building or female transsexuals who receive testosterone injections (and block the effects of estrogen) all report increased sex drive, enlargement of the clitoris, and male typical arousal patterns.

Love and the Brain

Recent fMRI studies on love suggest that there may be certain brain centers that are responsible for our ability to fall in love. In Kleinfelter's syndrome, the genes responsible for this disorder also make it impossible for some individuals with Kleinfelter's disorder to ever experience falling in love. This finding raises some interesting questions about the neurobiology and neuroscience of love. Fisher's book, *Why We Love*,[21] studied the effects of brains in love by measuring blood flow via fMRI. Two areas of the brain associated with the reward system (Caudate nucleus) and the neurotransmitter dopamine (in the ventral tegmental area) were implicated in brain states of people in love. There is a neurobiology of love.

Cautionary Thoughts

While sex and gender are based on the neurocircuitry of the brain and brain hormones, this is not to say that parents and culture do not have an influence over their children in terms of appearance, dress, and role modeling for stereotypical male/female behaviors. What it means, however, is that the fundamental variance along the dimensions of arousal, gender identity, sexual orientation, and love relationships are primarily determined by the organization of specific brain circuitry during fetal development. Parental influences may help shape gender and sex, but they are not responsible for it.

Social-Cultural Theories

These theories focus on the nature/nurture debate, and regard the influences and effects of culture, family process, ethnic, religious, and spiritual process on gender development as being predominant. The most prominent social theory in gender development was espoused by Money[22] who said that it was not the sex of determination at birth or the nature of the brain that was responsible for gender identification, but the gender in which the parents raised their child. Money viewed sex and gender as binary, and concluded that for male children with ambiguous, deformed, or absent genitalia, to be a boy or a girl you had to have the right sex organs. He argued that for children with inadequate or absent sex organs, if sex reassignment was done before age two (the developmental epoch in which the child can verbalize its gender) and the parents reared their male child as female (male), the child would become female (male). While this theory has been disproved, it served to generate a lot of cultural interest in the 1980s.

GENDER NONCONFORMITY: THE CLINICAL PERSPECTIVE

For the clinician, gender conflicts may first appear in a parent's struggle with dilemmas over their children's sense of being male or female (what is now called childhood gender nonconformity [CGN]). In the consultation room, it may appear when a mother says that her son's favorite game is dress-up. "Every chance he gets," says mother, "he wears my clothing or his sister's clothing and says he wants to be a girl. He puts on makeup and says that when he grows up he wants to be a woman. He plays with princess dolls and identifies with female roles." Girls also present with CGN, but focus their dysphoria on their wish to be a boy and have a penis. For some individuals, gender nonconformity (GN) may first appear in their adolescence or adulthood.[23] For the clinician, the first indication that there is a problem arises when a parent, spouse, or other authority figure comes into awareness and conflict with their child's, spouse's, or individual's cross-dressing.

Cross-Dressing

Cross-dressing (wearing the clothes of the opposite sex) is a phenomenon that has drawn much interest. Indeed, there is a considerable body of cultural, historical, literary, cinematographic, and autobiographical accounts of individuals who have cross-dressed. In a thought provoking book, Garber[24] pointed to both the interest and the cultural anxiety that underlies the phenomenon.

Cross-dressing may also be viewed as playful and representing a normal developmental stage in exploring one's sexuality and personhood. Cross-dressing can appear at all stages in the life cycle and be incorporated into creative self-expression or lead to neurotic anxiety, guilt, and shame. In the bedroom, cross-dressing can be used as part of normative arousal or stir up considerable guilt, shame, and anxiety because of its forbidden aspects. If cross-dressing behavior becomes compulsive and the person is preoccupied with it and experiences intense frustration, anxiety, and dysphoria when they are thwarted from cross-dressing, the behavior can be viewed as symptomatic of an underlying distressing conflict regarding the self.[25] It is at this point in time that the clinician may be asked to evaluate an individual who is dysphoric over their cross-dressing or cross-gender behavior. Often the request for an evaluation comes from the partner who is dysphoric.

In some cases when an individual cannot achieve orgasm without wearing clothing of the opposite sex, the condition is called fetishism or transvestism and is viewed as a paraphilia (the new term for perversion).[26] Cross-dressing can serve many psychological motives and functions, and there is no one explanation for why a person cross-dresses. These motives may include the following: being impulsive as part of one's character; being defensive against underlying sexual/gender conflicts; anxiety allaying and exciting; reflecting impaired narcissism and the search for perfection in the self; employed to repair a damaged self-system; and serve as a bridge to self-fulfillment and wholeness.[27] Along with these psychological explorations of gender experience and conflicts, scientific studies have pointed to possible neurobiological underpinnings of cross-dressing as part of gender identification as related to evolutionary adaptation. Of course there are those who cross-dress for other reasons including: social events such as drag shows, part of one's gender rebellion, as part of female or male impersonation, secondary to participating in theater roles, and for disguise.[26]

In the 1980s, when Richard Green[7] was studying the phenomenon of cross-dressing and cross-gender identification in children, he wrote his seminal book on so-called sissies and tomboys. In that book he reported that 40 percent of gay males recalled cross-dressing and having GD as children. However, none of these boys went on to have serious gender identity problems or were committed to a career of cross-dressing. Eventually, all of them announced their homosexual orientation in adolescence. Green was aware of Ehrhardt and Meyer-Bahlburg's[12] scientific findings pointing to the relationship between the drug diethylstilbestrol that women took to preserve their pregnancy and its effect on female fetal brain development leading to tomboyism in girls (that is, finding a relationship between brain development and gender expression). Green's findings provoked a lot of thought about what the meaning of cross-dressing is for different groups of individuals. That is, cross-dressing and suspected GID might not be part of a mental illness in a subgroup of boys, but heralding later homosexuality in gay latency age boys. In this sense, one had to revisit the prescription of behavior therapy with these boys to make them stop cross-dressing.

Gender Nonconformity and Cross-Gender Identification

How do we understand cross-gender identification (CGI) or GN in children and adults? While current research stresses that the foundations of GN are biologically based, leading to specific brain activity for sexual arousal, gender identity, sexual orientation, and love relationships, the specific form an individual's gender identity takes is psychological. As neurobiological processes dovetail with parental rearing, the result is gender variance between and within each individual as the norm rather than the exception. When CGN presents in children, their gender-variant behavior (part of the normative spectrum of gender as expressed in children's development) needs to be recognized as normal.[29]

Clinicians and educators need to be active in recognizing and confronting genderphobia (a phenomenon akin to homophobia) in those social systems that promote ignorance and harm directed towards individuals with CGN. This is important for many reasons, not the least of which is the violence directed by some forms of our society against transgendered individuals (cf., the movie *Boys Don't Cry*). Gender conformity/nonconformity begins at the moment of birth when the announcement of, "It's a girl," or, "It's a boy" is made. Initially, the child's gender is assigned by the visual inspection of the genitals. For those children who have ambiguous genitalia, the sex and gender of the child may be difficult to assign. Many of these individuals are now designated as intersexed. During the first two years of the child's life, it is the parents or the maternal object who contain an image of the child's gender (that is, their projection of what they want their child's gender to be).

Most Western societies have identified a seemingly unambiguous developmental construct, gender identity, as coalescing in the individual around age two and leading to the child's first verbal announcement that, "I am a boy," or, "I am a girl." Although the child seems certain in his or her gender announcement, he or she may also go on to say, "When I grow up I will become a mother/father." For the two-year-old, everything is in flux because of their early stages of cognitive development and the lack of causation in their thinking. While gender conformity may appear to be the norm, the subjective life of the child suggests considerable internal conflict over one's sense of self. Individuals who are struggling with their gender identity are not a rare phenomenon.[30] The statistics of transgenderism from the United Kingdom, the United States, and India suggests that the occurrence/ratio of transgendered conditions is 1/300, 1/500, and 1/1000 births, respectively. Being transgendered is not a rare phenomenon but a variant of a typical gender identity outcome (a rare occurrence would occur 1/50,000). Moreover, we know that the occurrence/ratio of homosexuality in the United States is 5/100, hardly a rare phenomenon.

For those individuals who experience suffering and conflict around their sense of gender and self (men and women who experienced subjective distress over their gender, some of whom wish to change their sex and live in the opposite gender roles), the medical/psychological term GD was introduced to label their perceived distress. As a descriptive term, GD focused the dysphoria on the individual and not on the society that may be gender phobic.[31] Some of these children are labeled as GN, a label that has potentially serious consequences for the child.

Recently, the term transgender has been used as the generic construct to embrace all gender conforming individuals. The term encompassed those individuals who experienced themselves as blending aspects of femaleness and maleness into their gender identity. Bolin[32] viewed transgenderism as "a community term denoting kinship among those with gender-variant identities. It supplants the dichotomy of transsexual and transvestite with a concept of continuity" (p. 461 Bolin, using a deconstructivist model, argued that "transgenderism (has) perpetrated the disassembling of gender," as "the transgenderist harbors great potential either to deactivate gender or create in the future the possibility of 'supernumerary' genders as social categories no longer based on biology ... the transgenderist has pushed the parameters of the gender paradigm even further by disputing the entire concept of consistency between sexual orientation and gender" (p. 485). As we enter the 21st century, postmodern gender theorists have challenged the view of absolutes in the social sciences, and stress the notion of ambiguity to describe the richness of human experience in terms of gender identification. In this sense, the meaning of gender nonconformity changes from an identity to a role concept.

Because gender variance better explains the diversity of gender roles and identities that exist in culture, the concept of transgenderism is a more appropriate term to describe individuals who defy the binary classification system of gender.

Nature versus Nurture: The Bruce/Brenda Controversy

While *nature* plays the pivotal role in the organization of gender identity, *nurture*, or parental influence, also plays a critical role in helping the child develop the appropriate level of emotional connectedness, affect regulation, and the quality of relationships so that he or she can have a meaningful, pleasurable, spiritual, and satisfying life in whatever is his or her gender adaptation. The dyadic bond between mother and child is critical during the early phase of bonding and the infant's security around its genital and gender self-development. While the child's gender self-experience develops along a continuum, both nature and nurture contribute to the ultimate shaping of one's sense of self and gender.

When gender theory is emphasized over empiricism, however, the results can be disastrous, as seen in the Bruce/Brenda Reimer case. The case played out in the scientific literature, but was given wide audience by Colapinto[33] in his book that summarized the debate. In the case involving identical twins, one twin had his penis burned off during a botched circumcision and was eventually raised as a girl based on John Money's influence.[34] Money tenaciously believed that a child's gender was determined by the sex rearing practices (nurture) of the parents and not by biology (nature). These ideas, which stood in the path of emerging scientific evidence, were enthusiastically supported by those who wanted to politically downplay the differences between gender and sex.

Called in as a consultant, Money argued that Bruce did not have a penis and should be raised as a girl, provided genital surgery to transform him to a female, and have the parents support her female role development. Because Bruce had an identical twin whose penis was not harmed, Money used the twin as control. Money's views on gender and sexuality seemed rooted in a naïve assumption that a boy without a penis was no boy at all, and that he would fare better socially as a girl. Money argued that if the parents dressed their boy child as a girl and raised him as a girl, he would become a girl. Diamond and Sigmundson[34] thought this was nonsense, as Professor Diamond's research findings revealed that the brain's circuitry was wired male or female. It was not the penis that made a boy male. It was his brain.

Money's follow-up article suggested that Brenda (originally born Bruce) was doing well, completely feminized, and was adjusting and living as a female. His findings were proof of his theory, and practitioners incorporated them into their theories of sexuality and gender. Diamond, however, tenaciously held onto his views and asked Money if he could interview the child and see for himself. Money refused.

The outcome of Money's crucial experiment was ultimately found to be specious, unscientific, and based on manipulation. Brenda hated being female and when she discovered her origins, she changed her sex/gender back to male. She always knew she was a male. Bruce married and seemed to be making a good adjustment. However, the trauma inflicted was too much, and Bruce committed suicide in 2004 (soon followed by her identical twin's suicide). The outcome was a tragedy.

No one should conclude from the outcome in the Bruce/Brenda Reimer case that parental rearing has no influence on childhood development. Nor should one read into these conclusions that gender identity simply follows an absolutely predictable binary structure, as there is diversity within the constructs of male and female gender identity. Parents can have an enormous effect on their children's social-emotional development, safety, development of self-regulation and internal controls, moral and spiritual development, and can shape the direction in which gender expression may evolve. However, according to Diamond and Sigmnudson,[34] Roughgarden,[5] and others, after the second trimester of fetal development, parental rearing has no discernible effect on the child's brain structures for gender self-identity that are formed prenatally and can only be titrated, not completely altered, without disaster, as in the Bruce/Brenda case.

Clinical Manifestations of Gender: Identity and Role

The clinical concepts of gender role and identity were introduced by Money[22] and Stoller,[16] and elaborated on by clinical observations in naturalistic settings, developmental research, and the treatment of individuals who were experiencing extreme dysphoria over their gender role and identity. While most individuals take their gender role and identity for granted, there are many individuals for whom the consolidation of gender role and identity is only achieved with great difficulty, in many cases as the result of a tumultuous process.

In order to further one's understanding of the complexities of gender role, identity, arousal, and sexuality, consider the following vignette, one that I find increasingly common in clinical practice in which one's subjectivity and fantasy play a key role in gender development, and supports the richness of gender variance, not only as a biological construct, but as a psychological construct as well.

Ian subjectively experiences himself as a male and his sex partners and friends know him as a man (his biologic and social presentation of sex). In the past, he had sexual experiences with males, females and transsexuals. As an adult, he is a sexually anxious man who is narcissistic, and identifies as primarily heterosexual. In his current relationship, his girlfriend, Joan, left her passive, ineffectual, and addicted husband for Ian. She enjoys Ian's masculinity, his sexual energy as a man, and his large penis, which she worships. During sex, she gets fulfillment from his male sexuality. Ian, on the other hand, subjectively fantasizes himself as bigendered and having female sex organs. He knows that he is a male and loves his masculinity, but during sexual arousal he can only attain orgasm thinking of himself as a woman with female genitals. He is able to become erect through the physiological sensations associated with male sexuality. However, his orgasm is determined by another brain circuit related to his subjective sense of his gender variance and his arousal system.

Joan knows nothing of Ian's fantasy. His transgendered experiences take place in the privacy of his subjective fantasy. One might well ask, what is his gender identity? Ian would say masculine. What would his partner say if she knew his fantasy life? He is not gender dysphoric over his transgender fantasy because he enjoys the orgasm associated with his female fantasy. Moreover, his gender variance does not impact on his work or love relationships.

The subjective experience of gender identity conflicts are rarely shared with significant others. Some individuals, however, develop GD that begins in early childhood, and this is where our journey begins.[35] As evident in the above vignette, the experience of one's gender is a complicated concept in which subjectivity and fantasy provides important clues as to how gender identity is related to one's self-system.

The earliest report on childhood cross-gender preferences was of an 18-month-old boy.[36] Moreover, childhood transvestism has been recognized as a distinct clinical phenomenon. For young children, gender is determined not by the genital but by appearance. For the child, the world is knowable and everything fits into black and white categories until symbolization and abstract reasoning emerges. The child under the age of five identifies someone as a boy if he has short hair and wears pants. Likewise, a boy may be identified as a girl if he has long hair and wears pants.

Boys who are gender variant are often labeled as sissies if they show any deviation from culturally enforced norms of dress and behavior. Subsequent bullying and teasing may lead to impaired self-esteem, depression, and suicidal behavior. It is imperative that parents form a bulwark against these condoned behaviors.

The next major developmental landmark occurs around age three when the child discovers the anatomical differences between the sexes. This discovery has as much to do with gender as with narcissism. What we find is that the moment the child discovers the genitals of the opposite sex, he or she immediately tries to deny their existence. Prior to the recognition of anatomical sex differences, the child believes that all things are possible (the grandiose position), that the world is unlimited and the child can become anything it wishes including the opposite sex/gender. At the same time, the child also entertains the opposing belief that all things are identical and there are no differences. Once the child recognizes the difference of another human being, he or she realizes that there are some limits to his or her possibilities. This realization often leads to a normal depression that is time-limited. The depression has to do with the realistic understanding that the child's capabilities are not limitless.

The following vignettes reveal the childhood origins of CGN and GD as viewed through the lenses of actual children as they experience early childhood genital anxiety (genital dysphoria, the urge to harm or remove the penis) focused on their penis as a symbol of their male gender. These cases raise important issues about the young child's understanding of sex, gender, and the body.[37]

Elliot (age five), who had a strong desire to be a girl, said, "When my penis goes up I get mad and angry. I hate it when it goes up. I want to shoot it off with a gun. I want to get rid of it. I want to shoot myself and die." He once tried to cut off his penis but was thwarted. His mother also intercepted his attempt to get his father's gun in order to shoot his penis.

Robert (age 4) believed that he had a vagina. He wanted to be a girl and told his mother that he wished he was born a girl. When his penis became erect he would pull back his testicles and bending his penis, would threaten to cut off his penis with a knife. Robert told his mother, "I want it to come off, it's ugly, I don't like it."

The wish to harm the penis is a primitive, concrete thought in these children and must be treated as soon as possible. While many children are self-destructive and harm their bodies, only gender dysphoric children try to harm their penis. None of the parents of these boys immediately contacted their pediatricians when their sons' expressed confusion, anxiety, and hatred towards their penis and maleness. This subgroup of children is at risk for genital mutilation without immediate psychological intervention.

Prior to their threats to genitally mutilate themselves, all of the boys were acting like girls, cross-dressing, and expressing a desire to be a girl. In some cases, the parents downplayed the urgency for a consultation because of the embarrassment and pain it stirred up in them. Indeed, the children's genital hatred and mutilation fantasies stirred up intense feelings of anxiety, fear, disgust, and terror in caregivers. Interventions that focused on latent gender conflicts in the family system led to the resolution of the genital dysphoria. However, as expected, the cross-dressing and cross-gender wishes of these children persisted, and the GD was experienced more acutely by their parents than the children.

While latency age girls with GD rarely exhibit genital dysphoria, their case presentations around the issues of GD are almost identical to the boys. These girls only want to wear unisex or boy's clothing. They refuse to wear dresses or anything frilly. They engage in rough and tumble play, and are labeled as tomboys. They believe they were born males with a female body. Like their male counterparts, cross-dressing for these girls is the norm. Girls with GD may want to have a penis. Many of them are creative in how they use various prosthetics to simulate a penis. As young children they do not, however, attempt to mutilate their female genitals, but fantasize and create a real or imagined phallus to serve as a bridge to resolve their GD. With the onset of adolescence and the development of their female genitals and bodies, some of these girls may bind their breasts and mutilate their vulva to allay their gender anxiety.

As the child enters adolescence, new stresses facilitate a reorganization of gender self-structures and lead to a new level of GD in boys and girls. With the entry into adolescence, the onset of the transsexual wishes and transgendered behavior may be accelerated and correlated with psychological stressors including, but not limited to: (a) a recent loss or change in a relationship which reactivates separation anxiety, (b) physical maturation of the body which threatens the gender self-system,

(c) stigmatized homosexuality, or (d) a flight from guilt-ridden masturbatory activity, leading to the belief that being the other sex would eliminate their conflicts. Children with gender identity conflicts have been identified as having comorbid separation anxiety. For these children, therapy must be intense, dynamically oriented, and linked with treatment of the parents.[38]

During adolescence, gender identity and role are subject to the vicissitudes of bodily changes, surging hormones, and powerful emotions that may be experienced as disorganizing in the transgendered young adolescent who is gender dysphoric and in the process of a reorganization of the adolescent self. For those males and females that experienced childhood GD, the onset of adolescence and the surfacing of powerful sexual feelings, in the context of the development and enlarging of their genitals, can be alarming as nature informs them that there is no turning back from their biological sex. Atypical depression among adolescents often signals an underlying disturbance in one's sense of maleness or femaleness.[39]

Because of legal issues and informed consent, there is virtually no possibility of a transgendered teen legally obtaining hormones and surgery until adulthood. Consequently, many gender dysphoric teenagers live in turmoil and chaos until young adulthood when they have the possibility of entering into more complex relationships and not be so isolated. The younger the child when GD is first identified, the more difficult is the transition to young adulthood. This difficulty relates to the lengthy period of time in which the child's impulsivity, mood destabilization, and problems relating to the social environment may intensify to catastrophic or suicidal proportions. Fortunately, with increasing awareness of the vulnerabilities of GLBT teens, support groups to help them manage their anxiety and alleviate their stress, thereby reducing their suicidal thoughts and plans, have been organized.

In an attempt to provide some narrative concerning this stage of development for the transgendered adolescent, consider the following case vignettes.

Earl, a 15-year-old African American male, lived with his schizophrenic mother and younger 12-year-old sister. He was referred for evaluation because of cross-dressing and truancy in school. He came to his appointments dressed in female clothes. Around age nine, he began to experience an increased sense of urgency to cross-dress and assume a female role after his father's and cousin's death.

Eva, a 16-year-old white female, had a history of moves, abandonment, child abuse, and neglect. At the age of seven she weighed 30 pounds and required surgery for a stomach tumor. Her father died soon after her surgery. As she entered preadolescence, she began cross-dressing as a male. At the time of the evaluation, she was afraid that her female lover would abandon her unless she obtained sex reassignment surgery and became a real man.

Persistent and enduring cross-dressing in these teens reinforced the opposite gender role for them. Their feelings of wholeness while cross-dressed also helped to solidify their new identities and shape the form of their transsexual/transgendered identification. During this period, a small percentage of teens who are diagnosed with schizophrenia also experience gender hallucinations and delusions about their genitals. They are not classified as having a GID in *DSM–IV*.[3]

Some teens with GD reacted with disgust and horror to unwanted bodily changes such as the dev elopment of breasts, testes, menses, and penis size at puberty. These teens may try to ward off their developing male or female bodies by dramatic acting-out rituals, including self-mutilating and suicidal behaviors. As latency aged children, they may have prayed each night that they would wake up transformed into the opposite sex and gender. However, the reality of mid-adolescence set in as each morning they awake and look at themselves in the mirror and feel the intensity of disgust and horror at their bodies.

Family systems and dynamics play a pivotal role in the child's evolving sense of security about his or her gender identity. As seen in many of the case vignettes, GD in the transgendered child is often amplified by the societal and familial response to their biology and rejection of their gender variant status. For these children, GD and subsequent GN behavior begins as a struggle in the family, necessitating family intervention. GD in the child may often be the result of genderphobia in the parents.

The act of masturbation in adolescence provides an important link to the development of the body image, the consolidation of the self and ego functions, and the development of reality testing. Masturbation fantasies provide the teen with inner access to his or her subjective experience. With the onset of puberty, the body becomes a continuous source of ambivalent, but hopefully pleasurable, genital sensations which may threaten to overwhelm the gender variant adolescent's ego. For the transgendered teen, the perception of the genitals as disgusting and shameful exist alongside the perception of his or her genitals as potential sources of intense pleasure. These experiences of pleasurable genital sensations are an ever-present reminder of one's anatomical sex, and can cause an emotional crisis for transgendered teens.

Myrna, an 18-year-old white female, recalled her conflict over masturbation. Although she felt compelled to respond to her genital excitation through masturbation, she despised her female sexual organs. She could only attain orgasm by fantasizing that she had a penis and was penetrating a female. Afterwards she felt guilty and empty.

Some gender dysphoric teens try to ignore their genital sensations. However, when their denial breaks down, intense feelings of guilt and shame may lead to genital mutilation.

As a result of lifelong gender confusion, many transgendered adults may have set aside their cross-gender wishes to marry or raise a family only to eventually find themselves inundated with urges to change their sex and live out their lives in a new role. These experiences were documented in a 2004 HBO movie, *Normal*, about a transgendered middle-aged, married man (with children) who was going through a sex change. Diedre McClosky's autobiography of undergoing a sex change at age 52 after marrying, fathering children, and working as a male also underscores the lifelong power of cross-gender wishes.[40]

The aging gender dysphoric individual has to deal with increased loneliness, isolation, and the realization that his or her narcissistic pursuit of perfection is bound to fail. The many biographies of transgendered individuals stand out as points of illumination for those individuals in search of happiness. The aging gender dysphoric individual also hopes that change is possible and that the self can be integrated and whole.

There are many gender variant individuals who never experience the surfacing of clinically distressing symptoms. These individuals received the support they need to consolidate a healthy self in their variant-gender adaptation and do not experience GD. They reflect what Roughgarden[5] and others have come to describe as gender variants of evolution's rainbow (diversity, gender, and sexuality in nature and people). While they may have to deal with society's transgenderphobia, they have had support from caretakers that gave a positive voice to their gender variance.

As can be seen in the case material presented, depending on the lens one uses, these individuals can be diagnosed as being mentally ill, according to *DSM–IV*,[3] or they can be viewed as normal and gender variant. My clinical experience suggests that a combination of the individuals confusion about one's self, combined with parental and societal rejection, often leads to comorbid psychiatric disorders of mood, substance abuse, alcoholism, and personality disorders that account for their suspected mental illness that is incorrectly associated with their transgendered status and gender variant behavior.

Future Directions for Gender Identity

Gender identity formation is a complex and dynamic process that changes over one's lifetime. Evident by age two and a half, one's gender identity changes over the life cycle depending on many factors, including but not limited to the following: the individual's personality; level of intelligence and executive functioning; central nervous system based brain circuitry for sex; arousal and gender; level of childhood anxiety and conflict over one's gender identity; experience of trauma; having adult links to paraphilias that enhance gender confusion; history of drug and alcohol abuse and dependency (especially the type of drug used, with amphetamines and cocaine being identified as sexual/gender stimulants and activators); and the cultural and familial values, support systems, and self-object relationships that the individual interacts with providing access to, or inhibition from, creative gender self-expression.

In the 1960s, Robert Stoller, a prominent psychoanalyst and gender researcher, offered an explanation of the etiology of transsexualism based on the binary model. Abandoning the conflict model of psychoanalysis, he accepted Money's imprinting, nonconflictual model to explain transsexualism.[41] He postulated that the child's so-called blissful symbiosis with the mother was responsible for the imprinting of a cross-gender identity in males. Under the sway of Stoller's influence, his own psychoanalytical colleagues abandoned their critical thinking and put aside the conflict model of personality that is at the heart of psychoanalysis. While Stoller's views are now discredited by developmental psychologists and neuroscientists, the influence he swayed over his colleagues revealed how implausible hypotheses may be appealing no matter how implausible.

Newer findings from fMRI studies suggest that brain circuitry and specific brain nuclei may be responsible for organization and arousal, gender identity, sexual orientation, and love relationships. Brain imaging studies help us to understand the underpinnings of core brain structures on the behavioral expression of gender. However, the specific ways in which gender identity is expressed in each individual appears related to the complex and unique organization of the person, parental, and social influences.

Pediatricians and gender surgeons need to have their practices informed by the more current research findings on gender. The brain is the biggest and most important sex organ. Secondary sexual characteristics may change, but one's basic sense of self is biologically rooted in the development of the brain. In the case of Brenda, she always knew something was wrong and that she was a boy. In the cases of the Dominican Republic females who changed into males at puberty, they knew well in advance that they were not females. Their brains informed them so long before the actual changes occurred. For those individuals who feel trapped in the wrong body, perhaps their brains are telling them something important that all of us have to listen to.

On the basis of misleading and inaccurate findings, about 100 children in the United States and 1,000 children worldwide are provided sex reassignment surgery before age two. This practice has to stop. Recently, children previously identified as hermaphrodites and now labeled intersex as adults have been very vocal about why genital surgery should not have been done on them as children.

They argue correctly that the biological basis of maleness or femaleness is rooted in deep brain structures and that any surgical interventions should have been delayed until adulthood when they could give consent.

You cannot make a boy female by giving him female genitals or a girl male by giving her male genitals. Gender is a brain construct. Intersex and transgendered children and adults need to be listened to and provided the acceptance and dignity they deserve. It is up to society to accept these findings into the mainstream of psychology, and to petition for changes both in medical and social practices about how genderphobia and scientific ignorance have only prolonged unnecessary suffering in transgendered individuals.

The medical diagnosis of GID reflects a view of gender identity as binary and is under attack from the scientific and GLBT community. As the American Psychiatric Association begins its work towards the publication of *DSM-V*, the question of whether GID will be listed as a disorder is being debated. The main objections focus on (1) the fact that gender is now defined as a continuum concept and not a disorder; (2) that the dysphoria associated with GID is probably related to the individuals assimilation of society's genderphobia of the transgendered individual; (3) children who present with atypical gender self-expression may be prehomosexual or gender variant but do not have a disorder; and (4) scientific evidence suggests that gender variance is the norm.

The main support for GID comes from several sources: (1) individuals who want transsexual surgery and want a diagnosis in order to have their insurance pay for it; (2) to assure a medical diagnosis in order to pay for psychotherapy treatment, and (3) as long as society remains homophobic and genderphobic, children will suffer and be in need of help.

The elimination of GID as a distinct *DSM* diagnosis would begin to address society's transgenderphobia and the violence directed against some GLBT youth and raise important social policy issues about providing prospective medical payments for those individuals who require medical treatment for their distress and suffering without labeling gender variance as an illness. In the future, while more sophisticated brain research will provide additional scientific evidence linking gender and brain structures, newer gender variants will arise and challenge our present assumption about the etiology of gender. For the present, individuals with GD will continue to present clinically, and their issues will need to be addressed sensitively, ethically, and compassionately. There is much to learn about the science of sex and gender and the social-emotional distress caused by gender phobia. Hopefully, public policy will address the inequities and discrimination that transgendered individuals experience, and as a result of the scientific findings, help to dispel the ignorance and fear directed towards them.

REFERENCES

1. American Psychiatric Association. (1980). *Diagnostic and statistical manual of mental disorders* (3rd ed.). Washington, DC: Author.

2. American Psychiatric Association. (1987). *Diagnostic and statistical manual of mental disorders* (3rd ed., rev.). Washington, DC: Author.

3. American Psychiatric Association. (1994). *Diagnostic and statistical manual of mental disorders* (4th ed.). Washington, DC: Author.

4. American Psychiatric Association. (2000). *Diagnostic and statistical manual of mental disorders* (4th ed., text rev.). Washington, DC: Author.

5. Roughgarden, J. (2004). *Evolution's rainbow: Diversity, gender, and sexuality in nature and people.* Berkeley, CA: University of California Press.

6. Conway, L. (2002). *How frequently does transsexualism occur?* Retrieved April 26, 2006 from http://ai.eecs.umich.edu/people/conway/TS/Tsprevalence.html.

7. Green, R. (1987). *The sissy boy syndrome and the development of homosexuality.* New Haven, CT: Yale University Press.

8. Lothstein, L. (1983). *Female-to-male transsexualism: Historical, clinical and theoretical issues.* London: Routledge & Kegan Paul.

9. Breger, L. (1981). *Freud's unfinished journey.* London: Routledge & Kegan Paul.

10. LeVay, S. (1996). *Queer science: The use and abuse of research into homosexuality.* Boston: MIT Press.

11. Hamer, D., & Copeland, P. (1994). *The science of desire.* New York: Simon and Schuster.

12. Ehrhardt, A., & Meyer-Bahlburg, H. (1981). Effects of prenatal hormones on gender related behavior. *Science, 211,* 1312–1317.

13. Abramowich, D., Davidson, I., Longstaff, A., & Pearson, C. (1987). Sexual differentiation of the human mid-trimester brain. *European Journal of Obstetrics, Gynecology, and Reproductive Biology, 25,* 7–14.

14. Money, J., & Ehrhardt, A. (1972). *Man and woman, boy and girl.* Baltimore, MD: Johns Hopkins University Press.

15. Baker, H., & Stoller, R. (1968). Can a biological force contribute to gender identity? *American Journal of Psychiatry, 124,* 1653–1658.

16. Stoller, R. (1979). A contribution to the study of gender identity: A follow-up. *International Journal of Psycho-Analysis, 60,* 433–441.

17. Imperato-McGinley, J., Peterson, R., Gautier, T., & Sturla, E. (1979). Androgens and the evaluation of male gender identity among male pseudo hermaphrodites with a 5-alpha- reductase deficiency. *New England Journal of Medicine, 300,* 1233–1237.

18. Wilson, G., & Rahman, Q. (2005). *Born gay: The psychobiology of sex orientation.* London: Peter Owen Publishers.

19. Cochran, G., Ewald, P., & Cochran, K. (2000). Infectious causation of disease: An evolutionary perspective. *Perspectives in Biology and Medicine, 43,* 406–448.

20. Lothstein, L. (1996). Antiandrogen treatment for sexual disorders: Guideline for establishing a standard of care. *Sexual Addiction and Compulsivity, 4,* 313–331.

21. Fisher, H. (2004). *Why we love: The nature and chemistry of romantic love.* New York: Henry Holt & Company.
22. Money, J. (1973). Gender role, gender identity, core gender identity: Usage and definition of terms. *Journal of the American Academy of Psychoanalysis,* 4, 397–403.
23. Corbett, K. (1999). Homosexual boyhood: Notes on girly boys. In M. Rottnek (Ed.), *Sissies and tomboys: Gender nonconformity and homosexual childhood* (pp. 107–139). New York: New York University Press.
24. Garber, M.(1992). *Vested interests: Cross-dressing and cultural anxiety.* New York: Routledge.
25. Lothstein, L. (1988). Self object failure and gender identity. In A. Goldberg (Ed.), *Frontiers in self psychology: Progress in self psychology* (Vol. 3, pp. 213–235). New York: The Analytic Press.
26. Arndt, W. (1991). *Gender disorders and the paraphilias.* Madison, CT: International Universities Press.
27. Lothstein, L. (1997). Pantyhose fetishism and self-cohesion: A paraphilic solution? *Gender and Sexuality Psychoanalysis,* 2, 102–121.
28. Newton, E. (1972). *Mother camp: Female impersonators in America.* New York: Prentice Hall.
29. Menvielle, E., Tuerk, C., & Perrin, E. (2005). To the beat of a different drummer: The gender- variant child. *Contemporary Pediatrics,* 22, 38–46.
30. Herdt, G. (1994). Introduction: Third sexes and third genders. In G. Herdt (Ed.) *Third sex: Beyond sexual dimorphism in culture and history* (pp. 21–84). New York: Zone Books.
31. Bockting, W., & Coleman, E. (1992). *Gender dysphoria: Interdisciplinary approaches in clinical management.* New York: Haworth Press.
32. Bolin, A. (1994). Transcending and transgendering: Male-to female transsexuals, dichotomy and diversity. In. G. Herdt (Ed.), *Third sex: Beyond sexual dimorphism in culture and history* (pp. 447–486). New York: Zone Books.
33. Colapinto, J. (2000). *As nature made him: The boy who was raised as a girl.* New York: Harper Collins.
34. Diamond, M., & Sigmundson, H. (1997). Sex reassignment at birth, long term review and clinical implications. *Archives of Pediatric and Adolescent Medicine,* 151, 298–304.
35. Zucker, K., & Bradley, S.(1995). *Gender identity disorder and psychosexual problems in children and adolescents.* New York: Guilford.
36. Galenson, E., Vogel, R., Blau, S., & Roiphe, H. (1975). Disturbance in sexual identity beginning at eighteen months of age. *International Review of Psycho-Analysis,* 2, 389–397.
37. Lothstein, L. (1992). Clinical management of gender dysphoria in young boys: Genital mutilation and DSM IV implications. In W. Bockting & E. Coleman (Eds.), *Gender dysphoria: Interdisciplinary approaches in clinical management* (pp. 87–106). New York: Haworth Press.

38. Coates, S., Friedman, R., & Wolfe, S. (1991). The etiology of boyhood gender identity disorder: A model for integrating temperament, development and psychodynamics. *Psychoanalytic Dialogues, 1*, 481–523.

39. Lothstein, L. (1980). The adolescent gender dysphoric patient: an approach to treatment and management. *Journal of Pediatric Psychology, 5*, 93–109.

40. McClosky, D. (2001) *Crossings: A memoir.* Chicago, IL: University of Chicago Press.

41. Stoller, R. (1968). *Sex and gender.* New York: Science House.

Chapter 11

Sexual Orientation and Mental Health: What the Behavioral Sciences Know about Sexual Orientation and Why It Matters

John C. Gonsiorek

Recent decades have seen a seemingly endless array of public policy controversy regarding sexual orientation, almost all of it focused on same-sex attraction, or homosexuality. Civil rights for homosexual citizens, gays in the military, homosexuality and child abuse, the fitness of gay men and lesbian women to parent, and most recently, same-sex marriage, have been debated extensively, although often in ways that shed more heat than light.

One might conclude from these contentious and unresolved disagreements that the behavioral sciences are as divided and befuddled as the rest of the public on these issues. In fact, however, there is generally rather strong consensus about these issues in the behavioral sciences, and typically in a manner that would be construed, at least within the terms of these polarized debates, as "progay"; although most behavioral scientists would likely see their positions as proscience, in that they are following the available data. These data, and the perspectives of the behavioral sciences, are introduced in this paper across a few basic topics, followed by concluding suggestions on the meanings and implications of these debates.

Primary among these topics is perhaps the most basic one: how sexual orientations are defined and measured. Surprisingly, for phenomena that generate so many dogged opinions, sexual orientations are remarkably elusive to define and measure. As will soon be seen, the objects of such intense disagreement come close to being ephemeral.

THE DEFINITION AND MEASUREMENT OF SEXUAL ORIENTATIONS

There are a number of good sources available for readers interested in a more detailed explication of the challenges of defining and measuring sexual orientation.[1,2] One of the first challenges involves differentiating various behaviors and attributes that have been confused with sexual orientation. Shively and De Cecco[3] early on developed a useful distinction in dividing sexual identity into four parts; their model has remained robust over the years. The first is *biological sex*; the genetic material encoded in chromosomes. The next is *gender identity*; the psychological sense of being male or female. *Social sex role* is adherence to the culturally created behaviors and attitudes that are deemed appropriate for males or females. Finally, *sexual orientation* is erotic and/or affectional disposition to the same and/or opposite sex. The first three bear no necessary relationship to sexual orientation in any given individual, although each has been confused with sexual orientation.

The work of Kinsey and his associates ushered in the modern era of scientific measurement of sexual behavior.[4,5] These were based on in-depth interviews with approximately 17,000 subjects covering a wide range of human sexual activities. Kinsey's data indicated an amount of homosexual activity greater than previously acknowledged in U.S. society. Kinsey's data cannot be used uncritically. They describe a particular sample population at a particular time, and the Kinsey group used sampling techniques and methodologies that were innovative in mid-20th century, but flawed by current standards.

Kinsey's group conceptualized sexual behavior as falling on a seven-point continuum from exclusively heterosexual (score of zero) to exclusively homosexual (score of six). A person in the middle of the scale (score of three) would be more or less evenly bisexual, for example. Kinsey's work was revolutionary at the time because it suggested more same-sex behavior than was previously anticipated, and also more clearly developed the notion of bisexuality. Kinsey's notion of a heterosexual-homosexual continuum challenged the dichotomous, either-or view of sexual orientation.

There may be significant problems, however, with a single continuous scale. Shively and De Cecco[3] expanded the Kinseyan continuum concept, adapting another researcher's revisions of the concepts of masculinity and femininity. Shively and De Cecco suggested that a single continuous scale like Kinsey's might be insufficient to explain sexual behavior and orientation. They suggested that sexual orientation can be better conceptualized with two continuous scales. Separate ratings for homosexual and heterosexual behavior can then be made, and the ratings then graphed on "Homosexuality" and "Heterosexuality" axes that are perpendicular to each other. Their proposed scheme would eliminate a restrictive implication of the Kinsey scale, namely that the bisexual positions can appear to be watered down mixtures of the two dichotomized components and that one form of sexual expression is at the expense of the other. For example, in their scheme it would be possible to differentiate an individual who has a high degree of homosexual interests and concurrently high degree of heterosexual interest from an individual who has a minimal degree of homosexual interest and simultaneously a minimal degree of heterosexual interests; clearly, these are very different people. Such a differentiation is not possible with the simple Kinsey scale, which would code both examples as a three, because the proportion of same versus opposite sex interests and behaviors are equal, even though the intensities vary dramatically.

There are other considerations in the definition of homosexuality: what variables are counted. The original Kinsey continuum readings used composite scores of sexual behaviors and fantasy (attraction) to arrive at the ratings. It may be the case that a third aspect is also important; affectional, as opposed to sexual, orientation. This aspect refers to the sex with whom an individual prefers to relate on an affectional, intimate, or friendship-based level, as opposed to sexual behavior or sexual fantasy level. As these three aspects may not be congruent, it may be useful to rate individuals separately on the three aspects of sexual behavior, sexual fantasy, and affectional orientation, which Klein, Sepekoff, and Wolf[6] attempt with their Sexual Orientation Grid. Others have examined the eroticization of friendship as opposed to body shape in some detail, and suggested this as an important component.

But here, a significant problem emerges. Suppose one uses separate two-axis grids to describe sexual orientation via behavior, fantasy, and affectional variables. What do you name an individual who is not congruent across these variables? The dilemma is that while it is clear that a simple Kinsey continuum fails to capture the complexities of sexual orientation, those models that do capture the complexity rapidly lose utility as the complexity becomes unmanageable, both in a research sense, and simply in terms of common sense understanding.

In addition, psychological processes may intervene to restrict the accuracy of this information. Many individuals deny their same-sex feelings, and for other individuals, self-identity and behavior are not necessarily congruent. For example, an individual may call herself lesbian and by that mean any complex arrangement of sexual, affectional, or political variables at a point in time. Gay men and lesbians may differ in the bases for self-definition, perhaps related to gender differences. Golden[7] describes how many lesbian women, and some heterosexual women as well, perceive choice as an important element in their sexual orientations; Baumeister[8] also suggests significant gender differences. Lesbians appear to perceive affectional orientation and political perspectives as central to self-definition, while gay males appear to view sexual behavior and sexual fantasy as central. Since the organized lesbian and gay communities are nascent, the bases for self-definition can change over time as these communities evolve. How a given individual defines these variables, and more importantly, whether this point in time predicts past or future behavior, is difficult to ascertain. It can safely be assumed that there is no necessary relationship between a person's sexual behavior and their self-identity unless both are individually assessed.

Perhaps the most dramatic limitation of current conceptualizations is change over time. There is essentially no research on the longitudinal stability of sexual orientation over the adult life span. In other words, even if one could satisfactorily measure the complex components of sexual orientation as differentiated from other aspects of sexual identity at one point in time, it is still an unanswered question whether this measure will predict future behavior or orientation. Certainly, it is not a good predictor of past behavior and self-identity, given the developmental process common to most gay men and lesbians (i.e., denial of homosexual interests and heterosexual experimentation prior to the coming out process).

A major problem facing such studies is the risk involved in self-disclosure, especially where the studies fail to ensure complete anonymity. In many places, homosexuals remain potential and even likely targets for embarrassment and harassment. Some homosexuals, particularly those who are successful and established professionally, may be unwilling to take the risks involved in being subjects of research. This may be informative about those homosexuals who are willing to be researched. For example, Burdick and Stewart,[9] on the basis of their research study, theorized that there is a tendency for homosexuals who readily volunteer for psychological research to be less well-adjusted than those who do not. While this conclusion requires more research, it does raise questions about whether homosexual volunteers for research are representative samples.

Most studies determine homosexual orientation by asking the individual, but a few studies use physiological measures to determine sexual orientation. The work of Kurt Freund is perhaps the most rigorous work in this area.[10,11] Freund invented a device called a plethysmyograph that fits over the penis and directly measures its blood volume; an analagous device can measure female genital blood flow. Sexual orientation—or, in Freund's terminology, "erotic orientation to body shape"—is observed by recording genital blood volume responses when the subject is shown photographs of naked people of various ages, appearances, and sexes.

Numerous studies have demonstrated the fundamental reliability and validity of this technique. Not surprisingly, plethysmyography does not work well with involuntary subjects, as anyone wishing to fool the procedure can simply fantasize something other than the visual stimuli presented, without external indications this is occurring. It is therefore impractical to use it to determine the prevalence of sexual orientations in the population at large. Nor can we assume *a priori* that erotic orientation to body shape correlates in any simple way with self-identification as homosexual or bisexual. The technique is scientifically useful, however, in demonstrating that sexual orientation (or erotic orientation) is not merely sexual behavior, nor is it just a behavioral choice. Freund suggests that there are responses that are embedded in the nervous system that are related, however imperfectly, to what people term sexual or erotic orientation. Those responses are distinct from actual sexual behavior.

By far the most common measurement has been verbal self-report. There are significant limitations to this method. First, individuals must accurately appraise their own degree of same-sex interests. As described by Gonsiorek and Rudolph,[12] individuals prior to the coming out process (and at times during and after this process), often distort their degree of same-sex interests as a way to defend against this realization. Therefore, *when* one asks an individual (over the course of adolescent and adult development) about same-sex interests is crucial. This issue is particularly acute in measuring sexual orientation in adolescents, whose sexual orientation may not yet be manifest or may be unclear to them, or whose level of (mis)information may result in their verbal report not meaning the same thing as the researcher understands.

Further, given the social condemnation of homosexuality, there are other constraints on verbal self-report. Research subjects who have reasons to doubt the confidentiality or anonymity of the data or who are simply frightened of negative repercussions, regardless of guarantees of safety, are likely to under-report same-sex orientation. For example, as one researcher noted in a cross-cultural sample of men from Ireland, Finland, Australia, and Sweden, individuals expecting the most negative reaction from others to their homosexuality are less likely to report homosexual activity in themselves. It is likely that self-report measures represent an underestimate, to an unknown degree, of homosexual orientation. There are some suggestions that those who refuse to respond to questions about homosexual behavior may be disproportionately likely to have substantial homosexual experience.

Given such significant measurement problems, one could conclude there is serious doubt whether sexual orientation is a valid concept at all. In fact, one theory, *social constructionism,* suggests that there is nothing "real" about sexual orientation except a society's construction of it. *Essentialism* suggests that homosexual desire, identity, and persons exist as real in some form, in different cultures and historical eras. Not surprisingly, social constructionists generally reject the possibility of biological factors in sexual orientation, while essentialists can accept (but do not necessarily require) biological factors. Regardless of these significant methodological concerns, most present-day North Americans tend to label themselves as homosexual, heterosexual, or bisexual despite the fact that these labels do not capture the full range of complexity of sexual orientation and sexual identity. But it is important to acknowledge that despite the acceptability of such terms in common parlance, their scientific meaning is quite unclear.

It would not be at all surprising if future research suggests that with our current tripartite division of sexual orientation into homosexual, heterosexual, and bisexual, we are cutting the pie in the wrong way, and that there are homosexualities, heterosexualities, and bisexualities as different within class as between classes—or even that other variables are better candidates for constituting a class. What might the sexual orientations look like if ordered primarily by patterns of affiliation, or by particular chromosomal patterns, or by propensity to engage in particular sexual behavior? Or that the bases for sexual orientation differ in women and men? Such possible radical restructurings of the way we conceptualize the sexual orientations are by no means a foregone conclusion, but neither is it a foregone conclusion that much of our current conceptualizations will survive future research findings and theoretical development.

THE RELATIONSHIPS BETWEEN SEXUAL ORIENTATION AND MENTAL HEALTH

Homosexuality first evolved into a medical "illness" in the late 19th or early 20th century, depending on the country. In 1973, the American Psychiatric Association removed homosexuality as a diagnosis of illness, replacing it with ego-dystonic homosexuality, a vague and problematic concept that attempted to label dissatisfaction with same-sex orientation as an illness.[13] In early 1975, the governing body of the American Psychological Association voted to support the 1973 action of the American Psychiatric Association. Ego-dystonic homosexuality was itself removed in 1986, probably because it created more confusion than illumination.

In 1957, University of California, Los Angeles, psychologist Evelyn Hooker published research which challenged the illness model when she reported that a panel of psychological testing experts was unable to differentiate samples of homosexual from heterosexual men using a battery of tests measuring mental health problems. At the time, this finding was surprising and inaugurated two and a half decades of experiments using psychological testing in an attempt to differentiate homosexual from heterosexual samples. This literature has been summarized by a number of authors,[14,15] who can be consulted for greater detail. The findings from this literature overwhelmingly supported a rejection of the illness model of homosexuality. In fact, it is fair to say these results are sufficiently consistent and compelling, and that current theories which purport a scientific basis for an illness model of homosexuality represent egregious distortions of these data.

This literature was the empirical basis for the depathologizing of homosexuality in the early 1970s. Most of the studies involved were unable to differentiate with any consistency homosexual from heterosexual populations. It is important to recognize, however, that this level of "proof" is actually unnecessary to depathologize homosexuality.

The illness model of homosexuality maintains that the existence of persistent homosexual feelings and/or behavior in an individual is in and of itself absolutely predictive of psychological disturbance. Findings supportive of *any* group of homosexual individuals who are not psychologically disturbed refute this model. One could even push the argument, then, that the comparative rates of psychological disturbance in homosexual and heterosexual populations are irrelevant to whether homosexuality is an illness. The only relevant issue is whether *any* non-pathological homosexual individuals exist. The psychological test literature suggests that many non-pathological homosexual individuals exist; and that in addition, homosexual and heterosexual individuals cannot be reliably differentiated, much less one group ascribed psychopathology.

Further, there are some reasons, such as facing increased levels of external stress, to believe that certain measures of disturbance may be higher in some homosexual populations as well as in other disparaged groups. This also can be congruent with an assumption that homosexuality itself is not indicative of psychological disturbance. If homosexuals as a group are subject to high levels of external stress, then a proper comparison group may not be heterosexuals in general, but heterosexuals with roughly equivalent external stress. As noted below, there are some measures of psychological difficulties in which there are clear indications that homosexual and heterosexual populations differ.

For example, higher rates of alcoholism and substance abuse, suicide attempts, depression, and other problems have been both suggested, but also disputed, as higher in lesbian and gay samples.[16] While the actual prevalence remains unclear, it would be unsurprising and expected if some of this were so, since it is a truism that economic, social, and/or political discrimination, among its other effects, results in enhanced risk of medical and mental health problems, regardless of the targeted group.

A final line of research findings are intriguing in the context of mental heath and sexual orientation: what characterizes those homosexual individuals who are well-adjusted psychologically? The factors that have emerged include features such as: (1) homosexual individuals who are well-adjusted rejected the idea that homosexuality is an illness, had close and supportive associations with other homosexuals, and were not interested in changing their homosexuality; (2) positive commitment to homosexuality was related to good psychological adjustment and the existence of significant others who support that identity; (3) membership in homosexual groups had positive psychological effects or was predictive of self-esteem; (4) among rural gay men and lesbians, having a supportive community is psychologically beneficial; and similar findings.[17]

In summary, when examining what is known about mental health problems of homosexual populations, the findings are somewhat complex. There is no indication that homosexuality in and of itself is predictive of mental illness. There are suggestions, but no certainty, that in some subgroups of gay and lesbian individuals there may be increased health and mental health risk, consistent with comparable risks in other disparaged groups. It is also clear that positive attitudes towards one's homosexuality and implementing those attitudes into behavioral form, such as maintaining relationships with other lesbian and gay individuals and becoming socially and politically active in lesbian and gay communities, tend to increase psychological adjustment in gay and lesbian populations.

It is important to comment on a particular distortion that has developed regarding the depathologizing of homosexuality; namely, that it occurred primarily due to political pressure.[18] There is little question that the this change was accompanied by unpleasant infighting within the American Psychiatric Association at the time, but the basis for the change was the overwhelming lack of empirical support for the illness model. This declassification must also be situated in the larger context of the sea-change that occurred in the diagnostic nomenclature as the theoretically driven and psychodynamically oriented *Diagnostic and Statistical Manual of Mental Disorders*, Second Edition *(DSM–II)*[13] gave way to the empirically driven and biologically oriented *Diagnostic and Statistical Manual of Mental Disorders*, Third Edition *(DSM–III)*.[19] Simply stated, the declassification of homosexuality was an early and relatively minor skirmish between these opposing forces in psychiatry in the run up to the publication of *DSM–III* in 1980.

On a more basic level, it is absurd to maintain that a rag-tag band of gay liberationists without any established power base could, in 1973, cause a capitulation of the American Psychiatric Association, which was then successfully resisting calls for change from much more powerful social and economic forces.

Rather, it was useful politically for empirically driven biological psychiatry to allow the humiliation of the old psychoanalytic guard with this issue in order to weaken them for more important battles to come. The old guard could be so easily humiliated on this issue because the data were so clear.

In summary, despite the tactic, by those who believe homosexuality must be an illness because they find it unacceptable, of coyly fretting over supposedly unresolved issues about the relationship between mental health and sexual orientation, there is overwhelming consensus in the mental health professions that same-sex orientations are not indicative of mental illness. There is much work that remains in this area, but it is in the area of how to identify and assist those subgroups of sexual minorities who are at enhanced risk for psychological and medical problems. In other words, the primary issue is how to reduce vulnerability and enhance resiliency. This is the public health challenge for all of humanity, and it is typically especially pointed for those individuals who are members of disparaged and/or disadvantaged groups.

CURRENT CONCEPTUALIZATIONS OF THE "CAUSES" OF SEXUAL ORIENTATIONS

One might easily imagine after the discussion about definitions and measurement above, that approaching the nature and causes of sexual orientations would be enormously complicated. Indeed it is, and an adequate coverage of this topic would require a volume of its own. Some words are in order, however.

Simply stated, there is currently no consensus about the causes of sexual orientations. The choice of these last words is careful: any good theory of sexual orientations must work across a range of same-sex, opposite-sex, and both same and opposite sex eroticism, and be able to handle the kinds of variation within each category suggested in the earlier section above on definition and measurement. It must also be able to embrace the possibility that there are multiple varieties of homosexuality, heterosexuality, and bisexuality as different within category as these categories are from each other. Many have suggested that the biggest challenges of any theory involve: retaining explanatory power across genders, adequately explaining the bisexualities, and providing a reasonable framework to understand the considerable cross-cultural variations observed. This is a VERY tall order.

Recent decades have not seen much in the way of primarily environmentally based comprehensive theories of the sexual orientations, perhaps because earlier illness-based psychodynamic theories were such a disappointment. There have been impassioned antibiological arguments made, especially from feminist and social constructivist sources. These have been useful in prodding biologically oriented scholars to adopt more nuanced, primarily interactionist models. This has had the ironic effect of improving the quality of biological models, especially as these critiques have offered little in the way of alternatives to the biological approaches they critique.

While biological models (or rather interactionist/biological models, since almost all serious biological models are now interactionist) have provided some tantalizing suggestions that may address parts of the puzzle, no comprehensive picture has emerged here either. This may well be a credit to appropriate caution on the part of many biological scholars, as well as the apparently daunting complexity of the sexual orientations.[20–23] Another intriguing development has been the deeper appreciation of the extent and complexity of same-sex behavior among other species[24]; but again, no comprehensive certainty about the nature and causes of sexual orientations in our species has emerged.

This lack of certainty should not be taken to mean that fruitful ideas are not being put forward. In fact, the current dilemma seems to have inspired a good deal of creative thinking from a variety of vantage points. However, little of this has filtered down to public policy debates, which seem to move little beyond sloganeering that people "choose to be gay" or are "born that way." It can safely be said that the first of these is simply without scientific foundation or even logic, and the second is so simplistic as to bear scant resemblance to any serious model.

ATTEMPTS AT "CONVERSION" AND "REPARATION" OF HOMOSEXUALITY

Prior to the depathologizing of homosexuality, there were a number of theorists, primarily psychoanalytic, who described in detail the alleged psychopathology of lesbian and gay individuals. Most of their work was based on psychoanalytic speculations about populations of troubled homosexuals who appeared for psychotherapy. Some of these theorists purported to conduct research which supported their views, although in fact it represents a parody of research.

For example, the Bieber et al research[25] is really a case study in researcher bias. They compared male homosexual and heterosexual patients in psychoanalysis. The same group of psychoanalysts developed a theory about homosexuality; developed a questionnaire to test their theory; designed the research study; served as analysts for the patient-subjects; served as raters in the research project on their own patients; and interpreted results. It is not surprising that they concluded that their theory had been verified. It is difficult to build more potential for researcher bias into experimental procedures than that which is evident in the Bieber group.

Unlike behavioral therapists who by and large dropped their attempts to "cure" homosexuality after homosexuality was depathologized, some psychoanalysts have continued expounding an illness model of homosexuality. Concurrent with these attempts, however, has been the development of fairly elaborate psychoanalytic models that do not view homosexuality as an illness, but rather as a normal variant in the human condition, and proceed to describe how psychoanalytic methods can be useful in understanding and assisting gay, lesbian, and bisexual individuals who may have difficulties; essentially, gay/lesbian affirmative psychoanalytic perspectives,[26,27] which gradually seem to be becoming mainstream within psychoanalysis.

Perhaps the most vocal of current illness theorists tend to be fundamentalist Christian therapists. These are church affiliated individuals who purport to cure homosexuality through a combination of religious exhortation, often intermingled with fragments of 12-step self-help programs.

There are a number of common features of these religiously oriented repathologizing attempts. First, they focus on changing sexual orientation, and do so almost exclusively with males. These efforts generally assert, based on no discernable data, that its members have been cured of homosexuality. On closer examination, many of them acknowledge that homosexual desire remains, but the individuals have "chosen" to lead a moral, heterosexual life. In effect, what they are occasionally capable of doing is utilizing group pressure and brainwashing to coerce gay males into not acting upon same-sex feelings. It is a comment on the pervasive sexism of these groups that lesbians are of little interest and rarely attract their so-called therapeutic efforts. It appears only males are important enough to warrant such interventions.

Another feature of this new fundamentalist repathologizing of homosexuality is the creation of bogus scientific institutions and foundations. They often have substantial funding and are usually headed by obscure individuals who are self-proclaimed authorities in the field. They frequently have well-orchestrated media contacts, usually in the wake of a legislative or court controversy, and often disappear and reemerge as needed. The substantial funding, nationwide coordination, and well-executed access to media suggest that many of these foundations, if not most, are part of a coordinated effort.

A recent hybrid is the appearance of professional-appearing attempts to "cure" homosexuality, usually couched in a 1950s style psychoanalytic approach. Case examples, but no scientific data, "prove" the authors' points. Most of these, on closer examination, bear clear indications of their religious affiliation.[28] A common feature of this pseudoscientific, covertly religiously oriented approach is to ignore the scientific information discussed above and to repose questions regarding psychopathology and homosexuality which have been decisively answered, under the guise of scientific inquiry and curiosity about these "unanswered" questions. Attempts are made to create false confusion regarding scientific information about homosexuality. No new scientifically verifiable evidence is produced. Their assiduous distortions of current research, reliance on case studies, and use of obsolete literature and ways of understanding sexual orientation effectively make the point that the depathologizing of homosexuality is robust.

Despite refutations of this literature, and its becoming even more ethically and professionally tenuous on the publication of guidelines for effective clinical work with non-heterosexual populations,[29] conservatively religious conversion or reparation therapists have become increasingly aggressive, both in attempting to gain legitimacy in the field, and in advocating a discriminatory political agenda.

A number of authors have offered thoughtful analyses of such so-called therapy.[30-32] The core dilemma with such therapies is that a non-heterosexual orientation is not a mental illness (despite repeated attempts by conversion therapists to reframe homosexuality as mental illness in need of change). Attempts to convert homosexuality to heterosexuality are of questionable efficacy, and are ethically compromised and heavily reliant on misinformation and disinformation. They also pose serious problems of informed consent, and a moderately high likelihood of adverse sequellae. Yet, conservatively religious clients sometimes request such therapy, some conservative Christian institutions actively foster social conditions to maximize distress for such clients about their sexual orientations, and these institutions simultaneously promote conversion therapy as the solution to this distress.

Conservatively religious Christians, while giving passing acknowledgement to Christian traditions other than their own, typically proceed as if the only alternative to their theology is loss of faith. This is an exaggerated dichotomy; perhaps a specific version of faith may be lost, but the loss is not one of Christian faith. Within Christian traditions in general, and even within conservative Christian traditions, there is considerable difference of opinion, even turmoil, regarding sexual orientation. Simply stated, any viewpoints other than strict adherence to orthodoxy are viewed as a crisis of faith and allegiance within Christian conservative orthodox thinking. This crisis is predominantly created by religious orthodoxy, and is part of a larger effort to constrain and suppress theological diversity within these traditions. Religiously conservative Christian hierarchies do not speak for Christianity or even conservative Christianity; the voices of Christianity are multiple and varied.

On the other hand, conflicts between religious belief and sexual orientation can be truly distressing. In fact, this has been a commonly recognized experience in current sexual minority communities, who have been seeking resolution of spiritual concerns since there were such modern communities.

Religious organizations have consistently been among the largest within sexual minority communities, usually surpassing political action organizations. Virtually every denomination, including religiously conservative denominations, has an equivalent organization in the lesbian/gay community whose purpose is to reconcile that particular faith tradition with a positive sense of lesbian/gay identity. These organizations vary in the degree to which the specific denomination welcomes them, but have been durable despite this.

Sexual minority communities have been working for decades to integrate spiritual life and sexuality, while conservative religious traditions have simply condemned this search because it does not conform to notions of orthodoxy and threatens to elicit other aspects of theological heterodoxy within conservative Christian communities. Conservative Christian hierarchies reject as unacceptable any view that diverges from its orthodoxy. Sexual minority communities have aspired to craft solutions that integrate both sexuality and religious tradition. These aspirations are ignored and disparaged by religious Conservatives, who disapprove of them on theological grounds.

Such disapproval can and does create psychological distress for those caught in between, particularly when accompanied by militant social and political activism to assure second-class status for sexual minorities, and planful measures to create misery and distress for those deemed second-class. The effects are psychological, but the problem is one of theology run amok, attempting to impose theocracy.

Recently, integrative solutions to this conflict have emerged. These generally share a view that all aspects of a client's self or identity are worthy of respect, and that the therapeutic goal is to assist the client in finding a solution, when different components clash, in which all will find some place at the table. These integrative solutions offer no decisive resolution, but rather a process of persevering in the attempt to craft a solution by valuing both sexuality and spirituality, addressing psychological conflict and distortion when they appear to be interfering, and trying to find a middle path in which no component of the individual is violated or disparaged. In essence, these approaches assert that for clients who are both same-sex attracted and conservatively religious, effective therapy cannot have a sole focus on either, but must work to integrate both if it is to be effective and beneficial in its effects.

This is a perspective that reaches beyond this particular controversy. A major work on cultural diversity suggests a comparable middle path in which the mental health professional should neither invalidate a client's cultural beliefs, nor support indoctrination into cultural beliefs. Implicit in the approach being suggested here is that mental health professionals remain in role as professionals in handling such issues, providing information, helping clients integrate various issues, reducing the impact of personal pathologies and liabilities that might impair resolution, serving as a source of neutral but concerned feedback, and similar therapeutic functions. This role, however, does not include posing as spiritual guides; operating as theological, cultural, political, or sexual enforcers; or rescuing clients from grappling with their own existential, spiritual, and philosophical dilemmas when the various components of who they are in their human fullness do not easily coexist.

It is difficult to think of another situation where such a clash allegedly exists between the principle of respecting diversity and other aspects of ethical conduct and professional practice responsibilities. I suggest that this dilemma so resists resolution because it is being misstated. The problem can be more clearly addressed if the underlying rationale of conversion therapies is fully articulated. At their core, conversion therapy seeks to legitimize the use of mental health techniques and behavioral science to enforce compliance with religious orthodoxy. The dilemma resists solution because it cannot be solved. Either the mental health professions are co-opted into abdicating their ethical principles, professional practice standards, and scientific base, or they soundly reject the enforcement of religious orthodoxy as a legitimate goal of mental health practice. Conversion therapists are asking the mental health professions to endorse and sanction the theologically based creation of psychological distress in sexual minority individuals, and this distress is then rationalized as an acceptable justification for conversion therapy.

HOMOSEXUALITY AND FITNESS: MILITARY AND PARENTAL

The volume by Herek, Jobe, and Carney[33] provides a strong platform for understanding the issues involved in gay and lesbian service personnel in the military. To briefly summarize their findings, there is no sound basis for excluding gay and lesbian personnel from the military. Such personnel have been successfully integrated into armed forces around the world, including many key U.S. allies, and the challenges of integrating gay and lesbian personnel are akin to those of integrating African American personnel into the U.S. military, a task which the military actually tackled successfully prior to the success of the civil rights movement in the broader society.

Ironically, given the military's history of denying that gay and lesbian people exist in military service and the attempted exclusion of gay and lesbian people from their ranks, some of the most interesting research with large sample sizes comes from the United States Department of Defense. Two internal studies were leaked early in the debates about the suitability of gay, lesbian, and bisexual citizens in the U.S. military. McDaniel[32] posed the question whether homosexuals would be suitable for national security clearances. He collected information about educational experiences, alcohol and drug use, criminal activities, and other factors on a self-report inventory, and then compared individuals who were discharged from the armed services for homosexuality versus other groups. McDaniel found that homosexuals had better preservice adjustment than heterosexuals in areas related to school behavior, that homosexuals displayed greater levels of cognitive ability than heterosexuals, and that homosexuals had greater problems with alcohol and drug abuse than heterosexuals. With the latter exception, homosexuals resembled those who had successfully adjusted to military life more than those who had been discharged for being unsuitable. This study concluded that the adjustment of male homosexuals tended to be better or equal to that of male heterosexuals, and that female homosexuals tended to score somewhat lower on preservice adjustment compared with female heterosexuals. Females as a whole, however, tended to have better preservice adjustment than males as a whole. Female homosexuals, while having poorer adjustment than female heterosexuals, had better adjustment than male heterosexuals.

Sarbin and Carols,[33] in their summary of the military suitability of homosexuals, concluded that homosexual orientation is unrelated to military job performance, and that the main problem facing integration of homosexual individuals in the military is primarily maintaining group cohesion within the general military structure when an unpopular minority group is absorbed. Similarly, Herek,[16] in his review of the social science data, concluded that denial or restriction of government security clearances for gay people has no rational or empirical justification. He also concluded that lesbians and gay men are no more likely than heterosexuals to be subject to blackmail or coercion, to be unreliable or untrustworthy, or to be likely to disrespect or fail to uphold laws.

The work of Patterson, Fulcher, and Wainright[34] has examined whether lesbian and gay individuals function effectively as parents. The research in this area is not new, but in fact was one of the first public policy concerns to be researched. The findings are similar to the military issue: research has consistently supported a position that sexual orientation does not predict parental fitness.

These two areas have garnered the bulk of research on fitness for various situations as related to sexual orientation. In neither case is there indication that sexual orientation is related to fitness.

WHY DO THESE ISSUES MATTER? THEIR MEANINGS AND IMPLICATIONS

It seems clear that issues regarding sexual orientation that seem unresolved in the public perception are quite resolved and essentially nonissues in the consensus of most behavioral scientists. In the sampling of issues covered in this paper, sexual orientation is unrelated to mental illness, sexual orientation is unrelated to the two aspects of fitness mot studied, parenting and military service, and attempts to change sexual orientation are ethically suspect of dubious efficacy and based on essentially fraudulent premises. There remain important and substantive questions regarding mental health and sexual orientation in areas such as mapping out how vulnerability and resiliency to health concerns work in sexual minority populations, and whether our current ways of defining and measuring the sexual orientations are accurate and optimal.

Yet such issues as these latter are virtually invisible in the public debates, and issues that to behavioral scientists are resolved have remained front and center in the public eye. What is going on here? I believe a closer examination of the issues underlying one of the topics covered in this paper, conversion therapy, might illuminate some of the latent issues here.

Religiously conservative ideologies typically are based upon certain values, which I suggest are incompatible with principles of scientific inquiry and professional psychological practice. Specifically, in faith-based thought, core aspects of understanding are theologically revealed, whereas in scientific inquiry, they are empirically derived. Theologically revealed truth is then the central operating principle around which understandings about various issues must align. There is no internal contradiction if arguments are circular, because at the center of this circle is truth.

Scientific reasoning, by contrast, assumes no central truth, and arguments must adhere to particular logical forms and methodological constraints, standing as valid on their own, without recourse to the validating anchor of a presumed central truth. Finally, faith-based thought rests on certainty about what is revealed. Scientific thought admits no ultimate certainty, as any finding can ultimately be usurped by another that is methodologically and empirically superior. Scientific thought, then, is at its core, evolving and ambiguous. I believe the above description is a fair characterization of certain aspects of conservative faith-based thought, although it may not be characteristic of other religious traditions. I am making no argument that such thought is necessarily flawed as theology, but that it is merely incompatible with scientific inquiry.

To pull these features together, I suggest that what is happening with the conversion therapy controversy is that conservative faith-based proponents offer an essentially tautological position, that their viewpoint must be accepted as one of a diverse range of options within psychology, in accordance with the psychological principle of respect for diversity. The point that is being overlooked is that respect for diversity does not require any scientifically based discipline to accept as scientific those positions which are not derived from scientific principles. Further, I suggest that the espousal of the idea of diversity by conservative faith-based proponents is not truly an operating principle or a held value, but merely a temporary strategy, a ruse essentially, geared toward the acceptance of a nonscientific theologically based viewpoint as legitimate science. In fact, such conservative faith-based systems operate on the assumption that truth is theologically revealed, and that different perspectives must be incorrect. One does not have to read much between the lines in the conversion therapy literature to conclude that there is also a strong undercurrent that certain others (unconverted homosexuals, unbelievers in general) are considered second-class. The progression, then, seems to be to use a diversity argument to gain acceptance for nonscientific thought as scientific, so that diversity of both ideas and people can then be attacked from within psychology. Conversion therapy, then, is a kind of intellectual virus as it operates within the mental health profession, attempting to trick a host into gaining entry so that it can attack it from within using its own mechanisms.

I do not view the statement above as alarmist or harsh. Consider the emergence of conservative faith-based so-called scientific contributions that offer creationism as equivalent to evolutionary biology, and disinformation on women's reproductive health, educational reform, adolescent sexuality, and sexual orientation presented as scientific data. Such information might more properly be called "scientistic": information that mimics science, but is not science in methodology, principle, or intent. Control of science is important to conservative Christian hierarchies because raw advocacy of theocracy is distasteful to many, whereas theocracy in scientistic drag is seen as more politically palatable.

In the recent United States Supreme Court case[35] which overturned sodomy statutes, one of the bases for that decision was that orthodox religious tradition was not a persuasive enough basis to outweigh the other legal principles that sodomy statutes violated. Anglo-American law has a tradition of including religious tradition, to a limited degree, as one of the bases for its structure. Nevertheless, the Court in *Lawrence et al. v. Texas* stated, " . . . for centuries there have been powerful voices to condemn homosexual conduct as immoral. The condemnation has been shaped by religious beliefs, conceptions of right and acceptable behavior, and respect for the traditional family . . . These considerations do not answer the question before us, however. The issue is whether the majority may use the power of the State to enforce these views on the whole society through operation of the criminal code." Quoting from another case, the Court goes on to note, "Our obligation is to define the liberty of all, not to mandate our own moral code." Why should the behavioral sciences, which have never accepted religious tradition as a basis, even consider abdicating professional responsibility to one variant of religious tradition, particularly one so at odds with the behavioral science's own traditions and methodologies?

What is at stake here is who will control science, specifically behavioral science. It is no accident where the battle lines are drawn. Sexual minorities remain the last target of societal bigotry that is socially acceptable in many quarters, and evolutionary biology is difficult to comprehend, easy to stereotype, and disquieting to many. These are ideal wedge issues to divide the general public from scientists and gain public support for theocratic control of science. A theocratically controlled or even theocratically influenced science is no science at all, however, but instead a weapon of theological enforcement.

What I am suggesting is that only those who operate via scientific principles have a legitimate place in the behavioral sciences, and those who aspire to manipulate and mimic science do not. This is what the considerable gulf between the behavioral sciences and public debate regarding sexual orientation is truly about.

ACKNOWLEDGMENTS

Parts of this chapter were previously published in: J. C. Gonsiorek, "Reflections from the Conversion Therapy Battlefield," *The Counseling Psychologist, 32,* no. 5 (2004): pp. 750–759; J. C. Gonsiorek, "Mental Health and Sexual Orientation," in *The Lives of Lesbians, Gays and Bisexuals: Children to Adults,* ed. R. C. Savin-Williams and K. M. Cohen, (pp. 462–478) (Fort Worth, Tex.: Harcourt Brace, 1996); J. C. Gonsiorek, R. L. Sell, and J. D. Weinrich, "Definition and Measurement of Sexual Orientation," *Suicide & Life-Threatening Behavior, 25* (1995, supp.), pp. 40–51. These can be consulted for more details and complete references.

REFERENCES

1. Gonsiorek, J. C., Sell, R. L., & Weinrich, J. D. (1995). Definition and measurement of sexual orientation. *Suicide & Life-Threatening Behavior, 25*(Suppl.), 40–51.

2. Sell, R.L. (1997). Defining and measuring sexual orientation: A review. *Archives of Sexual Behavior, 26,* 643–658.

3. Shively, M. G., & De Cecco, J. P. (1977). Components of sexual identity. *Journal of Homosexuality, 3,* 41–48.

4. Kinsey, A. C., Pomeroy, W. B., & Martin, C. E. (1948). *Sexual behavior in the human male.* Philadelphia: W. B. Saunders.

5. Kinsey, A. C., Pomeroy, W. B., Martin, C. E., & Gebhard, P. H. (1953). *Sexual behavior in the human female.* Philadelphia: W. B. Saunders.

6. Klein, F., Sepekoff, B., & Wolf, T. (1985). Sexual orientation: A multi-variable dynamic process. *Journal of Homosexuality, 12,* 35–49.

7. Golden, C. (1994). Our politics and choices: The feminist movement and sexual orientation. In B. Greene & G. Herek (Eds.), *Lesbian and gay psychology: Theory, research and clinical applications* (Vol. 1, pp. 54–70). Thousand Oaks, CA.: Sage Publications.

8. Baumeister, R. F. (2000). Gender differences in erotic plasticity: The female sex drive as socially flexible and responsive. *Psychological Bulletin, 126,* 347–374.

9. Burdick, J., & Stewart, D. (1974). Differences between "show" and "no-show" volunteers in a homosexual population. *Journal of Social Psychology, 92,* 159–160.

10. Freund, K. W. (1974). Male homosexuality: An analysis of the pattern. In J. A. Loraine (Ed.) *Understanding homosexuality: Its biological and psychological bases* (pp. 25–81). New York: Elsevier.

11. Freund, K. W. (1977). Should homosexuality arouse therapeutic concern? *Journal of Homosexuality, 2,* 235–240.

12. Gonsiorek, J. C., & Rudolph, J. R. (1991). Homosexual identity: Coming out and other developmental events. In J. C. Gonsiorek & J. D. Weinrich (Eds.), *Homosexuality: Research implications for public policy* (pp. 161–176). Newbury Park, CA: Sage Publications.

13. American Psychiatric Association. (1968). *Diagnostic and statistical manual of mental disorders* (2nd ed.). Washington, DC: Author.

14. Gonsiorek. J. C. (1991). The empirical basis for the demise of the illness model of homosexuality. In J.C. Gonsiorek & J.D. Weinrich (Eds.) *Homosexuality: Research implications for public policy* (pp. 115–136). Newbury Park, CA: Sage Publications.

15. Meredith, R. L., & Reister, R. W. (1980). Psychotherapy responsibility and homosexuality: Clinical examination of socially deviant behavior. *Professional Psychology, 11,* 174–193.

16. Herek, G. M. (1990). Gay people and governmental security clearances: A social perspective. *American Psychologist, 45,* 1035–1042.

17. Gonsiorek, J. C. (1996). Mental health and sexual orientation. In R. C. Savin-Williams & K. M. Cohen (Eds.), *The lives of lesbians, gays and bisexuals: Children to adults* (pp. 462–478). Fort Worth, TX: Harcourt Brace.

18. Bayer, R. (1987). *Homosexuality and American psychiatry: The politics of diagnosis* (2nd ed.). Princeton, NJ: Princeton University Press.

19. American Psychiatric Association. (1980). *Diagnostic and statistical manual of mental disorders* (3rd ed.). Washington, DC: Author.

20. Le Vay, S. (1996). *Queer science: The use and abuse of research into homosexuality.* Cambridge, MA: MIT Press.

21. Weinrich, J. (1987). *Sexual landscapes: Why we are what we are, why we love whom we love.* New York: Scribner's

22. Bagemihl, B. (1999). *Biological exuberance: Animal homosexuality and natural diversity.* New York: St. Martin's Press.

23. Bieber, I., Dain, H. J., Dince, P. R., Drellich, M. G., Grand, H. G., Gundlach, R. H., et al. (1962). *Homosexuality: A psychoanalytic study.* New York: Basic Books.

24. Isay, R. A. (1989). *Being homosexual: Gay men and their development.* New York: Farrar, Straus, & Giroux.

25. Friedman, R. C. (1988). *Male homosexuality: A contemporary psychoanalytic perspective.* New Haven, CT: Yale University Press.

26. Nicolosi, J. (1991). *Reparative therapy of male homosexuality.* Northvale, NJ: Jason Aronson.

27. Division 44/ Committee on Gay, Lesbian and Bisexual Concerns Joint Task force on Guidelines for Psychotherapy with Lesbian, Gay and Bisexual Clients. (2000). Guidelines for psychotherapy with lesbian, gay and bisexual clients, *American Psychologist, 55,* 1140–1451.

28. Shidlo, A., Schroeder, M., & Drescher, J. (Eds.) (2001). *Sexual conversion therapy: Ethical, clinical, and research perspectives.* New York: Haworth Press.

29. Haldeman, D. (2002). Gay rights, patient rights: The implications of sexual orientation conversion therapy. *Professional Psychology: Research and Practice, 33,* 260–264.

30. Religious beliefs and sexual orientation. [Special Issue]. (2004). *The Counseling Psychologist, 32*(5).

31. Herek, G. M., Jobe, J. B., & Carney, R. M. (1996). *Out in force: Sexual orientation and the military.* Chicago, IL: University of Chicago Press.

32. McDaniel, L. A. (1989). Preservice adjustment of homosexual and heterosexual military accessions: Implications for security clearance suitability (PERS-TR-89–004). Monterey, CA: Defense Personnel Security Research and Education Center.

33. Sarbin, T. R., & Carols, K. E. (1988). Nonconforming sexual orientation and military suitability (PERS-TR-89–002). Monterey, CA: Defense Personnel Security Research and Education Center.

34. Patterson, C. J., Fulcher, M., & Wainright, J. (2002). Children of lesbian and gay parents: Research, law and policy. In B. L. Bottoms, M. B. Kovera, & B. D. McAuliff (Eds.), *Children, social science and the law* (pp. 176–199). New York: Cambridge University Press.

35. *Lawrence et al. v. Texas,* U.S. 02–102 (2003).

Chapter 12

Conclusion: How Might We Prevent Abnormal Behavior from Occurring and Developing?

Thomas G. Plante

This book series has tried to bring the contemporary world of abnormal psychology and behavior to you in an informative, updated, and understandable manner. Hopefully, you have learned much about how abnormal behavior impacts all those around us including those we care most about. The book has tried to articulate what is currently known about a wide variety of abnormal psychology topics so that you will be much better informed about these issues that are often discussed in the news and elsewhere.

After reading and reflecting on these important topics, one might wonder what can be done to minimize, eliminate, or prevent these kinds of problems from occurring. There is clearly no simple answer to this question. There are a variety of reasons why abnormal behavior emerges and develops. Some are due to biological or physiological factors such as genetics, hormonal and biochemical influences, and the exposure to both legal and illegal substances. Others are due to internal psychological conflicts associated with personality, mood, and stress mechanisms. Still others are due to the interactions of many social and interpersonal relationships with loved ones, work or school associates, neighbors, and community members. There are many different roads that lead to abnormal and problematic behavior. However, this does not mean that we can't do much more to improve the odds that abnormal behavior won't develop within ourselves and others. We clearly can make a better world for ourselves and for society if we can follow some key principles of prevention. After reading this book series and carefully evaluating the advice of many leading experts, several important principles of prevention emerge as being especially important in preventing abnormal behavior from either developing or getting worse. While we cannot do justice to each prevention strategy articulated, we can at least introduce these seven principles to the reader. This list is not meant to be exhaustive or exclusive. It merely provides some very brief reflections and observations as well as prevention and coping principles.

AVOID ABUSE AND NEGLECT OF CHILDREN

As clearly articulated in several chapters of the series, the abuse and neglect of children occurs at alarming and disturbing rates. Abused and neglected children are much more likely to develop certain troubles with depression, anxiety, violence, substance abuse, interpersonal difficulties, and a host of other problem behaviors. Once developed, these problems impact others around them and can be passed on from generation to generation. Somehow, efforts must be increased to minimize child abuse and neglect. Public policy experts, child protection professionals, family attorneys, politicians, mental health professionals, and others must work closely to help children stay safe and to ensure that those entrusted with the welfare of children (e.g., parents, teachers, coaches, child care providers) are capable of providing the competent and effective care that children need, which is free from any abuse or neglect. While we can't totally eliminate child abuse and neglect, we can certainly try to minimize it by pooling our collective resources and expertise making a firm commitment to the safety and well-being of all children. Like a lot of things, it will take a selfless commitment of time, money, and other resources to make significant progress in this area. It will involve working with many different community, civic, religious, educational, law enforcement, mental health, political, and other agencies. Perhaps as former President Nixon argued for a "War on Cancer" or former President Johnson's "War on Poverty," we may need a "War on Child Abuse and Neglect."

MINIMIZE POVERTY

Those who are poor are less likely to have access to professional mental and physical health care services and are much more likely to be impacted by the stress that is associated with poverty (e.g., unemployment, poor housing, and exposure to community violence). As poverty levels increase and the gap between the rich and poor widens, it is likely that the psychological and behavioral problems associated with poverty will increase. Therefore, efforts to reduce poverty will likely minimize the development of or the worsening of a variety of abnormal psychology problems. Again, politicians, business leaders, mental health professionals, family advocates, and others must somehow work together in order to minimize poverty both here and abroad. Perhaps former President Johnson's "War on Poverty" needs to be waged once again.

MINIMIZE EXPOSURE TO VIOLENCE

Sadly, we live in an often highly violent world. Violence is not only perpetrated during wars and in street crime but also in the seclusion and privacy of one's own home. Domestic violence, child abuse, date rape, and other kinds of violence are all too common. Furthermore, research has clearly indicated that exposure to violence through entertainment sources (e.g., movies, video games) also increases the risk of both violence and other mental health–related problems among vulnerable viewers. The entertainment industry, politicians, mental health professionals, family advocates, and others must somehow work together in order to minimize violence exposure in entertainment, in the media in general, and in both public communities and private homes.

DEVELOP AND NURTURE EFFECTIVE AND AFFORDABLE TREATMENTS (INCLUDING PHARMACEUTICALS)

The development of quality and effective intervention strategies including pharmaceutical agents has the potential ability to greatly reduce the impact of abnormal behavior, assuming these options are available to all those in need. For example, medications such as Prozac and other selective serotonin reuptake inhibitors have revolutionized the treatment of depressive disorders during the past decade and a half. These medications, while not perfect or right for everyone with depression, have greatly improved the odds of effectively dealing with a number of psychiatric troubles including obsessive-compulsive disorder, depression, bulimia, and so forth. Recent quality research using empirically supported psychological interventions has also demonstrated remarkable results for a wide variety of abnormal behavior problems. Quality behavioral and psychological interventions for panic disorder, depression, eating disorders, posttraumatic stress disorder, and many other problems are available. Research and development on affordable medications and psychosocial interventions to help those who suffer from abnormal behavior offer hope to not only those afflicted with these conditions but also to those loved ones who suffer too.

However, medications in particular can often too easily be seen as a magic pill to solve all problems. Medications can also be extremely expensive in the United States in particular. A careful and thoughtful effort to make appropriate medications available to those who can truly benefit from them will likely help to minimize the severity of abnormal behavior for not only identified patients but also for all those who are connected to them via family, work, school, or other relationships. The best available research and practice is needed to ensure that interventions that can help people with abnormal behavior are readily available and used.

ALTER CULTURAL EXPECTATIONS ABOUT BEHAVIOR

In previous decades, children rode in cars without seat belts and rode their bikes without bike helmets. Parents physically hit their children at will and in public. People were allowed to smoke wherever they wanted to do so. Women who sought to work outside of the home were considered odd or too bold. Cultural expectations about how we live our lives that have impacted social customs and expectations can be applied to abnormal behavior risk factors as well. For example, violence exposure, maintaining zero tolerance for child abuse, alcohol and other substance abuse, poverty, and so forth may help to create a society where abnormal behavior cannot flourish. Public policy can be used to help decrease the odds that abnormal behavior risks are tolerated. Cultural expectations and policy decisions can be used to ensure that those who experience particular problems seek appropriate resources. There is too often a social taboo to request help from mental health professionals about abnormal psychology related problems. This resistance and avoidance tragically often allows potential problems to become more severe and serious.

AVOID EXPOSURE TO ABNORMAL PSYCHOLOGY RISK FACTORS

While Americans demand individual freedoms, exposure to particular risks increases the chance of abnormal behavior of developing. For example, legalized gambling in some form (e.g., Indian gaming, lotteries, Internet gambling) is now allowed in just about all states and is certainly not confined to Las Vegas and Atlantic City. Bars and liquor stores are open and available around the clock in just about every city. Pornography and online gambling are available on the Internet and thus just about everyone who has a computer or can get to one can be exposed to these influences. These trends increase the odds that those who are vulnerable to developing certain abnormal problems (e.g., alcoholism, pornography, gambling) will do so. As I have heard many times, "An alcoholic probably shouldn't work as a bartender." Controlling the environment so that temptations are not available very easily would go a long way in minimizing the development of many abnormal behavior problems. Furthermore, vulnerable children and those with predilections to particular behavioral problems can all too easily access materials that can contribute to further abnormal psychology problems. Therefore, being thoughtful about the environmental influences that increase the odds of developing problems later in life should make all of us more sensitive to these influences.

MAXIMIZE ETHICS—ESPECIALLY SOCIAL RESPONSIBILITY AND CONCERN FOR OTHERS

At the end of the day, somehow we all must find a way to live together, sharing the planet and its resources. If we have any hope of living in a world that is humane and just and where abnormal behavior and problems are managed better and minimized, we'll need to maximize our social responsibility and concern for others. The ethical treatment of all persons and our efforts to make the world a better place for all will hopefully prevent or at least minimize many of the troubles associated with abnormal behavior. A global effort to support ethical interactions among all may help us better live with social responsibility and concern for others.

While abnormal behavior is likely to be with us forever, there is much that we can do as a society to minimize the possibility that abnormal behavior will develop in at-risk individuals and groups as well as to help those who experience these troubles. Mental health professionals working with others including public policy leaders, industries such as the pharmaceutical companies, and experts in many other fields can help a great deal. Can our culture and society make the commitment to do this? Let us hope so.

Index

About the Editor and the Contributors

EDITOR

Thomas G. Plante, *PhD, ABPP*, is professor and chair of psychology at Santa Clara University and adjunct clinical associate professor of psychiatry and behavioral sciences at Stanford University School of Medicine. He has authored, coauthored, edited, or coedited six books including *Sin against the Innocents: Sexual Abuse by Priests and the Role of the Catholic Church* (Greenwood, 2004), *Bless Me Father For I Have Sinned: Perspectives on Sexual Abuse Committed by Roman Catholic Priests* (Greenwood, 1999), *Faith and Health: Psychological Perspectives* (2001, Guilford), *Do the Right Thing: Living Ethically in an Unethical World* (2004, New Harbinger), and *Contemporary Clinical Psychology* (1999, 2005, Wiley), as well as over 100 professional journal articles and book chapters. He is a Fellow of the American Psychological Association, the American Academy of Clinical Psychology, and the Society of Behavioral Medicine. He maintains a private practice in Menlo Park, California.

CONTRIBUTORS

Catherine C. Ayoub, *EdD*, is an associate professor at Harvard Medical School and Harvard Graduate School of Education. Her present research centers on the developmental consequences and emotional adjustment of children who have experienced mental illness, child maltreatment, homelessness, chronic illness, difficult parental divorce, and witnessed domestic violence. She also directs several research projects including a developmental study of maltreated children and their parents, a study of Munchausen by Proxy families, a project that explores the impact of conflicted divorce on children, and a project on Bolivian street children. Dr. Ayoub has published over 70 articles and book chapters relating to issues of childhood and adolescent trauma and risk.

Ruth E. Cook, PhD, is professor and director of Special Education and Early Intervention Services at Santa Clara University. Previously, she was the director of two inclusive early childhood centers, and is the lead author of *Adapting Early Childhood Curricula for Children in Inclusive Settings* (Prentice Hall) under contract for its 7th edition and coauthor of *Strategies for Including Children with Special Needs in Early Childhood Settings* (Thomson Delmar Learning, 2000). She serves as a technical consultant to the Morgan Center, a private, nonprofit school for children with autism spectrum disorders (ASD) that also provides comprehensive educational services to children with ASD.

Jennifer Couturier, MD, is assistant professor of psychiatry at the University of Western Ontario, in London, Ontario, Canada. She is also lead physician of the Eating Disorders Program for Children and Adolescents at London Health Sciences Centre. She completed her training in psychiatry and received a diploma in child and adolescent psychiatry at the University of Western Ontario. She also completed a postdoctoral research fellowship in the Department of Psychiatry and Behavioral Sciences at Stanford University in the Division of Child and Adolescent Psychiatry Eating Disorders Program with Dr. James Lock.

Elisabeth M. Dykens, PhD is professor of psychology and deputy director of the Vanderbilt Kennedy Center for Research on Human Development. Her research examines psychopathology and areas of strength in persons with mental retardation, especially those with genetic syndromes. Her studies focus on the development and correlates of psychopathology and behavioral problems in Prader-Willi syndrome, Williams syndrome, and Down syndrome. The author of numerous scientific articles and chapters, Dr. Dykens is also the coauthor of *Genetics and Mental Retardation Syndromes: A New Look at Behavior and Interventions* (2000, Brookes Publishing Company). She is also a consulting editor of *Mental Retardation* and an associate editor of the *American Journal on Mental Retardation*.

Angela Gavin is a graduate student in counseling psychology at Santa Clara University. She is a certified yoga instructor, and also runs body image awareness groups for adolescents.

John C. Gonsiorek, PhD, ABPP, is a past president of the American Psychological Association Division 44, and has published widely in the areas of professional misconduct and impaired professionals, sexual orientation and identity, professional ethics, and other areas. He is a fellow of APA Divisions, 9, 12, and 44. He is currently a full-time Core Faculty in the PsyD Clinical Psychology program at Capella University. For more than 25 years, he had an independent practice of clinical and forensic psychology in Minneapolis and provided expert witness evaluation and testimony regarding impaired professionals, standards of care, and psychological damages. His major publications include: *Breach of Trust: Sexual Exploitation by Health Care Professionals and Clergy; Homosexuality: Research Implications for Public Policy* (with Weinrich); *Male Sexual Abuse: A Trilogy of Intervention Strategies* (with Bera and Letourneau); and *Homosexuality and Psychotherapy: A Practitioner's Handbook of Affirmative Models.*

Robert M. Hodapp, PhD, is professor in the Department of Special Education and member of the Kennedy Center for Research on Human Development, both at Vanderbilt University. Dr. Hodapp worked for 10 years with Dr. Ed Zigler at Yale University before moving to University of California, Los Angeles's Graduate School of Education and Information Studies in 1992. In June of 2003, Dr. Hodapp moved to Vanderbilt University where he continues his research on the development of children with different genetic syndromes (specifically Down, Prader-Willi, and Williams syndromes), the reactions of parents and families to these children, and developmental issues in children with disabilities in general. In addition to publishing numerous scientific articles and book chapters, he is also the author or coauthor of seven books and serves on the editorial boards of *Mental Retardation* and the *American Journal on Mental Retardation.*

James Lock, MD, PhD, is associate professor of child psychiatry in the Department of Psychiatry and Behavioral Sciences at Stanford University School of Medicine. He is also the director of the Eating Disorders Program for Children and Adolescents at Stanford University. He is the author of numerous scientific and clinical papers on the subject of eating disorders in adolescents, and has spent the majority of his clinical and scientific career in treating adolescents with anorexia nervosa. Dr. Lock is currently the principal investigator of a study of family versus individual psychotherapy for anorexia nervosa supported by the National Institute of Mental Health.

Leslie M. Lothstein, PhD, ABPP, is an associate clinical professor of psychology in the Department of Psychiatry at Case Western Reserve University School of Medicine (tenured), adjunct clinical professor of psychology at the University of Hartford, and adjunct associate professor of psychology at the University of Connecticut Farmington Health Sciences Center. Dr. Lothstein is director of psychology of The Institute of Living, Hartford Hospital's mental health network. He has authored one book, *Female-to-Male Transsexuals: Historical, Clinical and Theoretical Issues* (1983), and authored or coauthored over 150 papers, book chapters, and reviews. Dr. Lothstein has evaluated and treated almost 2,000 individuals with gender identity disorders, and directed the Gender Identity Clinic for four years in Cleveland, Ohio.

Melissa A. Maxwell is currently a student of psychology and human development at Peabody College, Vanderbilt University. She graduated from Middlebury College in 2004, and is now a graduate student in clinical psychology at Vanderbilt University. She has research interests in psychopathology and treatment of individuals with mental retardation, particularly genetic syndromes, and sibling and family issues related to Prader-Willi syndrome and Williams syndrome.

Rudy Nydegger, PhD, is professor of psychology and management at Union College and the School of Management in the Graduate College of Union University. He is also chief of the Division of Psychology at Ellis Hospital in Schenectady, New York, and is past-president and chair of the Program Committee of the New York State Psychological Association. He is the author of many peer-reviewed articles and chapters in books, and is the author of "Gender and Mental Health," a chapter in the recently released book, *The Gender Handbook*, edited by Michele Paludi (Praeger, 2006). In addition to his academic responsibilities, he also has an active clinical and consulting practice in Schenectady, New York.

Michele Paludi, PhD, is research professor in the School of Management of the Graduate College of Union University. She has been a full and tenured professor at Hunter College. She has authored, edited or co-edited 23 books. Her book, *Ivory Power: Sexual Harassment on Campus* (1990), received the 1992 Myers Center Award for Outstanding Book on Human Rights in the United States. Dr. Paludi served as chair of the U.S. Department of Education's Subpanel on the Prevention of Violence, Sexual Harassment, and Alcohol and Other Drug Problems in Higher Education.

Carolyn Pender is a graduate student in the school psychology program at the University of South Carolina. She earned her bachelor of arts in honours psychology from McGill University in 2003. Her current research interests center around outcomes for children and adolescents with attention-deficit/hyperactivity disorder.

Marisa H. Sellinger is currently a student of special education at Peabody College, Vanderbilt University. Her research interests include abuse and victimization among children with mental retardation, as well as etiology-related maladaptive behaviors of children with genetic mental retardation disorders.

Shauna L. Shapiro, PhD, is an assistant professor of counseling psychology at Santa Clara University and adjunct clinical faculty of medicine and behavioral sciences at University of Arizona School of Medicine, Integrative Medicine Program. Her research and clinical work has focused primarily on mindfulness-based stress reduction across a wide range of populations, including breast cancer, insomnia, substance abuse, and eating disorders. Dr. Shapiro has studied mindfulness in Nepal and Thailand, as well as trained with Jon Kabat-Zinn, PhD, Jack Kornfield, PhD, and Sylvia Boorstein. She has published over two dozen articles and book chapters in the area of mindfulness, and has presented her research findings nationally and internationally.

Bradley Smith, PhD, is an associate professor in the department of psychology at the University of South Carolina. From 1993 to 1996, Dr. Smith was the clinical and research supervisor of the adolescent program at the Attention Deficit Disorder Program at the Western Psychiatric Institute and Clinic in the University of Pittsburgh Medical Center. Dr. Smith currently provides after school treatment for middle school students with learning or behavior problems, many of whom have attention-deficit/hyperactivity disorder (AD/HD). Dr. Smith's current scholarly interests are primarily focused on prevention or treatment of learning, behavior, and academic problems among adolescents and college students with AD/HD. Dr. Smith has published several journal articles on the diagnosis and treatment of AD/HD in adolescents and adults.

James E. Soukup, PsyD, is the founder and clinical director of Fairfield Psychological Center in Greensboro, North Carolina. He has a doctorate in psychology, a master of arts in counseling, and a master of business administration degree. In the past, he has served as a national trustee of Forest Institute of Psychology. He has also taught doctoral level courses in testing and psychometrics at the Adler Institute of Professional Psychology in Chicago, and was on the adjunct faculty. Dr. Soukup specializes in neuropsychological evaluation and treatment, and has developed a geriatric test battery for dementia in the elderly. He is the author of the books *Alzheimer's Disease: A Guide to Diagnosis, Management and Treatment* (Greenwood Press, 1996), and *Understanding and Living with People who are Mentally Ill* (1997). Dr. Soukup is currently involved in education and lecturing on the subject of Alzheimer's disease and dementia in the elderly.

About the Series Advisers

Patrick H. DeLeon, *PhD., ABPP, MPH, JD,* is a former president of the American Psychological Association and has served on Capitol Hill for over three decades working on health and educational policy issues. A fellow of the APA, he has been active within the APA governance, having been elected president of three practice divisions. A former editor of *Professional Psychology: Research and Practice,* he has been on the editorial board of the *American Psychologist* since 1981. He has received several APA Presidential citations as well as the APA Distinguished Professional and Public Interest Contributions awards. He has also been recognized by the leadership of professional nursing, social work, and optometry. He is a Distinguished Alumnus of the Purdue University School of Liberal Arts. He has authored in excess of 175 publications.

Nadine J. Kaslow, *PhD, ABPP,* is professor and chief psychologist at Emory University School of Medicine in the Department of Psychiatry and Behavioral Sciences. She is president of the American Board of Clinical Psychology, former president of the Divisions of Clinical Psychology and of Family Psychology of the American Psychological Association, past chair of the Association of Psychology Postdoctoral and Internship Centers, and associate editor of the *Journal of Family Psychology.* Her research interests and numerous publications focus on the assessment and treatment of suicidal behavior in abused and non-abused women, family violence (intimate partner violence, child abuse), child and adolescent depression, and training issues in psychology. She is currently principal investigator on grants funded by the Centers for Disease Control and Prevention on the treatment of abused suicidal African American women, the treatment of suicidal African American women. She is a licensed psychologist who maintains a psychotherapy practice in Atlanta, Georgia, for adolescents with eating disorders, adults, couples, and families.

Lori Goldfarb Plante, *PhD*, is a clinical lecturer at Stanford University School of Medicine. She conducts a private practice in clinical psychology in Menlo Park, California, where she specializes in the assessment and treatment of adolescents and young adults. She is the author of a book addressing chronic illness and disability within the family as well as the author of numerous professional articles on eating disorders, sexuality, and sexual abuse in adolescents and young adults.